Springer Proceedings in Business and Economics

More information about this series at http://www.springer.com/series/11960

Valentina Vasile

Editor

Caring and Sharing: The Cultural Heritage Environment as an Agent for Change

2016 ALECTOR Conference, Istanbul, Turkey

 Springer

Editor
Valentina Vasile
Romanian Academy
Institute of National Economy
Bucharest
Romania

ISSN 2198-7246   ISSN 2198-7254   (electronic)
Springer Proceedings in Business and Economics
ISBN 978-3-319-89467-6   ISBN 978-3-319-89468-3   (eBook)
https://doi.org/10.1007/978-3-319-89468-3

Library of Congress Control Number: 2018938370

Printed on acid-free paper

This Springer imprint is published by the registered company Springer Nature Switzerland AG
The registered company address is: Gewerbestrasse 11, 6330 Cham, Switzerland

Preface

Cultural heritage has an important potential for tourism sector development and to increase the share of tourism exports in GDP, is among the main factors of support competitiveness in tourism, local economic growth and social inclusion.

Digital technologies have created an important crossroads for onsite cultural heritage consumption and defined a new model of tourism. Social channels and mass media facilitate wider access to information about cultural heritage, providing both an increased and diversified demand. Current cultural consumption combines old fashioned models of cultural consumption with access and interactive participation, onsite innovation in terms of the consumption process, and facilitates environmental protection through non-invasive forms of heritage asset valuation. Younger generations conceptualize heritage assets valuing and capitalization in igneous ways, integrating perennial truths and historic values into modern cultural consumption models.

The attractiveness of cultural heritage to youths has multiple faces, from learning about national identity and perceived authenticity to discovering common regional/international roots, helping make sense of the past, and critically, prepare for the future. The recognition of community heritage and understanding cultural meanings for present and future, for individuals and groups, is a challenge for onsite visitor experiences (pre-visit, during visit, and post-visit) and also for providers of cultural products (the socio-economic impact of the business model). Cultural heritage consumption creates positive externalities, conveys values and meaningful messages for everyday life, and represents a vehicle for accepting diversity, embracing multiculturalism, and promoting understanding and peace. Sharing the experience through social media, revisiting the heritage sites (re)design or just confirming the business model relevance and efficacy, and increasing demand prove the cost-benefits efficiency both for consumer and provider. In the present, more than ever, past tangible heritage create/enrich contemporary intangible heritage of local communities and enrich local cultural identity.

The scientific and common approach to cultural heritage is based on the values of long-term cooperation between specialists/experts and locals in designing awareness for the need to preserve culture and its values, as well as the need for appropriate management of its sites.

Cultural heritage as a source of economic development creates synergies at the local level, develops networks of market providers, facilitates the design of a new framework for economic and social inclusion, create jobs, stimulates innovation and the cooperation between specialists, young entrepreneurs, artists, etc., and integrates knowledge with emotions in terms of designing new cultural goods and services. The benefits of investing in heritage are reflected in the livability of an area, job creation, and economic development (WB, 2012; EC, 2017). The need for a strategic approach was underlined (EHA3.3, 2012) in response to the Lisbon Treaty of the European Union, Article 3.3

The main facilitator of cultural heritage valuation is the travel and tourism sector, contributing to over 10% of global GDP, 30% of the world's service exports, and one tenth of jobs (WEF_TTCR, 2017). The World Economic Forum developed the Travel and Tourism Competitiveness Index to measure "the set of factors and policies that enable the sustainable development of the travel and tourism sector, which in turn, contributes to the development and competitiveness of a country." This composite index includes indicators that measure the direct, indirect, and induced economic effects of the heritage sector. The Heritage Economic Impact Indicator (TBR, 2016; Ortus 2017) and Heritage Counts (CHCFE Report, 2015) were also created to register the social and economic value of heritage to communities, individuals, and the economy.

The role of cultural heritage is still undervalued (EC, 2015) and a holistic impact assessment of the heritage sector on our lives and culture, both today and in the future, goes beyond quantitative measurements. This should not be just an EU or national key economic priority but should also contribute to enhancing Creative Europe, territorial cohesion, active inclusiveness, and multicultural convergence and harmony, in the short, medium, and long term. In this respect, identifying and disseminating good practice and multidimensional impact assessments represent just two examples of activities which ought to be conducted, based on EU funding, as well as public and private finance.

This volume includes the results of such initiatives to measure the socioeconomic dimension of the heritage sector and presents some good practices in terms of valuing and valuation of tangible (both natural and anthropic) and intangible cultural heritage assets.

The different approaches (scientific and practical) and diversity of research methodologies used in the chapters included in this volume comprise two parts:

- Part I "Economics of Heritage" is dedicated to scientific articles which present research results in an innovative manner. The research in these chapters highlights the proposed topics that make up the ALECTOR Project, and also some other research results on heritage and tourism topics for countries such as Bulgaria, Croatia, Russia, and Romania. The experts from the partner institutions in the ALECTOR project presented some of the results of the researches carried out during the project's implementation period, for countries such as Greece and Romania.

- Part II "Best Practices" presents and analyzes best practices in, experience gained from, and promotional plans for cultural heritage through tourism. Some tourist sites and thematic routes are presented from countries such as Bulgaria, the Republic of Moldova, Turkey, Russia, and Romania.

The present volume brings together the papers presented in international conference "Caring and Sharing: The Heritage Environment as an Agent for Change," organized as part of the ALECTOR Project—Collaborative Networks of Multilevel Actors to advance quality standards for heritage tourism at Cross Border Level, ENPI Cross Broader Cooperation Black Sea Basin Programme, JOP 2007–2013 (MIS ECT 2617 ALECTOR), http://www.alector.org. Partners in the project were from Greece, Romania, Bulgaria, the Republic of Moldova, Ukraine, Georgia, and Turkey.

Why ALECTOR Project? The necessity of the project was underlined by the following aspects:

- Cultural values are resources which depend on the capacity of people to interpret and use them for the benefit of society.
- There is a need to match supply (cultural values) and demand (cultural use) via new skills.
- Cultural heritage protection should match its use.
- Cultural values from tangible and intangible heritage should be better communicated.
- Trained human capital is required, along with the development of professional skills linked to heritage interpretation.
- Innovation should be enabled through knowledge pooling and management, and through the production and application of good practices in the interpretation of heritage.
- Involvement of key actors from the spheres of state, market, and civil society is needed to facilitate implementation.
- Strengthening the development capacity of the heritage interpretation sector is important, enabling the diversification of cultural heritage consumption through multi-sensorial end-user experiences.

The ALECTOR Project's international conference aimed to communicate to multiple public targets the project's results, methodologies, and planning strategies, local implemented pilot projects, using the international experience in the heritage sector and more particular in the conservation, protection, management and communication of heritage. At the same time the project offers an international forum on issues regarding sustainability and the dynamics of cultural values for regional and local development. In this way comprehension and support for local government and related decision makers, along with general public awareness, will be raised and maintained. The theoretical and empirical research papers presented at the conference addressed the following topics:

- Standardization in tourism—a new approach based on research and development and ICT.
- Local developments and international networking through heritage products and services.
- Climate change and the historic environment—natural and cultural heritage risks and hazards.
- Smart specialization and financing of local tourism development, based on heritage valuing and assessment.
- Teaching methods for novel professional profiles, developing future experts in heritage, tourism, and hospitality industries, including cultural communication and the interpretation of heritage.
- Anthropological cultural heritage—tangible and intangible heritage assets as the main identity pillars for socioeconomic development and community cohesion.
- Topics in natural heritage management, architectural conservation, and the protection of monuments and buildings.

These topics are closely related to the ALECTOR Project's objectives:

- Creation of a pool of knowledge needed to empower cross-border actors and decision makers to enhance the accessibility of heritage.
- Development of a participatory knowledge platform for the public to promote the values of historic environments.
- Producing standards for public access to cultural heritage assets needed to unlock their value for all of society.
- Helping territorial development and promoting cultural production and consumption.
- Promoting the development of actions for biodiversity preservation and natural and man-made heritage preservation.
- Enhancing the attractiveness of places by protecting cultural heritage.
- Creating transnational alliances in order to promote heritage entrepreneurship.
- Improving the perception and use of heritage.
- Involving new media tools to promote and add value to heritage tourism and cultural consumption.

The impact of the ALECTOR Project considered:

- Supporting entrepreneurial innovation by combined efforts of multilevel actors.
- Enhancing the access to knowledge of different actors from the public–private–third party, thus paving the way for entrepreneurial innovation, thanks to a highly skilled pool of certified specialists.
- Leveraging the economic usability of cultural heritage in the Black Sea Basin by producing standards for public access to cultural heritage assets.
- Unlocking heritage value for society.
- Facilitating transferability of good practice across the Black Sea region.
- Communicating heritage value and the potential of heritage assets to the public.

The results and outputs were designed:

- Provide a common tool for improving the management of domain-specific knowledge at the cross-border level.
- Develop new skills for individuals, experts, or associates.
- Design guidelines for increasing the accessibility of heritage tourism both for residents and non-residents/consumers.
- Formulate and substantiate recommendations for the development of accessible heritage tourism products and services.
- Identify good practices for heritage tourism products and services.
- Enhance guidelines for identifying and planning experience opportunities for visitors.
- Ground a common tourism planning methodology, adopted at the cross-border level.
- Create a database of heritage experts at the cross-border level.
- Set assessment criteria for the accessibility of heritage tourism products and services at the cross-border level.
- Design quality labels for heritage tourism products and services.
- Develop and implement pilot project plans in selected areas.
- Produce an open street museum and promote it as a permanent exhibition.

The project aimed to create stronger regional partnerships and cooperation in the Black Sea Basin, and promote development in a stronger and more powerful and sustainable way from the economic and social points of view in the Black Sea Basin region—promoting local competitiveness and the creation of strategic partnerships in the spheres of state, civil society, and the economy.

During the project's implementation, its partners looked to:

- Increase the attractiveness of the project's areas to tourists by promoting accessibility to cultural resources and heritage.
- Reconcile economic operators and decision makers through the convergence of measures of cultural protection and market philosophy.
- Promote local business incubators capable of producing and sustaining cultural goods, by preparing specific target groups of relevant actors.
- Provide local businesses with a range of tools and methods to design and implement cultural tourism products and services for the purpose of local economic regeneration.
- Communicate the values of cross-border culture to the local population.
- Promote the spirit of volunteering in the cultural sector, in particular through the involvement of young people.

We hope that the project's results presented during the conference, and the best practices disseminated to the project's participants, produces a "snowball" effect, generating an increased interest in other project proposals (financed through EU funds or from elsewhere) for heritage sector development through smart valuing and efficient valuation.

Bucharest, Romania   Valentina Vasile
                                                                         Romanian Academy
                                                                Institute of National Economy

Tărgu Mures, Romania   Daniel Stefan
                                                     "Petru Maior" University of Tărgu Mures
                                          Romanian Research Group for Corporate Finance

Tărgu Mures, Romania   Calin-Adrian Comes
                                                     "Petru Maior" University of Tărgu Mures
                                          Romanian Research Group for Corporate Finance

References

EC. (2015). *Towards an integrated approach to cultural heritage for Europe, Opinion of the European Committee of the Regions—COM (2014) 477 final.* http://eur-lex.europa.eu/legal-content/EN/TXT/?uri=celex%3A52014IR5515

EC. (2017). Cultural heritage counts for Europe report, publication coordination Joanna Sanetra-Szeliga, on behalf of the CHCfE Consortium. http://blogs.encatc.org/culturalheritagecounts foreurope//wp-content/uploads/2015/06/CHCfE_FULL-REPORT_v2.pdf

EHA3.3. (2012). Towards *an EU strategy for cultural heritage—The case for research 2012 European Heritage Alliance 3.3.* http://www.europanostra.org/wp-content/uploads/2017/02/Towards-an-EU-Strategy-for-Cultural-Heritage_final.pdf

ORTUS. (2017). *Heritage economic impact indicators 2017: Technical report.* https://content.historicengland.org.uk/content/heritage-counts/pub/2017/heritage-economic-impact-indicators-2017-technical-report.pdf

TBR. (2016). *Heritage economic impact indicators: Technical report for historic England.* Prepared by TBR's Creative & Cultural Team. https://content.historicengland.org.uk/content/heritage-counts/pub/2016/heritage-economic-indicators-sharing-best-practice-tech-note.pdf

WB. (2012). In: G. Licciardi & R. Amirtahmasebi (Eds.), *The economics of uniqueness. Investing in historic city cores and cultural heritage assets for sustainable development.* http://siteresources.worldbank.org/EXTSDNET/Resources/Economics_of_Uniqueness.pdf

Acknowledgements

This volume is the result of teamwork both from a content selection point of view as well as editorially. Following previous experience gained in the dissemination of research results and sharing best practices in terms of specific economic topics (i.e., http://www.rorcf.ro), for this volume, the editor closely cooperated with Dr. Daniel Stefan and Dr. Călin-Adrian Comes—both experts with good backgrounds in book editing, as well as being researchers in economics.

Sharing the ALECTOR Project's[1] results from the scientific community in the cultural heritage field was only possible because of the excellent cooperation given by the project's coordinators, Dr. Nikolaos Thomaidis and Dr. Dorothea Papathanasiou-Zuhrt, and the contributions of the partners and national teams involved from Greece, Bulgaria, Romania, Bulgaria, the Republic of Moldova, Ukraine, Georgia, and Turkey.

My special gratitude goes to all team members, for actively sharing their experiences and building together an emerging international cooperation network for cultural heritage sector growth, creating Europe's historical memory.

---

[1] The EU Neighbourhood Info Centre (ENPI) Cross-Border Cooperation (CBC) Black Sea Basin Programme, JOP 2007–2013 project *"Collaborative Networks of Multilevel Actors to Advance Quality Standards for Heritage Tourism at Cross Border Level"* (MIS ECT 2617 ALECTOR, www.alector.org).

Contents

Part I
Economics of Heritage

Chapter 1
Cultural Heritage Management (CHM) and the Sustainable Development Requirements

Gheorghe Zaman

Abstract The paper reveals some important characteristics of cultural heritage management (CHM) vis-à-vis the recent requirements of sustainable development (SD) taking into consideration the economic, social and environmental pillars of SD and the necessity of an adequate system of CHM indicators. The general conclusions are that CH, if well managed, represents an asset for a national economy with important contribution to GDP growth, employment and quality of life.

Keywords Cultural heritage management · Sustainable development
Pillars of SD · Integration of CHD into SD · Spillovers · Internalization of externalities

1.1 Introduction

The unanimous recognition of culture's and cultural heritage impact on economic and social development is a question not only of theoretical approach but of practical effective integration and mainstreaming of culture in strategies and policies at all levels and time horizons.

According to long and practical countries' experience, it is evident that the support of idea that cultural heritage as a direct result of cultural goods and services stemming from more or less recent past contribute in a complex and specific manner to development not only in terms of economic increase of GDP and employment but also of qualitative improvement of well-being and national wealth. Rising national and international awareness of the CHM contribution aiming at safeguarding cultural heritage and diversity require specific tools, economic and social mechanisms calling for its integration to development of practically social and economic domains.

G. Zaman (✉)
Institute of National Economy-Romanian Academy, Bucharest, Romania
e-mail: inst.ec.nat@gmail.com

© Springer International Publishing AG, part of Springer Nature 2019
V. Vasile (ed.), *Caring and Sharing: The Cultural Heritage Environment as an Agent for Change*, Springer Proceedings in Business and Economics,
https://doi.org/10.1007/978-3-319-89468-3_1

3

As an important component of cultural heritage, CHM belongs to the more general notions of Cultural Resources Management (CRM) category which is more widespread in the US literature.

Traditionally, CHM is dealing with the activities of identification, interpretation, maintenance, preservation and valorization of cultural goods and services, tangible and intangible, including traditional skills, languages, arts, other artistic activities, habits and handicrafts.

Green economy offers a large component of landscapes heritage which needs to prioritize both people and environment, provides an opportunity to revitalize the state, combats neoliberal primacy and drives progressive economic and environmental policy.

As social and environmental crises are deepening, the need for cultural heritage management is a complementary domain of sustainable growth, in parallel with the integration of culture into development strategies and policies in a distinct and adequate manner.

Recognition of cultural heritage influence, the safeguarding of world heritage and cultural diversity, contribute to development not only of quantitative economic growth (income, employment) but also of qualitative standards and well-being including the indirect propagation effects (spillovers).

The paper presents some general requirements of sustainable development in the field of cultural heritage management, taking into account the interdependence between the three pillars of sustainable development and the most important tools, methods, mechanism of CHM at macro- and microlevel for the large diversity of cultural heritage that can be considered not only an enhancer of national identity but also a genuine factor of economic growth, well-being and improved quality of life.

1.2 Integration of CHM into the Strategies of Sustainable Development

Although at first glance the topic of CHM could be considered as a separate domain not directly linked to the strategies of sustainable development, a large body of the literature demonstrates a more and more intense link between two processes under different forms of manifestation. That is why, in the last decades, a special attention is paid to the efficient integration of CHM into the strategies of sustainable economic and social growth taking into consideration the needs and criteria to be met for such an integration.

Figure 1.1 presented a general scheme of interference and integration between sustainable development pillars and the requirements to be met by CHM in order to contribute to a more consistent and resilient sustainable growth development. This figure can be developed, detailed and completed for each category of cultural heritage at different levels and territorial units in accordance with their particularities.

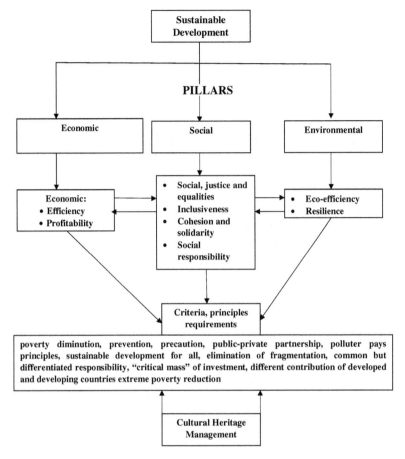

Fig. 1.1 Integration of cultural heritage management into the strategies of sustainable development

The ways of integrating CHM into strategies of sustainable development are specific for each category of cultural and natural resources. However, it is necessary to outline the necessity of taking into account some general common characteristic of CHM and sustainable development that are presented in the next chapter of our paper.

1.3 Common Characteristic of Sustainable Development (SD) and Cultural Heritage Management (CHM)

Common characteristics of both SD and CHM offer a better understanding and ways of integrating and bridging the two categories from both theoretical and practical viewpoints.

A first aspect is related to the characteristics of intergenerational cooperation and SD and CHM "for all" which offers comprehensive dimensions in time and space. Indeed both categories indicate the strategic goals on medium- and long terms and benefits offerings for all involved participants.

The high degree of complexity and diversity are common for SD and CHM inducing the necessity of systemic approach and structural analysis of interdependent and dynamic components which need multi-, intra-, inter-, pluri-disciplinary methods within which specialists of different domain have to cooperate in order to better respond to the inherent requirement of decision-making on different time horizon.

Not less important is the application of public–private partnership principle which imposes adequate schemes for the interlinked promotion between pure public and private goods and services. A series of important and complex criteria in approaching the topics of SD and CHM refer to applicability of strategic management in an interfering manner conducive to the convergence in reaching the medium- and long-term priorities, goals and objectives and meeting the requirement of combining static and dynamic methods of analysis and forecasting.

Another common characteristic refers to digitalization, R&D, IT&C representing very strong driving force and objective tendency in SD and CHM processes.

From the pure methodological viewpoint, the domain of SD and CHM are evolving from the linear to nonlinear modelling, with the scope of a better management, monitoring and solving the complex problems of risks, vulnerabilities and resilience.

The above-mentioned characteristics common to SD and CHM involve a specific manner of the values analysis of cultural heritage domain.

The diversity of CH imposes, as a consequence, a diversity of typology of values.

1.4   Valuation of CH—A Basis for an Efficient Management

The special literature (Bowitz and Ibenholt 2009) classifies effects of investment in culture in: direct, indirect, input–output, multiplies and acceleration effects ancillary spending, derived effects, gravitation, "non-economic", counteracting effects.

All the above mentioned effects can be identified at different levels of aggregation (local, regional, national and international).

In view the large diversity of CH which is practically covering almost all domains of human activity, the valuation methods are very diverse function of different types of value: cultural, historical, aesthetical, economic, financial environmental and educational (instrumental—intrinsic value).

A brief presentation of the techniques and methods used in economic and social valuation of cultural heritage (Fig. 1.2) shows a very close similarity with the methods of valuation of natural capital and resources.

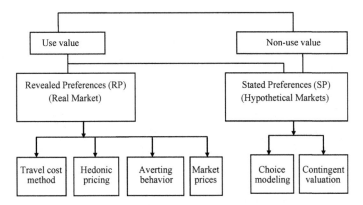

Fig. 1.2 Economic and social valuation techniques (*Source* Choi et al. 2010; Bateman et al. 2002)

For each group of CH, a certain system of valuation has to be elaborated and tested, including at the same time more or less rigorous determination of so-called positive and negative externalities which represent marginal external benefits and respectively costs (spillovers). The inclusion of spillovers by means of the internalization of externalities is possible by subsidies, in case of marginal external benefits, and by corrective or Pigouvian taxes for the marginal external costs.

In the framework of cost-benefit analysis applicable to CH valuation a very sensitive problem is the usage of different size discount rates specific for each category of CH.

Special techniques for determining net present value (npv) and internal rate of return (irr) for cultural heritage investment and restoration projects have to be applied in case of qualitative spillovers which, as a rule, are very difficult to be quantified in monetary terms (Zaman and Vasile 2010).

It is unanimously accepted that, in any situation, an efficient management of cultural heritage is directly dependent on the measurement of cultural and landscape capital.

In the CH valuation, it is also necessary to take into consideration a series of particularities of CH public goods and services non-rival, non-excludable and congestible, in parallel with pure private ones.

The valuation of intangible cultural heritage resources is much more different than in the case of tangible cultural heritage goods and services. The increasing role of intangible cultural heritage in supporting economic and social development as a result of knowledge-based society needs further efforts on improving valuation methods and contribution of this type of assets.

1.5 Policy Mix for CHM

An effective management and management plan is based on three prerequisites:

- A good objective understanding of cultural heritage by all stakeholders and effective cooperation between them;
- Clear methods of planning, implementing and monitoring the condition of identifying, maintenance, restoration, preservation and valorization of CH valuation and feedback;
- Preoccupation for economy the necessary funding.

Optimal policy mix in the field of CHM has to solve a series of problems related to the following aspects: subsidies versus regulations; direct versus indirect public support; incentives versus compulsory rules; local versus national, versus international interventions; centralization versus decentralization of decision-making, especially in the case of transition economy and transfer of cultural property goods; standard at national and international levels (Zaman et al. 2008).

The CHM needs highly qualified labour skills, a coherent and sustainable priority setting and an efficient investment policy, avoiding the shortcomings in investment process in different CH domain.

The experience of transition economies in the field of CH shows that privatization of cultural heritage was not a guarantee of "better off "for all cases (one size does not fit all!).

An effective CHM has to be inclusive and participatory, in order to meet some outstanding requirements of sustainable development such as development for all, a better decision-making etc.

CHM in terms of sustainability has to evaluate and combat a series of risks, vulnerabilities such as national hazard (floods, extreme climate changes, risks of war and terrorism, military conflicts, etc.). At the same time, special measure should be taken for CH resilience improvements based on adequate technologies, adaptation and alleviation measures, action plans and tools.

Integration of CHM into SD strategies is concerning the following major aspects:

- Constructive conservation and sustainable management;
- Public engagement and consultation;
- Capacity building and effective state involvement;
- Compatibility between general and specific priorities and objectives of SD and CHM at different levels;
- Long-term multi-annual budgeting;
- Joint monitoring and implementation procedure;
- The increase of absorption capacity of EU structural and cohesion funds;

Monitoring and evaluation of CHM as a continuous process and data collection has to be oriented towards detection of all deviations from the established tasks and goods. The monitoring process has to be based on good methodological basis in the following domains: specificity; measurability; accessibility; relevance and clarity; reliability; time-specific; cost-effective.

Ex-ante evaluation of CHM is pursuing the goal of a better preparation of management plan and evaluation ex-post examines the results achieved vis-à-vis the planned ones, the effectiveness and success of management plan.

1.6   Instead of Final Remarks

To answer the question If CHM is an asset or a liability, first of all you have to take into consideration the quality of CHM.

As a rule, CH at macro-level can be considered as an ASSET in case of its high quality and efficient management.

Given its social specificity, cultural heritage is "par excellence" a valuable public good transmitted from one generation to the next one.

References

Bateman, I. et al. (2002). *Economic valuation with stated preference techniques: A manual.* econweb.ucsd.edu/~rcarson/papers/BatemanBook.pdf.

Bowitz, E., & Ibenholt, K. (2009). Economic impacts of cultural heritage–research and perspectives. *Journal of Cultural Heritage, 10*(1), 1–8. January–March.

Choi, A. S., Ritchie, B. W., Papandrea, F., & Bennett, J. (2010). Economic valuation of cultural heritage sites: A choice modeling approach. *Tourism Management, 31*(2), 213–220.

Hoffman, P. T. (Ed.). (2006). *Art and cultural heritage: Law, policy and practice.* Cambridge, UK: Cambridge University Press.

Macmanamon, F. P., & Hatton, A. (Ed.). (1999). *Cultural resource management in contemporary society: Perspectives on managing and presenting the past.* London and New York: Routledge.

WCED. (1987). *Our common future.* Oxford: Oxford University Press.

Zaman, Gh., & Vasile, V. (2010). *Cultural creative industries (CCI)—economic and social performance.* Annals of the Ştefan cel Mare University of Suceava, Fascicle of The Faculty of Economics and Public Administration, Vol. 10, Special Number.

Zaman, Gh., et al. (2008). *Contribuţia economică a industriilor bazate pe copyright în România.* www.wipo.int/industry/ecostudy_romania. Oficiul Român pentru Drepturi de Autor, Centrul de studii şi cercetări în domeniul culturii, Institutul de Economie Naţională.

Chapter 2
Multi-sensory Experiences at Heritage Places: SCRIPTORAMA, The Black Sea Open Street Museum

Dorothea Papathanasiou-Zuhrt, Nikolaos Thomaidis, Aldo Di Russo and Valentina Vasile

Abstract Under the umbrella of the MIS ETC 2617 ALECTOR, a project within the *ENPI CBC BLACK SEA JOINT OPERATIONAL PROGRAMME 2007–2013*, a novel cultural heritage infrastructure with three components has been developed to communicate local heritage to international audiences. A cross-border partnership, operating in seven countries (Greece, Romania, Bulgaria, Ukraine, Georgia and Turkey), has developed standards for heritage tourism by involving key stake-holders, local communities and citizens into heritage planning in a bottom-up and training process. The project has been completed in a 30 month period with an overall budget of 1,065,894.00 EUR. The main result *SCRIPTORAMA*, a three-component Open Street Museum, accessible through 90 Quick Response Codes in the territory and as eBook at the Appstore and Google Play, is delivering the heritage experience by engaging in a constant dialogue heritage suppliers and heritage users. This paper examines (a) how cognitive-emotional and multi-sensory experiences can foster an (inter)-active knowledge acquisition pattern for non-captive audiences at heritage places; (b) how to integrate new technologies into the cultural heritage experience to support the informal learning modus; and (c) how to democratize the mission of heritage institutions by promoting self-reflective and critically thinking visitors who can perceive, reshape and orga-nize heritage places into a participatory public space accessible by all.

D. Papathanasiou-Zuhrt (✉)
University of the Aegean/The Wave Lab, Chios, Greece
e-mail: dorothea.papathanasiou@aegean.gr

N. Thomaidis
Drama Development S.A., Drama, Greece

A. Di Russo
ARTiFACTORY, Rome, Greece

V. Vasile
Institute of National Economy, Romanian Aacdemy, Bucuresti, Romania

© Springer International Publishing AG, part of Springer Nature 2019
V. Vasile (ed.), *Caring and Sharing: The Cultural Heritage Environment as an Agent for Change*, Springer Proceedings in Business and Economics, https://doi.org/10.1007/978-3-319-89468-3_2

2.1 Introduction

Although it is well organized and broken down by eras, genres or styles, the modern museum becomes a place where those who want to see everything, would finally not see anything. Eco's idea about an exhibition that emphasizes understanding through the definition of the historical, political, social framework building the prerequisite for cultural literacy is not necessarily a utopia (Eco 2003). But could, for example Botticelli's *Primavera*, the culmination of the Renaissance painting become such a universal value exhibit that can deliver a multi-sensory experience?

In the first hall there would probably be an introduction to the fifteenth century Florence revealing the rediscovery of the humanities with educational panels, exhibitions of books and engravings starting with incunabula, the earliest form of printed books. The objects aforementioned would remain *noli me tangere*, but nevertheless they would attract the audience's attention, to start with. Then the audience familiarizes with the works of the painters who preceded and inspired Botticelli, like Lippi and Verrocchio, and only after it would be introduced to the works of Botticelli before *Primavera*. The scene should be dominated by paintings with female faces that announce those created by Botticelli, to demonstrate that women were seen in a different way in those times and that it is Botticelli who has radically innovated the female social image. Music should be heard, like the one Botticelli must have listened to, along with the voices of poets and philosophers, whose works Botticelli must have studied. The audience would finally enter the central hall, to see *Primavera*, with the now trained eye of a Florentine of the fifteenth century. In the following hall, a screen would reveal all the details of *Primavera*: the pictorial solutions adopted by Botticelli, the comparisons with details of other painters. The last hall would be crowing the experience and would be dedicated to the legacy of Botticelli up to the Pre-Raphaelites.

As much as it is impossible to realize the multi-sensory experience in the bricks and mortar fashion using all authentic paintings in one place, it is feasible to deliver it using digital technology and digital reproductions. The new digital artwork would then allow every known masterpiece to be further spread and every unknown masterpiece to gain its place in the collective memory (Di Russo 2003). Along this line, *SCRIPTORAMA* is the first experiment to support *understanding* at the expense of *admiration* in the multi-ethnic and multi-cultural Black Sea Basin. In the eBook for iOS and Android operating systems, *The Will of Marco Polo: adventure with merchants, laborers and wise men*, the central hero is the visitor, who is travelling across the commerce roads that connect the East and the West: the *Golden Fleece*, the *Silk Road* and the *Golden Leaves*. On his reinvented trail of gold, silk and tobacco, this new *Marco Polo*, meets the Argonauts and the Ten Thousand, Roman and Byzantine Emperors, Mongol rulers, Ottoman Sultans, Western and Eastern travellers and modern era historic personage who share their thoughts and values. The new *Marco Polo* needs to know about the *European Discovery Age*, the *Modernity,* the late *Ottoman Empire*, the *Belle Époque*. Finally, he reaches *World War I* and *World War II* always trying to shed light to causality mechanisms, equipped with the main ingredient of civilization: human values and human rights. With the choral cantata 147 by J.S. Bach as background music, excellently performed by the children's choir of the Conservatorio di Cagliari under conductor Enrico Di Piana, the new heritage journey starts:

> *Marco Polo was travelling without maps,*
>
> *without streets, but following old tales.*
>
> *He wrote a story that still unites all of us.*
>
> *He did not want to convert anyone.*
>
> *He did not conquer any land.*
>
> *His will was the pursuit of knowledge.*
>
> *Be Marco Polo…and travel with us.*

In the meantime, pervasive media have already transformed the learning paradigm by providing unprecedented opportunities for self-directed learning, collaborative and lifelong learning. In contrast to the prevailing opinion, we argue that as pervasive media, continue to evolve (eBooks, apps, social media) supported by constantly advancing generations of data networking that move faster, the intangible nature of cultural assets will become either more important than the mere physical substance, or just an empty of content virtual shell. The rising tendency to rely on technology to convey cultural information off- and onsite does not necessarily lead to the acquisition of knowledge and the production of a heritage-driven value chain through shared practices: advanced ICT applications (apps, platforms) cannot convey meanings, if void of appealing and appropriate content. An improved understanding of heritage in the spirit of the knowledge economy, where creativity becomes a driver for development through active heritage consumption is the *conditio sine qua non* for the sustainability of heritage places (Francois 2012: 91). However, evidence form Structural Funds in the Programming Period 2007–2013 demonstrates the opposite: out of 347 billion, only 6 billion (1.7%) were allocated to culture. Two main conditions perpetuate this vicious circle:

(a) culture is thought to be of national interest and as such it is not export-oriented, and
(b) the contribution of culture is thought to be only an intangible benefit and as such it is not noticed by those who concentrate on the total value of the turnover as an indication of the significance of an industry (CSES 2013: 19–20).

The contribution of culture in the contemporary economic framework is connected to the obsolete conceptualizations of the relationship between cultural activity and the generation of economic value (Bucci and Segre 2009; Sacco 2011; Revelli 2013; Ates 2014). According to the EU Policy Handbook, in 2012 the economic contribution of the Cultural and Creative Industries (CCI) (2.1%) is higher than that of the sector of food, beverages and tobacco manufacturing (1.9%), the textile industry (0.5%) and the chemicals, rubber and plastic products industry (2.3%). Because culture is still thought to be the highly subsidized and low-productivity sector, it remains the easiest target for public funding cuts, especially in times of economic recession. This attitude disables the capacity of the CCI sector to contribute to future economic and employment growth. The networked economy demonstrates vacancies for professionals with digital skills, high-average wages, and persistent reports of skill shortages and use of migrant labour (Williams et al. 2012: 68). As a result, new products are delayed, orders are lost and competitiveness is weakened.

2.2   Research Methodology

The Project Area is peripheral and suffers a divergence of supply (heritage offers and businesses) and demand (heritage consumers), as informational asymmetries disable the access to heritage offers and eventually downgrade the onsite experience. In this way, the internationalization of culture through the selection and consumption of quality and highly customized heritage products and services fails. To effectively utilize the dynamics of culture for development, an alternative plan is sought: *SCRIPTORAMA*, a first attempt to operate a 24 h accessible museum in the Black Sea Basin. The range covers three EU NUTS II regions; three NUTS II equivalent regions in Moldova, Ukraine and Georgia and three regions in Turkey: EL51 (Drama in Eastern Macedonia and Thrace); Romania: RO223 (Constanta); Bulgaria; BG331 (Varna); Moldova, Chisinau; Ukraine, Donetsk Oblast, Mariupol; Georgia, Adjara, Batumi; Turkey:TR42 (Sile, Agva) and TR90 (Eastern Black Sea).

The design of multi-sensory experiences at heritage places remains an under-researched topic. The main objective within the ALECTOR Project is to set up a framework for the design of cognitive-emotional experiences for both the onsite and dislocated audiences considering the Project Area particularities and the conditions that regulate the informal learning environment. In contrast to prevailing opinions, we defend that the knowledge pattern of non-captive audiences in cultural heritage settings shall be reconstructed in line with Human Cognitive Architecture (HCA) to respond to the specific needs and requirements in the informal learning environment and thus contribute to successful heritage experiences and the appreciation of heritage. The conditions under which immersive experiences take place in heritage settings have been studied in the Project Area in a 30 month period from a transdisciplinary point of view, so that a new cultural heritage experience pattern based on shared practices could be designed. New services, generated in the creative economy, have been looked at from a technological point of view, so that a new travel motivation can be offered to dislocated audiences and an enriched experience is ensured for onsite visitors improving satisfaction and access to local product offerings.

2.2.1 Defining the Heritage Experience

The experience of visitors at heritage places is a complex and personal interaction between an individual and the heritage environment, natural, built or intangible. Experiential travel is rooted in the antiquity with Pausanias, producing the first travel documentaries, followed by the Grand Tour nobility travellers and later on the Baedeker readers. It regained contemporary understanding from the reference work *Experience Economy*, where the authors demonstrate that there is a fourth level of economic value called "experience" and that customers are willing to pay a premium for it (Pine and Gilmore 1999). The study *Economy of Culture in Europe* in 2006, and the UN report *Creative Economy* in 2008 establish the concept of creative economy and the domain-specific expertise. In 2014, the year of the digitalization of European cinema theatres, the INTERREG IVC report *Creative Industries* showcases that Europe has reached the point, where the internationalization and export of creative services and products will give new impetus to the cross-sectoral economy (Amann and Lange 2014). In the creative economy, the triangle technology, economy and society are converging and traditional skills are being challenged by a constantly changing knowledge ecosystem (HKU 2010: 3; Bruell 2013: 19). This semantic shift is generating new cultural consumers: individuals thinking and operating in the creative environment become exactly those skilled visitors who wish to be intellectually challenged, understand, appreciate and then participate and be involved at heritage places: (Armstrong and Weiler 2003: 14–16; Jurowski 2009: 1; Jager and Sanche 2010: 181; Tussyadiah 2014; Bulencea and Egger 2015).

The completeness and quality of the experience is influenced by the visitor's expectations, the setting, social interactions, degree of active participation (passive through to active), levels of immersion (emotional, physical, intellectual and spiritual engagement) and associated memories: to quote the American novelist Edward Streeter, "travel is ninety per cent anticipation and ten percent recollection" (Streeter in Sharpley and Stone 2012: 3). Although the four realms of experience (education, escapism, entertainment, aesthetics) are not always supported by empirical data, scholarly research provides insight into the experience motivations towards the enrichment of the personal cultural capital and the trend to understand the "other" by actively participating in the local life (Jurowski 2009: 6; TA 2008: 4; Shanks 2012: 21–43; Chen et al. 2014).

The post-war development of mass cultural tourism has led to a "serial reproduction" of culture and the onset of a "vicious cycle" of decline in leading cultural destinations (Russo 2002; Richards and Wilson 2006). Faced with mass consumption, critically thinking individuals seek refuge in less tangible forms of culture that require higher levels of cultural capital and competence to master (Richards 2012). It is exactly this gap that *SCRIPTORAMA* is called to fill offering a genuine cultural heritage experience by challenging intellectually both the onsite and dislocated audiences with audiovisual and media formats that require skills and participatory engagement. Ninety different experiences are formed at 90 heritage places through a combination of indoor and outdoor activities, settings and the personal connection that arises from the social interaction. An experience engages the senses; it is physical, emotional or spiritual (or all three). All ninety *SCRIPTORAMA* experiences go beyond nice places and good views. They are designed to offer discovery and enquiry learning and create strong memories. They all connect to *genius loci*, meeting visitor needs for unique, authentic encounters and the community need to narrate the cultural self. *SCRIPTORAMA* has practically developed and trained a new audience to demand and require a high-quality cultural experience directly connected to local services in the territory, one that creates higher yield opportunities at local level.

2.2.2   Surveys, Field Work and Involvement of Experts and Stakeholders

The Project Legacy includes a cultural heritage infrastructure with 11 highly repli-cable tools, a training programme in cultural communication, 5 publications, 5 project-driven networks, the *Black Sea Heritage Register* and *SCRIPTORAMA*, the first Open Street Museum in the Black Sea Basin. This legacy is of substantial value to be left without continuation and collective voice. A Cross-Border Non-Profit Non-Governmental Association, the *Black Sea Heritage Observatory,* is co-founded by Project Partners and cooperating organizations, to ensure further diffusion and sustainability of achieved results, most notably the ideals of *SCRIPTORAMA*. The *Black Sea Heritage Observatory* has adopted a common *Heritage Charter* and a common *Heritage Strategy* up to 2020 to ensure the viability of Project results. A Non-Statutory Cooperation Agreement has been signed by 132 multilevel actors from the three spheres of public administration, civil society, economy and the third sector such as local action groups, the private sector, professional unions, chambers of commerce, NGOs, local heritage organizations and initiatives. These actors have acquired access to project results and to praxis validated heritage planning and management tools. They thus ensure the continuation of the collective voice in the Project Area and promote entrepreneurial innovation in the heritage tourism sector.

   SCRIPTORAMA aims to create and globally launch a non-exchangeable, com-petitive cultural heritage place image in each of the nine heritage places in the Project Area in order to attract market segments from domestic and foreign tourism, stimulate new businesses in the CCI domain and enhance the performance of traditional tourism businesses at local level. Nine Pilot Projects have been therefore developed in the Project Area as follows (Tables 2.1 and 2.2):

   ALECTOR has explored the perceived image of each heritage area among domestic and foreign visitors to evaluate heritage offers and to provide suggestions to be fed back into the *SCRIPTORAMA* planning. An e-Survey has been conducted in national lan-guages by all Cross-Border Partners in 2015. 254 out of 459 respondents (56%) have stated that SCRIPTORAMA will attract the general public, while the rest 205

Table 2.1 The ENPI pilot projects

ENPI partners	NUTS III (equivalent)	Heritage project title	Subtitle
ENPI financial lead beneficiary: Drama development D.D.S.A., Drama, Greece	EL51 (Historic centre of Drama)	Tobacco perfumes	Drama 1840–1940. Stories, passions, protagonists
ENPI partner 1: National authority for tourism, Bucharest, Romania	RO 223 (Constanta)	Romania's ancient Black Sea coast	Greek colonists, Dacian kings and Roman legions
ENPI partner 2: Union of Bulgarian black sea local authorities, Varna, Bulgaria	BG 331 (Varna historic town)	100 years in 60 minutes	Varna, 1860–1960
ENPI partner 3: National association of rural, ecological end cultural tourism, Chisinau, Moldova	MO (Chisinau)	Tree of life	Discovering spiritual treasures
ENPI partner 4: Donetsk civic organization "Alliance", Donetsk, Ukraine	UKR (Mariupol)	The Greeks of Priazovie	Mariupol 1778-2016. History, customs and traditions
ENPI partner 5: The Batumi archaeological museum, Batumi, Georgia	GE (Adjara, Batumi)	Colchis, land of the golden fleece	Myths in places with real treasures

Source MIS ETC 2617 ALECTOR project record

Table 2.2 IPA heritage projects

ENPI partners	NUTS III (equivalent)	Heritage project title	Subtitle
IPA financial lead beneficiary: Governorship of Istanbul, Istanbul, Turkey	TR42 (Kocaeli, Sile)	Eastern Black Sea from the silk road to modern times	Sile, Turkey: a lighthouse, legends and mermaids
IPA partner 1: Eastern Black Sea development agency, Trabzon, Turkey	TR90 (Eastern Black Sea)	Legendary Journeys	Eastern Black Sea from the silk road to modern times
IPA partner 1: Bahcesehir University/METGEM development centre for vocational-technical education, Istanbul, Turkey	TR42 (Kocaeli, Agva)	A serenade in nature	Agva, Turkey. Birds, plants and poetry

Source MIS ETC 2617 ALECTOR project record

respondents (44%) considered that contents of the Pilot Projects would rather attract special interest groups. Although more than 50% of the respondents had some knowledge about local heritage assets, they could not connect mentally or emotionally to a certain thematic topic or a cohesive narrative that could express a validated cultural identity of the areas question. The e-Survey has revealed four prevalent suggestions:

- Get to know heritage places and create a greater understanding of the past;
- Exploit the technology intense experience to communicate heritage;
- Promote active visitor participation in the consumption of heritage;
- Identify what business opportunities can be created by originating a new race of entrepreneurs defined as cultural heritage suppliers, who are going to handle a mobile business that is highly customized for the client offering services that mass tourism by definition cannot offer.

The e-Survey has identified a target audience receptive to the Project Area heritage offers: the *heritage experience seeker*. This target audience is looking for unique, involving, customized experiences. It is less affected by the traditional barriers to consumption, like price, distance and time, favouring authenticity, uniqueness and originality at selecting heritage products and services, and is more informed, interested and curious about heritage places, traditional products and iconic values. The class of experience seekers who declare cultural heritage as important for everyday life arguably accounts for about 50% of cultural consumers from key source markets globally and can be found among all age groups, income levels and geographic locations (ATEM 2010; Bucci and Segre 2011; Eurostat 2011; Richards 2013; Eurobarometer 2013; Bui and Trupp 2014). This creative class shows commonalities across countries, placing high value on experiences and hence critically balances benefits with costs. These creative consumers are typically are open-minded and have an interest in world affairs, selective about their media consumption, well-connected, willing to learn from and share information with their peers and investigate cultural heritage options thoroughly. They spend more on quality and like to engage with the local people and lifestyles wishing to absorb and get involved in the day-to-day culture. Consequently, their tourism experiences are more engaging and they are likely to return to heritage places and cultural points of interest.

In their *Manifesto 2013,* the *Arts Council England* is stating: "Every taxpayer, every lottery ticket-holder, every donor, and every reader, theatre-patron and concert-goer is a stakeholder in our world-class arts and culture" (ACE 2013: 3). Embracing this integrative vision, ALECTOR has looked for ways to create the *Cross-Border Stakeholder Map* initiating the dialogue process with multilevel actors. Seeking opportunities to involve heritage authorities, government officials, heritage and tourism-related businesses, third-sector actors, special interest groups and citizens when planning the local Pilot Projects, creating the community story and commonly evaluating preliminary results have led to an intense and fruitful cooperation among local and cross-border stakeholders. To involve communities in the development process to feed back the pilot projects and secure ownership of the final result, was an important consideration right from the start. Locals understand the needs, opportunities, priorities, history and dynamics of the community in ways that professional non-residents do not. Users of services have perspectives and experiences that experts need to know of to develop a service for the market. Local populations are directly affected by problems and have therefore important insights about the causes of problems and ways to address problems. On the other hand without sufficient domain-specific expertise, it is difficult for communities to understand the underlying nature of heritage valuations or to develop effective and locally feasible solutions to address them. Eighteen field trips have been organized in 2015 in the Project Area to include local communities in the design and delivery of authentic experiences. Seven heritage experts from Greece, Bulgaria, Romania, Moldova, Ukraine, Georgia, Turkey and Italy have developed nine *SCRIPTORAMA* chapters, communicating with each other to ensure the quality of the desired heritage experience and produce a culturally cohesive multimedia narrative with market value.

A qualitative survey (face-to-face interviews) has been conducted with 107 stakeholders in the Project Area. It has been suggested that each Pilot Project within ALECTOR should offer a complex source of information concerning a summative tourist product: geographical location, climatic conditions, natural and cultural resources, local traditions, events and cuisine, major tourist attractions from the built and natural environment and accessibility opportunities. The opinion prevailed that cultural heritage attractions constitute a places' distinct features, its proper identity. But heritage assets cannot speak for themselves; it is therefore needed a holistic planning and management approach to provide for quality heritage experiences. It has been explicitly stated that in the Project Area many businesses offering a service or a product related to the heritage sector, cannot perform globally, because they have to apply local rules. In order to respond to this challenge, ALECTOR strived to identify the services and products that needed to be reshaped or launched and accordingly raise the awareness of the business sector in the Project Area. The participation of stakeholders in seven countries across the Project Area has opened a new dialogue format at cross-border level improving communication between individuals and organizations with an interest in heritage. A common vision has been built around a common view that has generated and enhanced the *SCRIPTORAMA* narrative. The active involvement of stakeholders in the planning process has led to more effective, feasible and responsive solutions, prevented the repetition of ill-advised decisions and enhanced the acceptance and legitimacy of decisions taken. The field work has proved that local stakeholders are empowered when they have the ability to exert control over forces that affect their lives, when have the knowledge, skills and resources to do so, and when they are actually involved in making decisions. These dimensions of local empowerment resonate closely with the basic tenets of participatory democracy. By actively taking part in making decisions and by determining the results of decisions, local stakeholders have gained control over their lives (Table 2.3).

2.2.3 Assessing the Significance of Heritage Resources

A heritage assessment has been undertaken in the Project Area to evaluate heritage assets at *spatial* (global, national, regional, local), *scientific* (research, technical), *historic, aesthetic, social* (national, community, group, family personal) and

Table 2.3 SCRIPTORAMA: stakeholder classification

Collective actors (327)	
1	Collective actors who clearly saw potential opportunities in the implementation and marketing of the Local Pilot Project (180)
2	Cultural heritage operators (museum, collection, heritage site, natural-protected area, women cooperatives on traditional products, etc.) (36)
3	Communities interested in the operation of the Local Pilot Project
4	Municipalities (111)
Individual actors (60)	
1	Individual actors who clearly saw potential opportunities in the implementation and marketing of the Local Pilot Project (56)
2	Heritage property owners within the Pilot Project Area (4)
Authorities (90)	
1	Agencies in charge of managing the heritage place (state, regional, municipal, local ministerial authorities, archaeological authorities, spatial planning authorities, etc.) (90)
Professional actors (209)	
1	Associations and professional unions interested in the operation of Cross-Border Projects (11)
2	Local businesses, especially those who would be affected by increased tourism flows that would positively impact the cultural consumption pattern (180)
3	Convention and Visitor Centres and Bureaus, Chambers of Commerce, and other local groups dedicated to promoting cultural consumption and tourism (18)

Source MIS ETC 2617 ALECTOR project record

spiritual (tradition, religion, rites and beliefs, lifestyles) level. A multi-criteria *Significance Assessment Tool* (SAT) has been applied to facilitate the selection of cultural heritage assets with interpretive potential (Papathanasiou-Zuhrt and Weiss-Ibanez 2014). Ninety heritage assets in seven countries are classified according to natural, man-made and spiritual heritage classes. All ninety assets and have been further evaluated according to the criteria described in the lists of designated monuments in Greece, Bulgaria, Romania, Moldova, Ukraine, Georgia and Turkey and the *Unesco Operational Guidelines*. A validated *Statement of Significance* has been formulated for each asset, generating the conservation motive for authorities and the travel and consumption motive for visitors (UNESCO 2012). The 90-asset-body forms the *Black Sea Heritage Registry* (Table 2.4).

Authenticity is a core value in cultural communication and central to the quality experience. Authenticity relates both to the representations of the past combined with visitor perceptions of authenticity, while from conservation management perspective it means to be as historically accurate as possible in the scientific representation of historical events, rehabilitation and restoration as per Venice Charter (1964); Amsterdam Declaration (1975); Florence Charter (1982); UNESCO (1994). In the development context of *SCRIPTORAMA*, visitors play an active role in the authenticity of heritage, rather than simply being a passive recipient of historical knowledge. It is of crucial importance to realize that the audience is not

Table 2.4 Heritage significance assessment process

Secondary criteria	Modifiers
Provenance	**1.1** Authenticity; **1.2** Originality; **1.3** Designation
Integrity	**2.1** Completeness; **2.2** Exemplarity; **2.3** Bio- and cultural diversity
Distinctiveness	**3.1** Novelty; **3.2** Familiarity
Accessibility	**4.1** Availability; **4.2** Carrying capacity; **4.2** Condition; 4.4 Facilities; **4.5** Service capacity
Interpretive potential	**5.1** Legal status; **5.2** Intervention possibilities; **5.3** Asset knowledge; **5.4** Knowledge of the audience; **5.6** Media selection; **5.5**. Experience opportunities

Source MIS ETC 2617 ALECTOR project record

only seeking knowledge but also enjoyment through the emotional interaction with the past. Presenting original assets and dry facts disconnect the audience from the experience vehicle and lead to an "in vitro image of the departed past" (Gyimothi and Johns 2001: 249). What *SCRIPTORAMA* wishes to avoid by all means is the "serial reproduction" of culture and the onset of a "vicious cycle" of decline in heritage places (Richards and Wilson 2006; Russo 2002).

2.2.4 Restructuring the Knowledge Pattern for Non-captive Audiences

SCRIPTORAMA aims to demonstrate the value of *Human Cognitive Architecture* for the recreational learning environment: the spatiotemporal gap generated by authentic heritage settings is produced by both the tangible (material substance) and the intangible (hidden meanings) dimension of heritage assets: architectural forms, inherent meanings, community values, universal values, state of integrity etc.,—and the inability of visitors without prior knowledge to access the bigger picture. This very particular time-distance condition is further sharpened by cultural and mentality differences, which impedes altogether non-captive audiences to grasp the value of heritage. The spatiotemporal gap is a matter of *cognition* closely linked to experiential learning as defined by Dewy (1938) and Kolb (1984) (Fig. 2.1).

Descriptions authored by the supply side (heritage authorities) are usually coded in the expert jargon. They are little adjusted to the eye-scan-path movement, the general cognitive ability **g**, the category learning, the ability to perceive and process information, retain and evoke mental representations, the capacity of working memory and the interactions of working and long-term memory and non-accidental connections between kinds and properties and grounded cognition (Baddeley and Hitch 1974; Prasada 2000; Barsalou 2008, 2010; Baddeley 2012; Baddeley et al. 2014). This vicious circle is responsible for the poor quality of onsite experiences, and as such it is generating significant revenues losses.

Fig. 2.1 Low readability panel in Turkish, Arabic and English with fragmented socio-historical information at the entrance of Ayasofya Museum in Trabzon, Turkey (*Source* The ALECTOR project record, 2015)

Cultural growth is linked to the presence of particular tangible assets, such as monuments, museums, heritage sites and historic cities, natural attractions and cultural landscapes. Tourism operators try to attract consumers, merely focusing on the tangible form of heritage assets, exploiting the iconic visibility at the maximum, while the intangible dimension, the meaning hidden in the tangible form, is neglected. On the other hand, cultural heritage authorities hold the monopoly of information and often reject the individual expressions and aspects about heritage assets as untrue. In fact some individual expressions can be hold true, while others cannot. Therefore, how to deliver validated knowledge patterns, how to establish a new learning paradigm and how to generate visitors that become self-providers and distributors of knowledge are the major research questions within ALECTOR.

We assume that non-captive audiences at heritage places are heterogeneous (multi-national, multi-cultural and multi-generational) groups, exploring information potentially connected with their own pre-understandings and prior knowledge. The main difference between learners in formal settings and non-captive audiences is the possibility to rehearse material. As the human working memory is limited in capacity with respect to the number of elements it can handle simultaneously, rehearsal is necessary to prevent information loss. This condition cannot be met with time-scarce and non-captive audiences. In order to create a mental bridge to selected phenomena, and make the novel seem familiar by relating it to prior knowledge and/or universal concepts in a much shorter time period and more entertaining way, a new approach is required: brain literacy is the *conditio sine qua non* to accurately identify opportunities for cognitive accessibility, exploiting both the visual, interactive and reading environment and list all features that enhance the perception. *SCRIPTORAMA* is an attempt to clarify the conditions in which understanding takes place. Among these, conditions are prejudices and fore-meanings in the mind of the interpreting visitor. Understanding is therefore interpretation, where one uses the own preconceptions so that the meaning of the object can really be made to speak or it can be altered in a non-desirable way. Understanding is a productive process, with interpretations keep changing during the process of what and when is being understood. An important condition in which understanding takes place is temporal distance: present and past are firmly connected and the past is not something that has to be painfully regained in each present, *if* the interpreter has the tool to decode it. One of the main problems is with is how to distinguish "true prejudices", by which we understand, from the "false" ones, by which we misunderstand. However, visitors at heritage places are not always aware of historic specificities. It is the knowledge of the undistorted history that is enabling the audience to put aside the own prejudices and evaluate heritage from a different light and multiple perspectives. But how to achieve this at heritage places and sites? *SCRIPTORAMA* relies on hermeneutics to bridge the spatiotemporal gap between the "object" and the "interpreter". Hermeneutics is a systems' logic that derives from the ability of humans to think in abstract and taxonomic categories, naming it categorical knowledge and that memories are composed of associations, as firstly put by Aristotle (Μανδηλαράς 2000). Mental activity does not occur in a vacuum, but is grounded in the type of worlds our bodies inhabit, meaning that humans use context to "guide the encoding and retrieve information" (Radvansky 2016: 17). Therefore, to link tangible aspects of heritage to their intangible meanings by connecting the visible form with the invisible meaning is an imperative task. Common threads between the asset and the rest of the world are needed to facilitate the understanding and appreciation of phenomena. If the audience understands how heritage is relating to the bigger picture, and why it is important, all connected services in heritage places acquire a special added value. To help the audience make sense of local phenomena, *SCRIPTORAMA* links them to the bigger picture employing storytelling in the format of audiovisual narratives designed in correspondence with the principles of Human Cognitive Architecture (HCA): the information architecture adopted by ALECTOR presupposes a limited working memory capacity to deal with visual, auditory and verbal material and an almost unlimited long-term memory, capable of retaining retain schemas, i.e. mental representations that vary in their degree of automation (Sweller 2008: 370–381; Paas et al. 2010; Baddeley et al. 2014; Radvansky 2016). Information units are chunked with three novel concepts per unit, below the limit proposed by Miller (1956, 2003). Graphic design is aligned with the eye-scan-path movement, and layering follows international standards for the interpretation of heritage (ICOMOS 2006). In order to decongest the working memory and redirect attention, metaphors, associations and universal concepts have been extensively utilized, and meanings are communicated through the use of universal concepts. Capitalizing on the attention-value-model suggested by Bitgood, a heritage narrative has been modelled in line with the cognitive load theory, to respond to the working memory constraints and the specific needs and requirements of attention and memory span in informal learning settings (Sweller et al. 2007; Bitgood 2013). The communication strategy considers an intrinsic, extraneous and germane cognitive load involving detailed didactic skills to model the narrative according to the findings obtained by empirical evidence in ninety heritage places across the Project Area. The model aims to demonstrate the value of a cognitive-driven narratology, making brain literacy educationally relevant for the museum sector, and provide the Project Area with cognitive-emotionally accessible heritage assets connecting them to local offers, products and services. Information management is concerned with the elimination of mental fatigue and the (re)direction of the attention with catchy elements. Ninety-six guidelines have been applied across five cognitive domains: Attention (28); Cognitive Chains (31); Comprehension (19); Decongestion of the working memory (36); Activation of Prior Knowledge (10).

2.3   SCRIPTORAMA Mise en Scène

SCRIPTORAMA, the first *Black Sea Open Street Museum*, has implemented a 90 geolocation connectivity map with 90 heritage assets with a total cost of 119.600 EUR (ENPI cost: 132.700; IPA cost 71.100 EUR). A scenario relates to 90 cultural heritage objects enabling visitors to select desired objects in the locations of interest. Heritage assets gain new significance, as they reclaim hidden values through a sophisticated audiovisual narrative that allows for cognitive-emotional encounters and stimulates imagination and participatory exchanges. *SCRIPTORAMA* is devoted to provide a deeper understanding of heritage places enriching the cultural experience. The 90 selected geolocations are accessible via QRC in the territory, and services attached around them, ensured through constantly updating Google map, integral part of the eBook for iOS and Android operating systems (Tables 2.5 and 2.6).

2.3.1   *Universal Values: The Open Street Museum Exhibition*

Heritage may broaden the audience's horizons by offering *distinctiveness* and *authenticity*, but at many heritage places a conflict is taking place: the one between *perception* and *understanding*, which is both of emotional and cognitive nature. Despite being driven by the "need of cognition", the visitor interest decreases as the museum visits progress (Cacioppo and Petty 1982; Davey 2005; Bitgood 2009). The same applies for the discovery process at heritage places. Working memory fatigue and other location-related inconveniencies trigger resignation in the last

Table 2.5 SCRIPTORAMA: the ENPI geolocations

ENPI funded partners	No	Monument	Geolocation
Greece: ENPI Financial Lead Beneficiary: Drama Development S.A.	1	Anastasiadis Tobacco Factory, 1875	41° 9′ 0.53″N, 24° 8′ 33.60″E
	2	Drama railway station, 1895	41° 8′ 26.20″N, 24° 8′ 51.18″E
	3	Portokaloglou Tobacco Factory, 1904	41° 9′ 1.45″N, 24° 8′ 20.80″E
	4	School of the Greek Orthodox Community, 1909	41° 9′ 9.46″N, 24° 8′ 19.14″E
	5	Michailidi Tobacco Factory, 1912	41° 9′ 4.13″N, 24° 8′ 30.46″E
	6	Olympia Cinema, 1920	41° 9′ 5.79″N, 24° 8′ 36.63″E
	7	Spierer Tobacco Factory, 1925	41° 9′ 2.07″N, 24° 8′ 31.20″E
	8	Tzimou Mansion, 1925	41° 8′ 58.60″N, 24° 8′ 18.14″E
	9	Feiss Mansion, 1927	41° 9′ 6.63″N, 24° 8′ 47.04″E
	10	National Bank, 1928	41° 9′ 4.96″N, 24° 8′ 48.13″E
Romania: ENPI 1, National Tourism Authority	1	Museum for National History and Archaeology Constanta	44° 10′ 25″N, 28° 39′ 29″E
	2	Roman Edifice with Mosaic	44° 10′ 25″N, 28° 39′ 29″E
	3	Constanta Archaeological Park	44° 10′ 16.79″ N, 28° 39′ 39.38″E
	4	Callatis Archaeology Museum	43° 49′ 2.2404″N, 28° 34′ 59.6568″E
	5	Callatis Fortress	43° 49′N, 28° 35′ E
	6	Tropaeum Traiani Monument	44° 6′ 7.2″N, 27° 57′ 18″E
	7	Tropaeum Traiani Fortress	44° 5′ 0″N, 27° 57′ 16″E
	8	Tropaeum Traiani Museum	44° 5′ 0″N, 27° 57′ 16″E
	9	Histria Fortress	44° 32′ 51″N, 28° 46′ 29″E
	10	Capidava Fortress	44° 29′ 37″N, 28° 5′ 25″E

(continued)

Table 2.5 (continued)

ENPI funded partners	No	Monument	Geolocation
Bulgaria: ENPI 2, Union of Bulgarian Black Sea Local Authorities	1	Varna Cathedral	43.205289, 27.909724
	2	The Tower Clock	43.204303, 27.910404
	3	The Drama Theatre	43.203708, 27.912550
	4	The Ethnographic Museum	43.201109, 27.913452
	5	The Roman baths	43.199965, 27.917392
	6	Varna history Museum	43.198661, 27.917994
	7	Varna Maritime Museum	43.200232, 27.921575
	8	Sea Garden	43.203758, 27.922318
	9	St. Nikolas thaugamature	43.204424, 27.917971
	10	Archaeological Museum	43.207389, 27.914961
Moldova: ENPI 3: National Association of Rural, Ecological and Cultural Tourism	1	National Museum, Chisinau	47° 1' 23.7252"N, 28° 49' 12.7848"E
	2	Wine Factory "Cricova"	47° 8' 17.3256"N, 28° 51' 20.9808"E
	3	Museum Complex "Orheiul Vechi"	47° 18' 10.9188" N, 28° 58' 02.1072"E
	4	Touristic halt "Vatra Stramoseasca"	47° 20' 27.0024" N, 28° 37' 24.2832"E
	5	Curchi Monastery	47° 20' 1.1256" N, 28° 39' 11.3112"E
	6	Soroca Fortress, Soroca	48° 9' 40.8168" N, 28° 18' 19.6632"E
	7	Domulgeni Village, Floresti	47° 47' 27.9276" N, 28° 26' 46.1904"E
	8	Ethno-cultural Complex "Vatra"	47° 10' 32.6568" N, 28° 29' 44.9664"E
	9	Wine Complex "Milestii mici"	46° 55' 11.5140" N, 28° 49' 17.1948"E
	10	"Carpe Diem" wine shop, Chisinau	47° 1' 48.4932"N, 28° 49' 50.9664"E

(continued)

Table 2.5 (continued)

ENPI funded partners	No	Monument	Geolocation
Ukraine: ENPI P 4, Donetsk Civic Organization "Alliance"	1	Mariupol Museum of local history	47° 5′ 34.2486″N, 37° 33′ 26.4594″E
	2	Mariupol art Museum "A. Kuindji"	47° 5′ 36.24″N, 37° 33′ 2.88″E
	3	"Meotida" cultural centre	47° 6′ 3.4128″N, 37° 31′ 29.067″E
	4	Church of St. John the Zlatoust	46° 57′ 44.856″N, 37° 16′ 9.6954″E
	5	Monument of metropolitan Ignatius	47° 5′ 46.0854″N, 37° 39′ 36.795″E
	6	Museum of Greek ethnography	47° 10′ 30.36″N, 37° 41′ 38.7594″E
	7	House of culture of Tamara Katsy	47° 10′ 13.7166″ N, 37° 41′ 20.3784″E
	8	Cultural Centre "Village of Vashura"	47° 0′ 13.0794″N, 37° 41′ 49.92″E
	9	St. Michael Church	46° 54′ 57.9918″ N, 37° 5′ 51.5862″E
	10	Mariupol Museum of folklife	47° 5′ 38.0394″N, 37° 33′ 0.7194″E
Georgia: ENPI 5, Batumi Archaeological Museum	1	Kvirike Mosque	41° 46′ 0.78″N, 41° 50′ 20.94″E
	2	Petra-Tsikhisdziri Fort	41° 46′ 6.39″N, 41° 45′ 13.12″E
	3	Batumi Botanical Garden	41° 41′ 48.08″N, 41° 42′ 48.26″E
	4	The Nobel Brothers Batumi Technological Museum	41° 39′ 42.31″N, 41° 40′ 49.45″E
	5	Batumi Fort	41° 39′ 49.42″N, 41° 40′ 57.98″E
	6	Art gallery Dotcomma	41° 38′ 54.68″N, 41° 38′ 2.81″E
	7	Batumi Boulevard	41° 39′ 17.14″N, 41° 38′ 4.58″E
	8	Batumi Archaeological Museum	41° 38′ 35.71″N, 41° 37′ 55.20″E
	9	Avgia Church	41° 34′ 27.21″N, 41° 35′ 18.07″E
	10	Gonio-Apsarus Fort and Museum	41° 34′ 23.64″N, 41° 34′ 24.55″E

Source MIS ETC 2617 ALECTOR project record

Table 2.6 SCRIPTORAMA: the ENPI geolocations

IPA Funded Partners	No	Monument	Geolocation
Turkey: IPA financial lead beneficiary Governorship of Istanbul	1	The sile lighthouse	41° 10′ 40.6″N, 29° 36′ 58.5″E
	2	Sile castle	41° 10′ 54.7″N, 29° 36′ 33.4″E
	3	Weeping rock	41° 10′ 31.6″N, 29° 37′ 27.2″E
	4	Fishing traditions	41° 10′ 52.7″N, 29° 36′ 25.2″E
	5	Historic ship rescue station	41° 10′ 31.3″N, 29° 36′ 29.4″E
	6	The Sile fabric	41° 09′ 20.8″N, 29°35′17.6″E
	7	Sofular's geology	41° 10′ 50.4″N, 29° 31′ 32.6″E
	8	Sile's past	41° 07′ 19.1″N, 29° 39′ 16.7″E
	9	Yenikoy's history	41° 07′ 19.1″N, 29° 39′ 16.7″E
	10	Yenikoy's beekeeping tradition	41° 07′ 19.1″N, 29° 39′ 16.7″E
Turkey: IPA 1, Eastern Black Sea development agency	1	Yason Cape, Ordu	41° 07′ 49″N, 37° 42′ 34″E
	2	Giresun Island, Giresun	40° 56′ 26″N, 38° 26′ 03″E
	3	Sümela Monastery, Macka	40° 38′ 27″N, 39° 41′ 18″E
	4	Ayasofya museum, Trabzon	40° 59′ 56″N, 39° 41′ 54″E
	5	Zil castle, Rize	40° 51′ 44″N, 41° 01′ 11″E
	6	Bedesten Bazaar, Trabzon	41° 00′ 11″N, 39° 43′ 56″E
	7	Memisaga mension, Surmene	40° 52′ 35″N, 40° 08′ 37″E
	8	Ataturk Pavillon, Soguksu	40° 00′ 13″N, 39° 17′ 51″E
	9	Trabzon museum, Trabzon	41° 58′ 33″N, 39° 44′ 15″E
	10	Santa Ruins, Gumushane	40° 58′ 33″N, 39° 44′ 15″E

(continued)

Table 2.6 (continued)

IPA Funded Partners	No	Monument	Geolocation
Turkey: IPA 2, Bahceseheir University/Metgem development centre for vocational-technical education	1	Akcakese's history & local culture	41° 08′ 33.2″N, 29° 43′ 04.2″E
	2	Akcakese's timber heritage	41° 08′ 33.2″N, 29° 43′ 04.2″E
	3	Traditional sile fabric embroidery	41° 08′ 37.7″N, 29° 41′ 18.1″E
	4	Poetry of the women in Sile and Agva	41° 08′ 33.2″N, 29° 43′ 04.2″E
	5	Agva's local culture	41° 08′ 20.3″N, 29° 51′ 18.7″E
	6	Natural heritage—birds	41° 08′ 03.6″N, 29° 50′ 24.1″E
	7	Natural heritage—plants	41° 08′ 18.6″N, 29° 50′ 55.3″E
	8	Kilimli cliffs ecosystems	41° 08′ 30.1″N, 29° 52′ 22.7″E
	9	Kilimli cliffs geomorphology	41° 08′ 31.0″N, 29° 52′ 13.0″E
	10	Kilimli cliffs—the future of heritage	41° 08′ 30.6″N, 29° 52′ 03.9″E

Source MIS ETC 2617 ALECTOR project record

phase of the visit. Given that the value of the read thread is known since the time of Theseus and Ariadne, a space without a read thread cannot become a successful attraction. However, telling the story is a creative process that cannot rely only on expert knowledge but shall include many types of synergies among stakeholders and the audience (Di Russo and Papathanasiou 2015: 6). Through the story, stakeholders can express what is unusual and special about their communities and heritage. Each heritage narrative created is the intentional, coordinated message that each heritage asset selected by the Cross-Border Partnership conveys to the audience. By producing the *Cross-Border Stakeholder Map*, the long-term viability of the operation is ensured.

The standardized heritage narrative is a max. 600 words long story structured in three subtitled and interconnected story segments. Each segment relates to the valuable traits of each individual heritage asset (museum item, monument, heritage place, cultural landscape, natural heritage phenomenon, place of memory, customs and traditions, traditional handicrafts, artwork, community innovation). Each narrative is tied to six intrinsic qualities: archaeological, socio-historical, artistic-cultural, natural, recreational and scenic (Wells et al. 2009: 25–27). These values are made explicit in the *Statement of Significance* for each of the 90 heritage assets included in the *Heritage Registry* of the MIS ETC 2617 Project ALECTOR. An asterisk section is included in the end of each story segment, not to disrupt the reading flow. At the end of each story, a connection is being made to other relevant stories in the same thematic chapter. Both the panels and the eBook keep the same story format; however, the eBook is interactive in many perspectives, while the access to the panels is ensured via the QRC in the territory scanned through a smart device.

Extensively capitalizing on the Narrative Museum in Castel La gopesole in Italy, *Il Mondo di Federico II. Tra storia e legende*, the historic personage is mise en scène, narrating in the first person to ensure direct emotional impact, always relating to a succinct and clear narrative, built on a well-documented historic fact (Papathanasiou and Di Russo 2015). The heritage narratives are connected with each other indicating the cultural bonds among the places:

WORLD TRAVELLER

EvliyaÇelebi*, the great Ottoman travel writer arrives in August 1640 in Trabzon, one of biggest merchant centres for silk and spices to Istanbul.

"I am Evliya* Çelebi, the *blessed one*. I was born in 1611 in the capital of our Empire*. I was fortunate enough to have received a good education. For 40 years now I am touring all the Ottoman lands. I have also seen Vienna, Nile, Caucasus and Persia. I travel on official business, but also for pleasure. My passion is to observe the everyday life: buildings, markets, landmarks and traditions. People call me scholar, raconteur, dervish, musician, and linguist. I call myself world traveler. My faithful companion is my ring with the inscription *The World Traveler Evliya*. I write down everything I see in my journeys, in my Book of Travels, the *Seyahatname*. The best place to observe life and customs is the Bazaar. Therefore I have visited the Trabzon Bazaar. It was originally built by Genoese merchants. Its shape is rectangular, like it is sitting on four elephant legs. In the course of the time it became the only single-domed covered bazaar among the covered bazaars of our Empire. It is a true Caravanserai with great stone doors. The interior walls are skillfully carved with seventy or eighty crowded shops inside with rich merchants and all kinds of tradesmen. They say that famous Marco Polo called the port of Trabzon on his way to Venice. The goldsmiths of Trabzon are the best in the world. Diamond and jewelry as precious as corn, dazzle in the wealthy merchants' cases! During the knight 60 watchmen safeguard the Bazaar.

*Greek: Evlogia; Latin: Benedictus.
**Present day Istanbul in Turkey.
*EvliyaCelebi: Seyahatname, (The Book of Travels), 1640.
For more adventures: *Follow Story no 8: THE GOLDEN PASSPORT.*

From: THE MARVELS OF TRABZON, Bedesten Bazaar, 1640.
In: LEGENDARY JOURNEYS: Eastern Black Sea from the Silk Road to Modern Times.
Source: MIS ETC 2617 ALECTOR Project Record

Layout and texts ensure that cultural assets are identified and that intangible meanings and universal concepts are linked to selected assets and generate a cohesive and memorable heritage narrative. To express the values of each asset monolithic interpretations are avoided, instead community values and a diversity of controversial aspects are included, so that visitors can make up their own mind in a reflective and dialogical process. Critical and political issues are providing multiples views and aspects and opinions, while relying validated socio-historical information. Thematic frameworks are developed by experts to connect non-captive audiences without a need for prior knowledge to the desired heritage experiences. The stories encompass the ordinary/every day and the extraordinary/unique and promoting the audience's capacity to reflect on the values of the assets presented, stimulating the visitor–monument–community interaction at a visual, haptic, cognitive and emotional level. All 90 selected heritage objects are integrated in the wider social community and the territory by including and involving specific interest groups (Table 2.7).

The smart device revolution has changed the way; software is distributed and used among consumers. The rise of (social networking) apps as a signal of maturation for the platforms opens new business opportunities. Smart devices are powerful, connected and always with consumers. The mobile telephony is marked by the dramatic rise of smartphones in the mainstream, the burgeoning of tablets and other web-enabled connected devices and a cultural shift towards cross-platform digital media consumption. Apps are a critical component of the mobile media ecosystem, playing an important role in consumers' mobile device purchase decision while shaping their engagement with mobile media content. They are used to share social experiences and can leverage the significance of heritage places, but can also act fame killers.

SCRIPTORAMA implements 90 *Quick Response Codes* (QRC) by directly guiding audiences to product information, without any other media intervention in the between. QR codes came onto the scene as a way to bridge mobile and traditional media across various mediums including print publications, product packaging, outdoor kiosks and more. A QR (Quick Response) code is a specific matrix barcode (or two-dimensional code) that is readable by smart devices with one touch only and do not require typing URL addresses or other tiring web searches. QR codes result in client offers, event information and location-based mobile check-in services to name but a few examples. Quality content that is built for mobile tagging and delivered through QR codes is designed with the mobile user experience in mind. *SCRIPTORAMA* understands how users are engaging with these codes and how these codes can complement the heritage experience in situ. The deployment of the *QRC Inventory* across the Project Area enables a vast customer pool to retrieve key media information, building thus an effective marketing tool (Figs. 2.2, 2.3 and 2.4).

Table 2.7 SCRIPTORAMA: heritage narrative sample

SCRIPTORAMA	
The black sea open street museum	
Partner	**DOKA** (Eastern Black Sea development agency)
Chapter	**Legendary Journeys**
Subtitle	Eastern Black Sea from the silk road to modern times
Monument	**Zil castle**
Story date	**1807**
Story title	**The golden passport**
Segment I	*Guardian of the silk road* In 1807 French Ambassador Gardane starts his journey from Istanbul to Persia. The diplomat Joseph-Michel Tancoigne keeps the journey's diary: "Our caravan reached on the 6th of October 1807 the fortress of Zil in the stormy valley of the Firtina River. The Castle was built in the reign of Emperor Justinian* and was used by the Empire of Trabzon**. It is now used by the Ottoman Sultan for military purposes passing on information to Rize Castle. Zil is built 750 m above the sea level and 100 m up the river bank. It has outer walls, middle walls and an inner castle. Zil lies on the historical *Silk Road* and functioned as a security and checkpoint. Silk was the most valuable product in the Mediaeval Ages after pepper. The *Silk Road* was a network of trade routes established in ancient China. It linked the East and the West from 130 BC to 1453 AD. When the Ottoman Empire closed the *Silk Road*, merchants took the sea route to continue trading. Thus the *Discovery Age** started in 1453"
Asterisk section	***Byzantine Emperor Justinian the Great (482–565 AD)* ***The Empire of Trebizond (1204–1461) was the longest survivor of the Byzantine successor states* ****European historical period (fifteenth–eighteenth century) with extensive overseas explorations*
Segment II	*MARCO POLO* Marco Polo was the only foreigner envoy at the Court of Kublai Khan* with a golden passport. Marco was born into a merchant family in Venice in 1254. He travelled with his father and uncle from Europe to Asia for more than 20 years (1271–1295). To make sure the Polos would be given any assistance on their travels *Kublai Khan* presented them with a *Golden Tablet of Command*, a 30 cm long and 2 cm wide! It was inscribed with the words: *By the strength of the eternal Heaven, holy be the Khan's name. Let him that pays him not reverence be killed.* It was a special passport, authorizing travellers to receive horses, lodging, food and guides throughout the dominions of the Great Khan. It took the Polos three years to return to Venice passing the South China Sea to Sumatra and the Indian Ocean to arrive at Hormuz in Persia, where they found out that Kublai Kahn died. However, his protection outlived him: the golden tablet protected them throughout the bandit-ridden interior. From Trebizond, the Polos went by sea to Bosporus and from there to Venice in 1295
Asterisk section	**Fifth Khan of the Mongol Empire, grandchild of Genghis Khan and founder of the Yuan Dynasty (1215–1294)* ***paiza in Chinese; gerege in Mongolian*

(continued)

Table 2.7 (continued)

SCRIPTORAMA	
The black sea open street museum	
Partner	**DOKA** (Eastern Black Sea development agency)
Segment III	***A MILLION LIES?*** After his return to Venice, Marco commanded a ship in a war against Genoa. He was captured and sent to a Genoese prison, where he met *Rustichello da Pisa* whom he described his journeys. *The Travels of Marco Polo* made Marco a celebrity, but few readers believed the tales. They called the book *Il Milione**, the million lies. After his release from prison, Marco marries in Venice and carried the family business for the next 25 years. He died at his home in 1324. As he lay dying he said: *I have not told half of what I saw.* His possessions of clothes, valuable pieces, brocades of silk and gold and other precious objects were exactly like those mentioned in his book. Among them, there was the *Golden Tablet of Command* given to him by the *Great Kublai Khan* on his departure from the Mongol capital
Asterisk section	**According to recent research Il Milione is correctly interpreted as a million miles*
Connection	For more adventures follow *STORY NO 3: THE MARVELS OF TRABZON*

Source MIS ETC 2617 ALECTOR project record

Fig. 2.2 ALECTOR QRC outdoor display label indicating heritage area, monument and geolocation (*Source* MIS ETC 2617 ALECTOR project record)

Fig. 2.3 ALECTOR QRC
gallery (*Source*
The ALECTOR project
record)

Fig. 2.4 SCRIPTORAMA, The Eurasian story (*Source* The ALECTOR project record)

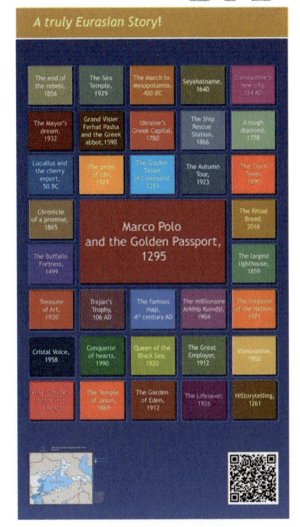

2.3.2   Information with Tourism Value: The Travel Aider

The *Travel Aider* is a printed booklet of 100 pages in an 24 * 26.5 cm which provides information with tourism value. It is perceived of as having a *floor plan* with a collection of *individual rooms* or *landscape units* that can be entered and experienced, like the rooms of a building. The intent of this task is to define the *Heritage Area Floor Plan* by identifying and mapping all of the individual units adding to a quality visitor experience. With regards to the natural heritage assets, topography, hydrology and vegetation will primarily define the landscape units; whereas cultural heritage assets are composed by the distinctive features of the built environment and the intangible cultural heritage assets, some of which are unique, at global level, are mapped according to their sociocultural significance. The *Travel Aider* is composing the bigger picture for *SCRIPTORAMA* connected to the larger storytelling of the eBook.

The *Travel Aider* includes an introduction to the heritage area, explicitly making a statement of significance for the cultural value of the each selected area. Each asset is presented with a short narrative, no longer than 400 words and a representative image. In this way, the *Travel Aider* embeds each heritage identity in a visitor floor plan with ten different heritage units per partner area. A section follows with accessibility information per asset and the QRC for each asset separately. By scanning the QRC, the visitor is accessing the bilingual panel with the heritage story in the national and English language. This integrative list allows the formation of experience diversity and promotes the customized selection of one or many experiences in the territory: visitors can decide which location to visit using the Google map that is incorporated to the eBook. Accessibility to attractions that meet changing needs of tourism markets will help local businesses to reach specific tourism development targets. Gunn emphasizes the repeated error in spontaneous tourism development: instead of developed and managed attractions heritage classes are listed to attract visitors: this practice often jeopardizes the nature of heritage and decreases the tourism experience (Gunn and Var 2002: 41) (Figs. 2.5 and 2.6).

To export the heritage experience in the Project Area to international markets, the *Travel Aider* groups the attractions according to location, key themes, operation and purchase information. Theme routes developed and heritage trails designed ensure the accessibility and proximity to tourism goods and services. Finally the *QRC Inventory* gives a further impetus to the desired travel motive at cross border level (Travel Aider, pp. 3–5).

2.3.3   The Power of Emotions: The eBook

As the Project Area is facing the lack of access points, which incorporate barriers for visitors and clients in terms of directly accessing local services and promoting

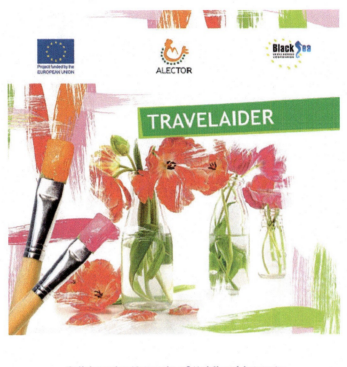

Fig. 2.5 MIS ETC ALECTOR, The travel aider (*Source* MIS ETC 2617 ALECTOR project record)

synergies among local businesses, the role of a new generation of web-based applications and services that leverage standards and open platforms involvement of key stakeholders, such as public bodies and businesses, with strong involvement of end-users and SMEs, is the only reality for the sector to face the financial crisis, with an instrument which connects and reshapes existing services, and formulates the ones that need to be invented.

The general aim of the ALECTOR eBook is to launch a new cultural consumption model by shaping and steering new integrative experiences able to deliver cultural values to consumers spreading local and regional boundaries with the use of mobile technologies. The eBook becomes thus an instrument which facilitates and stimulates the development of attractive services and applications, fostering

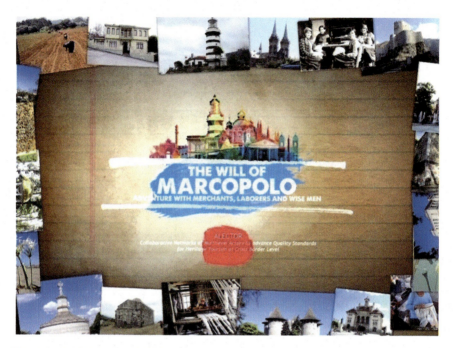

Fig. 2.6 ALECTOR eBook: Video section with interactive elements (*Source* The ALECTOR project record, 2015)

consumer demand. It shall further support the implementation of similar products and services in the Project Area and the uptake of innovation in cultural heritage production not only as a project-driven business model, but also as the proactive promoter of each participating region.

2.3.3.1 Technical Features

Any eBook can be purchased, borrowed, downloaded, and used immediately, whereas when one buys or borrows a tangible book, one must go to a bookshop, a home library, or public library during limited hours, or wait for a delivery. Unlike the paper book, an eBook can be backed up and recovered in the case of loss or damage to the device on which they are stored, and it may be possible to recover a new copy without incurring an additional cost from the distributor. Finally, an eBook has an infinite distribution potential, an unlimited capacity for updates, real-time synchronization with all the devices independently of place and time and can be disseminated by the AppStore and Google Play selling points.

The ALECTOR eBook is designed for both the iOS and Android operating systems in order to disseminate the heritage experience in the Project Area at a cross-platform level. It is creating a heritage corridor with 90 selected geolocations virally disseminating nine heritage identities on smart devices, phones, PCs and tablet applications, offered as a **free download** at the AppStore and Google Play and stimulates thus the individual travel motive in the Project Area. The ALECTOR eBook is not to be exchanged with any other digital format that belongs to certain categories and cannot be modified like .doc and .pdf documents. Instead, it uses a technology that includes and may converge various and different electronic formats in one format like pictures, sound, music, text, video, multi-visions and interactive pictures. Into the eBook, pages are embedded non-textual multimedia including interactive images and image galleries, videos, audio files and interactive animated and sophisticated graphic design. By adopting the eBook as a heritage communication medium, the Cross-Border Partnership offers to onsite and dislocated audiences a significance chance to create their personal place-bonding through a digital publication, consisting of text, images, interactive images, videos and multimedia and a variety of shared practices (Bookry/Reader Cloud; Google +; Facebook; Twitter; Email; Web embedding). Mobile availability is provided for users with a mobile data connection, alternatively a copy of the eBook can be stored on the device. In the space that a comparably sized print book takes up, e-readers can potentially contain thousands of eBooks, limited only by the storage memory capacity. The Partnership decision aimed to ensure a unique output that can exceed the project lifetime by far, available for further updates and considering transformations in the connected consumer market.

The ALECTOR eBook has not been created in isolation, but in collaboration with local stakeholders, whose valuable feedback has facilitated the crossing of the bridge of vision to the valley of implementation. It capitalizes on existing local resources to enable local businesses with proximity to the selected geolocations of the Open Street Museum to benefit by being present in the Google Map that leads to the enhanced visitor revenues. Connected to an interactive Google Map, the eBook inevitably becomes an agent for change per se: a model for cultural heritage products and services that is not yet in place, but needed in the context of the revalorization of the territory: consumers increasingly consult their trustworthy shopping companion—the smartphone—inside stores and at street level in format of downloadable videos, images to Whatsapp images, Instagram photos and geo-media location data. The Google Map integrates contents of the retail environment providing local SMEs with a significant opportunity to reach customers through a highly personal digital media channel incorporated into the eBook. In this way, a clear image of each local heritage identity is created, part of the Project Area identity, as understood and launched by the Cross-Border Partnership.

Added value and local expertise are mapped so that the Google Map becomes an *Inventory of Products & Services* in the Project Area. Through the Google Map, anyone interested may access all available consumption points in the territory: from hotels and restaurants to pharmacies and gas stations, from stores and souvenirs to hospitals and police stations. In this way, a business platform is operated for local products and services, an inventory linked to the local–global markets, proactively promoting the Project Area: the eBook launches *SCRIPTORAMA* as business venture in the Project Area identifying how consumer time is shifting across app categories and operating systems.

Shopping can also be very important for the visitor experience—memory shopping of material culture (Moreno et al. 2005; Yuksel 2005; Yuksel and Yuksel 2007). There is a certain need for visitors to buy things as memories of their holidays. Consuming quality goods onsite adds to the sense of place; consuming them in the permanent place of residence is adding to the memory: the location visited, its people and the climate acquire a special added value. By-products such as traditional gourmet products, handicrafts and participatory activities like cooking and language learning contribute to the *genius loci* as well. For example, a considerable amount of wine is bought at cellars around Drama (Greece), in Varna (Bulgaria), in Batumi (Georgia) and in Chisinau (Moldova); traditional silverware and jewellery are offered in Trabzon (Turkey); Sile (Turkey) is famous for its hand-made cloth and the prize-crowned chestnut honey; Batumi's artistic production has spread boundaries: the list of quality products is long in the Project area.

Factual information about selected geolocations is transformed into a fully comprehensible AV and multimedia narrative for a better understanding of cultural heritage and the improvement of independent travel practices. In this vein, the eBook ensures that cultural heritage assets become fully accessible across computers, smart devices and mobile phones, with the streetscape playing a protagonist role in the experience framework. However, as highly advanced this can be in terms of technical implementation, it is neither the hardware nor the device, nor the software that offer a cultural heritage experience, but the overall quality of contents: the cognitive-emotional experience and the possibility for immersion—the latter relates to the emotional, physical, intellectual and spiritual engagement in the activities in which skilled visitors participate. Quality assurance in regards to the specification for design and use is guaranteed by Apple Corporation. The ALECTOR eBook is accordingly registered at the Apple Store. The *eBook* is the registered name of the Apple software to produce electronic books for the iPad. The ALECTOR eBook will be uploaded at the Apple platform that is called eBook store. Apple allows producing it again for the competitor, who is Android, if it is made for free, e.g., it has not been destined to be sold for profit. Apple provides the creators with an ISDN for the official publication, which is an extra added value for the dissemination. The eBook will be produced in both versions to gain visibility and promote the efforts of the ALECTOR Cross-Border Partnership, by addressing the connected consumer market, e.g. both iOS and Android users. Depending on the device, the eBook may be readable in low light or in total darkness. Many newer readers have the ability to display motion, enlarge or change fonts, use text-to-speech software to read the text aloud for visually impaired, partially sighted, elderly or dyslectic people or just for convenience, search for key terms, find definitions or allow highlighting bookmarking and annotation. Additionally, the eBook allows readers to look up words or find more information about the topic immediately.

2.3.3.2 Content Design

The ALECTOR eBook is not a database of static facts about heritage places and sites but an interactive cognitive-emotional and dynamic experience collection which identifies and presents the diverse intangible values and universal meanings to the audience. It shows multiple perspectives and the relationships of events, encouraging visitors to derive personal meanings. It provides guidance on artistic and cultural achievements allowing readers to understand causal and functional relationships, alternative hypotheses and the nature of evidence. The interpretive nature of *SCRIPTORAMA* reflects the goals and objectives set by local stakeholders and the Cross-Border Partnership. To create powerful emotions, storytelling is applied: old as prehistoric times, storytelling is a powerful tool for conveying and sharing ideas, beliefs, values and traditions. All ninety heritage assets in SCRIPTORAMA have a variety of stories to tell. Not all stories have the same emotional impact, as they are addressing different ethnic, generational, religious and cultural audiences, but they convey the significance of the asset in terms of universal values. Interesting aspects connecting the asset with the audience are linked together in sequences. Creating emotional impact and regulating behaviour to embrace values of heritage including protection and conservation objectives, intercultural and interfaith dialogue and political awareness is the quintessence of a quality cultural heritage service. To focus on a concise story and avoid causing mental overload, the contents are organized into stories, with a main messages, the audience carries away. Meanings are easily communicated through storytelling that helps the audience appreciate what's special about heritage places. The repository of stories is well balanced between history and legend, between facts and imagination. It is based on historic evidence and research with archives and literature, so as to give the different audiences clear threads to follow, rather than a series of disconnected facts, but it is leaving significant space for the imagination and fantasy to capture the audience's attention and stimulate the cognitive-emotional interactivity with selected phenomena. The stories always support the significance and importance of the interpreted heritage assets. They are written in complete sentences focusing on a single message the audience is likely to remember, going beyond a mere description of facts. The level of details is presented is appropriate for the non-captive audiences linking tangible things to intangible ideas, allowing visitors to derive personal connections and discoveries.

A cognitive-driven instructional design strategy has been developed to facilitate knowledge transfer. It ensures cognitive accessibility by activating perception through provocation, by relating to prior acquired experiences with universal values, and by providing for novelty and variety, surprise and exploration. Capturing the attention means to create bridges between the inherent values of phenomena selected for presentation, and the audiences. Far beyond the dissemination of factual information, cognitive accessibility aims to create meanings, so that visitors can put a phenomenon into personal perspective and identify with it in a more profound and enduring way. Leaning on the concept of multi-vision (vast screens with a resolution unattainable by any other means creating thus the enabling technical environment to enhance the possibilities of the photographic medium in animation), the eBook has exploited animation possibilities and has extensively used static documents of any kind to produce cultural manifestations in an interactive continuum. This makes both the onsite and offsite place visit an integrative experience: visual, haptic, educational, physical and emotional. The artistic concept derives from the 3 major Eurasian trails:

A: the pursuit of gold in early antiquity, expressed by the myth of the *Argonautica* and the *Golden Fleece*;

B: the commerce of silk and spices in the Antiquity and the Middle Ages, manifested by the *Silk Road*, the commercial route that brought Asia to Europe and the Mediterranean shores;

C: the trade of the oriental tobacco, covering the period from the late Ottoman Empire until the World War II.

In this tapestry of human history, the Cross-Border Partnership includes regions that played major roles in all historic periods. The title, *The will of Marco Polo. Adventure with merchants, laborers and wise men,* is inspired by the legacy of Marco Polo as a merchant and discoverer, compared to the EU acquis for "free movement of people, goods and services" as established by the Treaty of Rome signed on the 25 March 1957 at the Capitoline Hill by the founding members of the now European Union: Belgium, Netherlands, West Germany, Luxemburg, Italy and France. *Marco Polo* is not the tautology of the historic personage, but left to the imagination of the reader, to identify or not with one or with many of the historic personages included in the cultural tapestry.

The eBook is the unique project output that has exploited the infinite potential of static documents such as photographs, documents, archival materials, parchments, newspapers by enriching them with new elements and integrating them into the new storytelling with unprecedented possibilities for the creation of emotions and effects. Thus, the eBook has enriched the reader experience with diversified media, which otherwise would have stayed in the archives. The use of digital graphics and videos has introduced further changes in the narration, enabling to infer the unknown from something known within the horizon of the readers. Heritage narratives presented in the eBook are not made only by documents, but by a cluster of links between each document that creates a bridge between each event, between a letter and photograph, an object and a label, i.e., multiple links between different elements. The eBook has merged static archival elements in one great ensemble that has the possibility to create emotions and thus interact with the reader. Photos, portraits and manuscripts of all kinds are carefully put together in a counterpoint of a contemporary event and thus facilitate the perception, bridging the spatiotemporal gap between the object and the reader. The interactive character of the eBook is not restricted to the technical feature provided by Apple, but is a cognitive-emotional effort to provide knowledge to non-captive audiences and thus stimulate social consensus. Therefore, subject matter knowledge and socio-historic documentation for each heritage chapter presented in the eBook is ensured through nine *Authentication Papers*: they testify the production of high-quality heritage narratives, plagiarism-free texts and AV materials with special permissions (paid royalties; in-house production; by courtesy of individuals or institutions, registered in EUROPEANA). AV materials have been produced in full conformity with the EU directive 013/37/EU laying down the general principle that documents from libraries, museums and archives shall be reusable for commercial and non-commercial purposes (European Commission 2014: 11) (Figs. 2.7, 2.8 and 2.9).

Fig. 2.7 Chapter Cover with embedded Google Map and Historic Photo Gallery (*Source* MIS ETC 2617 project record)

Fig. 2.8 Asset story cover with narrative (*Source* MIS ETC 2617 project record)

The fact is that the shipping route competition keeps the profit low and in the end the construction cost is 3 times higher than the receipts. Fortunately, the Sultan has granted our company the privilege to hold the railway revenues for 99 years.

Fig. 2.9 Readability and interactivity of text and image (*Source* MIS ETC 2617 project record)

2.4 Conclusions

The official discourse on EU integration focuses on identity for over 60 years with cultural heritage being the uncontested common thread for all Europeans. However, cognitive-emotional accessibility to heritage assets is alarmingly low. The ICT revolution has created a digitally innate youth; however, the latter acquires new digital literacies in a self-directed learning environment with no formal opportunity for meta-cognition and critical thinking. But the *conditio sine qua non* for the future of Europe is to develop as many as thinker-citizens as possible. In this vein, the need to develop critical skills among the youth and raise its awareness for semiotic codes through a new knowledge pattern in the heritage settings is a challenging opportunity the Union's future.

The Council of Europe (COE) demonstrates that the entire European digital industries sector experiences stagnation including television, cinema, video and video on demand (VoD). Contents and values in digital cinema, video games, broadcasting services pay-tv platforms and the production of online VoD are mainly controlled by US groups meaning that the European Audiovisual Sector (AV) lost 5.3% of its global market share in the period 2009–2013 despite a 133 billion revenue €. The competitiveness of the European Audiovisual industry depends increasingly on its ability to generate and manage knowledge innovation: it is cultural heritage that can contribute to the sector's desired knowledge innovation. Viewed from this angle the implementation of the ALECTOR Project has shed light into five areas of concern:

- **Supply-demand divergence**: Developments in ICT and mobile telephony have produced a new market, the digitally innate youth. The use of outdated languages and technology results in the loss of the audience in the sector. On the other hand, developments in the digital heritage sector stagnate in front of the fossilization of professions with outdated skills. Activating training of workforces that brings the work to follow the development and launching new professional profiles is the remedy to unemployment in the cultural heritage sector.
- **New skills for new jobs**: Traditional curricula in both the cultural heritage and tourism planning sector are not up to the task, as they address outdated organizational structures depending on individuals with outdated skill sets. Also the ICT sector is affected by skills–jobs mismatches: The European Commission is calling for a Grand *Coalition for Digital Skills and Jobs*, as Europe might face a shortage of up to 825,000 ICT professionals by 2020, risking its potential for growth, social cohesion and digital competitiveness. Outdated languages and technology result in the loss of the audience in the sector. Unidentified skills needs, mismatches, stakeholder fragmentation and the US control of the industry disable self-employment, SME development and public procurements. The facts aforementioned lead us to support the view that specific job-related competences learned throughout education and training must be underpinned by transversal competences, especially digital and entrepreneurial competences, in order to both encourage self-directed learning rather than simple reproduction of received knowledge and to better adapt to learners and employers' needs,

especially in the cultural heritage sector, where diversification of higher skills and competencies build the prerequisite for the final results.

- **Stakeholder fragmentation**: The cultural heritage sector, the main public employer, is extremely fragmented across the EU because: (a) different institutional/legal structures and frameworks/capacities with overlapping state–regional–local government responsibilities perpetuate tensions in the policy context; (b) different perceptions of culture by different actors at different levels give rise to competition between the public–private sector actors. A more flexible structure is urgently needed to plan success stories and yield the potential benefits: a public–private–third-sector partnership in the spirit of social economy could become an agent of change.

- **Violence Contamination of the AV Sector**: The transformation of film theatres to digital has been completed in 2014. The process cannot be considered an evolution without the cultural impact that the new distribution system has over the territory and identity of Europe. This last aspect has to be guided by a cultural policy, which can result in a virtuous connection between the public and private sector and contribute to the programming of media events related to cultural heritage. European AV productions are being contaminated by alienated contents with own languages, which lie outside of the European cultural values, human rights and education to democratic citizenship. Too often violence is shown as a solution for daily problems, which if it remains uncontested, will be producing **horror insensitive youth**. Bollywood, disputable social contents in-game alternate realities, discrimination, race and political incorrectness invade the screens and the minds, without possibility for critical reflection and resistance. Although the CREATIVE EUROPE MEDIA offers continuous training for AV skills regarding technology, much lesser attention is allocated contents promoting cultural heritage values and human rights.

- **A new narrative for Europe** is needed intends to share and spread European values, enhance citizen reflection and sociability performance, interlink nations through a new trans-generational digital cultural learning, deconstruct violence and promote abstract thinking and scientific ethics is utilizing new iconic AV languages with high-quality contents is not a utopia. Content literacy is enhanced with transversal key competences, integrating acquired skills and media formats into the labour market through the creation of a new value-driven heritage narrative with commercialization potential. The digital revolution has altered the production of various industrial sectors, the AV market in particular. New communication patterns define new market preferences, while the constant use of e-devices in daily life impacts the common sense through the interpretation of visual codes. It is only in May 2016 that the European Commission has amended the Audiovisual Media Services Directive (AVMSD), requiring from international broadcasters like Netflix and Amazon to invest about 20% of their revenues into making or commissioning original content and to spend at least 50% of their time showing European works, including materials made in their own country. The amendment of the AVMSD in 2016, pursuing also the creation of new symbols or phrases that would warn viewers of potentially harmful video content—such as bad language, sex or drugs—shall be used across the EU by both broadcasters and internet-based platforms, is a clear indication that policymaking has acquired a deeper understanding of the situation and is determined to move towards a better and visible Europe. Following this path, the ALECTOR Project is making a conscious effort to uptake innovative heritage-based ICT solutions to improve the cultural experience on a social inclusion basis: local communities and businesses have been trained and involved in the heritage planning, as they have shared their profound knowledge and have provided for the storytelling that package tours cannot deliver.

The *European Heritage Audiovisuals Market* is an underestimated opportunity for combatting unemployment and brain drain. Europe needs to define a strategic approach to this market and connect higher skilled AV and multimedia workers to the educational, cultural heritage and the entertainment sector. The digital heritage audiovisuals offer more than any other medium the possibility for image manipulation of the image and incorporate the most advanced technologies available while it becomes a stimulus for future creations, exploiting Europe's vast static archives. Sites such as EUROPEANA, the European Film Gateway or EU Screen allow to access picture and sound recordings dating back to the very birth of cinema. However, the digital shell does not necessarily embed quality, citizen education and the shared European identity. The digital audiovisual, although extensively utilized, is under-researched as communication production pattern, and seldom taught in the tertiary education. This default is currently disabling the European heritage industry to develop with new digital heritage artworks. In times where the European identity is contested by the economic global economic crisis, refugee flows and terrorist attacks, it is imperative to rethink the mission of the heritage sector to shape citizen attitude and its capacity to establish ideas for an improved society. It is necessary to determine the quintessential steps to define a strategic approach to the *European Cultural Heritage Market* and find new opportunities for research, application and creation of new iconic contents to design and deliver cognitive-emotional experiences.

The recent economic recession is urgently calling for productivity and innovation, capabilities increasingly dependent on new skills and education. The ALECTOR Project has built a first attempt to invest in human capital in the Black Sea Basin by creating an open and participatory knowledge exchange platform for new competences, utilizing imagination, creativity and place knowledge of local populations to facilitate, through the deployment of mobile services, the transformation of the Project Area to a node for culture without frontiers. Supporting the provision of multi-sensory experiences and innovation in cultural heritage consumption, *SCRIPTORAMA,* the *Black Sea Open Street Museum,* becomes an instrument to facilitate and stimulate the development of heritage offers to serve the rising demand for services that are not yet in place, but are needed as agent for change in the context of sustainable development and cultural diversity.

References

Academy of Tourism Research and Studies (ATEM). (2010). *Biannual report analysis of the greek tourism activity.* Athens: The Tourism Research Unit of the Athens Institute for Education and Research (ATINER).

Amann, S., & Lange, B. (2014). *Creative industries.* Lille: INTERREG IVC (2007–2013).

ΑΡΙΣΤΟΤΕΛΗΣ. (2000). *Ὄργανον 1, Κατηγορίαι, Περί Ερμηνείας* (Vol. Τόμος 23). Επιμέλεια, Β. Μανδηλαράς, Αθήνα: ΕκδόσειςΚάκτος.

Armstrong, K., & Weiler, B. (2003). *Improving the tourist experience: Evaluation of interpretation components of guided tours in national parks.* Gold Coast, Queensland: CRC for Sustainable Tourism.

Arts Council England. (2013). *Great art and culture for everyone.* 10 Year Strategic Framework 2010-2020. Manchester, UK: Arts Council England.

Ates, O. (2014). *The valuation of cultural capital: A case study.* Paper presented at the 18th International Conference on Cultural Economics. Montreal, CA: University of Quebec (UQAM), 24–27 June.

Baddeley, A. (2012). Working memory: Theories, models, and controversies. *Annual Review of Psychology, 63,* 1–29.

Baddeley, A., & Hitch, G. J. (1974). Working memory. In G. Bower (Ed.), *Recent advances in learning and motivation* (pp. 47–90). New York: Academic Press.

Baddeley, A. D., Eysenck, M., & Anderson, M. C. (2014). *Memory.* Hove: Psychology Press.

Barsalou, L. (2008). Grounded cognition. *Annual Review of Psychology, 59,* 617–645.

Barsalou, L. (2010). Grounded cognition: Past, present, and future. *Topics in Cognitive Science, 2,* 716–724.

Bitgood, S. (2009). Museum fatigue: A critical review. *Visitor Studies, 12*(2), 93–111.

Bitgood, S. (2013). *Attention and value: A key to understanding museum visitors.* London, New York: Routledge.

Bruell, C. (2013). *Creative Europe 2014–2020.* A new programme—a new cultural policy as well? ifa-Edition Culture and Foreign Policy.

Bucci, A., & Segre, G. (2009). *Human and cultural capital complementarities and externalities in economic growth* (Working Paper No. 05). Milano: Universita degli studi di Milano.

Bucci, A., & Segre, G. (2011). Culture and human capital in a two-sector endogenous growth model. *Research in Economics, 65*(4), 279–293.

Bui, H., & Trupp, A. (2014). The Development and diversity of Asian tourism in Europe: The case of Vienna. *International Journal of Tourism Sciences, 2,* 1–17.

Bulencea, P., & Egger, R. (2015). *Gamification in tourism. Designing memorable experiences.* Norderstedt: Books on Demand.

Cacioppo, J., & Petty, R. (1982). The need for cognition. *Journal of Personality and Social Psychology, 42*(1), 116–131.

Center for Strategy and Evaluation Services (CSES). (2013). *Enhancing the Competitiveness of Tourism in the EU.* An evaluation approach to establishing 20 cases of innovation and good practice, Kent, UK.

Chen, L., Scott, N., & Beckendorff, P. (2014). *An exploration of mindfulness theories in eastern and western philosophies.* Paper presented at the Tourism and Hospitality in the Contemporary World: Trends, Changes & Complexity (CAUTHE).

Davey, G. (2005). What is museum fatigue? *Visitor Studies, 8*(3), 17–21.

Dewey, J. (1938). *Experience and education.* New York: Collier Books.

Di Russo, A. (2003). *Caravaggio una mostra impossibile.* RAI: Rome.

Di Russo, A., & Papathanasiou, D. (2015). The end of entertainment: Castel Lagopesole, the new rising power of cultural communication for local development, collective identities and sustainable place-making. *Elsevier Procedia—Financing sustainable economic growth for security and wellbeing. 4th edition of Emerging markets queries in finance and business* (in press).

Eco, U. (2003). Il Sole24ore, 5th of October.

Eurobarometer 370. (2013). *Attitudes of Europeans towards tourism*. Brussels: DG Enterprise and Industry.

European Commission. (2014). *Mapping of cultural heritage actions in European Union policies, programmes and activities*. Brussels: Directorate-General for Education and Culture (DG EAC).

Eurostat. (2011). *Cultural Statistics*. Luxembourg: Publications Office of the European Union.

Francois, M. (Ed.). (2012). *Policies and good practices in the public arts and in cultural institutions to promote better access abd wider participation in culture*. Brussels: European Union.

Gunn, C., & Var, T. (2002). *Tourism planning: Basics, concepts, cases* (4th ed.). New York and London: Routledge.

Gyimothi, S., & Johns, N. (2001). In S. Drummond & I. Yeoman (Eds.), *Quality issues in heritage visitor attractions* (pp. 243–266). London and New York: Routledge.

HKU. (2010). *The entrepreneurial dimension of the cultural and creative industries*. Utrecht: Hogeschool vor de Kunsten.

ICOMOS. (1964). The venice charter for the conservation and restoration of monuments and sites, 2005. http://www.international.icomos.org/e_venice.htm.

ICOMOS. (1975). *The declaration of Amsterdam*. http://www.icomos.org/en/charters-and-texts/179-articles-en-francais/ressources/charters-and-standards/169-the-declaration-of-amsterdam.

ICOMOS. (1982). The florence charter for historic gardens.

ICOMOS. (2006). Ename Charter for the interpretation of cultural heritage sites. Preamble. Objectives. Principles. *The George Wright Forum, 23*(1), 34–39. Available from: http://www.jstor.org/stable/43597974.

Jager, E., & Sanche, A. (2010). Setting the stage for visitor experiences in Canada's national heritage places. *The George Wright Forum, 27*(2), 180–190.

Jurowski, C. (2009). *An examination of the four realms of tourism experience theory*. Paper presented at the International CHRIE Conference-Refereed Track. Paper 23.

Kolb, D. (1984). *Experiential learning: Experience as the source of learning and development*. Englewood Cliffs, NJ: Prentice Hall.

Miller, G. A. (1956). The magical number seven, plus or minus two: Some limits on our capacity for processing information. *The Psychological Review, 63*, 81–97.

Miller, G. A. (2003). The cognitive revolution. A historical perspective. *Trends in Cognitive Sciences, 7*(3), 141–144.

Moreno, Y. J., Santagata, W., & Tabassum, A. (2005). *Material cultural heritage and sustainable development*. Torino, Italy.

Paas, F., van Gog, T., & Sweller, J. (2010). Cognitive load theory: New conceptualizations, specifications, and integrated research perspectives. *Educational Psychology Review, 22*, 115–121.

Papathanasiou-Zuhrt, D., & Weiss-Ibanez, D. F. (Eds.). (2014). *Designing the roving museum*. Athens: South East Europe Transnational Cooperation Programme.

Pine, B. J., & Gilmore, B. H. (1999). *The Experience economy: Work is theatre & every business a stage*. Cambridge: Harvard Business School Press.

Prasada, S. (2000). Acquiring generic knowledge. *Trends in Cognitive Science, 4*(2), 66–72.

Radvansky, G. (2016). *Human memory* (2nd ed.). UK: Routledge.

Revelli, F. (2013) Tax incentives for cultural heritage conservation. In I. Rizzo, A. Mignosa, & E. Elgar (Eds.), *Handbook on the Economics of Cultural Heritage* (pp. 129–148).

Richards, G. (2012). *Tourism, creativity and creative industries*. Paper presented at the Creativity and Creative Industries in Challenging Times, NHTV Breda, November 2012.

Richards, G. (2013). Creativity and tourism in the city. *Current Issues in Tourism, 17*(2).

Richards, G., & Wilson, J. (2006). Developing creativity in tourist experiences: A solution to the serial reproduction of culture? *Tourism Management, 27*, 1209–1223.

Russo, A. P. (2002). The "vicious circle" of tourism development in heritage cities. *Annals of Tourism Research, 29*, 165–182.

Sacco, P.-L. (2011). *Culture 3.0: A new perspective for the EU 2014–2020 structural funds programming*. European Expert Network on Culture (EENC).

Shanks, M. (2012). *The archaeological imagination*. Walnut Creek, CA: Left Coast Press.

Sharpley, R., & Stone, P. R. (Eds.). (2012). *Contemporary tourism experience. Concepts and consequences*. New York: Routledge.

Sweller, J. (2008). Human cognitive architecture. In J. Spector, M. D. Merill, J. van Merrienboer, & M. P. Driscol (Eds.), *Handbook of research on educational communications and technology: A project of the association for educational communications and technology* (pp. 370–381). New York, London: Taylor & Francis.

Sweller, J., Ayres, P., & Kalyuga, S. (2007). *Cognitive load theory*. New York: Springer.

Tourism Australia. (2008). *The experience seeker*. Sidney: Tourism Australia.

Turku School of Economics and MKW Wirtschaftsforschung. (2006). *The economy of culture in Europe*. European Commission, Directorate-General for Education and Culture.

Tussyadiah, I. (2014). Toward a theoretical foundation for experience design in tourism. *Journal of Travel Research, 53*(5), 543–564.

UNDP. (2008). *Creative economy. The challenge of assessing the creative economy: Towards informed policy making*. Geneva: United Nations.

UNESCO. (1994). *The nara document on authenticity*. Paris: UNESCO World Heritage Center.

UNESCO. (2012). *Operational guidelines for the implementation of the world heritage convention*. World Heritage Center, Paris, France: UNESCO. Intergovernmental Committee for the Protection of World Cultural and Natural Heritage.

Wells, M., Lovejoy, V., & Welch, D. (2009). *Creating more meaningful visitor experiences: Planning for interpretation and education*. Denver, Colorado: United States Department of the Interior, Bureau of Reclamation, Policy and Program Services, Denver Federal Center.

Williams, M., Hillage, J., Pinto, R., & Garrett, R. (2012). *Sector skills insights: Digital and creative (Evidence Report no 49)*. London: UK Commission for Employment and Skills.

Yuksel, A. (2005). Tourist shopping habitat: Effects on emotions, shopping value and behaviours. *Tourism Management, 28*(58), 58–69.

Yuksel, A., & Yuksel, F. (2007). Shopping risk perceptions: Effects on tourists' emotions, satisfaction and expressed loyalty intentions. *Tourism Management, 28*(3), 703–713.

Chapter 3
Heritage Tourism and Neo-Endogenous Development: The Case of the Black Sea Project "Alector"

Nikolaos Thomaidis and Dorothea Papathanasiou-Zuhrt

Abstract The neo-endogenous development paradigm advocates the democratic use of local resources in order to improve the quality of life of local residents in a given area through intense social and economic interaction with the global system. A theoretical basis for this development paradigm could be the "culture economy", which dictates that a locality, through its local institutions and the civic society, should promote its self-perceived distinct territorial identity both at the local and the extra-local level in order to achieve its development goals, especially through tourism. This is due to the fact that the local identity has been recognised as a decisive factor that favours neo-endogenous development through the processes of democratic legitimacy and community empowerment. Herein, we examine the practical implementation of the European Union "Alector" project and its local pilot implementation project "Tobacco Perfumes. Drama 1840–1940. Stories, Passions, Protagonists" under the theoretical framework of the culture economy in the specific area of Drama, Greece. The "Alector" project, implemented by nine (9) multi-level partners in seven (7) countries (namely Greece, Romania, Bulgaria, Moldova, Ukraine, Georgia and Turkey) from 2014 to 2016 was funded by the Black Sea Basin Joint Operational Programme 2007–2013. The project sought to develop quality heritage tourism standards in selected areas of the Black Sea Basin; as such it demonstrated a great potential in as far as cultural assets' rejuvenation and local identity formation and promotion is concerned both at the local and the extra-local level. We argue that local cultural assets, despite the current practical difficulties of their rejuvenation due to the economic crisis in Greece, can contribute to the formation of a specific place identity that could in turn trigger a broader post-productive development process. In this respect, it is of utmost importance to ensure the initiation of an involvement and consumption process by all segments of local society in order to ensure the sustainability of the culture economy approach and the creation of a long-term development repertoire for the locality. We finally

N. Thomaidis (✉)
Drama Development S.A, Drama, Greece
e-mail: n.thomaidis@aned.gr

D. Papathanasiou-Zuhrt
The Wave Lab, University of the Aegean, Mytilene, Greece

© Springer International Publishing AG, part of Springer Nature 2019   51
V. Vasile (ed.), *Caring and Sharing: The Cultural Heritage Environment as an Agent for Change*, Springer Proceedings in Business and Economics, https://doi.org/10.1007/978-3-319-89468-3_3

provide practical implementation suggestions for similar projects falling into the culture economy approach.

Keywords Heitage · Neo-endogenous development · Black Sea Programme Culture economy

3.1 Introduction

3.1.1 Endogenous Development

The theoretical debate on endogenous development has mainly focused on the level of dependence of the local to the extra-local level. As Lowe et al. (1999) put it, there are two examples or models of endogenous growth introduced in this debate. The first and more extreme is the one that gives emphasis on self-reliance, which challenges the very dependence on the extra-local level. This position is supported by scholars such as Friedmann (1986), who argues that the only appropriate response for a locality when lagging behind is taking absolute control of resources at the local level. A necessary condition for this transition is the establishment of institutions with considerable autonomy at the lowest possible level.

The second example, which is dominant within Europe nowadays, supports integration of the local into the global economic system. Generally, and as described by Lowe et al. (1999), it is a paradigm of development based on extra-local resource mobilisation, yet "coloured" by the local system. The basic assumption of this development model is that a local community, through the process of empowerment, will be in the end capable of implementing initiatives triggered by the extra-local level to the local context, in a democratic way. This process is illustrated in Fig. 3.1.

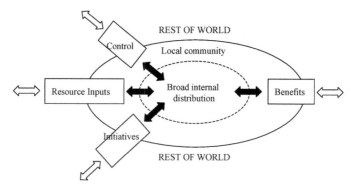

Fig. 3.1 Spatial levels and development. *Source* Stöhr (1990: 32)

3.1.2 Neo-Endogenous Development

The addition of the prefix "neo" to endogenous development should not be regarded as an attempt to devise new terms for already known concepts. On the contrary, the addition of the prefix "neo" emphasises the importance of extra-local intervention to the local milieu. Indeed, the neo-endogenous development as described by its introducer Ray is "endogenous-based development in which extra-local factors are recognised and regarded as essential but which retains a belief in the potential of local areas to shape their future". (2001: 4). In the neo-endogenous paradigm, development is triggered by three possible sources, which act either separately or jointly—firstly, by local factors; secondly, by national governments and/or the European Union; thirdly, it can be driven from an intermediate level, in particular by development agencies or other bodies. The emergence of neo-endogenous development in a territory will be the result of various combinations of extra-local and intermediate activities that interact with the local level (Ray 2001: 8–9).

A key component of the success of neo-endogenous development—which mainly concerns the interaction between the local and the extra-local level—is the democratic, social and political reorganisation at local level. This reorganisation ensures representation of all interests and use of all potential. This kind of "governance" is extremely important, mainly to intermediaries of neo-endogenous development (e.g. NGOs or development agencies) and recognises: "(a) the respect of human rights and especially of vulnerable groups, (b) respect for the law, (c) the policy for transparency and broad participation in the decision-making process, (d) accountability and transparency, and (e) administrative efficiency" (Work 2001: 22).

3.1.3 Culture Economy: Implementing Neo-Endogenous Development

One of the most suitable approaches to theorise neo-endogenous development is the idea of the culture economy. Culture economy places emphasis on production and consumption. The place is considered to be a "productive" unit, the resources of which can be mobilised and where local community can manage resource consumption by the extra-local level. In short, the economy of culture examines the relationship between the local and the extra-local level as a producer—consumer relationship. In this respect, natural and cultural assets are the regulatory factors of supply and demand. A very important aspect of neo-endogenous development (and of the culture economy) is the territorial identity. The more "visible" this identity is the greater the probability of a successful exercise of neo-endogenous development. Also, the stronger this identity is, the greater the possibility that the relationship with the central government is viewed as a "partnership" and not as a top–down relationship. But what is the relationship between the local culture and local identity? As Ray argues: "Culture" is, in a sense, a synonym for "territorial identity"; it is the way in which humans create, and then perceive, the differentiation of space (albeit on overlapping layers) and which can differ from the mosaic of politico-administrative boundaries that exist at any moment. However, in another way, "culture" signals a reorientation in thinking towards what is produced and consumed (rather than where); that is, "it is partly a shift towards a post-industrial, consumerist economy" (2001: 16).

This shift to a post-industrial economy is particularly evident in the efforts of local players to enhance endogenous resources directly related to culture such as food, languages and dialects, crafts, folklore, visual arts, theatre, literature, history, landscapes, flora, fauna. This restructuring effort of local economy with emphasis put on such resources has been defined as the economy of culture (cultural economy) and was proposed by Ray (1998). For a better understanding of the culture economy, Ray (2001) proposed an initial typology through four operational modes. This typology is illustrated in Fig. 3.2.

Mode I may be defined as the process of commoditisation of local heritage. In essence, it refers to the creation (or valorisation) and use of resources that express the place's identity and can be "sold" directly or indirectly. Typical examples of such resources are nature and manmade heritage assets, listed buildings, monuments, etc. Other resources may be intangible, e.g. local food products and local craftsmanship. Mode II is defined as the process of construction or rejuvenation of local identity and its promotion to the extra-local level.

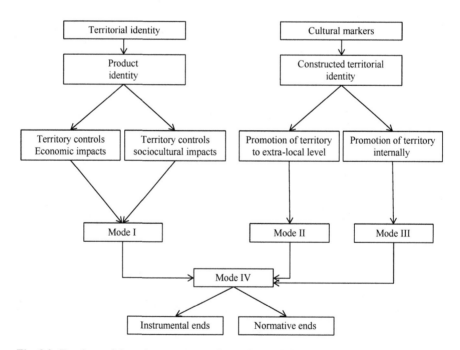

Fig. 3.2 Typology of the culture economy. *Source* Ray (1998: 6, 2001: 19)

The emphasis that is put here is to the creation of a "corporate" identity for promotional purposes. This is the aspect of culture economy that is directly related to tourism. The easiest and more popular way of selling a place at the extra-local level is for it to become a destination, if assets allow this of course. A locality can also sell itself to the extra-local level through the export of products that define the territorial identity.

In Mode III, emphasis continues to be placed on the promotion of the local identity yet the target group changes. The recipient of promotion is not the extra-local, but the local level with its communities, businesses, associations and official institutions. This internal "advertisement" of the "local to the local" is an important element of the theory of Ray which has particular application to marginalised, vulnerable or declining areas with a "weak" self-perceived identity. The application of this mode may lead to increased self-esteem of local residents and, subsequently, to building confidence in their own abilities to manage local resources. This process may lead to new economic opportunities, innovation and sociocultural revitalisation. It should be noted here that this task of "selling the place to the place" can be difficult in those cases where the relationship between the central state and the region has not been regarded as a "partnership" in the past. In such cases, spatial development strategies should emphasise the creation of a new, or rather reconstructed, identity through the process of "historical revisionism".

Finally, Mode IV can be described as a process in which the local economy by shifting to endogenous resources can create the conditions for the introduction of various development strategies with specific implementation tools and regulatory instruments. Development can mean many different things and the area may select one or more of these strategies. The logic of neo-endogenous approach, irrespective of whether the initial development "boost" comes from above or below is that this area can generate its own development "repertoire". The term "repertoire" is used by Ray to indicate a stock or techniques that can be used depending on the specificities of a given situation. In that respect, a territory—besides its set of endogenous resources—must also rejuvenate (or establish anew) its political culture with emphasis put on participation and collaborative planning.

3.2 The EU "Alector" Project

3.2.1 General Information

The "Alector" project was funded by the Black Sea Basin Joint Operational Programme 2007–2013 through ENPI and IPA funds. Its implementation lasted thirty (30) months starting from January 2014. The project was implemented by nine (9) partners from seven (7) countries, namely: ENPI Financial Lead Beneficiary (Drama Development S.A., Greece); ENPI Partner No. 1 (National Authority for Tourism, Romania); ENPI Partner No. 2 (Union of Bulgarian Black Sea Local Authorities, Bulgaria); ENPI Partner No. 3 (National Association of

Rural, Eco-logical end Cultural Tourism, Moldova); ENPI Partner No. 4 (Donetsk Civic Organisation "Alliance", Ukraine); ENPI Partner No. 5 (The Batumi Archaeological Museum, Georgia); IPA Financial Lead Beneficiary (Governorship of Istanbul, Turkey); IPA Partner No. 1 (Eastern Black Sea Development Agency, Turkey); IPA Partner No. 2 (METGEM Development Centre for Vocational Technical Education, Turkey). Three active associate partners were also involved, namely: Associate Partner No. 1 (University of the Aegean Research Unit, Greece); Associate Partner No. 2 (Institute of National Economy of the Romanian Academy, Romania); Associate Partner No. 3 (Ukrainian Network for Education of Adults and Development of Innovation, Ukraine).

The full title of the project "Collaborative Networks of Multilevel Actors to advance Quality Standards for Heritage Tourism at Cross Border Level" clearly suggests that its main objective was the development of quality heritage tourism at local and cross-border level through the application of interpretation and signage standards. In order to achieve this objective, the project aimed at: enhancing partners' skills mainly through education, on-site training activities and manuals; creating innovative tourism promotion products based on quality standards and state-of-the-art technology; involving local decision-makers in the design of the project. The "Alector" project produced a considerable number of deliverables, the main being: the first Black Sea Basin "Open Street Museum" consisting of ninety (90) Interpretive Panels (bilingual), a Travel Aider and an e-Book; an e-course on Heritage Tourism Planning and Management; four (4) transnational meetings with parallel seminar sections; one (1) international conference; a series of studies—tools —manuals on tourism accessibility, heritage planning, etc.; surveys for end-users and decision-makers; dissemination material. The "Alector" project focused on creating skills and competencies and then applying them to valorise cultural heritage assets at local level through the implementation of the so-called local pilot projects. These local pilot projects concerned the selection and interpretation often (10) local heritage assets in each partner area. The interpretive texts of all these assets were subsequently included in the "Open Street Museum" mentioned above. Specific attention was given, as the texts were of interpretive character, to link the assets with specific stories, myths, people and events that can be easily associated with tourists and locals, thus generating experience rather than mere knowledge. The cross-border character of the "Open Street Museum" is evident in the project's e-book which collates the interpretive information on all ninety (90) assets chosen by the partnership. In each partner area, a main "theme" was selected in order to create a "story" or a distinct "theme trail". The titles of the local pilot projects are presented in Table 3.1.

3.2.2 The Local Pilot Project of Drama

The pilot project of Drama "Tobacco Perfumes" was dedicated to the Golden Age for the tobacco industry in Drama (1840–1940) and included ten (10) selected listed

Table 3.1 "Alector" local pilot projects

Partner	Local pilot project title
Drama Development S.A., Greece	Tobacco perfumes. Drama 1840–1940. Stories, passions, protagonists
Governorship of Istanbul, Turkey	A maritime heritage. Sile, Turkey. A lighthouse, legends and mermaids
National Authority for Tourism, Romania	The trail of the Romania ancient history at the Black Sea coast. 2000 years of history in 2 days
Union of Bulgarian Black Sea Local Authorities, Bulgaria	100 years in 60 min. Varna 1860–1960
National Association of Rural, Ecological end Cultural Tourism, Moldova	Tree of life. Discovering spiritual treasures
Donetsk Civic Organisation "Alliance", Ukraine	Greeks of Priazovie. Mariupol 1778–2016. History, customs and traditions
The Batumi Archaeological Museum, Georgia	Colchis, land of the Golden Fleece. Myths in places with real treasures
Eastern Black Sea Development Agency, Turkey	Legendary journeys. Trabzon from the silk road to modern times: heroes, myths and narratives
METGEM Development Centre for Vocational Technical Education, Turkey	A serenade in nature. Agva, Turkey. Birds, plants and poetry

Source Drama Development S.A. "Alector" project record

buildings in the city of Drama with each one of them presenting their stories, passions and protagonists in Greek and English. These are: A. Anastasiadis Tobacco Factory, 1875; B. Drama Railway Station, 1895; C. Portokaloglou Tobacco Factory, 1904; D. School of the Greek Orthodox Community, 1909; E. Michailidis Tobacco Factory, 1912; F. Cinema Olympia, 1920; G. Spierer Tobacco Factory, 1925; H. Tzimou Mansion, 1924; I. Feiss Mansion, 1927 and J. National Bank, 1928.

The route was designed in order to tell the story of the city as a processing and export centre of the famous oriental tobacco, the transition from the Ottoman Empire to the newly born Greek State, the rise of the upper middle class, the tobacco workers' movement and the Europeanisation of the city at the beginning of the twentieth century. The project had a range of three historical periods covering the rise and fall of the production and marketing of tobacco in Europe and the USA, the globalisation of the smoking habit, the economic and social changes made in the area of the tobacco producers, brokers and tobacco merchants along with the tobacco monopolies and the tobacco workers' movement dominating during the fall of the Ottoman Empire, the Balkan Wars, the First World War and the Greco-Turkish War. The Asia Minor Catastrophe of 1922 and the population exchange in Asia Minor, Pontus, Crete and Thrace, the Crash of 1929 with the consequent social instability, the bloody strikes of tobacco workers of 1936, the Nazi Germany as the last large-scale customer and the tobacco supplies for the army complete the last chapter.

Table 3.2 "Tobacco Perfumes": Assessing the significance of heritage assets

Basic criteria		Multi-criteria matrix
1	Provenance	1.1 Authenticity; 1.2 Originality; 1.3 Designation
2	Integrity	2.1 Completeness; 2.2 Exemplarity; 2.3 Bio- and Cultural diversity
3	Distinctiveness	3.1 Novelty; 3.2 Familiarity
4	Values	4.1 Natural 4.2 Archaeological–historic; 4.2 Social–economic; 4.3 Scientific; 4.5 Aesthetic
5	Accessibility	5.1 Ownership; 5.2 Condition; 5.3 Availability; 5.4 Carrying capacity; 5.5 Facilities
6	Interpretive potential	6.1 Asset knowledge; 6.2 Audience knowledge; 6.3 Authority permissions; 6.4 Media selection; 6.5. Experience opportunities

Source Papathanasiou-Zuhrt and Weiss-Ibáñez (2014: 309)

Information on the listed buildings included in the "Tobacco Perfumes" route is accessible via Quick Response Codes (QRC) in the territory. Upon scanning with any smart device a QRC on a lasted building leads to a bilingual cultural heritage narrative. It is further supported by an e-Book for iOS/Android operating systems and a printed "Travelaider" entailing information with tourism value. The concept heavily capitalises on the EU funded Project Sagittarius, where a cognitive-driven communication pattern has been developed and adapted to the conditions regulating the recreational learning environment (Babic et al. 2014). In order to select the monuments, the project team originally approached the Municipality of Drama and organised a front-end evaluation meeting with the participation of experts. The suggestion of the municipality representatives was to capitalise on an earlier cultural route that was designed by them, the so-called Cultural Route of Drama; this included a variety of listed buildings—monuments dating in different historical periods and were included in a tourist guide that had no interpretive but standard information for the monuments and the tourists. In close collaboration with Drama's municipal authorities, the project team has concluded the formative evaluation stage having assessed the significance of the selected ten (10) listed buildings (see Table 3.2). This task was necessary in order to ensure that an adequate interpretive narrative can easily trigger the interest of visitors (Papathanasiou-Zuhrt and Weiss-Ibáñez 2014: 309).

In this vein, "Tobacco Perfumes" addresses non-captive audiences, e.g. multi-national, multi-cultural and multi-generational groups, visiting heritage places being potentially connected with their own pre-understandings and prior knowledge. The interpretive design strives therefore to create a mental bridge to selected phenomena and make the novel seem familiar by relating it to prior knowledge and/ or universal concepts in a much shorter time period and more entertaining way, information architecture must consider working memory limitations to deal with visual, auditory and verbal material stimuli (Papathanasiou-Zuhrt 2014). In this respect heritage contents are organised as (a) a direct relationship with tangible-intangible aspects of selected assets through an analytical, cognitive approach to the other knowledge fields in order to document asset value and promote recognition, and (b) as presentation, interpretation and communication of heritage values embedded in the interactive learning space of the iOS/Android e-Book, where non-captive audiences are stimulated to think contextually and express views through valid statements.

At a later stage (August 2015), and after the project team has concluded with the remedial evaluation, a draft of the pilot project has been presented to decision-makers from the local government, decentralised state institutions, tourism bodies, etc. Drama Development S.A. has also organised an e-survey addressing potential users and a survey addressing local decision-makers. Approximately one year after this planning meeting, Drama Development S.A. finalised the pilot project. It was first presented in May 2016 to a local audience consisting of experts and decision-makers from the central, regional and local government in Drama during the project's info day. It was also presented at an international audience in Istanbul during the project's conference in June 2016.

3.3 Examining the "Alector" Pilot Project of Drama in the Context of Culture Economy

The "Alector" project is one of the most characteristic examples of post-productive development intervention. As a project addressing heritage tourism and partially designed by local actors, it can be regarded as a classic example of the neo-endogenous development approach, as this was generally described above. In that respect, we will examine it in the context of culture economy.

As far as Mode I of culture economy is concerned (process of commoditisation of local heritage), it is clear that the "Alector" project made use of endogenous heritage resources that express the territory's identity, at least in its historical dimension. Indeed, the ten (10) listed buildings that were selected are associated with a specific "derelict" identity (i.e. the Golden Age of tobacco) which is however still vivid in the historical memory of local people. Evidence of the above is that from a small-scale web survey we conducted in the framework of the project, it was made clear that the majority of local people regard these assets as part of the area's identity. The same positive "ownership" feeling was also expressed by decision-makers during the project's promotional events. The positive stance of locals towards the attempt to commoditise these assets at the urban context of Drama should be seen as encouraging in the urban context, as previous research in the countryside of Drama (Thomaidis 2003) showed that rural residents were—on the contrary and by large—not recognising cultural assets as key components of rural tourism initiatives.

A major issue that arises at this point is to see what does "commoditise" meant in the context of the project. Out of the ten (10) listed buildings, four (4) were privately owned and were used to house businesses, one (1) was a private residence, two (2) were used to house public services and the rest were derelict and inaccessible. An obvious question that was thus posed during the project's info day was how the interpretation and promotion of these assets via the projects "Open Street

Museum" would contribute to economic growth. The answer to that is that the commoditisation of the resources at this stage is only indirect. In this heritage tourism "immaturity" stage, inaccessible heritage assets act as attractors rather as "in situ experience" poles (e.g. museums, cultural centres).

Mode II, defined as the process of construction or rejuvenation of local identity and its promotion to the extra-local level, is of particular importance in the context of Drama and the pilot project. This is due to the fact that similar assets associated with the currently derelict tobacco industry may be found elsewhere in Greece. Does this mean however that this lack of "global" uniqueness makes these assets less attractive? The answer is "no" as these attractions are not only associated with their material characteristics but also to their particular location, i.e. Drama. In this sense, every tobacco factory, every school, every listed building in the world is unique and linked to a specific locality, specific stories, specific people and specific myths. Thus, the assets of the "Alector" pilot project may function as magnets that would entice a person to travel to Drama in order to discover the "sense of place" (Richards 2002: 1048; Leiper 1990: 381; Swarbrooke 2002: 44). Sense of place is a social phenomenon that exists independently of any one individual's perceptions or experiences, dependent yet on human engagement for its existence: the attribution of non-material characteristics to a place creates the soul and spirit of a place; its genius loci. A set of personal, family, and community narratives include features of a place. Taken together, these narratives constitute an attachment to places. The unique identity of and feelings associated with a place can be acquired by a visitor through interpretation: visitors develop a "sense of place" through experience and knowledge of a particular area.

When the pilot project of Drama was examined in retrospect in the context of Mode III (selling the local to the local), it was realised by the authors—and managers of the project—that further work could be made towards this direction, i.e. towards participative planning and civic involvement. The project was, indeed, promoted internally to decision-makers and key institutions. However, large-scale informational events and wide participation processes have not taken place. On the contrary, it could be argued that the project was designed by experts in a top-down fashion (within the community however). A limited number or professionals also attended the e-course on heritage management. The dissemination of the assets' associations with the place was not wide, especially among youth, and this could be regarded as a negative aspect in the project's life cycle. However, it should be mentioned that a large-scale participatory and collaborative planning approach in heritage planning should constitute a capitalisation project by itself.

3.4   Conclusions

Heritage tourism development initiatives like the EU "Alector" project can contribute greatly to triggering neo-endogenous development. In order to examine the practical application of the project in the area of Drama, we applied Ray's culture economy theory. Indeed, we demonstrated how the above-mentioned project contributed to facilitating certain aspects of the culture economy, namely the commoditisation of local heritage, the promotion of the place to the outside world and, to a limited extent, the promotion of the place to the place. We argue that one of the most necessary enhancements in Ray's culture economy theory would be to include the interpretive approach as a key component of Mode II, i.e. of the process of construction or rejuvenation of the territorial identity and its promotion to the extra-local level. Indeed, heritage assets succeed as a tourism product only through the process of cognition. Full of symbolic elements, these assets should become "mentally, emotionally and spiritually accessible in order to survive and satisfy the needs and expectations of experience-seeking visitors" (Papathanassiou-Zuhrt et al. 2007).

The interpretive approach is also necessary in Mode III of the culture economy, i.e. in the process where the local system sells itself internally. If ownership of development ensures sustainability then it is necessary to find ways of ensuring the first. The youth, in particular, seem to detach themselves from territorial identity. If it is presented to them in such a way that would trigger their interest (interpretive techniques, state-of-the-art technology, etc.) then it is most likely they initially become consumers and then planners of local heritage.

Overall, righteous governance at local level with the establishment of more inclusive multi-level institutions seems to be the major factor that facilitates the process of neo-endogenous development. Heritage, as a public good with deep historical roots in people's hearts and minds, is an ideal resource for testing the ability of local communities to respond to global challenges and claim their role in the global post-productive system.

References

Babic, D., Papathanasiou-Zuhrt, D., & Vasile, V. (Eds.). (2014). *Heritage as a development mediator: Interpretation and management.* Zagreb: Faculty of Humanities and Social Sciences, University of Zagreb.

Friedmann, J. (1986). Regional development in industrialised countries: Endogenous or self-reliant? In M. Bassand, E. A. Brugger, J. M. Bry-den, J. Friedmann, & B. Stuckey (Eds.), *Self-reliant development in Europe* (pp. 203–216). Aldershot: Gower.

Leiper, N. (1990). Tourist attractions systems. *Annals of Tourism Research, 17,* 367–384.

Lowe, P., Ray, C., Ward, N., Wood, D., & Woodward, R. (European Foundation for the Improvement of Living and Working Conditions). (1999). *Participation in rural development.* Luxembourg: Office for Official Publications of the European Communities.

Papathanasiou-Zuhrt, D. (2014). *Heri-journey. A good practice guide in heritage interpretation. Experiences in South East Europe.* Athens: South East Europe Transnational Cooperation Programme.

Papathanassiou-Zuhrt, D., Sakellaridis, O., Doumi, M., Tsimitakis, M. & Thomaidis, N. (2007). *Promoting a non-exchangeable destination image: The tourism cluster in the prefecture of Drama, Greece and its final product "Ecstasy".* Paper presented at the 1st Biannual International Conference on "Strategic Developments in Services Marketing", Chios, Greece, September 27–29, 2007.

Papathanasiou-Zuhrt, D., & Weiss-Ibáñez, D. F. (2014). *Cognitive processing of information with visitor value in cultural heritage environments. The case of the SEE TCP SAGITTARIUS 2011–2014.* Paper presented at the Procedia Economics and Finance Emerging Markets Queries in Finance and Business (EMQ 2013). Accessible at: http://www.sciencedirect.com/science/article/pii/S2212567114005097.

Ray, C. (1998). Culture, intellectual property and territorial rural development. *Sociologia Ruralis, 38*(1), 3–20.

Ray, C. (2001). *Culture economies.* Newcastle upon Tyne: Centre of Rural Economy-Press.

Richards, G. (2002). Tourism attraction systems. Exploring cultural behaviour. *Annals of Tourism Research, 29,* 1048–1064.

Stöhr, W. B. (1990). Introduction. In W. B. Stöhr (Ed.), *Global challenge and local response: Initiatives for economic regeneration in contemporary Europe* (pp. 20–34). London: Manshell.

Swarbrooke, J. (2002). *The development and management of visitor attractions.* Butterworth and Heinemann: London and New York.

Thomaidis, N. (2003). *Rural tourism and endogenous development: A case study of a mountainous area in Northern Greece* (Unpublished Ph.D. thesis submitted to the University of Aberdeen).

Work, R. (2001). Decentralization, governance, and sustainable regional development. In W. B. Stöhr, J. S. Edralin, & D. Mani (Eds.), *New Regional development paradigms (Vol. 3): Decentralization, governance, and the new planning for local-level development* (pp. 21–33). London: Greenwood.

Chapter 4
Information Services Industry in Tourism

Tagir Saifullin and Maria Lomovtseva

Abstract Information appears as a commodity in modern society and the sphere of tourism is defined as an information-rich service that speaks of a direct information connection from tourist activity. Tourism in the modern interpretation cannot exist without the transfer of information. It acts as an information-rich service that shows once again the important role of information in the field of tourism. In this context, there is the phenomenon of tourism as an industry of information service. The paper deals with the information services industry and information technologies and focuses on its implementation in tourism industry. The researchers try to find a solution on how information technologies could increase the effectiveness of tourism business, so they introduce a model that consists of eight components (information, users, information resources, suppliers, information system, information processes, etc.). Then, the model is tested in hospitality and tourism industry companies. As a result of the test, the authors highlight some points to be improved in the model. To sum up, the model in its final version can assist and allow increasing the competitiveness of the tourism business. The authors conclude that the performance of the company also can be improved through computerization and informatization processes, especially in such an information-rich industry as tourism.

Keywords Information services · Technology · Tourism · Online tourism

4.1 Introduction

In today's world, informatization is one of the most prominent features of the social relations system of developed countries. Humanity has entered into a stage of civilization in which the information and knowledge play a crucial role in all spheres of human activity. This information is, in today's society, the most important factor of economic growth.

T. Saifullin (✉) · M. Lomovtseva
Kazan Federal University, Kazan, Russia
e-mail: limonogon@gmail.com

© Springer International Publishing AG, part of Springer Nature 2019   63
V. Vasile (ed.), *Caring and Sharing: The Cultural Heritage Environment as an Agent for Change*, Springer Proceedings in Business and Economics,
https://doi.org/10.1007/978-3-319-89468-3_4

It should be understood that the advances in technology today is not only a major factor in ensuring the welfare of the nation but also an important condition for its sustainable development process. At the same time, priority should be given to the informational technologies, which due to their special catalytic properties actively promote the technological breakthrough of the country not only in the information spheres but also in many other important ways. In modern information society, they increase the value of information as a commodity. This is due to the overall growth of information needs and expression of the information services industry development, including the sphere of tourism. Evidence of this is increasing in the information sector's contribution in the creation of national wealth. Informatization of the economy is the transformation of information into an economic resource of primary importance. This occurs on the basis of computerization and telecommunications, providing the fundamentally new opportunities for economic development, multiple increases of labor productivity, the solution of social and economic problems, and the formation of a new type of economic relation.

4.2   Literature Review

The most outstanding works in this area are "Information technology in hotel and tourism businesses" (1999) Rodigin L. A. and "The role of information in tourism" (2010) Cherepanova K., in which the authors identify specific aspects of information systems in the tourism industry as well as offer a methodology to assess the impact of these components on the tourism business. Also, Cherepanova K. writes that information is a communication center, which allows hold of various manufacturers within the tourism industry, while the flow of information rather than products provides communication between producers of tourist services. There is a significant shortage of quality tourist information, especially concerning Russian domestic tourism products, which negatively affects the satisfaction of the growing demand, hindering its development. Another specialist Kupeshev A. claims that IT plays an important role as application in the development of tourism. His study identified the main directions of the use of IT in tourism. Kupeshev A. emphasizes the importance of the transformation of tourism into a profitable branch of the national economy by creating highly profitable tourism industry, able to produce and sell high-quality, competitive conditions in the international tourist market of the product; increase the tourist potential of the republic; conservation and management of cultural, historical, and natural and recreational resources; accessibility of tourist resources for all segments of the population, the maximum satisfaction of requirements of tourist services; promotion of employment; improving the efficiency of interaction between public and private entities in the tourism sector; the development of small business and private entrepreneurship. In our paper, we propose a new supplemented model containing eight components of information services industry in tourism as well as the impact of these aspects on the efficiency of business activities in tourism, that is, the scientific novelty of the article.

4.3 Information Services Industry in Tourism

Modern tourism is one of the largest, high-yielding, and most dynamic sectors of the global economy. The successful development of tourism has an impact on key sectors such as transport and communications, trade, construction, agriculture, consumer goods, and others. Creating a developed tourist industry has a great importance in the effective direction of structural adjustment of the Russian economy. Information services industry (information sector) of tourism consists of the following components:

1. Information;
2. Users (consumers) of the information;
3. Information resources;
4. Suppliers (owners) of the information and the resources;
5. Information systems;
6. Booking and sales systems;
7. Information processes;
8. Means of ensuring of information systems and technology (Means of maintenance of automated information systems and technologies 2012).

Rodigin L.A. defines the information as a link of tourist activities (Rodigin 1999: 33). Thus, information is the communication center, holding various producers within the tourism industry. The information flows, rather than products, provide links between producers of tourist services; they not only have data stream forms but also act as the form of services and charges. Services, for example, overnight hotel stay, car rental, package tours, and places in airplanes, are not sent to travel agents who, in their turn, do not keep it for as long as they sell it to consumers. They transmit and use the information on the availability, cost, and quality of these services. In the same way, actual payments are not transferred from the travel agents to suppliers and commissions—from suppliers to travel agents. Actually, the information about payments and revenues is transferred. There are not a lot of other industries in which the collection, processing, using, and transferring of information would have been as important for daily operation as in the tourism industry. Services in tourism cannot be exhibited and examined in the sales offices, as consumer or industrial goods. It is usually something you buy in advance and far away from the place of consumption. Thus, the tourism market almost completely depends on images, descriptions, communication means, and information transmission (Rodigin 1999: 33). The consumers of information products in tourism are individual tourists, travel agencies, hotels, airlines, railways and shipping companies, car rental firms, etc.

According to the federal target program "Development of tourism in the Russian Federation," it provides the creation of a unified information support system in the field of tourism, including the creation of a unified tourist information network in Russia and its integration with international systems (Information processes in socio-cultural service and tourism 2011). It assumes the formation of data banks (tourism information resources) on the foreign firms in domestic market, tours, routes, and transport and tourist accommodation facilities. With the sales of tourism products, another important function of travel agencies and other suppliers of information and resources in tourism is the provision of information services. Only 48% of customers know where they want to go, 35% have a vague idea about it, and 17% do not have it at all (Provision of information services 2009). Travel agents inform potential buyers about the tourism areas, transport timetables, accommodation options, current pricing and help to count an approximate travel costs. Communication with customers and searching demanded proposals occupy more than half of the spent time. For its efforts, the travel agency receives a commission (7–15% of the tour price). In some cases, it can be increased (for example, in the case of sales of tourism services in excess of the agreed amount). Modern computer technologies are actively implemented in the sphere of socio-cultural service and tourism business. Their use is becoming an integral part of successful operations. There has been observed an active use of information and communication technologies in tourism, which is also a priority sector of the Russian economy. Use of information technology (information systems) in the field of tourism is one of the key points of development and can significantly increase its economic and qualitative indicators. Information and communication services are directly related to the development of tourism. Using tourist telephone communication networks, Internet access systems, and a variety of technical means during the participation in the activities that meet the requirements of tourism is characterized by strong intensity. They significantly increase the load and, therefore, the demand for information services and resources in modern conditions play a crucial role in ensuring information availability of the tourism region (Burkutbaeva 2011: 6). There is a significant shortage of quality of tourism information, especially concerning the Russian domestic tourism products, which negatively affects the satisfaction of the growing demand and impedes its development (Cherepanova 2010: 1). Therefore, a new form of regional tourism development is the creation of tourism information centers, which provide a variety of travel information to tourists and generating feedback to the tourism market. Formation of the qualitative information infrastructure is an important task. Information services are needed for both tourists and tourism organizers. An important role is played by modern electronic media, especially the Internet, where on their Web sites, regions can offer users a detailed description of the tourism centers, services, attractions, to create a kind of virtual journey, including museum exhibitions (Burkutbaeva 2011: 6).

The fact that tourism is a sphere of the growing use of information technology explained by the characteristic features of the tourism: tourism is a diverse and integrated services trade; tourism is a complex service; tourism is an information-rich service. It is necessary to designate the concept of information technology. Thus, information technology is concentrated expression of scientific knowledge and practical experience, presented in the form of the project, i.e., in a formalized manner, which allows in a rational way to organize one or another frequently repeated information process (Panchuk 2010: 43). Information processes include registration, data collection, transmission, storing, processing, information providing, and management decision-making procedures (Information processes in socio-cultural service and tourism 2011). The modern tourism industry in recent years has undergone greatly significant changes due to the introduction of new computer technologies. The successful functioning of any company in the market of tourism business is almost impossible without the use of modern information technologies. The specifics of technology of the development and the implementation of tourism products require such systems that in the shortest possible time can provide information about the availability of transport and the possibilities of tourist accommodation, would ensure rapid booking and reservation, and automation of solving of the supporting tasks in the provision of tourist services (parallel issuance of such documents like tickets, invoices, guides, software and computational background information). This can be achieved on the condition of widespread use of modern computer technologies for processing and transmission of information in tourism (The classification of information technologies in tourism 2012). Figure 4.1 gives information about different types of information technology systems.

Information technology (IT) is only one of the branches of scientific and technological revolutions, which are taking place nowadays and can provide a much more powerful "long wave" than its predecessors. The intersection of telecommunication and information problems and means of solving it are inevitable. To the greatest extent, it relates to the Internet as the most large-scale information and telecommunication facilities. Information technologies have four characteristic features (Information processes in socio-cultural service and tourism 2011):

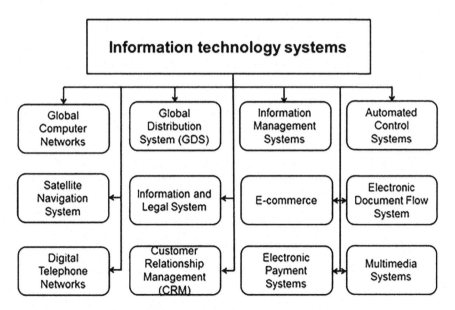

Fig. 4.1 Information technology systems (*Source* The classification of information technologies in tourism 2012)

- It has permeation character;
- It contributes to more efficient operation of markets by simplifying and improving access to information, the removal of barriers to new entrants, thereby admitting many buyers and sellers on the market, reducing operating costs up to the zero mark;
- It has a global distribution; therefore, a huge amount of knowledge can be stored, forwarded, and become the property of people anywhere in the world; and
- It accelerates the innovation process, enabling to process huge amounts of information easier and cheaper and reducing the time required to develop new products.

The value of information technology is caused by creation of possibilities to collect, analyze, and transmit the information at any place, instantly and with minimal costs. The structure of information technologies of management in the field of socio-cultural service and tourism (hereinafter SCST) (Information processes in socio-cultural service and tourism 2011):

- General-purpose software;
- Tour operators and travel agencies automation software;
- Hotel automation software packages;
- Human resources management automated systems;
- Entertainment industry automation software;
- Searching and tours' booking systems;
- Online hotels, excursions, cars, and other travel services' booking systems;
- Global reservation systems.

Modern computer technologies are actively being implemented in the tourism business, and their application has become an indispensable condition for increasing the competitiveness of any tourist enterprise. The tourism industry allows using all the variety of computer technology, from specialized software products for single travel agency management to the application of global computer networks. Nowadays, tourism applies the latest technologies in booking systems, integrated communication networks, multimedia systems, and management information systems. Computer technologies have the greatest impact on the promotion of tourism products—distribution and sales; it is possible to create new marketing channels of promotion and sales of tourism products. In the field of advertising, the widespread way is direct mailing of tourism information via e-mail. The majority of travel agencies create their own Web sites on the Internet. In western countries, online booking prevails over the traditional tourist industry. There are already electronic travel agencies, allowing anyone with a credit card to buy a tour, book a seat on the plane or hotel, buy tickets to entertainment events, or rent a car. Thus, computer technologies have provoked the creation and application of innovative electronic marketing channels of promotion and sales of tourism products (Information processes in socio-cultural service and tourism 2011). In the tourism industry is also widespread the video text, combining the possibility of reservation computer systems, e-mail, telex, electronic newspapers. In the UK, about 90% of travel agencies use the system of visual data Prestel, which the British Telecom supports. This system provides information on travel and tourism, and also the tour operators, rail lines, ferries, hotels, and airlines' offers, with easy accessible for consumers. The latest news and changes in all these areas are regularly added to the system. The main components of the Prestel system are TV acting as a display, a keyboard for data entry, and an adapter that provides a link between travel agency and the central computer, avoiding telephone lines. Videotext technology has also enjoyed success in France, where the Minitel system is applicable. At the same time, use of the videotext in the USA is limited (The classification of information technologies in tourism 2012). The appearance of multimedia technologies found rapid application in SCST (Information processes in socio-cultural service and tourism 2011). The main feature of the multimedia computer is the presence of additional devices, such as sound card, speakers, and others. Currently most represented PCs at the market are multimedia, and these devices included in standard equipment. Multimedia technology provides the ability to work with audio and video files, which opens up new ways of using computer technology in the field of SCST, in particular, the development of virtual tours of museums and travels. Virtual excursions and travels are presentations that allow viewers to explore the main objects of interest (museums, sights) before their actual visit. It can be freely moving panoramas of objects of any size (exhibits of museums and art galleries, hotel rooms, streets and buildings of the city, parks, alleys, views from the bird'-s-eye view, and so on). Panoramas are interconnected by simulated longitudinal movements within the object so that it creates the illusion of actual movement along the inside of the object with the ability to stop the circular inspection in the most interesting places. The viewer can arbitrarily change the direction, use the zoom function, move forward and backward, left, and right. There are the possibilities to add audio supporting, explanatory notes to the presentation and integration into the virtual tour geographic maps and plans of the premises with the possibility of orientation. One of the most common ways of application of multimedia technology in the field of SCST is the creation and use of encyclopedic, reference, and promotional CDs. There are currently a large number of information and reference materials to museums and various tourist destinations, including Moscow, St. Petersburg, the resorts of Caucasian Mineral Waters, Sochi, etc.

Many businesses in SCST sphere, most often museums, travel agencies and hotels, create their own CDs, containing reference and advertising information. Typically, multimedia catalogs do not contain frequently changing information, such as data on prices. Thus, the growing application of information technology in the tourism sector is explained by the characteristic features of tourism:

- Tourism is a diverse and integrated services trade;
- Tourism is a complex service;
- Tourism is an information-rich service.

4.4   Resulting Components of Information Services
        Industry in Tourism

Information services industry (information sector) of tourism consists of the following components:

1. DVGWVDHA Information. Information is the link between tourism activities, holding various producers within the tourism industry. This is due to the fact that the tourism market almost entirely depends on images, descriptions, means of communication, and transmission of information, because the service of tourism cannot be exhibited and examined in the sales office—it is usually buy in advance and far away from the place of consumption.
2. Users (consumers) information. Consumers of information products in tourism are individual tourists, travel agencies, hotels, airlines, railways and shipping companies, car rental firms, etc.
3. Information resources. These are data banks on foreign firms at domestic market, tours, routes, transport and tourist accommodation facilities.
4. Suppliers (owners) of information and resources. Information services provide travel agencies and other suppliers the information and resources in tourism.
5. Information systems. The information technologies act as information systems —presented in the form of the project, i.e., in a formalized manner, concentrated expression of scientific knowledge and practical experience, which allows in a rational way to organize one or another frequently repeated information process. The structure of information technologies of management in the field of SCST are: general-purpose software; tour operators and travel agencies automation software; hotel automation software packages; human resources management automated systems; entertainment industry automation software; searching and tours booking systems; online hotels, excursions, cars and other travel services booking systems; global reservation systems. The tourism industry allows using all the variety of computer technology, from specialized software products for single travel agency management to the application of global computer networks. Nowadays, tourism applies the latest technologies in booking systems, integrated communication networks, multimedia systems, and management information systems. Computer technologies have the greatest impact on the promotion of tourism products—distribution and sales; it is possible to create new marketing channels of promotion and sales of tourism products. In the field of advertising, the widespread way is direct mailing of tourism information via e-mail. The majority of travel agencies create their own Web sites on the Internet.
6. Booking and sales systems. The specifics of technology of the development and the implementation of tourism products require such systems that in the shortest possible time can provide information about the availability of transport and the possibilities of tourist accommodation, would ensure rapid booking and reservation, and automation of solving of the supporting tasks in the provision of

tourist services (parallel issuance of such documents, like tickets, invoices, guides, software and computational background information). This can be achieved on the condition of widespread use of modern computer technologies for processing and transmission of information in tourism—online booking systems and global computer systems (such as Amadus, Galileo, Worldspan).

7. Information processes. Information processes include registration, data collection, transmission, storing, processing, information providing, and management decision-making procedures.

8. Information systems and technologies means of maintenance. Means of ensuring of automated information systems and technologies—in the Russian Federation legislation—programmatic, technical, linguistic, legal, organizational means used or created in the design of information systems and ensure their operation, including computer programs; computer and communication equipment; dictionaries, thesauri, and classifiers; instructions and techniques; provisions, regulations, job descriptions; schemes and its descriptions; other operational and supporting documentation.

4.5 Conclusions

The industry of information services ("information industry," "computer science industry," "information services industry") is the production of information goods and services based on information technologies. The information industry is the newest branch of the world economy, which is still an evolving industry. The aim of this new industry is to collect and process the information, and provide information services to consumers by means of modern techniques and technologies. Increasing role of information technology in the tourism sector explained by the fact that tourism is the information-rich service. Information services industry (information sector) of tourism consists of the following components:

1. Information;
2. Users (consumers) information;
3. Information resources;
4. Suppliers (owners) of information and resources;
5. Information systems;
6. Booking and sales systems;
7. Information processes;
8. Information systems and technologies means of maintenance.

The resulting model has limited scope for use only in the field of socio-cultural service and tourism. In future, it is planned to further develop this model, making it universal for use in wider areas.

Acknowledgements This research was partially supported by Timur Absalyamov. We thank our colleagues from Kazan Federal University who provided insight and expertise that greatly assisted the research, although they may not agree with all of the conclusions of this paper. We thank Islam Fayzullin for assistance with particular methodology and Edward Madirov for comments that greatly improved the paper. We are also immensely grateful to Vladislav Zenin and Stanislav Zenin for their comments on an earlier version of the manuscript, although any errors are our own and should not tarnish the reputations of these esteemed persons.

References

Absalyamov, T., Absalyamova, S., & Absalyamova, A. (2014 May 14) Private museums as a form of preservation of cultural heritage. *Procedia—Social and Behavioral Sciences, 188*, 218–221.

Absalyamova, S. G., & Absalyamov, T. B. (2015). Remote employment as a form of labor mobility of today's youth. *Mediterranean Journal of Social Sciences, 6*(1S3), 227–231.

Burkutbaeva, N. A. (2011). *The development of the regional infrastructure in tourism.* Elista: Kalmyk State University.

Cherepanova, K. (2010). *The role of information in tourism.* Shadrinsk: Shadrinsk State Pedagogical Institute.

Financial dictionary. (2010). [Online]. Available: http://dic.academic.ru/dic.nsf/fin_enc/25594. November 27, 2015.

Geography of the world information industry—General characteristics. (2012). [Online]. Available: http://geographyofrussia.ru/geografiya-mirovoj-informacionnoj-industrii-obshhyax arakteristika. November 27, 2015.

Information processes in socio-cultural service and tourism. (2011). [Online]. Available: http:// gendocs.ru/page=16. November 27, 2015.

Kupeshev, A. (2013). *The effectiveness of the use of information and communication technologies in tourism.* Republic of Kazakhstan: University Miras.

Means of maintenance of automated information systems and technologies. (2012). [Online]. Available: http://www.finam.ru/dictionary/wordf02B55/default.asp?n=27. November 29, 2015.

Panchuk, E. I. (2010). *Basics of tourism and hospitality industry: A bachelor's degree program for students entering in the direction of preparation 100400 tourism.* Vologda: Vologda Institute of Business.

Provision of information services. (2009). [Online]. Available: http://popturizm.ru/Turoperator_i_ turagentPredostavlenie_informacionnyh_uslug.html. November 27, 2015.

Rodigin, L. A. (1999). *Information technology in hotel and tourism businesses.* Gloucestershire: RIAT.

The classification of information technologies in tourism. (2012). [Online]. Available: http://www. npark.ru/klassifikaciya-informacionnyxtexnologij-v-turizme-page1.html. November 27, 2015.

Chapter 5
The National Heritage of Călimani Mountains: Peering Inside Unspoiled Wilderness

Călin-Adrian Comes and Maria-Alexandra Popa

Abstract Călimani National Park is situated in Transylvania, Romania, and was established with the purpose of helping to preserve biodiversity of flora and fauna, to maintain the natural geographic framework and natural habitats. Also, the sustainable development of the area is aimed at the efficient use of natural resources, so as to meet the main objective of the Park. It is desirable to create conditions for the development of educational activities, scientific research and recreation, beneficial activities for the preservation and transmission of local traditions to tourists. In this respect, local and national authorities want to invest in infrastructure, education, and research to turn Călimani National Park into a national and international tourist attraction, involving locals in the development, conservation, and sustainability of the region. The aim of this research is to identify the needs for improval in fulfilling the main objective of the Park and to seek solutions to preserve popular culture through smart economy.

Keywords Conservation policy · Călimani National Park · Popular culture
Smart economy · National heritage · Deforestation

5.1 Introduction

Călimani National Park is a protected area of national interest that corresponds to the national park category; a special conservation area located in the central-northern part of Romania, on the administrative territory of the counties: Mureș, Suceava, Harghita, and Bistrița-Năsăud.

C.-A. Comes (✉)
Faculty of Business and Law, Petru Maior University of Tirgu-Mures,
Nicolae Iorga, 1, Tirgu-Mures 540088, Romania
e-mail: calin.comes@ea.upm.ro

M.-A. Popa
School of Accounting, 1 Decembrie 1918 University of Alba-Iulia, Alba, Romania

© Springer International Publishing AG, part of Springer Nature 2019
V. Vasile (ed.), *Caring and Sharing: The Cultural Heritage Environment
as an Agent for Change*, Springer Proceedings in Business and Economics,
https://doi.org/10.1007/978-3-319-89468-3_5

Călimani occupies the northwestern part of the central group of the Eastern Carpathians, representing the largest volcanic mountain in Romania. It is conducted to the north–west–south–east and is bordered to the north by the depression of Dorna (Wah) and Bârgăului Mountains; east—string depressions Păltiniş Drăgoiasa, Bilbor, Secu separates from the high mountains of Bistriţa and Giurgeului (Southeast); south—Mureş gorge forms the boundary Gurghiului volcanic mountains; in the west—Piedmont hills of Călimanului moving toward the eastern part of Transylvania Plateau.

Eastern boundary marks the contact between the crystalline mountains and volcanic massif of Călimanului near Bistriţa. From the town Panaci, it is moving toward the southeast along the stream Călimănel and crosses depressions Paltinis Dragoiasa, Bilbor, to the southeast following the Secului and Topliţei Valley, to the town of the same name. The southern limit is pegged to cross the valley of the Mureş (Topliţa-Deda Gorge) which separates Călimani of Gurghiu Mountains. This region consists of a series of basins scattered human settlements, interposed sectors narrower aspect keys. Western boundary begins north of Hill Tănase, passing west of peaks Păltinului or Pârjoliturii (1147 m), Black Hill or Raglitci (1152 m), Pleşa (1136 m), Bistra (1144 m), south of Hill Vătavii up the Bistra valley, where can be found the confluence with the Mureş. Călimanului contact with Transylvanian plateau is through broad porches—Piedmont Călimanului—that ensures the transition to depressions Orchards-Bârgău, Budac, Deda-Bistra Sieului peak bounded on the west by hills and other hills of Bistriţa. This delimitation corresponds Massif Călimani regarded as mountain unit itself, but in terms of tourism, the area of influence gravitates toward Wah (starting point for routes 1 and 8), comprising Country Dorna (drained by rivers Şarului and Dorna with Dornişoara). Located on the northern flank of the massif, Country Dorna descends gradually forming a broad valley nestled in the heart of the mountains. To the northeast area of influence includes the Bistriţa Valley with a resort Colibiţa future—gateway to the trails that lead to high Călimanului ridge.

The natural area extends to the northeastern part of Mureş County, the southwestern part of Suceava County, the northwestern part of Harghita County, and the southeastern part of Bistriţa-Năsăud County.

In the central-northern area of the Oriental Carpathians, the Călimani Mountains are the most enlightening example of the mass of neogen volcanism, the colossal forces that created the Mount through various explosive, effusive, and intrusive processes. The Călimani massif extends to almost 2000 km^2, with a quasi-rectangular shape of 30/60 km. The higher central area has lagoon placers, craters and volcanic caldera, huge pyroclastic deposits, traces of impressive phenomena that have produced reinforced lava in andesite rocks, but also breccia, volcanic tuffs, etc. This central area is surrounded by a large volcanic plateau, developed especially on pyroclastic deposits, which are now shaped as wider, heavily forested valleys.

In the central-northern part of Călimani Mountains is located a large volcanic caldera with a diameter of approximately 10 km, horseshoe-shaped to the north, surrounded by peaks over 2000 m altitude, being the biggest volcanic caldera in southeastern Europe. The caldera is the result of the collapse of cameras of magmatic reservoirs inside the volcanic apparatus. The higher peaks are the Pietrosul peak of 2100 m, Negoiul Unguresc peak of 2081 m, Răchițiș/Rețițiș peak of 2021 m; the jagged ridge between the peaks Negoiul Unguresc and Pietrosul has alpine characteristics on approximately 4 km long. The Călimani Mountains are the only volcanic mountain area in Romania that carries the traces of the quaternary glaciation, making possible the existence of glaciers.

These stratovolcant mountains are made up of reinforced lava, alternating with pyroclasts and intrusive bodies. In the first stage of formation, in the lower Pliocene, the underwater volcanism developed in the marine waters of those times led to the accumulation of volcanic matter combined with marine sediments, which now constitutes the lower compartment underlying these mountains, deposits which are 100–500 m thick. The second phase of the Upper Pliocene led to the construction and operation of approximately 12 volcanic devices that produced the superstructure, the upper floor of the Călimani Mountains.

The Călimani National Park shelters few lakes. Lake Iezer is a natural dam lake, located near the largest volcanic caldera. Lake Tăul Zânelor is a lake formed by successive frosts and thaws from the high mountains, located in the northern part of the Călimani Mountains.

Probably the best known and most accessible tourist attraction in the Călimani Mountains is the 12 Apostoli Nature Reservation stretched between the Neagra Șarului brook and the Poiana Negri brook, on the surface of which are various unusual rocky formations. At 12 Apostles, you reach the village of Gura Haitii on a spectacular tourist route. The reserve is made up of several huge rocks, carved in the form of human and animal figures which gave birth to some legends. The legend says that this attraction was a place where Dacian used to encounter and to hold holy rituals. It was said that the 12 rock statues were made of sinners punished by God and turned into rock. The locals, together with the priests, followed a tourist route from the southern Călimani Mountains to the north at the 12 Apostles each summer solstice for a Christian Orthodox ceremony. Rituals were performed at the temple of the 12 Apostles until the tradition was stopped in 1914 by national authorities. Nowadays, the road to 12 Apostles is marked in the form of tourist route with a red cross being named Maria Theresia Road, being the longest path in Romania and the only path in National Parks with a length of 42 km.

Another exciting topic related to the Călimani Mountains is the presence of some legends, some famous as Pintea or others less known as Pohontu, Plesca, Miu, and last but not least Haralambie Niculiță. Their story combines moments of manhood, thirst for righteousness with hard life in the heart of the mountains. There are traces of hidden treasure in caves guarded by the courage. Pintea's hand is inlaid in the rock at Apa Rece. Also nearby is Pintea's Spring.

With the Călimani Mountains being classified as a national park, touristic activities started to appear, but the lack of accommodation places and the great distances to be walked significantly reduce the tourist impact in the area. Also, the poor infrastructure related to roads, railroads, touristic paths, the lack of sewerage, and gas infrastructure contribute to the unfavorable regional development, both economically and tourism.

5.2   Literature Review of Călimani National Park

Natural area stretches in the northeastern county of Mureş (on administrative territories of municipalities Răstoliţa and Stânceni); the southwestern county of
Suceava (territories communes Dorna Candrenilor, Panaci, Poiana Stampa and Şaru
Dornei city and Wah); the northwestern county of Harghita (the municipality and
the city Topliţa Bilbor); and the southeastern county of Bistriţa-Năsăud, on the
administrative territory of Bistriţa Bârgăului (Cruceanu et al. 2015a, b; Dincă
2004).

In Călimani Mountains area can be found approximately 100,000 ha of forest.
Places there are wild, rarely walked by people, making perfect room for the quiet
habitat of bears, deer, and other wild animals. The beech forests (Fagus sylvatica)
are located at 600–1000 (1200) m altitude, then the beech, spruce, and fir (Abies
alba) mixture, followed by 800–1000 m above the spruce (Picea abies) sporadically
sprinkled with Sorbus aucuparia. In these forests, there are isolated specimens of
several other tree species, such as Acer pseudoplatanus, Larix decidua. Tisa (Taxus
baccata) is a tree looking for its resistant wood, and today, it almost disappeared
from the area. The compact spruce forests climb to Călimani up to an altitude of
1756 m (Fekete and Blattny 1913).

Pinus cembra is a glacial relic species and is present in juniper trees, on cliffs and
possibly in spruce forests at their upper limit. Interesting is the spruce-smelling
association, a rare combination through the Carpathians but present in Călimani: the
Cembreto-Piceetum abietis association existing at 1610–1780 m altitude on the
northern slope of the Pietricelu Peak (Chifu et al. 2004).

The first proposal establishing the Călimani National Park held in 1975; it will
be declared a protected area by Law No. 5 of March 6, 2000 (the approval of the
National Landscaping—Section III—areas protejate). In 2003, by Government
Decision no. 230 of March 4 concerning the delimitation of biosphere reserves,
national parks, and the establishment of their administrations, the main objective of
the authorities is to restore the boundaries and surface of national parks, including
Călimani National Park (Chirita and Matei 2012).

The Pinus mugo scientific reserve stretches over an area of 384.2 ha and was
established in 1971. Lake Iezer Reservation has an area of 322 ha, protecting the
scenery in the vicinity of the lake. The 12 Apostoli Reservation is extended to
200 ha and features volcanic cliffs of interesting morphology.

5.2.1   Natura 2000

Natura 2000 is a program developed by the European Union and aims to develop a
network at the level of the member states of the European Union to allow the
monitoring and conservation of rare habitats and of animal and plant species in the
partner countries.

The basis for sustainable development is the need to integrate economic activities with environmental and environmental protection requirements, as prioritizing economic and economic growth by excluding environmental protection has resulted in environmental damage by degradation of environmental components.

The Natura 2000 program also includes the National Park Călimani, being an important shelter for rare habitats, sprinkled with animal and plant species protected by national legislation. The Călimani–Gurghiu site (pSCI) covers most of the two volcanic massifs—Călimani Mountains and Gurghiului Mountains which are mountains with volcanic origin with large slopes (average over 30°), extremely varied and crafted relief, with volcanic agglomerations that give specific reliefs of a great scene. The morphology of relief alongside specific bio-pedo-climatic characteristics favors the maintenance of a particularly valuable biodiversity. Here, the varied morphology of the relief combined with the pedo-climatic aspects favored the preservation of a valuable biodiversity, representative of the volcanic mountains in the Carpathians. This has also contributed to the existence of large-scale natural-fundamental forests (over 100,000 ha); their area not significantly altered by anthropogenic activity, preserving the variety of habitats and species. In this area, habitats of European interest are predominant, being spread, according to the Habitats Manual, on 95% of the surface. Here, conifer forests (about one-third of the wooded area) and mixed forests (more than one-third of the wooded area) predominate. Also in this region can be found one of the most highly evaluated populations of carnivores in the Carpathians: brown bear (Ursus arctos)—over 500 specimens, wolf (Canis lupus)—100–120 specimens, and lynx (Lynx lynx)—70–80 specimens. An important factor which made possible the preservation of the value of biodiversity was the lack of human settlements throughout this vast territory, except the Mureş gorge. Traditional management has established a balance between human activities and nature and remains unchanged over time.

According to the Habitats Manual, the Călimani–Gurghiu site hosts 13 habitats, of which 4 are of great importance: 18 bird species, 9 mammalian species, 2 reptiles, 5 fish (including Hucho hucho), 6 invertebrate species (including Rosalia alpina), and 8 species of plants are of community interest.

The implementation of Natura 2000 program in Călimani National Park demonstrates the importance of the place in matter of heritage. The local and national authorities are concerned with creating the necessary framework for the preservation of the area considered a geographic and biological heritage of great national interest. In this respect, it is noted a growing emphasis on the awareness of the population about the importance of the area through various information campaigns, the imposition of restrictions in the Park, the involvement of authorities in research and conservation projects, and sustainable regional development through various mechanisms and concepts, including smart economy.

5.3 Approach

5.3.1 Popular Culture

The extraction of wood from the forests was of small magnitude and of local interest until the time of the flood. Records of the amount of wood that has been flooded since 1711–1714 can be found in Târgu-Mureş local library.

The Saxons in Reghin took over the business in the 1850s, setting up the Floscompany. Beginning with the 1860s, they descended each year through the gorge 1600 floats with approximately 400,000–600,000 cubic meters of wood from Călimani Mountains. Floating was carried out with the help of experienced Italians in this occupation, coming from South Tyrol. The descent with the rafts was done especially in spring, on the big waters, and it was reached with them to the corners of the country. Riding through the gorge was one of the traditional occupations, but it fell after the construction of the railway that became operational in 1909, as well as the highway that passes through the gorge.

Currently, we can speak of several ethnicities present in this geographical area, most of them Romanians, followed by Hungarians, Roma, Saxons. The population here is aging, most of those born in these areas being established in the cities near the Călimani National Park (Târgu-Mureş, Reghin, Bistriţa, Suceava, Cluj Napoca, etc.).

According to recent statistics, most of the population in the Călimani National Park who are over 30 years of age have a medium-level education at high school/ vocational level and are not being educated in order to be able to preserve the reservation in which they live. Moreover, the cultural mix in this region (Romanians, Roma, Hungarians, Saxons, Russians) raises problems of behavior among the population. From this, on the one hand, it can be said that the environment is directly affected by multiculturalism, under these conditions. On the other hand, multiculturalism itself has shown considerable benefits for the reservation, as local, regional, and regulatory authorities have acted together, involving several political parties (Romanian, Hungarian) in taking measures to conserve the Călimani National Park. Moreover, there are several ethnic non-governmental organizations that deal with the maintenance of the Călimani National Park. There are several shelter points in the Călimani Mountains, where most of the Hungarians are volunteers of Hungarian ethnicity who take care of mountain markings and intervene in emergencies.

In spite of all the measures taken to protect this area, illegal deforestation, with a significant negative impact on the ecosystem in the area, is continuing, the destruction of some formations of the type of volcanic caves, unique in the country, for the purpose of exploiting resources leading to the definitive loss of the history of this area. Moreover, the exploitation of sulfur proved to be very toxic significantly pollutes the surroundings, and there also exists the risk of poisoning with uranium, a natural resource specific to the Călimani Mountains. Recent studies show that there are several springs of radioactive mineral water in the affected area that endanger the health of locals (especially those in the eastern area of the mountains).

5.3.2 Smart Economy

As mentioned above, the population in this protected area is aging, due to the living conditions of this place. Young people want to go to the nearby cities to have better living conditions and to have the chance to practice any job they want. The Călimani National Park area limits economic development in several areas.

Călimani National Park is a poor, high cultural risky area, given the significant population decline in the last few years and the economic underdevelopment specific to the Park. The main industrial activities carried out here are in the wood and food processing industry (bakeries, mineral water). Illegal mass deforestation is an essential risk factor that leads to the destruction of the cultural and natural assets in this area. Most of whom practice it have a need to resort to this method in order to survive in this economically poor environment. There are old locals who are very skilled at various local old jobs, risking that these jobs disappear due to the fact that there is no longer a young population willing to learn the trades and stay in the villages.

Although it is an area with real potential for tourism, there are very few accommodations, resorts, and restaurants in this area. From our point of view, this area could grow economically by investing in tourism, by bringing together plant and animal experts to inform local people about protected species, by accessing national and European funds for opening agritourism boarding houses several strategic points in the Mureș Gorge and Călimani National Park where tourists learn from the locals the art of craftsmanship but also so that they can see how they live in this area in order to spread the local folk culture in order to be able to preserve traditions and do not lose the identity of the area. Also, tourists could make hiking trails alongside locals, learn the law-protected species in that area, and enjoy the wonders of nature.

It is desirable to promote the places inside the Călimani National Park by bringing tourists from and outside the country and their accommodation in these agritouristic hostels. Tourists can be also conducted into itineraries in Călimani Mountains to discover the beauty of nature by the locals; they can have the advantage to exchange experiences and to preserve the area's culture.

In this context, we can talk about the concept of smart economy taking into consideration that it is expected a slow development of the Park area and the economic growth targeted is focused on the quality of the local people's quality of life and the raising of the living standard, incorporating the innovative elements for its realization. Moreover, with local people's help, local traditions can be spread, thus preserving the cultural heritage of this special and unique area.

5.4   Conclusions

Călimani National Park presents a real risk of cultural heritage loss, considering all the factors presented above.

Multiculturalism influences positively and negatively the conservation of the area. The negative influence is due to the cultural differences between the locals, and the positive influence is caused by the involvement of all authorities, parties, associations in preserving the Park.

Illegal clearing and tracing or breaking of legally protected species that lead to their disappearance over time, as well as the destruction of geomorphological formations preserved over time to exploit resources, are leading to the loss of the specific identity of the area, drastically decreasing the country's natural wealth.

Local and national authorities have begun to focus on preserving the area by attracting European funds and by constantly monitoring protected species and habitats. In this respect, an increase in the population of protected species can be noticed, especially in terms of brown bears.

There are solutions to these issues; local and national authorities are considering more measures to improve both the lives of people in this area and to reduce illegal practices that would lead to the destruction of the protected area.

Although tourism has not been highlighted so far, this sector in the economy is becoming increasingly demanding, representing a real potential, both for regional development and for combating illegal deforestation.

References

Chifu T., Sârbu I., & Ştefan N. (2004). Fitocenoze din ordinul Quercetalia pubescentis Br.-Bl. 1931 em. Soó 1964 pe teritoriul Moldovei (România). In *Bul. Grăd. Bot. Iaşi.* (Vol. 12, pp. 17–44).

Chirita, V., & Matei, D. (2012). The relational articulation between communities and protected areas in the Dorna—Calimani Mountains Area (The Eastern Carpathians of Romania). In *International Multidisciplinary Scientific GeoConference: SGEM: Surveying Geology & mining Ecology Management* (Vol. 4, p. 1177).

Cruceanu, A. D., Muntele, I., & Cazacu, M. D. (2015a). The management of tourism and development in Vatra Dornei health resort from the sustainable development. In *PEEC-Ecological Performance in a Competitive Economy—Conference Proceedings*, Bucharest, Romania, March 5–6.

Cruceanu, A. D., Muntele, I., & Cazacu, M. D. (2015b). Ways of valorization of the touristic potential in Tara Dornelor. *SEA-Practical Application of Science*, (7), 193–202.

Dincă, I. (2004). *Apa şi peisajele din Munţii Călimani.* Cluj Napoca: Editura Dacia.

Fekete, L., & Blattny, O. (1913–1914). *Die Verbreitung der forstlichwichtigen Bäume und Sträucher im ungarischen Staate.* Selmecbanya.

Government Decision No. 230 from 4 March 2003 on the Delimitation of Biosphere Reserves, National Parks and Natural Parks and the Constitution of Their Administrations, Published in The Official Monitor, no. 190 in 26 March 2003.
Law no. 5 from 6 March 2000 on the Approval of the National Territory Planning Plan—Section III—Protected Areas, Parliament of Romania, published in The Official Monitor, no. 152 in 12 April 2000.

Chapter 6
Statistical Correlation Between Tourism and Poverty in EU Countries

Carmen Boghean and Mihaela State

Abstract Tourism is a crucial factor that contributes to a country's economic growth. Nowadays, one of the greatest challenges worldwide is to diminish poverty since an increasing number of individuals suffer from this phenomenon. Throughout time, in many countries, tourism worked and still works as an economic development engine, contributing both directly and indirectly to the creation of working places in the economy. Tourism is one of the sectors of economic activity that can offer multiple opportunities to stimulate labour market growth with profound implications for the economic development level of countries that have a high level of poverty. Therefore, for some countries tourism represents the main source of foreign currency. If these revenues are directed towards poverty diminishing, the poorer categories can benefit from the inclusion of the local people in tourism activities, with positive effects on the attenuation of the current level of poverty. The aim of this research is to analyse the correlation between the activities from the tourism industry and the poverty level in the countries of the European Union. The employed research methodology relies on the correlation analysis, accomplished through the use of the data sets collected from the Web page of the European Commission related to the revenues obtained from tourism and the poverty level in the countries of the European Union. In order to highlight the differences existing between the EU member states, we will make a comparison using the cluster analysis. This paper aims to reveal that tourism cannot be regarded as the only factor for poverty diminishing but may have an extremely important contribution. Taking into account the size of the tourism industry in many countries of the European Union, we can state that a change of the approach regarding this industry's importance for the economic development may have remarkable effects on diminishing the level of poverty.

Keywords Poverty · Tourism industry · Cluster analysis · Economic growth

C. Boghean (✉) · M. State
Faculty of Economics and Public Administration,
Ştefan cel Mare University of Suceava, Suceava, Romania
e-mail: carmenb@seap.usv.ro

© Springer International Publishing AG, part of Springer Nature 2019   83
V. Vasile (ed.), *Caring and Sharing: The Cultural Heritage Environment as an Agent for Change*, Springer Proceedings in Business and Economics,
https://doi.org/10.1007/978-3-319-89468-3_6

6.1   Introduction

Tourism is one of the determining factors for foreign trade and prosperity. One of the major global challenges is the reduction of poverty. The relationship between tourism development and reducing the level of poverty is found in the area of concern both of researchers but also of international institutions. Many researchers have investigated the impact of tourism development on reducing the level of poverty in different countries or groups of countries (Bazini 2008). They have started from the premise that the revenues from tourism represent an important factor in increasing living standards in poor areas, representing at the same time a sector of economic activity that can assimilate the available workforce (Jamieson et al. 2004).

Ashley and Goodwin (2007), appreciate that the impact of tourism on decreasing poverty level is higher in those areas where micro-businesses have access to capital, receive significant support in business and have a skilled workforce. This will mean the implementation of measures at a local level, which will contribute to increasing competitiveness, improving the business environment and creating new opportunities for the labour market, with direct effects on the living standards of the population in poor areas (Goodwin 2008).

To reduce poverty through tourism, a number of principles need to be implemented (UNWTO and SNV 2010):

- All governments should include poverty reduction as a key objective of developing tourism and consider tourism as a possible tool for reducing poverty.
- All tourism enterprises should be concerned about the impact of their activities on local communities and should make sure that the poor benefit from their actions.
- Tourism planning and development should involve the participation and representation of poor communities.
- Projects involving the poor should be considered a priority.

6.2   The Analysis of the Link Between Tourism and Poverty Level in EU Countries

6.2.1   The Evolution of Receipts from International Tourism in European Union Countries in the Period 2010–2014

The countries that recorded the largest share of receipts from international tourism in total exports are Croatia, Greece and Cyprus. The lowest shares are registered in the Netherlands, Romania and Slovakia (Fig. 6.1).

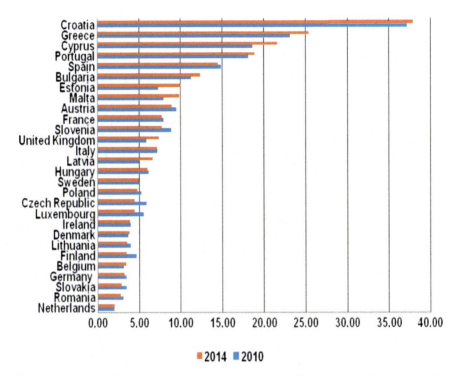

Fig. 6.1 International tourism receipts (% of total exports) in EU countries in 2014 compared to 2010 (*Source* Our own elaboration based on World Bank data, www.worldbank.org)

The results of the descriptive data analysis on receipts from international tourism in the EU countries for the two years under analysis are presented in Table 6.1. The average of the receipts from international tourism in 2014 (8.91%) is not different from the average in 2010 (8.61%).

The grouping of countries by receipts from international tourism in 2014 resulted in two clusters:

Table 6.1 Descriptive statistics

	N	Minimum	Maximum	Mean	Standard deviation
International_tourism_receipts_2010	28	1.93	37.14	8.61	7.64
International_tourism_receipts_2014	28	2.01	37.88	8.91	8.17
Valid N (list-wise)	28				

Source Calculation performed with SPSS software

Table 6.2 Average values

	Cluster	
	1	2
International_tourism_receipts_2014	6.08	25.92

Source Calculation performed with SPSS software

- Cluster 1, which consists of 24 countries (Netherlands, Slovakia, Germany, Belgium, Finland, Denmark, Luxembourg, Czech Republic, Poland, Sweden, UK, Slovenia, France, Austria, Malta, Romania, Lithuania, Ireland, Hungary, Latvia, Italy, Estonia, Bulgaria and Spain), has an average of receipts from international tourism of 6.08% (Table 6.2), lower than the EU average;
- Cluster 2 which consists of four countries (Portugal, Cyprus, Greece and Croatia) has an average of receipts from international tourism of 25.92%, higher than the EU average; tourism planning and development should involve the participation and representation of poor communities.

The difference between cluster 1 and cluster 2 in terms of international tourism receipts is 19.84.

6.2.2 Changes in the Evolution of the Poverty Level in the EU Countries in the Period 2010–2014

The largest shares of people at risk of poverty or social exclusion in total population are recorded in Bulgaria, Romania and Greece. The lowest shares are registered in the Czech Republic, Netherlands and Sweden (Fig. 6.2).

The results of the descriptive data analysis on poverty level in the EU countries for the two years under analysis are presented in Table 6.3. The average poverty level in 2014 (24.85%) is not different from the average in 2010 (24.57%). However, there is a reduction between the maximum poverty level in 2010 (49.20%) and 2014 (40.10%), the standard deviation decreasing as well. The data representing poverty level in 2014 are more homogeneous than in 2010.

Considering the poverty level registered in EU countries in 2014, we can identify two clusters:

- Cluster 1, which consists of 15 countries (Netherlands, Slovakia, Germany, Belgium, Finland, Denmark, Luxembourg, Czech Republic, Poland, Sweden, UK, Slovenia, France, Austria and Malta), has an average poverty level of 19.55% (Table 6.4), lower than the EU average;
- Cluster 2, which consists of 13 countries (Romania, Lithuania, Ireland, Hungary, Latvia, Italy, Estonia, Bulgaria, Spain, Portugal, Cyprus, Greece and Croatia), has an average poverty level of 30.98%, higher than the EU average;

The difference between cluster 1 and cluster 2 in terms of poverty level in 2014 is 11.43 (Table 6.5).

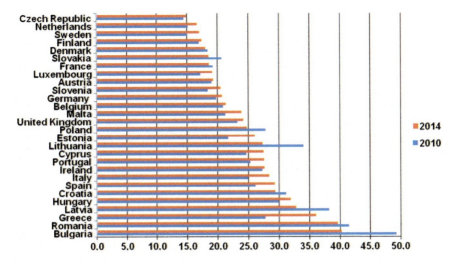

Fig. 6.2 People at risk of poverty or social exclusion (percentage of total population) in EU countries in 2014 compared to 2010 (*Source* Our own elaboration based on Eurostat data, http://ec. europa.eu/eurostat)

Table 6.3 Descriptive statistics

	N	Minimum	Maximum	Mean	Standard deviation
Poverty_level_2010	28	14.40	49.20	24.57	8.34
Poverty_level_2014	28	14.80	40.10	24.85	6.94
Valid N (list-wise)	28				

Source Calculation performed with SPSS software

Table 6.4 Average values

| | Cluster | |
	1	2
Poverty_level_2014	19.55	30.98

Source Calculation performed with SPSS software

Table 6.5 Spearman correlation coefficient

		Poverty_level_2014	International_tourism_receipts_2014
Poverty_level_2014	Correlation Coef.	1.000	0.454
	Sig (2-tailed)		0.015
	N	28	28
International_tourism_receipts_2014	Correlation Coef.	0.454	1.000
	Sig (2-tailed)	0.015	
	N	28	28

*Correlation is significant at the 0.05 level (two-tailed)
Source Calculation performed with SPSS software

6.2.3 Correlation Between Tourism and Poverty Level in EU Countries

The graphical representation of the two variables analysed is performed in Fig. 6.3.

Based on the results for the Spearman correlation coefficient, we can say that there is a direct link between tourism and poverty level in the European Union.

In order to have a clearer understanding of the impact of tourism sector development on alleviating poverty level, it is necessary to consider the GDP per capita in the European Union countries. The grouping of countries by GDP per capita 2014 resulted in three clusters:

– Cluster 1 consists of one country (only Luxembourg);
– Cluster 2 consists of 11 countries (Netherlands, Germany, Belgium, Finland, Denmark, Sweden, UK, France, Austria, Ireland and Italy) has a GDP per capita higher than the EU average;

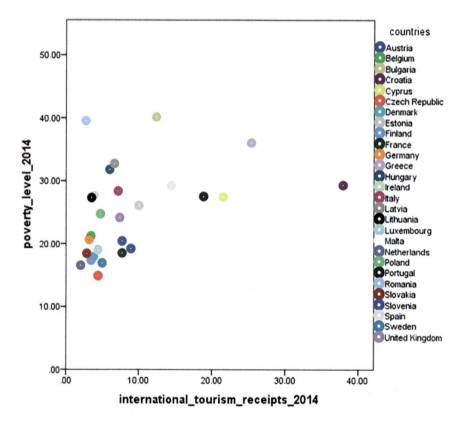

Fig. 6.3 Correlation between international tourism receipts and poverty level in EU countries in 2014 (*Source* Our own elaboration based on Eurostat and World Bank data)

Table 6.6 Average values

	Cluster		
	1	2	3
GDP_per_capita_2014	87,600.00	37,500.00	14,106.25

Source Calculation performed with SPSS software

– Cluster 3 which contains 16 countries (Bulgaria, Croatia, Cyprus, Czech Republic, Estonia, Greece, Hungary, Latvia, Lithuania, Malta, Poland, Portugal, Romania, Slovakia, Slovenia and Spain) has an average GDP per capita lower than the EU average.

The difference between cluster 1 and cluster 3 in terms of GDP per capita is 73,493.75 (Table 6.6).

Figure 6.4 shows the distribution of EU countries that have similar characteristics in the same cluster. A low level of GDP per capita is found in countries that have a high level of poverty.

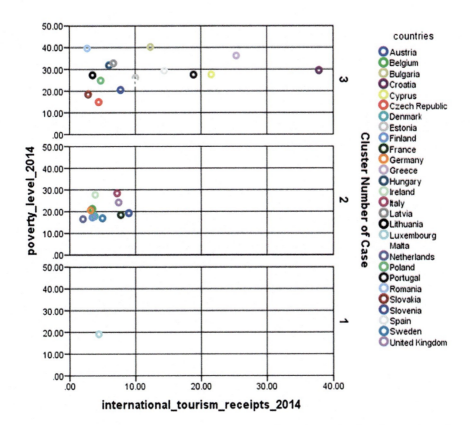

Fig. 6.4 Distribution of EU countries into clusters according to international tourism receipts and poverty level in 2014

6.3 Conclusion

Tourism is for many countries the best choice for a sustainable development. If tourism is managed with a strong focus on poverty reduction, it can directly bring benefits to the poorer groups by engaging local people in tourism enterprises that have a positive impact on reducing poverty levels.

There is a direct link between tourism and poverty level in the European Union. In countries like Romania and Bulgaria, with high levels of poverty, the share of international tourism receipts (total exports) is quite low. In these countries, the development of the tourism sector could contribute significantly to the economic development and poverty reduction through the positive effects it generates on the labour market (by engaging the population from poorer areas) and the national accounts (through increase in international tourism receipts).

References

Ashley, C., & Goodwin, H. (2007, June), *'Pro poor tourism': What's gone right and what's gone wrong?* Overseas Development Institute. https://www.odi.org/sites/odi.org.uk/files/odi-assets/publications-opinion-files/778.pdf;evelopment.

Bazini, E. (2008). Impact of the tourism development on poverty reduction in Albania as a country in transition. *The Annals of the "Ştefan cel Mare" University Suceava.* Fascicle of the Faculty of Economics and Public Administration, No 8/2008. http://www.seap.usv.ro/annals/ojs/index.php/annals/article/viewFile/23/22.

Goodwin, G. (2008, December). Tourism, local economic development, and poverty reduction. *Applied Research in Economic Development,* 5(3). http://haroldgoodwin.info/uploads/ARED2008goodwin_online_v5n3_propoor_tourism.pdf.

http://ec.europa.eu/eurostat.

Jamieson, W., Goodwin, H., & Edmunds, C. (2004). *Contribution of tourism to poverty alleviation pro-poor tourism and the challenge of measuring impacts.* For Transport Policy and Tourism Section, Transport and Tourism Division, UN ESCAP, November 2004. http://haroldgoodwin.info/resources/povertyalleviation.pdf.

Manual on Tourism and Poverty Alleviation, Practical Steps for Destinations. UNWTO and SNV 2010.

Tourism and Poverty Alleviation. http://step.unwto.org/content/tourism-and-poverty-alleviation-1.

Tourism and Poverty Reduction—Overseas Development Institute. https://www.odi.org/resources/docs/5725.pdf.

www.worldbank.org.

Chapter 7
Patterns in Romanian Tourism Activity—A Factorial Analysis

Cristina Boboc, Simona Ghita and Valentina Vasile

Abstract According to the data provided by the National Institute of Statistics, in Romania, in 2015, there were recorded almost ten million tourist arrivals in accommodation establishments, of which foreign tourist arrivals represented less than a quarter (22.55%). After 2000, tourist arrivals have registered an upward trend, interrupted only during the global economic and financial crisis in 2008–2009. Over 57% of foreign tourists arrivals in Romania in 2015 came from the European Union (mostly from Hungary and Bulgaria), and from Republic of Moldova and Ukraine. In 2014, only 5% of companies in Romania were operating in the hotel and restaurant industry, their turnover representing less than 1% of the total value. The average length of stay for Romanian tourists ranges between 2 days (at the mountain) and over 3 days (at the seaside). Foreign tourist arrivals are mostly concentrated in mountain areas, in Bucharest, and in other cities as well. This paper identifies and explores—using methods of descriptive statistics and factor analysis—patterns existing in relationships between different tourism statistical indicators (arrivals of Romanian tourists, arrivals of foreign tourists, overnight staying for Romanian and foreign tourists, tourism accommodation capacity, tourism accommodation establishments, favorite tourism destinations). Thus, there are analyzed the essential components and characteristics of the main types of tourism developed in Romania and some measures of economic and social policy are proposed, aiming at optimizing tourism activity in Romania.

Keywords Tourism · Romania · Tourism indicators · Factorial analysis
Descriptive statistics

C. Boboc (✉) · S. Ghita
Bucharest University of Economics, Bucharest, Romania
e-mail: cristina.boboc@csie.ase.ro

V. Vasile
Institute of National Economy, Romanian Academy, Bucharest, Romania

© Springer International Publishing AG, part of Springer Nature 2019
V. Vasile (ed.), *Caring and Sharing: The Cultural Heritage Environment
as an Agent for Change*, Springer Proceedings in Business and Economics,
https://doi.org/10.1007/978-3-319-89468-3_7

7.1 Introduction

In the last 10 years, tourism market in Romania has registered some positive developments, particularly in terms of extensive issues of the tourism supply and demand. Favorable aspects were maintained in 2015, when tourism market grew by 5.3% (August 2015), specialists forecasting a continuing increase in 2016 as well (by 10–12%). Thus, in 2015 we have noted an increase in tourist arrivals by over 17% compared to the previous year, both for the Romanian and foreign tourists. The number of tourist arrivals reached almost ten million tourist arrivals in accommodation establishments, of which foreign tourist arrivals represented less than a quarter (22.55%). The number of overnight staying has increased with a similar annual average rate (almost 16%), while the net use index of accommodation places has increased from 26.2% (2014) to 28.8% (2015). Regarding tourism supply indicators, there have existed here some favorable developments too, such as an increase in the number of establishments of tourist reception with functions of tourist accommodation by 11%. On the side of efficiency in tourism activity, Romania has to perform some more improvements. Thus, over the last 10 years, the net use index of accommodation places has followed a downward trend, from 33.6% in 2006 to 28.8% in 2015. Also, the average time of stay has experienced a decrease, from 3.06 days in 2006 to 2.37 days in 2015. It is well known that generally, tourism activity has a strong seasonal character. Analyzing the net occupancy rate in hotels and similar establishments, over the period 2012–2015, it was revealed that the seasonal indices recorded a maximum value of 139% in the third quarter and a minimum value of 72.1% in the first quarter.

This paper identifies and explores—using methods of descriptive statistics and factor analysis—patterns existing in relationships between different tourism statistical indicators. Understanding and analyzing the relational patterns in tourism activity could facilitate highlighting weak links in the cause-effect chain, identifying the factors with highest influence on outcome indicators of tourism activity. The analysis focused on the following statistical indicators of tourism demand and supply: the number of tourist arrivals (for Romanian and foreign tourists), the number of overnight staying (for Romanian and foreign tourists), the existing tourist accommodation capacity, and the average length of overnight staying (for Romanian and foreign tourists). Thus, there are analyzed the essential components and characteristics of the main types of tourism developed in Romania and some measures of economic and social policy are proposed, aiming at optimizing tourism activity in Romania.

7.2 A Brief Overview of the Literature

The key role of tourism in amplifying the output of economic activity was revealed many decades ago. Thus, Krapf (1961) identified a tourism special function, with a particular role in development, by generating significant capital amounts in tourism-related economic sectors (trade, industry, construction, telecommunications, transport) (the multiplier effect of tourism). For small developing economies, tourism can be an engine to boost economic recovery, by providing external financial resources (Dwyer and Forsyth 1993).

Mowforth and Munt (1998) saw the tourism as a product with special status, different from all the other products, an export product or even as a complex of products and services, purchased by tourists (Song and Witt 2000).

Governments realized that tourism can be used as a political tool for maintaining peace and good relationships with other countries (Hall 2000). Therefore, it is necessary to allocate substantial funds to support and promote tourism, in a joint effort of governmental, public, and private institutions.

A number of empirical studies have focused on analyzing satisfaction in tourism. Thus, Suanmali (2014) identified the main factors that influence satisfaction in tourism: the staying costs, attractions of destination area, accessibility, and infrastructure.

Another category of studies focused on international tourism demand and searched for a way to quantify it and to determine its influence factors (Lim 2006), using the number of tourist arrivals as a tourist demand indicator, and even more advanced models such as Almost Ideal Demand System (AIDS) or Time-Varying Parameter (TVP).

Hanke et al. (2001) analyze macroeconomic aggregate demand, using models to identify the trend component, the seasonal component, and the cyclical component. Nicolau and Más (2005) have performed—using multiple regression—a model of tourist spending depending on a number of factors, including the decision to go on a vacation and the length of stay.

Aguilo Perez and Juanedasampol (2000) and Wang (2000) have analyzed tourist expenditures, separating them into two groups: expenditures in the origin country and expenditures in tourism destination country, measuring the extent to which different factors influence the expenditures variability.

Most studies include economic, social, and psychological variables as explanatory variables of tourism expenditure. They have certified a significant effect of income on tourism demand, especially in the case of longer stays (Jang et al. 2005; Lehto et al. 2004; Mehmetoglu 2007). Tribe (2005) highlights the inverse influence of prices on tourism demand, taking into account individual behavior.

When it comes to introducing the socio-demographic variables in explaining behavior patterns of tourism demand, studies have often revealed contradictory results. Some of these factors considered in most studies are: gender, age, education level, marital status, household size.

7.3 Tourism Indicators in Romania

Tourism market in Romania follows an upward trend, and 5–10% increases in recent years could amplify to 10–12% in the coming years—believe specialists. A report released in 2015 by World Travel and Tourism Council shows that the direct contribution of travel and tourism industry in Romania amounted to 1.6% of GDP in 2014, while the total contribution amounted to 4.8% of GDP in the same year. The impact of tourism on employment is illustrated by the fact that it directly supported 205,000 jobs in 2014 (representing 2.4% of total employment) and 467,500 jobs indirectly (representing 5.5% of total employment). Referring to tourism investments, the same report reveals that in 2014 they represented 7.3% of the total investment, being expected an increase to 7.6% by 2025. In a world country ranking, Romania ranks 62 in terms of the absolute contribution of tourism on the economy (out of 184 countries).

In the last 10 years, tourist arrivals have experienced an upward trend, from 6216.1 thousand in 2006 to 9930 thousand in 2015, with an average relative change of 5.3% per year. The share of foreign tourist arrivals in accommodation establishments ranged between 22.2% (2006) and 22.6% (2015), reaching a minimum of 20.8% in 2009 (Fig. 7.1). In 2015, tourist arrivals in hotels represent around 73% of the total number of tourist arrivals. In 2015, most of the tourist arrivals are located in Bucharest and county residence town (51.24%), in mountain resorts (15.4%) and to the seaside (8.27%).

Analyzing the monthly evolution of tourist arrivals in 2015, a peak can be observed in August (1420.1 thousand arrivals) and a minimum in January (498.4 thousand arrivals). Compared to 2014, the highest relative increase appeared in July (24.8% in July 2015, compared to July 2014), while the lowest relative increase was in February (9.09% in February 2015, compared to February 2014) (Fig. 7.2).

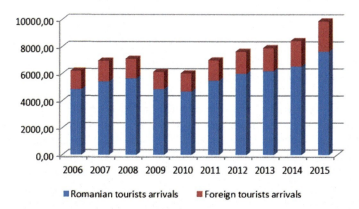

Fig. 7.1 Tourist arrivals (thousand) in Romania, by types of tourists, 2006–2015 (*Source* Authors' processing, based on data provided by the National Institute of Romania, TEMPO online —Tourism)

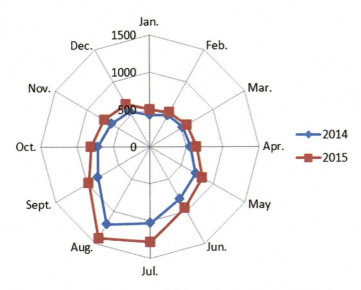

Fig. 7.2 Monthly tourist arrivals (thousand) in Romania, in 2014 and 2015 (*Source* Authors' processing, based on data provided by the National Institute of Romania, TEMPO online—Tourism)

Tourists' favorite destination in 2015 was Bucharest and county residence towns (51.24%), followed by mountain resorts (15.4%), and seaside (8.27%).

The number of overnight staying has recorded an upward trend, interrupted by a decrease in 2009 and 2010, due to the global financial crisis. The indicator level has increased on average by 2.4% per year, from almost 19,000 thousand to 23,445 thousand.

In the period 2006–2015, the average time of stay has experienced a decrease, from 3.06 days in 2006 to 2.37 days in 2015, with an average annual relative change equal to 3% (Fig. 7.3).

The number of establishments of tourism reception with functions of tourism accommodation has followed a general increasing trend, from 4710 (2006) to 6821 (2015), with an average annual relative change of 11%. It was interrupted by a few short decreases (in 2007 compared to 2006 and in 2011 compared to 2010) (Fig. 7.4).

Less than a quarter of tourist accommodation establishments are hotels (1522 hotels, in 2015, of which more than 86% have private integral ownership) and over a quarter of the total number of establishments is in mountain resorts (1822). More than half of the hotels are three stars hotels, almost a quarter are two stars hotels, and only 2% are five stars hotels (Fig. 7.5).

In terms of net use index of accommodation places, Romanian tourism has experienced a general decrease in the last 10 years, from 34% in 2006 to 29% in 2015 (by 1.7%, on average per year). The entire period can be divided into two sub-periods, with different directions of evolution of the indicator level. Thus,

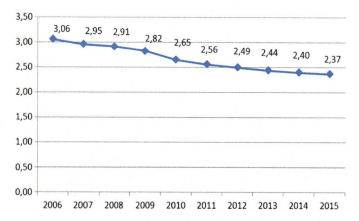

Fig. 7.3 Average time of stay (days), 2006–2015 (*Source* Authors' processing, based on data provided by the National Institute of Romania, TEMPO online—Tourism)

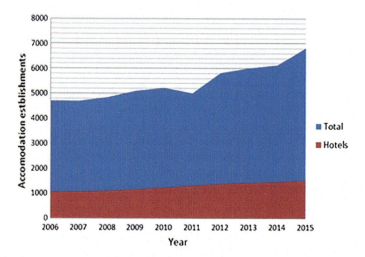

Fig. 7.4 Tourist accommodation establishments in Romania, 2006–2015 (*Source* Authors' processing, based on data provided by the National Institute of Romania, TEMPO online—Tourism)

between 2006 and 2010, the indicator declined more pronounced, with an average annual rate of nearly 7%. Then, between 2010 and 2015 the indicator level rebounded, growing by a lower average annual rate of 2% (Fig. 7.6).

The net use index of tourism accommodation capacity in function differs by the type of ownership. Thus, the indicator has recorded the highest value for the accommodation establishments in state property (almost 50%), followed by establishments in foreign property and private property (almost 40%). The lowest net use index was recorded in case of accommodation establishments in cooperative

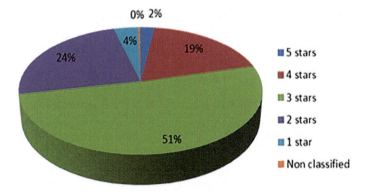

Fig. 7.5 Hotels in Romania, by category of comfort (%)—2015 (*Source* Authors' processing, based on data provided by the National Institute of Romania, TEMPO online—Tourism)

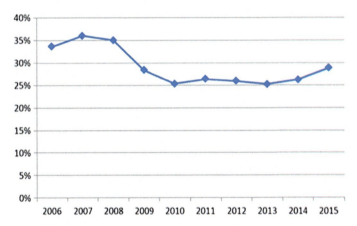

Fig. 7.6 Net use index of accommodation places (%), 2006–2015 (*Source* Authors' processing, based on data provided by the National Institute of Romania, TEMPO online—Tourism)

property (21.3%). Apartment hotels recorded the maximum net use index of accommodation capacity (46.7%), while camping recorded the lowest value (13%).

7.4 Which Are the Main Patterns of Tourism Activity in Romania?

In order to identify the main patterns of tourism activity in Romania, we have used the national statistics for the period 2011–2015. We have chosen four indicators for tourism activity:

- The number of tourists arrivals—for Romanian and foreign tourists (NRTA, NFTA),
- The number of overnight staying—for Romanian and foreign tourists,
- The existing tourist accommodation capacity, and
- The average length of overnight staying—for Romanian and foreign tourists.

In order to obtain a suggestive representation of the patterns of tourism activity on Romanian regions and on types of accommodation, a multiple correspondence analysis (MCA) is applied. MCA is a technique used to reduce multidimensional data sets to lower dimensions, when the variables included in the analysis are categorical. MCA is mathematically defined as an orthogonal linear transformation that projects the data to a new coordinate system (principal components) in order to obtain the greatest variance explained by this projection of the data (Table 7.1; Fig. 7.7).

Table 7.1 Model summary

Dimension	Cronbach's alpha	Variance accounted for		
		Total (Eigen value)	Inertia	% of variance
1	.753	2.514	.503	50.272
2	.590	1.893	.379	37.852
Total		4.406	.881	
Mean	.683	2.203	.441	44.062

Source National Institute of Statistics, 2016, authors' calculations using SPSS software; observation period: 2011–2015

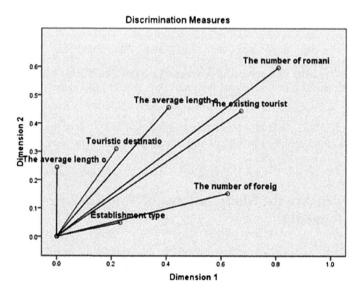

Fig. 7.7 Discrimination measures extraction method: multiple correspondence analysis (*Source* National Institute of Statistics, 2016, authors' calculations using SPSS software; observation period: 2011–2015)

Examining the descriptive statistics output for the variables considered, we can observe that most of them present higher variability, except for the length of staying for Romanian and foreign tourists. All the distributions are positively skewed, prevailing small values of the variables.

The projection of data on the first axis explains 50% of the total inertia. The best discrimination measures on this axis are: the number of foreign and Romanian tourist arrivals and the existing tourist accommodation capacity. The projection of data on the second axis explains 38% of the total inertia. The best discrimination measures on this axis are: the number of Romanian tourist arrivals, the average length of overnight staying for Romanian tourists, and the existing tourist accommodation capacity (Fig. 7.8).

By analyzing the projection of categories on the first two axes, it could be observed that during the analyzed period (2011–2015) the average length of overnight staying for Romanian tourists at seaside is higher than 2.5 nights and for foreign tourists is higher than 3.7 nights. In mountain resorts, the average length of overnight staying for a Romanian tourist is between 1.6 and 2.5 nights and they prefer hotels/motels or hostels as accommodation types. In Bucharest or other destinations, foreign tourists have an average length of overnight stay that is less

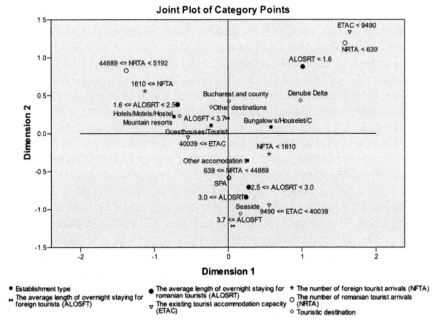

Fig. 7.8 Joint plot of category points. Extraction method: multiple correspondence analysis (*Source* National Institute of Statistics, 2016, authors' calculations using SPSS software; observation period: 2011–2015)

than 3.7 nights. In Danube Delta, Romanian tourists stay in average up to 1.6 nights. According to these results on the existing tourist accommodation capacity, we can say that the Danube Delta and seaside regions should be developed for improving the tourism activity in Romania.

7.5 Conclusions

In the last 10 years, tourism market in Romania has registered some positive developments, particularly in terms of extensive side of the tourism supply and demand. Specialists reveal that Romanian tourism market increased by 5–10% in recent years, and could amplify to 10–12% in the coming years. A report released in 2015 by World Travel and Tourism Council shows that the direct contribution of travel and tourism industry in Romania amounted to 1.6% of GDP in 2014, while the total contribution amounted to 4.8% of GDP in the same year. Most statistical indicators in tourism domain have experienced favorable evolutions, interrupted by brief periods of decline due to the global financial and economic crisis. However, the analysis revealed some negative aspects in the evolution of net use index of accommodation capacity and of the average time of stay.

Using methods of descriptive statistics and factor analysis, the authors identified and analyzed patterns existing in relationships between different tourism statistical indicators. The analysis was based on the following statistical indicators of tourism demand and supply: the number of tourist arrivals (for Romanian and foreign tourists), the number of overnight staying (for Romanian and foreign tourists), the existing tourist accommodation capacity, and the average length of overnight staying (for Romanian and foreign tourists). Thus, by analyzing the essential components and characteristics of the main types of tourism developed in Romania, the following outcomes were obtained: The average length of overnight staying for Romanian tourists at seaside is higher than 2.5 nights and for foreign tourists is higher than 3.7 nights. In mountain resorts, the average length of overnight staying for a Romanian tourist is between 1.6 and 2.5 nights and they prefer hotels/motels or hostels as accommodation types. In Bucharest or other destinations, foreign tourists have an average length of overnight stay that is less than 3.7 nights. In Danube Delta, Romanian tourists stay in average up to 1.6 nights. According to these results on the existing tourist accommodation capacity, we can say that the Danube Delta and seaside regions should be developed for improving the tourism activity in Romania.

A condition to ensure the success of the Romanian tourism industry in the next period is a better adaptation of tourism to novelties in e-commerce activity. The studies have shown an increase in the penetration rate of information through e-commerce channels, and especially an increase in the speed response to information received through online channels. In this way, a better promotion of traditional tourist destinations and products can be achieved (Danube Delta, seaside region), and a better joint between the tourism demand and supply is required, as well as an improvement of the seasonality in tourism activity.

References

Aguilo Perez, E., & Juanedasampol, C. (2000). Tourist expenditure for mass tourism markets. *Annals of Tourism Research, 27*(3), 624–637.

Dwyer, L., & Forsyth, P. (1993). Assessing the benefits and costs of inbound tourism. *Annals of Tourism Research, 20*(4), 751–768.

Hall, C. M. (2000). *Tourism in Indonesia: The end of a new order.* Oxford: Butterworth-Heinemann.

Hanke, J. E., Wichern, D. W., & Reitsch, A. G. (2001). *Business forecasting* (7th ed.). Upper Saddle River: Prentice Hall.

Jang, S., Cai, L. A., Morrison, A. M., & O'Leary, J. T. (2005). The effect of travel activities and seasons on expenditure. *International Journal of Tourism Research, 7*(6), 335–346.

Krapf, K. (1961). Les pays en voie de developpement face au tourisme:Introduction methodologique. *Tourism Review, 16*(3), 82–89.

Lehto, X. Y., Cai, L. A., O'leary, J. T., & Huan, T.-C. (2004). Tourist shopping preferences and expenditure behaviours: The case of the Taiwanese outbound market. *Journal of Vacation Marketing, 10*(4), 320–332.

Lim, C. (2006). A survey of tourism demand modelling practice: Issues and implications (pp. 45–72). In L. Dwyer & P. Forsyth (Eds.), *International handbook on the economics of tourism.* Cheltenham, UK: Edward Elgar 26 Publishing.

Mehmetoglu, M. (2007). Nature-based tourists: The relationship between their trip expenditures and activities. *Journal of Sustainable Tourism, 15*(2), 200–215.

Mowforth, M., & Munt, I. (1998). *Tourism and sustainability. New tourism in the third world.* London: Routledge.

National Institute of Statistics. TEMPO online database—Tourism. http://statistici.insse.ro/shop/index.jsp?page=tempo2&lang=en&context=63.

Nicolau, J. L., & Más, F. J. (2005). Heckit modelling of tourist expenditure: Evidence from Spain. *International Journal of Service Industry Management, 16*(3), 271–293.

Song, H., & Witt, S. F. (2000). *Tourism demand modelling and forecasting: Modern econometric approaches.* New York: Pergamon.

Suanmali, S. (2014). Factors affecting tourist satisfaction: An empirical study in the northern part of Thailand. In *SHS Web of Conferences* (Vol. 12, p. 0102).

Tribe, J. (2005). *The economics of recreation, leisure and tourism* (3rd ed.). Oxford: Elsevier.

Wang, N. (2000). *Tourism and modernity: A sociological analysis.* Oxford, UK: Pergamon Press.

World Travel & Tourism Council, & Travel & Tourism Economic Impact. (2015). Romania, 2015. https://www.wttc.org/-/media/files/reports/economic%20impact%20research/countries%202015/romania2015.pdf. Accessed May 15, 2016.

Chapter 8
Tourists Attitudes Toward Autochthonous Product Quality and Placement—The Case of Dubrovnik, Croatia

Ivica Popovic and Marija Dragicevic

Abstract The Republic of Croatia is a country with significant number and large variety of autochthonous products. In recent years, more attention is paid to the importance of local products and their protection at national and even European level. Autochthonic products in Croatia can be protected by the marks of origin, geographical origin, and traditional reputation. Although there are great numbers of authentic products in Croatia, just some of them are protected. Very important are autochthonic ecological products (in the first order produced on the organic farms and agricultural households in Croatia), but they still do not have adequate market position. The aim of the paper is to explore domestic tourists' perception toward autochthonous products quality and placement. For the purpose of this paper, we have carried out the primary research in the area of Dubrovnik. According to the results of the research which included the sample of 120 respondents, it is visible that tourists are satisfied with the autochthonous products quality, but on the other side they are not satisfied with availability, promotional activities, and distribution channels which have been used in autochthonous product placement policy. The domestic tourists think that there are only few outlets where they can buy autochthonous products what is huge disadvantage because the participants want to buy products but they do not know how and where (because of bad product availability, inadequate promotion, and small number of retail outlets). They find out that the price is acceptable, but they also find that there is not always value for money. It is sure that autochthonous products have target group in the market, but it is necessary to protect it better (and more) and take care that all elements (not only quality) fit to the clients. They create national identity, but also make recognizable tourist destination on the domestic and international markets.

Keywords Autochthonous product · Tourists · Quality · Placement Dubrovnik

I. Popovic · M. Dragicevic (✉)
University of Dubrovnik, Dubrovnik, Croatia
e-mail: marija.dragicevic@unidu.hr

© Springer International Publishing AG, part of Springer Nature 2019
V. Vasile (ed.), *Caring and Sharing: The Cultural Heritage Environment as an Agent for Change*, Springer Proceedings in Business and Economics,
https://doi.org/10.1007/978-3-319-89468-3_8

8.1   Introduction

The creation of identity and recognition adds value, contributes to the visibility of the destination, and thus contributes to rural development. Recognized and autochthonic products are important factor for Croatian positioning domestic and at the international touristic market. Some of the autochthonous products and services are protected (by the marks of origin, geographical origin, and traditional reputation), but a lot of them are not under protection and it has to be one of the main tasks for the producers and local community in the future.

The subject of this paper refers to the perception of domestic tourists toward quality and placement of local products. The issue will be explored theoretically and based on the empirical research. The main objective of the research is to analyze the satisfaction and perception of domestic tourists toward the quality and other elements of placement.

8.2   Autochthonous Products in Croatia

Protection of agricultural products within the Croatian systematic procedure is defined by the Ministry of Agriculture of the Republic of Croatia (http://www. svijet-kvalitete.com, 27.08.2015). Autochthonous products have technological, nutritional, and organoleptic specific features. Quality and uniqueness compete with other food products. Protection of autochthonous products falls within the legally defined area. Geographical indications are labels where European Union has prescribed under the EU Regulation No. 1151/2012. In Croatia in force are also two regulations, agricultural law (Official Gazette 30/15) and regulation of protected mark of origin, geographical indication and traditional specialties (Official Gazette 65/15).

The category refers to the autochthonous products protection by designation of origin that includes registration of 11 autochthonous products, and they are, respectively,: (1) Istrian extra virgin olive oil; (2) olive oil from Korcula; (3) olive oil from Krk; (4) olive oil from Solta; (5) lamb from Pag; (6) mandarina from Neretva; (7) extra virgin olive oil from Cres; (8) pickled cabbage from Ogulin; (9) Varazdin greens; (10) prosciutto from Istria; (11) Dalmatian marasca cherry.

The category refers to the protection by GI currently including nine products which are: (1) Kulen from Slavonia; (2) Kulen from Baranja; (3) Dalmatian prosciutto; (4) prosciutto from Drnis, (5) prosciutto from Krk; (6) potatoes from Lika; (7) turkey from Zagorje; (8) soparnik from Poljice; (9) Virovitica pepper (www.mps.hr, 12.06.2015; Radman et al. 2006; www.ebrd.com, 16.10.2015; www. croatiaweek.com, 15.10.2015).

There are a significant number of associations which protect authentic products, and their contribution in this field is very important. They were working on products specifications. For example, the Association "Dalmatian prosciutto" has prepared specification for Dalmatian prosciutto (Kos et al. 2015), the Association of Kulen from Baranja producers has given specifications for Kulen from Baranja (Kusec 2014), and the Association of Cabbage from Ogulin producers has given specification for cabbage from Ogulin (Dobricevic 2014). Prosciutto from Krk is the first product in Croatia with the mark of geographical origin (www.index.hr, 8.10.2015).

There are also examples of good business practice in the Bosnia and Herzegovina which have preserved production of milk products; in the first order it refers to cheese, such as Kajmak, cheese from Travnik, and cheese from Livno (Saric and Bijeljac 2003). The preservation of products and tradition in Croatia is important from cultural, ecological, social, and economic point of view, and relations should be considered as triangular (Conti et al. 2003: 8).

8.3 Methodology of the Research

For the purposes of the paper, empirical research has been done which includes the sample of 120 respondents. The questionnaire consisted of 15 open, closed, and combined type questions. The limitation of the survey refers to the limited number of tourists and interviewing only domestic tourists. In this research, we have not included the category of foreign tourist, but we find it obligated in the future, due to the fact that the share of foreign tourist in the area of Dubrovnik is significant.

For the purpose of this paper, we have stated the min hypotheses:

- H1. Domestic tourists are satisfied with the quality autochthonous products, but they are not satisfied with availability, promotion activities, and distribution channels which have been used in placement policy.

8.4 The Results of the Research

According to data collected by survey carried out in Dubrovnik, Croatia, on the sample of 120 respondents, it is visible that the largest number of respondents is between 51 and 65 (35%), followed by respondents between 35 and 50 years (23%), 19 and 34 years (20%), and 65 and over (15%). The smallest number of respondents (7%) had less than 18 years (Table 8.1).

According to the data obtained in this study, for the majority of respondents (65%) it is important to buy local products, followed by the respondents who think that it is not at all important buying local products (25%). The certain number of respondents considers buying autochthonous products is extremely important (20%) (Table 8.2).

Table 8.1 Importance of local product buying

Importance	The share of respondents (%)
Extremely important	20
Important	65
Neither important, nor unimportant	–
Not important	–
Not important at all	25
Total	100

Source Authors

Table 8.2 Buying locally produced products

The intensity	The share of respondents (%)
Often	82
Rarely	12
Never	6
Total	100

Source Authors

The share of 82% respondents often buys local products, while 12% of respondents rarely buys local products, and 6% of respondents never buy authentic products (Table 8.3).

According to the results of the research, for 32% of the respondents placement is not satisfying, 39% of respondents neither agreed nor disagreed that it is satisfying, and 29% thinks it is satisfying.

We have also explored the tourists' satisfaction with the promotional activities. The most of them, that is 72% of respondents, believe that indigenous products in Croatia are not well promoted in the market, while 28% believe that they are adequately (Table 8.4).

The share of 46% respondents is neither satisfied nor dissatisfied with the availability of the product. According to the results of the survey, it is evident that 14% of respondents are generally satisfied with the availability of local products in the market of Croatia, while 5% of respondents are fully satisfied with the availability of the autochthonous product on the market. The rest of respondents (35%)

Table 8.3 Placement of local products on the market

Placement	The share of respondents (%)
Have satisfying placement	29
The placement is neither satisfying nor dissatisfying	39
The placement is not satisfying	32
Total	100

Source Authors

Table 8.4 Promotional activities

Satisfaction	The share of respondents (%)
Well promoted products	72
Not well promoted	28
Total	100

Source Authors

Table 8.5 Availability of autochthonous products

Availability	The share of respondents (%)
Have satisfied availability	19
The availability is neither satisfied nor dissatisfied	46
The availability is not satisfied	35
Total	100

Source Authors

are not satisfied with the availability of the local autochthonous products (Table 8.5).

The proportion of respondents who are dissatisfied is 15%, while 19% of respondents are neither satisfied nor dissatisfied with the quality of the product. The most important fact is that 66% of respondents are fully satisfied with the quality of local products.

The survey found that 24% of respondents so far bought "Extra virgin olive oil from Istria," 27% of respondents bought "olive oil from Korcula," 24% of respondents "olive oil from Krk," and 18% of them "olive oil from Solta." "Potatoes from Lika" so far purchased 77%, "mandarina from Neretva" 83%, 62% of them bought "lamb from Pag," 75% "cabbage from Ogulin," and 65% "greens from Varazdin." "Turkey from Zagorje" so far bought only 27% of respondents, 13% bought "soparnik from Poljice," 6% purchased "Croatian plum," and 6% bought "Croatian liquor." "Prosciutto from Istria" so far purchased 48% of domestic tourists, "Kulen from Slavonia" 56%, "Kulen from Baranja" 50%, "Dalmatian prosciutto" 70% of them, "prosciutto from Drnis" 40%, and "prosciutto from Krk" 31% (Table 8.6).

According to the results of the study, the data indicate that 38% of respondents monthly spend up to 500 kunas to buy local products, 48% of them spend between 501 and 1000 kunas, 6% between 1001 and 1500 kunas, while 8% spend more than 1501 kunas (Table 8.7).

The share of 24% of respondents do not consider that there is a fully value for money, and 43% of respondents generally do not considered that they have received value for money. The share of 23% believes that they fully receive value for the money.

Table 8.6 Autochthonous products

Type	The share of respondents (%)
Extra virgin olive oil from Istria	24
Olive oil from Korcula	27
Olive oil from Krk	24
Olive oil from Solta	18
Potatoes from Lika	77
Mandarina from Neretva	83
Lamb from Pag	62
Cabige from Ogulin	75
Greens from Varazdin	65
Turkey from Zagorje	27
Soparnik from Poljice	13
Croatian plum	6
Prosciutto from Istria	48
Kulen from Slavonia	56
Kulen from Baranja	50
Dalmatian prosciutto	70
Prosciutto from Drnis	40
Prosciutto from Krk	31

Source Authors

Table 8.7 Costs per month

Cost (kunas)	The share of respondents (%)
Up to 500	38
501–1000	48
1001–1500	6
1501 and more	8
Total	100

Source Authors

8.5 Conclusion

In recent years, more attention is paid to the importance of local products and their protection at national and even European level, so some of the local products of the Republic of Croatian have been protected. The producer's consciousness of auto-chthonous quality product has risen. Based on the results obtained from the empirical research in Dubrovnik, Croatia, it is clear that the quality is undoubtedly for the high level of respondents. The domestic tourists find very important to purchase autochthonous products. They find out that the price is acceptable, but they also find that there is not always value for money.

On the other side, domestic tourists are not satisfied with the other element of placement. The domestic tourists think that there are only few outlets where they can buy autochthonous products what is huge disadvantage because the participants want to buy products but they do not know how and where, because of bad product availability, inadequate promotion, and small number of retail outlets. According to the results of this and other researches (Perucic et al. 2011), it is sure that autochthonous products have target group in the market and is necessary to protect it better (and more) taking care that all elements fit to the clients.

References

Conti, T., Watson, G. H., & Kondo, Y. (2003). *Quality into the 21st century, perspectives on quality and competitiveness for sustained performance*. Milwaukee, Wisconsin: ASQ Quality Press.

Dobricevic, N. (2014). *The specifications for "Cabige from Ogulin"*. Ogulin: Association of Ogulin Cabige Producers.

EU Regulation No. 1151/2012.

http://www.croatiaweek.com. October 15, 2015.

http://www.ebrd.com. October 16, 2015.

http://www.index.hr. December 8, 2015.

http://www.mps.hr. June 12, 2015.

http://www.svijet-kvalitete.co. August 27, 2015.

Kos, I., Mandir, A., & Toic, U. (2015). *The specification for "Dalmatian prosciutto"*. The Association "Dalmatian Prosciutto".

Kusec, G. (2014). *The specification for "Kulen from Baranja"*. BeliManastir: Association of Kulen Producers.

Official Gazette No. 30/15.

Official Gazette No. 65/15.

Perucic, D., Dragicevi, M., & Pavlic, I. (2011). Consumers' attitudes towards organic food: The case of Dubrovnik bitter orange jam. In H. R. Kaufmann (Ed.), *International consumer behaviour: A mosaic of eclectic perspectives*. UK: Access Press.

Radman, M., Mesic, Ž., & Kovacic, D. (2006) Geographical indications in Croatia: A case study of Virovitica pepper [online]. http://www.origin-food.org. October 16, 2015.

Saric, Z., & Bijeljac, S. (2003). AutohtonisireviBosne i Hercegovine. Mljekarstvo, No. 2, pp. 135–143.

Chapter 9
Financing Tourism Companies Through the Capital Market

Angela-Nicoleta Cozorici, Gabriela Prelipcean and Liliana Scutaru

Abstract The main problem facing tourism companies, but not their only problem, is lack of finance. Banks provide financial solutions, but expensive ones, difficult and inconvenient but with their own money, companies cannot grow too much and then surely we have to look at what other chances, what other possibilities the companies have for financing themselves. One possibility is financing through the securities market. This chapter includes an array of information about funding and capital markets as well as how to attract investors to support a company's development.

Keywords Tourism companies · Capital market · Financing · Development

9.1 Introduction

Tourism activity, according to the economic effects it produces (after trade, tourism is the second most important branch of the service sector), is considered to be one of the most dynamic and promising areas of development.

Small and medium-sized enterprises (SMEs) are the main engine of all other economies and the most important source of economic development—creating jobs and innovation in developed countries and also in those that are still under development. From this point of view, governments provide these companies with various methods of credit, guarantees, and some other sources of support in order to facilitate their access to capital.

Bank loans are the main source of financing SMEs. However, the economic and financial crisis has shown that financing through banks is not a secure method of financing, especially in times of instability. In addition, regulatory measures adopted after the crisis, such as strengthened rules on capital requirements, have

A.-N. Cozorici (✉) · G. Prelipcean · L. Scutaru
Stefan Cel Mare University of Suceava, Suceava, Romania
e-mail: angelac@seap.usv.ro

© Springer International Publishing AG, part of Springer Nature 2019
V. Vasile (ed.), *Caring and Sharing: The Cultural Heritage Environment as an Agent for Change*, Springer Proceedings in Business and Economics, https://doi.org/10.1007/978-3-319-89468-3_9

created new challenges for SME financing through bank loans. In these conditions the use of diversified sources of funding for SMEs is required.

At the moment, SMEs everywhere use very little financing through capital markets, although these markets offer an alternative source of financing over long periods of time.

9.2 Methods of Financing the Activities of a Company

Funding is the process of making available money resources that an enterprise, institution, or non-governmental organization (NGO) needs to pursue its business activities. Funding can be achieved by resorting to its own resources or from external sources outside the firm. Details of these funding sources are shown in Fig. 9.1.

The advantages and disadvantages of different sources of funding are listed in Table 9.1.

9.3 Financing Through the Capital Market

Many people know the stock market only in terms of purchases and sales of shares and earnings that can be obtained from them. However, the stock market fulfills another important role: attracting financing for companies that want to grow their businesses.

Development projects of companies require substantial financial sources, often not available from the company itself, therefore, capital market financing may be the solution, enabling companies to ensure future development. The capital market, and in particular the Bucharest Stock Exchange (BSE), represent the institution that

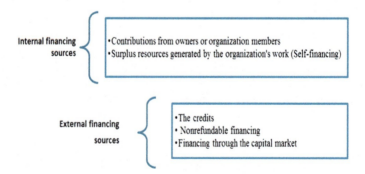

Fig. 9.1 Sources of finance

Table 9.1 Advantages and disadvantages of different sources of funding

		Advantages	Disadvantages
Sources of internal finance		• Maintain independence and financial autonomy because it does not create additional obligations (interest, guarantees) • Does not affect an organization's ability to borrow • Constitutes a reliable means to cover the financial needs of the organization	• Owners have fewer funds with which to invest in more profitable activities other than the activity which generated the financial surplus
Sources of external finance	Credit/ loan	• Short-term access to necessary financial resources • Accessible at any time • Ability to obtain a variable amounts of financial resources • Possibility of negotiating repayment conditions.	• Emergence of additional obligations (interest rate, collateral) • Existence of mandatory formalities to be fulfilled (documentation, periodic reports, etc.)
	Grants	• Activities may be funded without using or borrowing from own resources • Maintains the independence and financial autonomy of the organization	• Difficult to access (funds are awarded periodically, usually based on selections) • Strict controls in place for use of funds from donors, including thorough cooperation with other specialized institutions

Source Authors

reconciles the two categories of participants: those who need capital and those who provide capital.

Most companies are reluctant to attract investors into their businesses, something which is a normal feeling held by small companies, where entrepreneurs are in the procurement phase and want to develop their businesses themselves, rather than relying on someone else. At some point, however, a company may need more visibility, substantial funding, or need to reduce its dependence on the banking system as well as being positioned accurately in a competitive environment. Listing with the BSE is one solution, with companies being seen to mature as they take this step.

Some businesses worry about listing on the grounds that they should display a certain transparency related to mandatory reporting of financial data obtained each quarter, semester, or year. Others consider that financing on the capital market is quite expensive, however, if you compare it to a bank loan where you pay interest of the amount borrowed, financing through capital markets involves the issuance of financial instruments (shares), the company is not obliged to return the funds raised, but only to increase shareholder value and pay dividends. In other words, capital market financing is not obtaining money to be returned, but instead yielding shares of a company.

9.4 Sources for Raising Capital for Companies in the Field of Tourism

The main problem facing Romanian tourism companies is related to financing their activities. Although the country has significant tourism potential and entrepreneurship, financing tourism projects can sometimes be a major obstacle in turning a business idea into a commercially viable project.

The most commonly used method of financing, which companies in the local tourism industry have resorted to, is traditional bank financing. Regardless of the size of the operation or the type of project that requires funding, bank loans are often used to finance working capital requirements, for both short-term and long-term capital projects. Because changes in lending policy have reshaped the banking industry, tourism firms are now seeking new funding opportunities for their businesses without taking on excessive and unrealistic financial leverage.

The development projects of tourism companies require substantial financial sources, often not available from their own resources. In such cases, capital market financing may be the solution, enabling companies to ensure future development projects.

In this context, companies have tried, and succeeded effectively, to gain access to the capital market in Romania, but given the more restrictive conditions required for listing on the regulated market they have chosen an alternative trading system. Most companies in the tourism sector are SMEs, some of which operate with less than 10 employees. Therefore, in this context, the listing conditions for these companies might seem quite expensive considering the limited resources available to them. It should be noted that one of the major constraints for SMEs in the tourism industry is increasing funding from capital markets.

9.5 AeRO Market, an Alternative Means of Financing

In 2015 the BSE, through AeRO market financing, began supporting those companies who are unable to satisfy the criteria of size or operational length in order to be listed on the BSE regulated market. The AeRO market was created from the need to provide entrepreneurs alternative finance for development and is a dedicated segment within the equities alternative trading system of the BSE. This market segment is dedicated to listing companies wishing to finance their investment projects, enhance their visibility, and contribute to business development. Based on the BSE's alternative trading system, existing since 2010, the AeRO market was launched on February 25, 2015, as a redesigned and rebuilt concept.

The alternative trading system does not constitute a regulated market for the purposes of European Directives and Romanian legislation on the capital market, but is governed by rules and requirements set by the BSE. The AeRO market was created by the BSE with the aim to offer a market with fewer reporting requirements by issuers, yet with a sufficient level of transparency that would motivate investors to make transactions.

Companies which want to list on this market must take the steps outlined in Fig. 9.2.

The requirements that listed companies must meet on the AeRO market are less stringent than those of the regulated market. The minimum requirements for admission are that companies need to be established as joint stock companies and that they are not bankrupt. For the admission in the alternative trading system of the Bucharest Stock Exchange, no criteria regarding equity / early capitalization should be met. Admission to trading procedures are simplified—it is not necessary to draw up a prospectus for admission to trading, the only necessary document is a presentation of the company. Listed companies must meet certain requirements related to transparency and reporting on three levels:

- Annual reports, which include financial statements, notes to the financial statements, directors' report, and the audit report.
- Half-yearly reports, including balance sheet, income statement, and management report.
- Current reports on the decisions of the General Meetings of Shareholders or Boards of Directors, as empowered by the shareholders, mergers/divisions, litigation, insolvency proceedings, reorganization, or bankruptcy (and other).

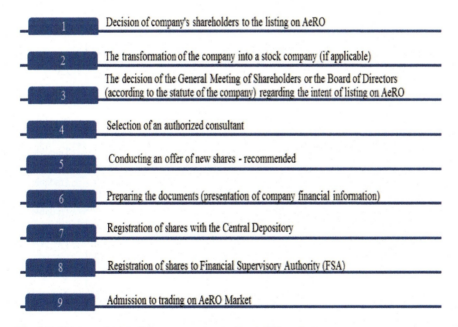

1 | Decision of company's shareholders to the listing on AeRO

2 | The transformation of the company into a stock company (if applicable)

3 | The decision of the General Meeting of Shareholders or the Board of Directors (according to the statute of the company) regarding the intent of listing on AeRO

4 | Selection of an authorized consultant

5 | Conducting an offer of new shares - recommended

6 | Preparing the documents (presentation of company financial information)

7 | Registration of shares with the Central Depository

8 | Registration of shares to Financial Supervisory Authority (FSA)

9 | Admission to trading on AeRO Market

Fig. 9.2 Steps required to listing a company on the AeRO market

9.6 Listing Tourism Companies in the Alternative Trading System

Funding through the capital market is an alternative that needs to be taken more and more seriously, given that the overwhelming majority of companies are at the disposal of banks and their regulations in order to obtain the necessary funds. In the case of public issues (stocks or bonds), the issuing company dictates the conditions by which the sale is made (of course, these conditions must also be pleasing to investors for the sale to be successful). Thus, any company can diversify its funding structure and include the capital market in its plans.

Of the 388 firms listed on the BSE, 28 are from the tourism industry, which represents 7.22%. The 28 companies listed are presented in Table 9.2.

Table 9.2 Tourism companies listed on the BST

	Issuer	Symbol	County	Exchange section	Category	Status
1.	Compania Hoteliera Intercontinental Romania SA Bucuresti	RCHI	Bucharest	ATS	AeRO premium	Tradable
2.	Resib SA Sibiu	RESI	Sibiu	ATS	AeRO standard	Suspended
3.	Terra Estival 2002 SA Neptun	TERA	Constance	ATS	AeRO standard	Suspended
4.	Clabucet Estival 2002 SA Neptun	UCET	Constance	ATS	AeRO standard	Suspended
5.	Romanta Estival 2002 SA Neptun	ANTA	Constance	ATS	AeRO standard	Tradable
6.	Sifi Cluj Retail SA Bucuresti	ARCU	Bucharest	ATS	AeRO standard	Tradable
6.	Athenee Palace SA Bucuresti	ATPA	Bucharest	ATS	AeRO standard	Tradable
7.	Tratament Balnear Buzias SA Buzias	BALN	Timis	ATS	AeRO standard	Tradable
8.	BTT SA Bucuresti	BIBU	Bucharest	ATS	AeRO standard	Tradable
9.	Balea Estival 2002 SA Neptun	BLEA	Constance	ATS	AeRO standard	Tradable
10.	Banat Estival 2002 SA Olimp	BNAT	Constance	ATS	AeRO standard	Tradable
11.	Cicero SA DR. T. Severin	CICE	Mehedinti	ATS	AeRO standard	Tradable
12.	Hotel Club Estival 2002 SA Neptun	CLUB	Constance	ATS	AeRO standard	Tradable
13.	Dorna Turism SA Vatra Dornei	DOIS	Suceava	ATS	AeRO standard	Tradable

(continued)

Table 9.2 (continued)

	Issuer	Symbol	County	Exchange section	Category	Status
14.	Euxin SA Constanta	EUXI	Constance	ATS	AeRO standard	Tradable
15.	NEPTUN Olimp SA Neptun	NEOL	Constance	ATS	AeRO standard	Tradable
16.	Nord SA Bucuresti	NORD	Bucharest	ATS	AeRO standard	Tradable
17.	Palace SA Sinaia	PACY	Prahova	ATS	AeRO standard	Tradable
18.	Parc SA Caracal	PARC	Olt	ATS	AeRO standard	Tradable
19.	Prahova Estival 2002 SA Neptun	PRAH	Constance	ATS	AeRO standard	Tradable
20.	Regal SA Galati	REGL	Galati	ATS	AeRO standard	Tradable
21.	Tusnad SA Baile Tusnad	TSND	Harghita	ATS	AeRO standard	Tradable
22.	TURISM Covasna SA Covasna	TUAA	Covasna	ATS	AeRO standard	Tradable
23.	Turism Covasna SA Covasna	TUAA1	Covasna	ATS	AeRO standard	Tradable
24.	Casa de Bucovina-Club de Munte	BCM	Suceava	BSE	Standard	Tradable
25.	Sif Hoteluri SA	CAOR	Bihor	BSE	Standard	Tradable
26.	Turism, Hoteluri, Restaurante Marea Neagra SA	EFO	Constance	BSE	Standard	Tradable
27.	Turism Felix SA Baile Felix	TUFE	Bihor	BSE	Standard	Tradable

Source Author's information, according to data from http://www.bvb.ro
Note ATS, alternative trading system

Of the 28 tourism companies, 4 companies are listed on the regulated market of the BSE and 24 companies on the alternative trading system (ATS), developed by the BSE, 3 of which were suspended from trading: Resib SA Sibiu, since 14 October 2015; Terra Neptune Estival 2002 SA, since 11 February 2014; and Clabucet Neptune Estival 2001, since 11 February 2014.

Twenty-one tourism companies are currently being traded on the alternative trading system of the BSE from a total of 280 companies, of which one is in the Premium category and 20 in the Standard category. On 30.12.2015 they had a stock market capitalization of 152,358,388 lei, respectively 3.96% of the total of 3,852,011,574 lei.

The geographical distribution of these companies is shown in the Fig. 9.3.

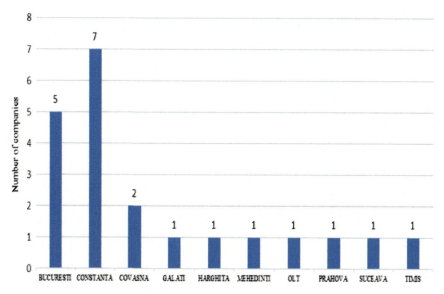

Fig. 9.3 Number of tourism companies listed on the ATS—by county

As can be seen from Fig. 9.3, the county of Constanta has 7 tourism companies listed on the ATS, followed by Bucharest with 5 companies, Covasna with 2 companies, and then the counties of Galati, Harghita, Mehedinti, Olt, Prahova, Suceava, and Timis each with 1 company.

We may conclude that the Romanian capital market does not currently fulfill the role of financing the economy, although financing through the stock market brings greater benefits than traditional financing through bank loans. The most important aspect of capital market finance is the fact that it does not burden a company with costs like interest or principal repayments.

Over the years it has been shown that an initial public offering is quickly analyzed and assimilated both by speculators and investors of portfolios. With frequent use of market instruments a company can hold the attention of investors, after admission to trading of shares, to ensure a continuous inflow of financial resources associated with investors' expectations regarding their profitability and prospects.

9.7   Conclusion

Romania's tourism industry is still in development and has the potential for growth. The capital market provides companies with a comprehensive range of finance. At a company level, managers need to choose between all the available resources and combine them, thus shaping the company's financial policy. The main advantage of listing firms on the capital market is that through this action companies' shares acquire greater liquidity and bring rewards and financial freedom for both founders and employees.

Financial resources on capital markets can be a significant component of funding for companies that are acceding to this market and using its tools.

This alternative to financing through the capital market represents a much cheaper alternative, it outpaces bank loans and is more accessible to firms due to market dynamics and investor perceptions.

The AeRO market follows the successful model already proven in major world stock, bringing to Romania one of the most innovative and rich patterns of growth and financing through the financial instruments market. The main advantage of listing in an ATS is that it caters for all joint stock companies, with less stringent criteria compared to regulated markets both in terms of admission requirements and company reporting.

We should mention that relatively rigid legislation, costs, technical aspects of trading infrastructure, and difficulties with compliance to transparency and corporate governance are still perceived as the negative factors of the capital market in Romania. Financing through the stock market is an alternative to be taken into consideration, given that the overwhelming majority of Romanian companies use the banks, with their associated regulations, in order to obtain funds.

References

Bădulescu, D. (2013). *Dezvoltarea şi finanţarea afacerilor antreprenoriale: particularităţi în turism*. Presa Universitară Clujeană.

Mowforth, M., & Munt, I. (2015). *Tourism and sustainability: Development, globalisation and new tourism in the third world*. Routledge.

Paicu, C., Hristache, E., & Andreia, D. (2013). Implicaţiile economice şi comunicaţionale ale turismului din România. *Economie teoretică şi aplicată, 20*(7), 584.

Scutaru, L., Prelipcean, G., & Cozorici, A.-N. (2014). Financing SMEs from the tourism sector and valorization of local cultural heritage. In *Paper presented at the International Conference "Heritage as an alternative driver for sustainable development and economic recovery in South East Europe"*, Basilicata, Italy, 11–14th April 2014.

Financing of SMEs through Capital Markets in Emerging Market Countries. (2013). *ICSA Emerging Markets Committee*. Available at http://the-insider.biz/index.php/issues/vol-iii-issue-12/item/358-capital-market-financing-opportunities-for-the-local-tourism-industry.

http://www.bursa.ro/suplimente/.

http://www.bursa.ro/_pdf/publicatii/bvb_2016/supliment_bvb_2016.pdf.

http://www.bvb.ro/ForCompanies/AeroForShares/ListingProcess.

https://www.ssifbroker.ro/operatiuni-corporate/finantare-prin-bursa.html.

http://macintsol.ro/stock-market/.

http://www.wall-street.ro/.

http://www.amib.com.mx/images/Financing%20of%20SMEs%20through%20Capital%20Markets%20in%20Emering%20Market%20Countries(2013.2).pdf.

Chapter 10
Stressing the Urge for Awareness to Climate Change Impact on Natural and Cultural Heritage: A Romanian Perspective

Marius-Răzvan Surugiu and Camelia Surugiu

Abstract Climate change is an important and immediate threat, while the effects are felt in various sectors, including agriculture, fishing, transportation, construction, tourism, insurance. Nowadays, climate change impact is felt more strongly (e.g. heat and cold waves, modification of season's heavy rainfall and floods, prolonged droughts), requiring adaptation and mitigation measures for stakeholders at various social and economic levels. In this regard, awareness strategies and formulation of adaptation measures are necessary. In addition, in order to become aware of the climate change effects on natural and cultural heritage, communication campaigns across all sectors are required in near future. The present paper aims to underline the impact of climate change on natural and cultural heritage, to identify the particularities of climate change effects in Romania and to formulate some recommendation to raise awareness on climate change impact among stakeholders involved in protection and conservation of natural and cultural heritage.

Keywords Awareness · Climate change · Impact · Natural heritage
Cultural heritage · Romania

10.1 Introduction

Natural and cultural heritage is very important for worldwide nations, representing unique and irreplaceable treasures of different time periods, regions, and countries. Climate change effects are more present in the recent years, more often observed in various parts of the globe, starting with glacier retreat, extreme weather events, changes in the timing of seasonal events, sea level rising, higher temperature,

M.-R. Surugiu (✉) · C. Surugiu
Institute of National Economy-Romanian Academy, Calea 13 Septembrie,
050711 Bucharest, Romania
e-mail: mariussurugiu@yahoo.com

© Springer International Publishing AG, part of Springer Nature 2019
V. Vasile (ed.), *Caring and Sharing: The Cultural Heritage Environment as an Agent for Change*, Springer Proceedings in Business and Economics,
https://doi.org/10.1007/978-3-319-89468-3_10

121

changing landscapes, etc., with different effects on various sectors such as agriculture, transportation, insurance, forestry, energy, constructions, tourism and recreational activities. The researches on climate change impact were mainly focused on ecology and agriculture, and there are not many studies developed which assess the impact on cultural and natural heritage.

There are a number of climate change factors that may have adverse effects on buildings or other cultural heritage sites (on materials such as metal, stone, wood), and on natural heritage sites. Firstly, differences in temperature may present an impact on buildings, mainly on the materials from which the facades or roofs are made (e.g. if metal panels are used outside for the roof of a building and high temperature differences occur, such as differences from 40–45 °C in summer or more to −25 °C or less in winter). Rising temperatures may have an impact also on natural heritage sites, such as parks, coastlines, forests, gardens. Secondly, the rainfalls may have an important impact on buildings and other cultural heritage sites, because increased precipitation may adversely affect materials such as wood or stone, but also metals. Rainfalls may be followed in various areas by floods or landslides, with serious impact on immovable heritage.

Natural heritage sites are also endangered by these phenomena. In addition, pollution remains a risk factor for any site, which may contribute to acid rains, to their harmful effects on various materials (may cause paint to peel, corrosion for metals, and erosion for stone), plants, animals, and so on. Extreme weather events (strong wind, heavy rainfall, and drought) have an increased risk of damage on natural and cultural heritage sites. Rising sea level may present a risk of damage on buildings from coastline and other important heritage sites. When these sites are lost, important items of great value are lost, and sources of knowledge, important resources for society, local communities, individuals, will no longer exist. This is why finding heritage sites which are vulnerable to damage as a result of climate change is important.

In Romania, there are seven cultural and natural heritage sites registered at UNESCO: Churches of Moldavia, Dacian Fortresses of the Orastie Mountains, Historic Centre of Sighisoara, Danube Delta, Monastery of Horezu, Villages with Fortified Churches in Transylvania and Wooden Churches of Maramures. In addition to this list, other sites are included on UNESCO tentative list: Slatioara Secular Forest, Byzantine and Post-Byzantine Churches of Curtea de Arges, Densus Church, Trei Ierarhi Monastery of Iasi, Monumental Ensamble of Targu Jiu, Rupestral Ensamble at Basarabi, Neamt Monastery, Historic Town of Alba Iulia, Cule from Oltenia, Retezat Massif, Pietrosul Rodnei Massif, Sanpetru Formation, the Historic Centre of Sibiu and its Ensemble of Squares, the Old Villages of Hollókő and Rimetea and Their Surroundings, and Extension to the Joint World Heritage Property "Primeval Beech Forests of the Carpathians (Slovak Republic and Ukraine) and the Ancient Beech Forests of Germany (Germany)".

The present paper aims to underline the impact of climate change on natural and cultural heritage, to identify the particularities of climate change effects in Romania and to formulate some recommendations in order to raise awareness on climate change impact among stakeholders involved in protection and conservation of natural and cultural heritage. The paper is structured as follows: the second section presents some aspects analysed in the literature concerning the climate change impact on natural and cultural heritage. In the third section, some effects of climate change in Romania are presented. Fourth section discusses some measures to raise awareness on climate change impact on natural and cultural heritage. The final section concludes the paper.

10.2 Climate Change Impact on Natural and Cultural Heritage

Climate change is part of the reality we live, and nowadays its effects are felt more often. Climate change brings different threats to society and economy. This can have undesirable effects, from the occurrence of droughts to the effect of rising sea level, affecting primarily low-income individuals, ecosystems, buildings that were not part of a conservation programme, etc. These undesirable results may have in the future negative effects on historic buildings, parks, forests, etc.

Challenges to the historic environment appear because of climate change. These challenges may be represented by weather events with an extreme character such as heat waves, which may determine fires in forests. Other effects may refer to the erosion of the coastal areas and wetlands, emergence of new pests and in some cases even diseases.

More frequent wetting and drying and the attack from pests have impact on collections, floods will have an impact on movable and immovable heritage (Cassar 2010). Increased soil moisture has an impact on heritage sites, thus becoming more vulnerable to various risks of which floods, landslides, earthquakes and so on.

The change of the temperatures may lead to increased frequency of heat waves, with impact related to deteriorating facades of buildings, building's interior, etc. The sea level rise or other assimilated changes have impact on landscapes, parks and buildings with historical significance, archaeological remains, gardens and so on (CADW, Welsh Government 2013). Also, rising sea levels can lead to risks such as flooding in coastal areas, generating permanent loss of land located in low-lying areas.

Heritage sites are vulnerable to various risks. These risks can have negative influences on the value of historical sites and on their important features for communities, local economy, tourists and so on. Also, increases in the number of days with storms can lead to structural damage on sites. Other risks of climate change may be related to abundant rainfall, changes in the chemical composition of the soil, groundwater composition changes, etc. The climate change impact on heritage sites is stressed by the damage of mural paintings, erosion of various construction materials caused by floods, etc.

Air pollution has an impact on heritage, and it is related to the effect of gases (the corrosive effect, when acid chemicals are found in rain, snow, fog) and black particles on light-coloured surfaces (making them dirty) (Hamilton and Crabbe 2009). Atmospheric pollution is an important factor which has effects on heritage assets, such as erosion, perforation, cracking, deterioration, soiling, attack from pests. Therefore, it is important to develop a detailed list with actions for preservation of heritage assets in each country, and to continuously update this list.

Recent studies underlined that climate change will affect heritage sites and values, including buildings, monuments, natural resources of cultural importance, ecosystems, archaeological sites and the losses will be magnified if appropriate mitigation measures and strategic projects are not implemented in the future (McIntyre-Tamwoy 2008). Sites, objects and ways of life are all under threat requiring alternative management or prompting specific climate change adaptation (Harvey and Perry 2015).

In conclusion, climate change will show effects in future on cultural heritage sites, and these represent damage and losses. But on the other side, climate change may lead to discovery of new artefacts and sites (Kaslegard 2011). Melting snow or coastal erosion may lead to new archaeological discoveries. This will bring new perspectives about the ancient world. Nevertheless, the existing sites must be protected, even if new ones will be found.

10.3   Romania Facing the Climate Change Effects

The guide on adapting to climate change effects developed in 2008 by a working group comprising representatives from all vulnerable sectors states that compared to the annual global average temperature increase of 0.60 °C during 1901–2000 period, the annual average registered an increase in Romania of only 0.30 °C. During 1901–2006 period, the increase was of 0.50 °C compared with the global level increase of 0.740 °C (1906–2005). Similarly with the global level situation, some changes in extreme events regime were emphasized (based on the analysis of data from several weather stations): increased annual frequency of tropical days (daily maximum >30 °C) and decreased annual frequency of the winter days (daily maximum <0 °C); significant increase in the average summer minimum temperature and in the average winter and summer maximum temperature (up to 2 °C in the south and southeast in the summer). In terms of rainfall for 1901–2000 period, the analysis shows a general downward trend of annual precipitation quantities and a boost in drought phenomenon in the south of the country after 1960. Consistent with this result, an increase in the maximum duration of the intervals without rainfall was identified in the southwest (in winter) and west (in summer).

Romania expects that the annual average temperature will register an increase. Thus, there may be differences of about 1.0 °C from 2020 to 2029. Also, there may be differences of about 3.0 °C from 2090 to 2099. In the south and southeast of Romania and for the period between 2090 and 2099, the most models underline the occurrence of drought in the summer.

In Romania, average annual temperatures increase by more than 1–2 °C will first have as consequence aridization of some areas from south, with negative impact on forests. Another consequence would be the increase in the incidence of attacks from insects.

According to the European Climate Adaptation Platform (Climate-ADAPT), Romania has recorded in the past years high temperatures, and historic floods which caused deaths and significant property damage. Flooding has impacted the agricultural land, roads, railway, and bridges. Also, in past years, Romania was impacted by droughts, water scarcity, and wildfires.

Recent studies developed for Romania underlined that climate change generates various effects on different economic sectors, namely biodiversity, agriculture, water resources, forestry, infrastructure, constructions, transport, tourism, energy, industry and health. Climate change has an impact on agriculture, and the main agricultural area of Romania (Baragan Plain) is exposed to drought periods and water deficit in summer, with negative impact on crop yields, the projected climate change scenario underlying an enhancement of dryness and drought phenomena (Institute of Geography, Romanian Academy 2014).

According to climate change scenarios developed by Cuculeanu et al. (2002) for Romania up to 2075, the effects of climate change may appear on various sectors, especially maize crops, forest species and water resources. Domnişoru (2007) analysed the effects of drought on water availability and quality in the Arges catchment from Romania, noting that soils and agriculture (the irrigated maize crop) seem to be affected. The results for 1999–2004 period underline that emission reduction is the dominant driving factor in water quality of the catchment.

Climate change has also an impact on the Romanian coastline, which requires some adaptation measures to cope with climate change effects, to sustain tourism development, to support economic development and to reduce negative social effects, such as job losses and income decreases (Surugiu et al. 2010a). Regarding tourism activity in mountain resorts, this one became vulnerable in Romania to meteorological parameters (temperature and snow-cover depth), with a negative relationship between temperature and tourism parameters (Surugiu et al. 2010b). The rise of the Black Sea level may determine beach erosion or put under threat the coastal ecosystems. Also, historical tourist attractions with valuable heritage may be flooded. Floods, drought, deteriorating water quality and declining fish reserves have negative effects on the communities from the Danube region and biodiversity of the Delta. In the Danube Delta, the average annual air temperature will increase by 1–1.5 °C by 2050, leading to more hot days and shorter snow-cover period. Also, extreme weather events may appear more often (droughts, heat waves, floods, windspouts, showers, storms and hail) (World Wide Fund for Nature 2013).

In July 2013, the Romanian Government adopted Romania's National Strategy on Climate Change 2013–2020 which specifies that extreme weather events will affect infrastructure, historical and architectural heritage and the seasonality. The National Strategy for Sustainable Development of Romania developed in 2008 and having as national coordinator the Ministry of Environment and Sustainable Development specifies that adaptation to climate change is a complex process because the severity of the impacts varies from region to region, depending on physical vulnerability, the degree of socio-economic development, natural and human adaptive capacity, health services and disaster surveillance mechanisms. The strategy emphasizes the importance of the national cultural and natural heritage protection and states that the connection to European norms and standards regarding the quality of life must be accompanied by revitalization in modernity of some ways of traditional living, especially in mountain areas and in wetlands.

10.4 Rising Awareness on Climate Change Impact: The Need for Adaptation and Mitigation

Climate change impact is more strongly felt in recent years (e.g. heat and cold waves, changing the structure of the seasons, floods and massive rainfall, prolonged droughts), and adaptation and mitigation measures for stakeholders from cultural and natural heritage sector are necessary. In this respect, formulation of concrete awareness measures is required.

It is important to facilitate the dialogue between stakeholders on the topic of climate change impact in heritage sector. This may turn into a learning process that will permit to find new solutions to current problems. Among the measures which may provide benefits are the following:

- Promotion, support and dissemination of research projects regarding climate change impact on natural and cultural heritage;
- Government and educational efforts to translate and make the researches results known to public, increasing the sector attractiveness by highlighting its specificity;
- Development of a database with statistics on the impact of climate change on the heritage sector, and scenarios on climate change;
- Exchange experience programmes with partners who already face such problems and identified a number of solutions to climate change effects on natural and cultural heritage;
- Development of school curriculum including specific environmental topics, tourism, heritage sites preservation, environmental protection, with user-friendly platform;
- Development of interactive exhibitions and scientific events to make the local population aware of the consequences of climate change and the solutions that are required;
- Development of communication campaigns through various media channels to inform general public on the effects of climate change.

It is important to identify natural and cultural heritage sites which are at risk and to build a database about changes to those sites because of climate change. Also, it is important to engage local communities in the process of preparing the measures to respond to the impact of climate change on heritage.

10.5 Conclusions

Natural and cultural heritage sites are threatened by climate change and are subject to risk because of floods, heavy rainfall, rising sea levels, storms and so on. This is why it is important to analyse the climate change impact on heritage sites in order to develop sustainable adaptation and mitigation measures. Extreme weather events driven by climate change affect the natural and cultural heritage. Protecting heritage sites to cope with these threats represent a real challenge. This paper is motivated by the necessity to understand the phenomenon of climate change by the stakeholders from natural and cultural heritage sites. In this regard, a number of actions may be undertaken by stakeholders to be informed about its effects and thus the climate change challenges to be understood by each actor from the sector. This study aims to underline the necessity to reduce the vulnerability of natural and cultural heritage at climate change through specific awareness actions for general public, businesses, tourists, etc., at local and national level.

Climate change will have an effect on heritage sites because the changes in the environment lead to changes in the conservation conditions. Authorities' involvement is needed in order to take measures to assess the impact of climate change. Some measures may refer to creating a database and dissemination of relevant data related to the effects of climate change among stakeholders from heritage sector.

References

CADW, Welsh Government. (2013). *INTERREG IVC project CHARTS Good Practice Guide "Preparing the historic environment to meet the challenges of climate change".*

Cassar, M. (2010). Principles of mitigation and adaptation of cultural heritage to climate change. In R. A. Lefêvre, C. Sabbioni (Eds.), *Climate Change and Cultural Heritage, Proceedings of the Ravello International Workshop*, 14–16 May 2009 and Strasbourg European Master-Doctorate Course, 7–11 September 2009, Edipuglia, Bari.

Cuculeanu, V., Tuinea, P., & Balteanu, D. (2002). Climate change impacts in Romania: Vulnerability and adaptation options. *GeoJournal, 57,* 203–209.

Domnişoru, A. (2007). *Long term effects of climate change on Europe's water resources.* Case Study Romania, Techneau.

European Commission. (2015). *European climate adaptation platform (Climate-ADAPT).* http://climate-adapt.eea.europa.eu/countries/romania .

Guvernul Romaniei, Ministerul Mediului si Dezvoltarii Durabile, Programul Natiunilor Unite pentru Dezvoltare, Centrul National pentru Dezvoltare Durabila. (2008). *Strategia Nationala pentru Dezvoltare Durabila a României.* Orizonturi 2013-2020-2030, Bucuresti.

Hamilton, R., & Crabbe, H. (2009). Environment, pollution and effects. In J. Watt, J. Tidblad, V. Kucera, & R. Hamilton (Eds.), *The effects of air pollution on cultural heritage.* Springer.

Harvey, D. C., Perry, J. (2015). Heritage and climate change: The future is not the past. In D. C. Harvey, J. Perry (Eds.), *The future of heritage as climates change: Loss, adaptation and creativity.* Routledge.

Institute of Geography, Romanian Academy. (2014). *Report on climate change effects for Baragan Plain, Romania, ECLISE—Enabling Climate Information Services for Europe.*

Kaslegard, A. S. (2011). *Climate change and cultural heritage in the Nordic Countries.* Copenhagen: Nordic Council of Ministers.

McIntyre-Tamwoy, S. (2008). The impact of global climate change and cultural heritage: Grasping the issues and defining the problem. *Historic Environment, 21*(1).

Ministerul Mediului si Dezvoltarii Durabile. (2008). *Ghid privind adaptarea la efectele schimbarilor climatice—GASC,* Monitorul Oficial nr. 711 din 20 octombrie 2008.

Ministerul Mediului si Schimbarilor Climatice. (2013). *Strategia nationala a Romaniei privind schimbarile climatice 2013–2020.*

Surugiu, C., Breda, Z., Surugiu, M. R., & Dinca, A. I. (2010a). Climate change impact on seaside tourism. Portugal and Romania: Two different case studies with strong particularities. *Revista Economica, Nr., 1*(54), 113–135.

Surugiu, C., Dincă, A. I., & Micu, D. (2010b). Tourism destinations vulnerable to climate changes: An econometric approach on Predeal resort, Buletinul Universitatii Petrol—Gaze din Ploiesti. *Seria Stiinte Economice, 62*(1), 111–120.

World Wide Fund for Nature. (2013). *Vulnerability of the danube delta to climate change.* www. panda.org/dd_climate_adaptation.

Chapter 11
Generation Y—Challenges for Heritage Planning

Doru Marian Tudorache, Alina Niculescu, Marioara Musteață-Pavel and Adriana Radu

Abstract Millennials or Generation Y are young people born in the last two decades of the past millennium. They represent the most dynamic generation in history, with a high-purchasing power, which due to the increased technological environment has behaviours, values and attitudes different than previous generations. Given the importance that the younger generation will have in the near future enhancement of heritage objectives should take account of the wishes of this large segment of consumers. This study aims to find solutions to development planning one of the most iconic heritage objectives near the capital of Romania—Palace Mogoşoaia, considering ideas received from representatives of Generation Y.

Keywords Generation Y · Cultural heritage planning · Cultural tourism

11.1 Introduction

Although the specialists' opinions are divided, generally, they consider that the "Millennials" (Howe and Strauss 1991) or Generation Y (Ad Age editorial 1993) are young people born in the last two decades of the last millennium (1980–2000).

They grew up in a period of very rapid technological developments, during which the computer and the Internet came into people's homes (Palfrey and Gasser 2008). In these conditions, "Millennials" have learned behaviours, values and attitudes differently than previous generations (Draves and Coates 2004).

It is considered that the most important feature of these people is the constant need to be connected to those around them. Millennials have as primary interest—friends, fun and digital culture. Generally, they are described as optimistic, team-oriented, high-achieving, rule-followers (Howe and Strauss 2003). Thanks to

D. M. Tudorache (✉) · A. Niculescu · M. Musteață-Pavel · A. Radu
National Institute for Research and Development in Tourism, Apolodor 17, Bucharest, Romania
e-mail: tudoru007@yahoo.com

© Springer International Publishing AG, part of Springer Nature 2019
V. Vasile (ed.), *Caring and Sharing: The Cultural Heritage Environment as an Agent for Change*, Springer Proceedings in Business and Economics, https://doi.org/10.1007/978-3-319-89468-3_11

the progress in the digital field, this generation has a better level of education and presents a comprehensive and entrepreneurial thinking.

From an economic perspective, they are the most active market segment. Although currently they only represent about 25% of the EU population and only 40% of them have now entered the labour market (Eurostat 2012), Generation Y already has a tremendous purchasing power. As a generation that grew up in a society based on consumption and the influence that they have on parents (Kennedy 2001), it is considered that Generation Y has more money available than any group of young people in history (Morton 2002).

Inside the family, they were protected and helped, but expectations from them have always been high.

In everyday life, they prove a lot of energy and appreciate teamwork. They always connect with others through modern communication tools, leading to the idea that they can be often influenced by friends, family or colleagues. The young people of this generation greatly appreciate the independence and freedom to make their own decisions, but also to compensate for lack of experience, they wish to have access to a coach or mentor with whom to consult when needed.

As employees, they are very interested in the diverse opportunities and challenges. They focused on development opportunities because they are concerned about their long-term career. Therefore, they are likely to prefer organisations which make the development they need available (Eckert and Deal 2012). Young people from the former socialist countries, as is the case of Romania, want to get away as quickly as possible of the old patterns of thinking and attitude of the communist period, which has left traces on the older representatives of this generation and tries to anchor onto a more inclusive, socially engaged and transparent society.

Through their way of being, Generation Y has a profound impact on our culture. These people are in a constant search for information and new experiences. Those who are part of Generation Y are travelling more frequently, exploring more destinations and spend more when they are on vacation. Whether travelling for leisure or for business, they are interested in the local culture and seek experiences helping them understand local customs.

As consumers, they give importance to quick and quality services. For this generation, offering quick services is something even more important than the existence of personal contact (EY 2013).

They wish to disseminate experiences through social media channels, tools that enable a quick feedback from acquaintances. The development of Internet and the emergence of sites that offer the opportunity to evaluate certain services they receive (e.g. TripAdvisor) give them the occasion to share experiences. Also, when wanting to purchase a particular service, they consult assessments on such sites, taking informed decisions, trying to minimise any risks. This is a huge opportunity for the tourism industry, providing an inexpensive marketing tool, but also implies an increased responsibility to provide quality services.

They use the latest technology and want to stay connected to the Internet, and mobile applications are always present in their travels. They use the Internet both in decision-making but also as a help to get additional information at the destination.

It is estimated that in the next decade, once the youngest representatives of this generation will graduate, they will be the largest consumers of tourism and cultural products. Given the role, they occupy in the market today, but especially in the future, their needs and desires must be considered by marketers, and cultural and tourism products should be adapted taking into account their wishes.

This study explores a small group of Millennials—students in marketing, tourism, political and administrative studies—and aims to provide solutions in accordance with their wishes for the most visited heritage asset located near the Romanian capital—the Mogoşoaia Palace complex. The objective is to actively involve young public to cultural heritage planning actions, giving them the opportunity to express their creativity.

11.2 Methodology

The National Institute for Research and Development in Tourism (Romania) partner in South East Europe Transnational Cooperation Project SAGITTARIUS held the Young Archers—Local Thematic onsite visit for students in December 2012. At the event organised at the Mogoşoaia Palace complex, took part 20 students (85% female and 15% male, ranged in age from 19 to 22 years old, with a mean of 20 years old) from the University of Bucharest (Faculty of Business and Administration and the Faculty of Geography of Tourism) and from the National School of Political and Administrative Studies—SNSPA. The students have participated voluntarily and were given no incentive for their cooperation.

The study visit was finalised with an interactive workshop. In the first part of this event, they received additional information regarding the history of this place in national history (reign of Constantin Brâncoveanu, Phanariot period, Revolution of 1821, the national revival and the Revolution of 1848, Independence War, World War I—the Great Union, the interwar period, World War II, the communist period).

In the second part of the workshop, a questionnaire divided into a total of ten questions—closed questions and open questions, questions that provided an opportunity to present their own impressions and interpretations were used. For the survey, the young people were divided into five groups of four, each group having one moderator for completing the survey and to provide further explanation. Finally, free discussions took place between the five groups of students, based on the questionnaire, trying to systematise the information received.

The role of the survey was to notice how this cultural–historic objective is perceived by young people and identify, with their help, solutions for the complex problems facing currently. This approach was chosen because interaction and group dynamics can stimulate answers. Furthermore, experiments on problem-solving groups show that new ideas non-included in the individual solving of tasks appear in group discussion (Carey 1994).

11.3   Brief Description of Mogoşoaia Palace Complex

Mogoşoaia is one of the most attractive places located close to the City of Bucharest, in a picturesque natural environment, on the bank of Mogosoaia Lake and surrounded by a beautiful park. The whole architectural complex was built by Wallachian ruler Constantin Brâncoveanu in the late seventieth—early eighteenth century. Later restoration work was done by Princess Martha Bibescu, in the first part of the twentieth century. Mogoşoaia Palace is a representative element of the Brancoveanu architectural style and also one of the most representative elements of civil architecture preserved in good state of preservation from the time of the ruler. A wonderful loggia of Venetian inspiration, located on the lake façade, is considered "the most beautiful and richest model of Romanian civilian architecture" (Ionescu 1938).

In Romanian art historiography, the Brâncoveanu style characterises architecture and arts in the Wallachia Province during the reign of Constantin Brancoveanu (1688–1714) and during the first Phanariot rulers (members of Greek families residing in Phanar, the quarter of Constantinople) period, up to 1730. The Brâncoveanu architecture style is recognised today as "the first Romanian style". It combines local Wallachian artistic traditions, Byzantine traditions and oriental influences and even western forms of the Renaissance (www.cimec.ro). It adopted vegetal and floral motifs specific to Renaissance and Baroque—also being called "Baroque Brâncovenesc".

Completed in 1702 for his second son—Ştefan—the palace, like other residences of the Ruler (eg. Potlogi Palace) was built on the lake border, inside a rectangular enclosure. It is organised on two levels, above a high basement. The Palace on the yard side has a gazebo with scale and on the lakeside a beautiful Venetian loggia. Equipped with water adducts, with bathrooms and toilets, this princely residence offered unprecedented comfort for that period.

The palace courtyard is bordered by a monumental entrance gate with watchtower, a pyramidal-roofed building which was the former kitchen of the palace (cuhnia) on the right side of the entrance and by Elchingen Villa a massive construction, built in the second half of ninetieth century, on the left side of the entrance (www.palatebrancovenesti.ro).

On the exterior of the courtyard, it may find: the St. Gheorghe Church, built by Constantin Brâncoveanu in 1688; the English Park (1870) and Italian style gardens, design under the guidance of Martha Bibescu; the Bibescu chapel (19th century) a real family necropolis; the N. Bibescu Greenhouses—a French studio (1890).

After Prince's passed away (1714), the palace went through hardships. Only after World War I, Martha Bibescu, the new owner of the estate, performed extensive renovations of the palace and the whole architectural complex. In the history of the palace, a new epoch of reconstruction and pomp began and for more than three decades, the old Brancoveanu residence recovered the glamour it had in its days of yore (Ion 2004). Having in view the personalities visiting this place, during the interwar period it becomes "the social and diplomatic centre of the capital" (Pandrea 2001).

At present, the Palace is the host of the Aulic Tradition Museum (founded in 2000) and organises over the year many cultural events, temporary exhibitions, summer schools (e.g. Christmas Eve at The Palace, Summer School "Discover Bucharest"). A restaurant and an accommodation unit also functions here, in Elchingen Villa. A visit in this location can be very interesting both for those that wish to practice some outdoor activities and for those who are interested by the cultural and historic aspect of this place.

11.4 The Analysis of the Research Results

Following this visit and research, all participants said they had learned new and exciting things related to the history of Romania and Bucharest. For the majority of students, the information about Martha Bibescu and the role she played in the history of the complex were a novelty.

Although most of them knew something about this complex (associated with Constantin Brâncoveanu and certain moments in the national history), this location was seen more as a place to organise events. Also, due to poor marketing, it is still perceived as an old location, not restored and its multipurpose side is little identified.

Most students felt that it was a bivalent place combining contemporary history and art, representative for the Brâncoveanu architectural style. The focus is not on reconstructing the past but especially on hosting events belonging to contemporary art and culture.

In today's postmodern society, the heritage elements must become products which are promoted and adapted to some requirements of the market economy. That is why heritage resources should be recreated, created, modified and adapted to become marketable products. Following this study visit and having in view the surveys completed by students, several ideas for improvement suggested by the 20 students involved could be formulated.

Although most of those interviewed consider the visiting infrastructure appropriate, they however suggest a better organisation of the sightseeing circuit. They propose that the introduction of monitors/touch screen information displays and audio guides will be helpful for a better presentation of the exposed materials. In addition, they reported a lack of facilities for people with disabilities and proposed the adaptation of this location to the specific needs of these vulnerable consumers. Diversification of souvenirs sold within the existing mini-store, introducing a system of internal heating for visiting spaces (the visit took place in winter, and it was very cold inside) and creating selling points with hot drinks are other suggestions that they have made.

As a way to improve the image of the complex, young people emphasised that it was necessary to organise restoration works. They believe that mural paintings should be restored; replicas of the original furniture should be created in order to revive the atmosphere of those times. They suggested its transformation from museum of history in anthropology museum, illustrating the way of life in the early twentieth century, a period associated with Martha Bibescu. Restoration of rugs and tapestry, cellar and existing icons, renovating and refurbishing the concert hall should also be done.

For a better promotion of this attraction, they think that partnerships with other museum institutions should be signed for common promotion programmes, and the palace should be present more often in the Bucharest tourist tours that it should be promoted in the mass media, through advertisements, brochures and flyers, the events in the palace should be promoted more intensely. Also, they have mentioned that, in line with the new technologies, the promotion of the Mogosoaia Complex can be done through: social networks (especially promoting the events on the Facebook page), actualising and improving the Website, interactive 3D images and 360° movies panoramas.

A promotion achieved by highlighting the key features must beneficiate of the most modern digital communication means. Achieving such cultural products aimed for the profile market should be done only through partnerships (eventually cluster system) and a relational marketing involving several participants—travel agencies, tour operators, media, cultural marketers.

Concerning the interpretation of the heritage, in order to present the history of the place more pleasantly, they propose the use of images/pictures from the past so that visitors can make up an image about the way the palace and surroundings looked like. They also suggest to adapt the presentations according with the age of the public; to redecorate the rooms with epoch-like furniture and use people dressed with epoch-like clothes who would embody important personalities of the palace; to present details from the personal lives of the personalities of that time; and to offer the visitors the possibilities to wear garments of that epoch and take pictures of themselves dressed this way. Creativity and imagination are the most appreciated qualities in creating such an approach. These characteristics will help products exceed the expectations of visitors/tourists, be actively valued and promoted.

The phenomenon of artistic interpretation with a playful touch of a heritage item is aimed to amplify the visitors' emotions through stronger impressions, being a unique experience for them. The interpretation here intermingles with education and entertainment, as leisure activities. In recent years, this symbiosis between education and entertainment created the term "edutainment" (Swarbrooke 1994). Learning while having fun is an easier formula, better accepted by visitors/tourists irrespective of their education and cultural level or their age, income.

Respondents argued that the complex needs to reduce seasonality and increase the number of visitors. In this context, they proposed to organise festivals and carnivals with historic themes, where people are introduced to the atmosphere of the seventieth, eighteenth, ninetieth, early twentieth centuries. They support the idea of an additional number of outdoor and recreational nature activities in the park. It can be noted: the offer of recreational services (boating, sports activities on the lake); organisation of culinary demonstrations with traditional products; increasing the number of temporary exhibitions (eg. ice sculpture exhibition in winter); organising thematic workshops; arranging a summer theatre and organising concerts; contracting a band of actors to perform plays in the complex; organising musical evenings in the restaurant. One of the proposals was the creation of an annual event —"the Mogoşoaia Palace day", where anyone can participate and where they can serve meals from the epoch when Mogoşoaia palace was inhabited, to recall events in the history of this place.

One of the most vulnerable aspects of the complex is funding. From this point of view, young students thought that managers should "walk on all possible tracks", namely attracting European funds, private funds, donations from businesses, donations from art collectors. In addition, the income from visiting fees, fees for temporary rental of premises, organising leisure activities while food and accommodation services are important resources for the functioning of complex.

To increase revenues, they have proposed a better promote the guest house, reorganising the shops selling souvenirs and offering for sale pieces of furniture similar with the works of art belonging to the complex (pots, paintings, small furniture, towels, etc.), offering babysitting services with a special space where children can be kept while their parents visit the palace—thus new segments of visitors can be attracted.

The Programme of Ministry of Education and Research "Şcoala altfel" (engl. Different School), developed for one week each year, dedicated to curricular and extracurricular educational activities, creates new opportunities for all cultural institutions in the country. In this respect, the museum complex Mogosoaia should aim to work better with schools to create attractive offers for students. Also, through a permanent connection with the directions of higher education, they should find ways to combine academic training activities with cultural programmes generated by universities (faculties of history, arts, architecture, geography, tourism economy), financially supported by the school, various sponsors and students. In this way, our today young people will become lovers of art and culture of tomorrow and will educate their children in the same spirit of openness to cultural and heritage values.

11.5   Conclusions

Due to the cultural–historic resources, to which are added the natural conditions, the Bucharest surrounding area can contribute to the rising of the attractiveness level of the Romanian capital, representing the place where people go on trips at the end of the week. The most visited tourist spot of the Bucharest outskirts is the Mogosoaia Palace, representative heritage objective for the Brâncoveanu architecture, witness of the development of this area at the limit between Orient and Occident.

The economic activity intermingles harmoniously with the cultural activity inside the Mogoşoaia Complex, as a consequence of an inspired public–private partnership so here the cultural heritage is capitalised in different ways: different events are organised, permanent and temporary expositions are designed, a restaurant and an accommodation unit functions here.

The natural background brings added value to this place and creates new visiting opportunities. That's why hundreds of visitors come weekly to Mogoşoaia to enjoy the palace park and to escape the urban jungle for some hours.

Historical value is given by the personalities who have lived here or whose names may be linked to this place. There are many personalities and stories about this monument that could be exploited. The person that can even become a brand of the place is the Princess Martha Bibescu. Here can be recreated successfully the atmosphere of the ninetieth and the twentieth centuries.

Although this tourist location is already capitalised from the economic point of view, still, for enhancing the experience of the visitors and especially the most dynamic segment of these—Generation Y—new solutions and creative ideas are needed, closely connected to their wishes in order to make this place at least as attractive and appreciated in the future as it is in present.

References

Advertising Age. (1993). *Generation Y.*

Carey, M. A. (1994). The group effect in focus groups: Planning, implementing and interpreting focus group research. In J. M. Morse (Ed.), *Critical issues in quantitative research methods* (pp. 225–241). Sage Publications Inc.

Draves, W., & Coates, J. (2004). *Nine shift: Work, life and education in the 21st century.* Wisconsin: LERN Books, River Falls.

Eckert, R., & Deal, R. (2012). Generation Y—attitude and talent at work. IEDPRaport, developing leaders. *Executive Education in Practice* (6), 22–27.

EY. (2013). *Global hospitality insights.* Top Thoughts for 2014.

Howe, N., & Strauss, W. (1991). *Generations: The history of America's future, 1584–2069.* New York: William Morrow & Company.

Howe, N., & Strauss, W. (2003). *Millenials go to college: Strategies for new generations on campus.* Washington, D.C: American Association of Collegiate Registrars.

Ion, N. D. (2004). *The Brâncovan palaces. Historical guide, Mogoşoaia: The "Brancovan palaces" cultural center.*

Ionescu, G. (1938). *Bucureşti: Ghidistoricşi artistic, Bucharest: Fundaţiapentru Literaturăşi Artă "Regele Carol al II-lea".*

Kennedy, L. (2001). The up and coming generation. *Retail Merch, 41*(8).

Morton, L. P. (2002). Targeting generation Y. *Public Relations Quarterly, 47*(2).

Palfrey, J., & Gasser, U. (2008). *Born digital. Understanding the first generation of digital natives.* New York: Basic Books.

Pandrea, P. (2001). *Memoriilemandarinuluivalah.* Bucharest: EdituraAlbastros.

Swarbrooke, J. (1994). The future of the past: Heritage tourism into the 21st century. In A. V. Seaton (Ed.), *Tourism: The state of the art* (p. 225). Chichester: Wiley.

www.ec.europa.eu/eurostat.

www.cimec.ro.

www.palatebrancovenesti.ro.

Chapter 12
Heritage Component of Sustainable Development

Andreea Constantinescu

Abstract Due to the abundance of heritage issues interpretation and in order to facilitate analysis of the transformation of an object or site—through expertise and instrumentation—into a topic open to long-lasting cultural consumption, researchers have recently imposed the concept of patrimonialization. Being able to promote and manage sustainable development by capitalizing both natural segments, as well as the cultural and intangible segments of universal heritage, patrimonialization added—from an interdisciplinary perspective—to social interrogations of heritage interpretation, those specific for the necessity to ensure environmental, economic, and social sustainability. This paper will emphasize the importance of heritage component for sustainable development, as well as the fact that patrimonialization provides to sustainable development the opportunity to become part of the heritage. Following an integrated approach, patrimonialization implies that the implementation of all activities related to heritage will be introduced in the service of sustainable development. Thus, policies, strategies, and measures for conservation, protection, and promotion of heritage should stimulate, on the one hand, civic engagement and critical attitude towards protecting and respecting local and universal heritage values and, on the other hand, transnational cooperation in implementing the most appropriate ways for their integration. Therefore, having the quality of an alternative device for economic recovery, heritage of Southeast Europe must be patrimonialized to ensure sustainable reconciliation between entrepreneurship that reflects emergence of regional markets, and consumption of heritage, between economic development and the limitations of environmental protection and between museological local traditionalism and the expansion of international networks of living heritage interpretation. In the field of climate change, there is a clear opportunity for all sectors linked to sustainability and also for heritage. Many of the initiatives of heritage conservation stated that sustainability strategies and compliance are imposed by respect for the environment and climate change constraints. Despite the fact that identification of heritage items

A. Constantinescu (✉)
Institute of National Economy-Romanian Academy,
Calea 13 Septembrie, 050711 Bucharest, Romania
e-mail: andreea_constantinescu07@yahoo.com

© Springer International Publishing AG, part of Springer Nature 2019
V. Vasile (ed.), *Caring and Sharing: The Cultural Heritage Environment
as an Agent for Change*, Springer Proceedings in Business and Economics,
https://doi.org/10.1007/978-3-319-89468-3_12

was already resolved by instrumentalization of interpretation process, its placement in the field of sustainable development could be done only by interdisciplinary targeting of correlation elements.

Keywords Heritage interpretation · Patrimonialisation · Sustainable development Transnational cooperation projects

12.1 Introduction

Heritage interpretation gives distinct meaning to presented items, without resorting to scientific explanations. This concept was launched in "Interpreting Our Heritage" study made by journalist Freeman Tilden in 1957, for North American promoters of national parks. Tilden has selected some principles, which since then underpin the achievement of positive impact on heritage visitors, promoting a marketing centered on visitors' expectations and personality (AHI 2012).

In turn, sustainable development requires both a holistic approach and underlying elements of growth, which is why it finds in heritage interpretation support for achieving common objectives. Also, both put an emphasis on the role of education in developing the society ability to understand responsibility for the future.

Thus, once identified a heritage site or object—given obviously its economic, human, natural, and cultural features, it will be accompanied by a management and communication support to enable recognition of its popularity to stakeholders (Interpret Europe 2012). Heritage Interpretation becomes both a vital feature of how people share their experiences of places they visit as well as an artistic act that allows culture consumers to feel connected, inspired, and responsible equally for their past and future experiences. Therefore, the interpretation plan of a heritage site should contain among its central objectives caring for the natural and cultural environment, consistent with the need for social, financial, and environmental sustainability (ICOMOS 2008).

12.2 The Convergence of Conceptual Coordinates of Heritage Interpretation and Sustainable Development

Heritage Interpretation characteristics converge with those of sustainable development as both are complex activities with methodologies that cover specific needs, most often revealed after laborious analysis on a site, area or whole regions. At the same time, revealing new meanings and knowledge of the consequences of human activities, in accordance with sustainable development, it creates coherent and plausible events scenarios (e.g., impacts of climate change), which often cannot be perceived in their full extent. Thus, sustainable development researcher's mission meets the one of heritage interpreters—both requiring interdisciplinary knowledge using a variety of techniques in order to analyze consequences on many levels and to send effective messages about the need to preserve environmental conditions, i.e., natural or cultural history (Trans Interpret 2013).

An important step in this direction was made by the World Heritage Committee, which has adopted in 2004, the "Budapest Declaration on World Heritage" by which all interested parties are invited to support World Heritage conservation key objectives identified as "the 4 C's." Starting from here was realized the diagram of the "7 C's" so that heritage interpreters could better follow the feedback (Massung 2011). It is important that at the end of this cycle of interpretation does not result a new marketing cliché, but a high content of relevant meanings devoid of ostentation and deeply empathic. Despite the different methods used to achieve Heritage Interpretation, stages and its characteristic elements must ensure obtaining feedback which provides assurance that the information provided to consumers of culture enters a dynamic circuit (Fig. 12.1).

However, natural heritage tends to create a permanent picture of the present cultural heritage through its value and potential as renewable resource tends to be the key to include Heritage Interpretation between devices that sustainable development owns in order to ensure the evolution of society. Therefore, the knowledge and promotion of heritage particularly cultural heritage through an integrated interpretation of sustainable development objectives are a crucial mechanism to facilitate peaceful coexistence, acceptance of multiculturalism, and respect for the values and beliefs widely different (CoE 2005). This can be done based on many points of convergence between Heritage Interpretation and sustainable development, enhancing awareness about the need to create better living conditions for all humanity.

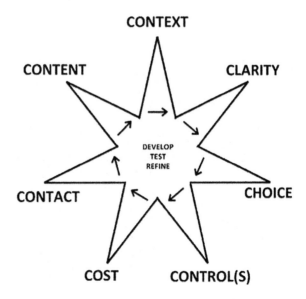

Fig. 12.1 Seven C's of heritage interpretation. *Source* Massung (2011)

Heritage Interpretation tried to integrate the economic dimension aimed at achieving welfare—after the model of sustainable development—both in its quantitative and qualitative aspects (Tweed and Sutherland 2007). At the same time, the social dimension of sustainable development is supported by the Heritage Interpretation in its ability to combine the imperative of increasing quality of life with increased growth of social justice so that all groups have equal access to resources, education, and livelihood.

12.3 Evolution of Heritage Interpretation to Patrimonialization—Heritage Hermeneutics

While presenting heritage remains a simple activity of information to the general public, heritage interpretation provided a structured concept, including its presentation, covering all activities that can be implemented to educate the public and make well worth the subject or heritage site in question. Tilden considered, referring to the US National Park Service, that heritage interpretation is a non-formal educational activity that reveals meanings and relationships, using original objects, direct experience, and illustration tools rather than simply communicate information and facts related to a particular destination (Interpret Europe 2013).

Thus, interpretation work may satisfy the requirements of the three pillars of establishing universal value of heritage: heritage inclusion, compliance of integrity, and protection and proper management (UNESCO 2012). Although the principles of Tilden remain widely available, other authors have sought to broaden his definition. Following this research, the term "Heritage Interpretation" describes how to use specific disciplines and communication in order to differentiate from other meanings in which appears the word "interpretation." This is due mainly to the fact that the "heritage" concept includes both natural and cultural world, which implies a too large expansion of meaning to explain issues and topics that are not usually considered strictly part of heritage issues although they have become extremely important, such as climate change and sustainable development (Uzzell 2000).

In this context, the notion of "interpretation" has become increasingly vague and permissive but also inclusive between information, pedagogy, planning, implementation of the heritage, culture, and tourism economy. Thus without denying the possible achievements by launching the concept of Tilden, the new theory of heritage finds applications in several areas of relationship management with various audiences. It aims to facilitate the understanding of need to integrate heritage elements into a unified framework that can highlight diversity of relationships among social actors interested in establishing collective strategies of heritage objects (Massung 2013). By focusing on the entire process related to heritage and not only public appearance of packaging, patrimonialization considers all elements related to the role and functionality of all categories of heritage. Thus became possible decantation of heritage components, from expert's decision referring to appropriate ranking to survey and collective perception, through putting into practice and feedback (Oers and Haraguchi 2003).

Patrimonialization refers to the dynamic establishment of heritage, managing to confer the status of every constituent representation, using management which gives it a central role in society. Thus, heritage exits the constraints of its dual significance—economy and social sciences—to join the general coordinates of sustainable development. If in the first sense, resulting in the concept of legal property, heritage related to individual assets owned by a person, and in the second, got a collective dimension, represented by the common heritage of which the holder is not the owner, but only manager (Landel and Senil 2008), by patrimonialization, heritage is perceived as a vector for sustainable development.

On the other hand, patrimonialization has the credit of taking advantage of new interpretation, learning, and participation strategy, taking into account the role of each stakeholder and establishing best ways in which they collaborate to highlight the importance of heritage. Thus, existing resources shall be used more efficient and shall be covered potential gaps that heritage interpretation would leave on its integration as a whole. However, patrimonialization helps maximize funding opportunities, given that sources of funding for heritage can now be attracted by other stakeholders than those enshrined including individual. Patrimonialization strategy provides an integrated approach to heritage interpretation and of all resources necessary for its exploitation, in order to involve as many partners in sustainable and open capitalization to universality of contexts in which it is placed (Carver 2011).

From this broad, conceptual development of idea of heritage has emerged the need for hermeneutics, conceived as an exegesis able to critically analyze various aspects of heritage, including the process of forming heritage. This leads to understanding and integration of heritage in general scientific discourse about human projection in fundamental relations (work, socializing, connecting with the environment), without particular emphasis on how to set up technical heritage body itself (Uzzell 2000).

Researchers who study heritage in order to use its assets as part of sustainable development share the common mission to discover importance and beauty of the natural environment, such that finding a noninvasive place for humankind, to make him cherish and preserve both nature and culture. Even if this philosophy—least possible interventionist—is accepted unanimously, this manifests itself differently from one country and region to another for reasons related to socio cultural or climatic context (Espace Naturel Régional 1999).

In the case of world heritage, wealth consists in diversity. Patrimonialization remains with the task of reconciling local trends to interpret heritage (focusing on landscape and local customs) with those regional, which considers environment as part of an assembly (Landel and Senil 2008).

12.4 International Networks Role for Heritage Interpretation

Once developed heritage interpreter profession by the US National Park Service, based on the approach of Tilden, programs that encourage visitors to respect environment sites acquired new meanings. Taking over this pattern, Britain and Canada began to introduce interpretation in conservation and recovery domain, primarily in natural environments and then into cities and their historical sites. Naturally, associations have emerged for interpreting heritage, both in Spain, Italy, and Scandinavia, which benefited from inspired mentors who have done heritage interpretation become a recognized technique and representative for management, especially of protected areas and sites (UNESCO 2012).

In 1999, at the Conference of heritage interpreters in Bournemouth, England, it was decided to form a European network of interpreters, which became official in 2010, in Slovenia, the European Association for Heritage Interpretation (Interpret Europe 2013). Recognizing that cultural dissemination and exploitation of cultural results requires new ways of production and consumption, all international networks of heritage interpretation aim exploiting its potential to stimulate creation of new jobs, economic growth and encourage sustainable economic development of all economic sectors involved. These issues concern not only promotion of modern cultural policy and sustainable culture economy, but also creation of national wealth through valorization of each of its coordinates social, economic, and political (AHI 2012). Also, these networks encourage investment in cultural resources and entrepreneurship to improve the quality of life in a given area by attracting new economic, financial, and human resources, improving social and territorial cohesion, and definition of new types of professions resulting from this collaboration.

Recognizing the capacity of cultural heritage concepts, intangible heritage, conservation, preservation, promotion, and interpretation thereof and importance of local identity affirmation and protecting heritage from joint initiative of European Commission and Council of Europe have been launched since 1999, European Heritage Days. Thus, the 50 signatory countries of European Cultural Convention have the opportunity to exchange experiences by opening sites and historic buildings that are normally closed to the public. This is not only a civic responsibility but also an opportunity to create benefits to local communities through tourism development and revitalization of crafts and traditions (EC, CoE 2013).

Such contributions to heritage valorization as a device of sustainable development made to establish itself in Strasbourg in December 2011 during the meeting of coordinators and national experts in heritage interpretation, the concept of European dimension of events related to heritage. It is characterized not only by working on multiple levels (local, regional, national, international, and transnational), but also by creating micro-networks to use technology in order to achieve information coverage on cultural diversity and small communities according to the text adopted by Council of Europe, European Commission, and UNESCO (Interpret Europe 2013).

On these considerations, in 1972 was created the World Heritage Fund which is aimed at helping Convention Parties States in identifying, preserving, and promoting World Heritage sites. Mandatory contributions are 1% of UNESCO annual funds, supplemented by voluntary contributions and other income from donations and sale of publications. The estimated four million dollars collected annually represents an insufficient amount to meet the growing needs for international assistance on heritage (UNESCO 2007). Therefore, these resources are supplemented by loans from World Bank who contributed even to creation of sustainable development plans of several historical cities. Among them stands city of Berat in Albania which was given the chance to human and financial resources and ensuring sustainable beyond the framework of a project (UNESCO 2012).

Concrete results of cooperation within interpretation networks enabled heritage assets to be considered today a key element of building peace and sustainable development and, at the same time, a source of identity and dignity for local communities and a source of knowledge that has the ability to share identity values. In addition, these networks have improved heritage interpretation capabilities, particularly through support for specific initiatives in three directions, represented by practitioners, institutions, and networks. This approach, outlined in Table 12.1, allows World Heritage to be addressed by stakeholders in various sectors, for example, from non-governmental organizations to directly concerned owner groups.

Table 12.1 Different categories of audiences and learning areas covered by networks of heritage interpretation

Where capacities reside: target audiences for capacity building	Principal learning areas
Practitioners (including individuals and groups who directly intervene in the conservation and management of World Heritage properties)	• Implementation of the Convention (tentative lists, nomination, etc.) • Conservation and management issues: planning, implementation, and monitoring • Technical and scientific issues • Resource utilization and management
Institutions (including state party heritage organizations, NGO's, the World Heritage Committee, Advisory Bodies, and other institutions that have a responsibility for the enabling environment for management and conservation)	• Policy-making for learning areas mentioned above • Legislative issues • Institutional frameworks/issues (governance, decentralization) • Financial issues • Human resources • Knowledge
Communities and networks (including local communities living on or near properties as well as the larger networks that nurture them)	• Reciprocal benefits and linking with sustainable development and communities • Stewardship • Communication/interpretation

Source Managing Cultural World Heritage, UNESCO 2013

The table highlights three target audiences for the purposes of determining learning needs of capacity building for heritage capitalization. Networks also have the role of extending training process to all those concerned—vital for broadening sustainable and efficient management responsibility of heritage. Thus, by increasing knowledge about heritage, development of responsible behavior of heritage management and conservation can be achieved improvement of institutional structures and processes at policy-maker's level.

12.5 Heritage Contribution to Economic Recovery Through Transnational Cooperation Projects

Needs of sustainable development highlighted by patrimonialization have made an increasing number of different actors to work together, thus helping to protect heritage and to include it among business opportunities taken into account by entrepreneurs who want to offer specific heritage sites goods and services.

Figure 12.2 shows the flow diagram of types of benefits arising from exploitation of protected area. These advantages can be divided into use and nonuse benefits which, in turn, can be subdivided into direct and indirect benefits and, respectively, inherited or present benefits. Various goods and services of protected areas fall within one or more of these categories.

Clearly, heritage has potential to become a "business" as far as the protected site is managed so that it can provide products and services that "sell," for example, the uniqueness and beauty of a habitat or its importance. An essential difference between world heritage management and usual business is the fact that the first must not undermine, but highlight and enhance the values for which the site was notified (Patry 2008). It is important for entrepreneurs to be aware of the challenges of management and the need to meet sustainability requirements before proceeding to analyze economic benefits (UNESCO 2012).

In terms of heritage, transnational cooperation promotes projects that engage countries in a specific region, focusing in particular on issues of sustainable development of cities, innovation, and environment. On these directions also goes Transnational Southeast Cooperation Programme which aims to define a common

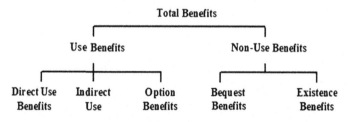

Fig. 12.2 Heritage protection beneficiaries. *Source* Patry (2008)

strategy of marketing heritage as means of transition towards European integration (Southeast Europe 2013). Regardless of level of integration of participating countries, regional cooperation in Southeast Europe becomes essential for stability, prosperity, and security in this area.

As well as European citizenship, heritage and common cultural values have resources to lead to overcoming the current crisis and stimulate further revision of EU policies so that they provide a solid basis for development of cultural heritage that future generations will consider as being truly European (EC 2013).

A good example to illustrate that transnational cooperation heritage can be helped to gain a sustainable European dimension, was My European City Project, which has provided partners (cities: Nantes, Caen, Le Mans, Laval, in France; Padova in Italy; Szczecin in Poland; and Sibiu in Romania) experience of common European interpretation of heritage and possibility of implementing an inclusive European route (My European City 2011).

12.6   Challenges for Heritage as a Mechanism of Sustainable Development—National Specificities

One of the most significant aspects of which—in the same way as sustainable development—heritage must face is its vulnerability to natural disasters and major climate change phenomena. Even if it is impossible at all times to prevent damage to sites, it is imperative to conduct research and take steps to avoid at least some favoring circumstances. For this, it is necessary to use a catalyst of climate change impacts on heritage awareness after discussions which propose to support climate change mitigation policies and to disseminate best practices from vulnerabilities evaluation projects, for adopting adaptation and mitigation strategies under the specific nature of each heritage (UNESCO 2007).

In the field of climate change, there is a clear opportunity for all sectors closely linked to achieving sustainability agenda, among which, also, falls heritage. Many of the initiatives promoted or practiced of heritage conservation institutions stated sustainability strategies and compliance with requirements imposed by respect for the environment and climate change constraints. Thus, the concept of low-carbon activities can influence the field of heritage under three possible scenarios: implementation of existing technologies, use of advanced technologies on goods and services, or acceptance of creative economy in terms of introducing new services to reduce demand and consumption of products that are not within rules (Brinkley et al. 2010).

Therefore, UNESCO World Heritage List is expanding very slowly, given the fact that inclusion of sites considered as having outstanding universal value must cope with increased demands. Currently, this list includes 981 properties from 160 countries, including 759 cultural, 193 natural, and 29 mixed sites. Romania appears with the following seven sites: Danube Delta Biosphere Reserve, Village settlements with fortified churches in Transylvania, Horezu monastery, painted churches of Northern Moldavia, Dacicum Fortress of Orăştie, Sighisoara town center, and wooden churches of Maramures.

Another issue that threatens the role of heritage in sustainable development is the lack of economic development prospects and the uncertain nature of property, which makes recording a heritage asset of outstanding universal value to come up against bureaucratic aspects which makes even more difficult a process already complex and long lasting (UNESCO 2012).

In the absence of such business plans, we are faced with the phenomenon of non-patrimonialization which unfortunately is manifested in Romania as irresponsible negligence. The effects of this lack of concern for community values, no matter of what explanations are offered, affects all social plans because of missing an excellent opportunity for socioeconomic and cultural development based on European synchronicity and encourage participation that leads to restoration of solidarity. Through such an approach could be resolved both spiritual heritage issues, and those related to employment and young people's interest to promote specific retrieved identity.

However, despite the fact that Romania has a highly valuable intangible cultural heritage, stored in popular practice, traditional artistic expressions and cultural associated spaces, lack of professionalism and even interest in its capitalization led to the proliferation of kitsch, hijacking, and improvisations. This is also the case for Bucharest's historic buildings that have not been properly capitalized until now. Instead, attention was given to fashionable activities of image and transient recognition of human performances for entry into the Guinness Book of Records. Therefore, communities, groups, and, in some cases, individuals are invited to get involved in recognition and proper management of their cultural heritage (Lira and Amoêda 2009).

Romania also faces the problem of unaltered transmission of intangible cultural heritage from generation to generation, under conditions of changing social structure and depopulation of villages, which makes its recognition no longer belong to community groups, but to some managers who have no direct interest in reviving its natural heritage and restoration interactions with nature and history. Moreover, if we consider only the example of organized hunting in Balc, Bihor County, we understand the danger of diversion of national heritage capitalization for private purposes only, which creates a dangerous precedent.

Another challenge that patrimonialization must face in Romania is the lack of funds raised so that, by using cutting-edge technology, visitors to national heritage to be able to overcome the position of passive recipients of information. On the other hand, it is true that being a delicate and difficult exercise, interpretation of a site and its patrimonialization reclaim a responsibility towards the heritage resource to be promoted, which often inhibits the stakeholders so much that is not anyone willing to take any initiative in this regard.

12.7 Conclusion

Considered an alternative device for sustainable development, patrimonialization can contribute to overall economic regeneration, especially in Southeast Europe, where the interpretation of heritage was not encouraged. This certainty resulted from the cultural heritage feature of putting cultural values in the service of sustainable development and creating links and multilateral interactions between cultures and different practices. If socioeconomic potential of heritage will be capitalized properly by the action of all stakeholders, the corollary of environmental, social, historical, aesthetic, spiritual, and economic values, promoted by sustainable development, will be found in all actions for promoting heritage.

Using as working method examination of recent bibliographic sources, the paper highlighted the relationship in three steps, between heritage and sustainable development. In the first stage, based on the common goals of sustainable development and heritage interpretation, we found that interpretation can be considered as part of sustainable development. From the second step, results that patrimonialization provided to sustainable development opportunity to become part of the heritage. And the third step, thanks to the integrated approach of heritage system that patrimonialization suggests, which allows implementation of all activities related to heritage in the service of sustainable development.

We also concluded that, despite the fact that identification heritage items were already resolved by instrumentalization of interpretation process, its placement in the field of sustainable development could be done only by interdisciplinary targeting of correlation elements. This opens the possibility for future research to examine the degree to which patrimonialization policies, as well as heritage interpretation strategies, integrates objective of making local heritage a universal essential vector, not only to improve access to natural and cultural heritage of humanity and support the management of these sites, but also a settlement factor of the local economic mechanism on sustainable development coordinates.

Although heritage can be analyzed and valued from several perspectives, the economic benefits arising from transnational cooperation projects on heritage is a challenge much too important to be left prey to contradictions and interests within a social system that tolerates non-patrimonialization and that threatens necessity of enrolling national and universal heritage on the sustainable development coordinates.

Acknowledgements This paper has been developed within the period of sustainability of the project entitled "Horizon 2020—Doctoral and Postdoctoral Studies: Promoting the National Interest through Excellence, Competitiveness, and Responsibility in the Field of Romanian Fundamental and Applied Scientific Research," contract number POSDRU/159/1.5/S/140106. This project is co-financed by European Social Fund through Sectoral Operational Program for Human Resources Development 2007–2013. Investing in people!

References

Association for Heritage Interpretation (AHI). (2012). *What is interpretation?* http://www.ahi.org. uk/www/about/what_is_interpretation.

Brinkley, I., Clayton, N., Levy, C., Morris, L., & Wright, J. (2010). *Heritage in the 2020 knowledge economy, a report for the heritage lottery fund.* http://www.hlf.org.uk/aboutus/ howwework/Documents/Heritage_2020KnowledgeEconomy.pdf.

Carver, E. (2011). Stonehenge, world heritage site. A Strategy for Interpretation, Learning and Participation, 2010–15, http://www.english-heritage.org.uk/publications/stonehenge-whs-interpretation-learning-participation-strategy/840210/.

Concil of Europe (CoE). (2005). *Convention on the value of cultural heritage for society.* http:// conventions.coe.int/Treaty/en/Treaties/Html/199.htm.

Drouin, M. (2007). *Un vieux débat toujours ranimé autour de l'interprétation du patrimoine, Téoros, 26-3/2007.* http://teoros.revues.org/1042.

Espace Naturel Régional. (1999). *Cahier technique "La demarche d'interpretation du patrimoine", Espace natural regional.* http://www.en....com.

European Commission. (2013). *Reflective societies: Cultural heritage and european identities.* http://ec.europa.eu/research/participants/portal/desktop/en/opportunities/h2020/calls/h2020-reflective-society-2015.html.

European Commission, Council of Europe (EC, CoE). (2013). *European heritage days.* User's manual, DGII/PAT/JEP (2013) Users Manual, http://europeanheritagedays.com.

Filip, G. F. (2008). Economia culturii în societatea informaţională bazată pe cunoaştere, Akademos nr. 4(11), decembrie 2008. http://www.akademos.asm.md/files/Academos%204%202008% 207%.

International Council on Monuments and Sites (ICOMOS). (2008). *Charter for the interpretation and presentation of cultural heritage sites.* http://quebec2008.icomos.org/en/pdf/Interpretation_ EN_10-04-07.pdf.

Interpret Europe—European Association for Heritage Interpretation. (2013). *Freiburg declaration on heritage interpretation.* http://www.interpret-europe.net/fileadmin/Documents/publications/ Fbg-declaration-web.pdf.

Interpret Europe. (2012). *What is heritage interpretation?* http://www.interpret-europe.net/top/ heritage-interpretation.html.

Landel, P.-A., & Senil, N. (2008). *Patrimoine et territoire, les nouvelles ressources du développement.* Développement durable et territoires, Dossier 12/2009, http:// developpementdurable.revues.org/7563.

Lira, S., & Amoêda, R. (2009). *Constructing intangible heritage, green lines institute for sustainable development.* http://www.greenlines-institute.org/greenlines-institute/Pdfs/pdfs_ bookstore/CIH_Contents.pdf.

Massung, E. (2011). *Sailing the seven Cs of heritage interpretation.* http://heritage.miss-elaineous. com/post/10402539989/sailing-the-seven-cs-of-heritage-interpretation.

Massung, E. (2013). *Interpretation strategies for museums and heritage sites.* http://www.miss-elaineous.co.uk/Heritage%20Interpretation/Chapter%202%20Elaine%20Massung.pdf.

My European City. (2011). *Europa aproape de mine.* http://www.myeuropeancity.eu.

Oers, R., Van Haraguchi, S. (Ed.), UNESCO World Heritage Centre. (2003). *Identification and documentation of modern heritage.* Paper no. 5. http://whc.unesco.org/documents/publi_wh_ papers_05_en.pdf.

Patry, M. (2008). *Business planning for natural world heritage sites.* UNESCO World Heritage Centre. http://whc.unesco.org/enbusinessplanningtoolkit.

Southeast Europe—Transnational Cooperation Programme. (2013). *Jointly for our common future.* http://www.southeast-europe.net...programme.

Sutherland, M. (2007). *Built cultural heritage and sustainable urban development.* http://www. sciencedirect.com.ux4ll8xu6v.useaccesscontrol.com/science/article/pii/S0169204607001442.

Trans Interpret. (2013). *Heritage interpretation.* http://www.transinterpret.net/insights/heritage-interpretation.

UNESCO World Heritage Centre. (2013). *Managing cultural world heritage.* http://whc.unesco.org/en/activities/703.

UNESCO. (2012). *Historic cities in development: Keys for understanding and action, Urban development plan and regulation for the city.* Case studies on the conservation and management of historic cities, http://www.ovpm.org/sites/ovpm/files.

UNESCO World Heritage Centre. (2007). *Climate change and world heritage.* http://whc.unesco.org/documents/publi_wh_papers_22_en.pdf.

Uzzell, D. (2000). *Interpreting our heritage: A theoretical interpretation.* http://www.academia.edu/301486/Interpreting_our_heritage_a_theoretical_interpretation.

Chapter 13
Cultural Heritage, Cultural Tourism, and Creative Economy Basis for Social and Economic Development

Maria Valkova Shishmanova

Abstract Observations show a growing interest in cultural heritage, which seems compensated and opposite to globalization. The individuality of a territory is determined by the cultural heritage, the culture of human relations, from the memory of what is the environment—a measure of quality of life. Cultural tourism is a process in which man strives to regain its proximity to a specific social and spatial environment with lots of authentic identity and memory. Cultural heritage must be present not only in the leisure of the individual and society, but to become part of their everyday life to enhance the value system. Cultural tourism is a major sector of the creative industry. Creative industries are an important tool for socioeconomic development and heralded for urban and regional revitalization. The economy is always influenced by consumption and "production" in the cultural sphere, creating cultural heritage—tangible and intangible, and creative products. The creative industry is working in close collaboration with the tourism industry. An important step in the development of creative industries, on which their growth depends, is to start to work on four themes: access to finance; construction of incubators; initiatives for clusterization; and professional interconnections within the creative industries. Cultural and creative industries usually include cultural tourism, which can increase the added value and create new jobs. By promoting creativity and innovation, the communities will retain their cultural diversity and will enhance economic performance. All activities in the creative industries could develop much more successfully if bound and are incorporated into a single mechanism, to set up and work creatively in tourist clusters.

Keywords Cultural heritage · Cultural tourism · Creative economy
Tourist cluster · Social and economic development

M. V. Shishmanova (✉)
Faculty of Mathematics and Natural Sciences,
South-West University "Neofit Rilski", Blagoevgrad, Bulgaria
e-mail: valkova_chich@abv.bg

© Springer International Publishing AG, part of Springer Nature 2019
V. Vasile (ed.), *Caring and Sharing: The Cultural Heritage Environment
as an Agent for Change*, Springer Proceedings in Business and Economics,
https://doi.org/10.1007/978-3-319-89468-3_13

13.1   Introduction

The individuality of a territory is determined by the cultural heritage, the culture of human relations, from the memory of what is the environment—a measure of the quality of life. An environment without memory has no future, and the legacy is a sign of the quality of the environment for the layers of elapsed time. Cultural tourism is a process in which man strives to regain its proximity to a specific social and spatial environment with lots of authentic identity and memory. Cultural heritage must be present not only in the leisure of the individual and society, but to become part of the daily routine to increase their value system and improve the comfort of the budget of their free time. The movement of people with cultural motivation—fine arts, sightseeing and cultural monuments, trips to festivals, feasts of traditional industries, folk holidays and festivals of arts, educational tourism, and other cultural events are determined by cultural tourism. It has a complex philosophy as it carries the code as culture and tourism. Each issue is complicated enough but together the problems multiply. Nexus and connection provoke merger between them as product and process. The present study examines the cultural tourism in aspect of movement towards cultural heritage, preparation of territory to take on this kind of tourism, as well as its exposure and commitment to creative industry.

13.2   Cultural Heritage and Free Time

13.2.1   Nature Cultural Heritage

The essence of cultural heritage and its importance are still valid, but expand the range of significance and evolve over time, including other elements in its nature. An example of this is the inclusion of cultural landscapes and cultural routes (Krastev 2005: 20–23).

The individuals must develop their attitude towards cultural and historical heritage. The concept of inheritance affects the perception of value, for its authenticity and uniqueness, the scientific, documentary, aesthetic and spatial value, and material characterization. Global trends are legacy to be used with the help of cultural tourism, as "unlimited" resource for sustainable social development. And it can be added to improve the quality of leisure in its inclusion in the balance sheet. The combination between the natural and cultural values tangibly enriches and completes breaks of free time to man, to the individual. So, leisure enters the evolution of values and promotes its enrichment. Leisure enriches its nature, including new aspects of items of cultural heritage.

Preservation and use of heritage require coordinated efforts and mutual understanding of the values of others. Cultural heritage should be seen as a resource for regional development, whose rational use would not only contribute to the recovery of invested funds, but would provide sufficient funds for its protection, mainte-nance, preservation, and development.

Judicious use of cultural heritage through the development of cultural routes would contribute to sustainable economic development and cooperation and the security in a region.

It is good that each country will have a unified strategy for sustainable devel-opment of cultural heritage. The idea is to create a network of cultural itineraries, outlining the macrostructure of this heritage, which is so far known only in narrow national frameworks. Cultural resources make rich these countries. Thus, it can promote the development of a regional cohesion in the whole region, for tolerance to the values of other countries in the spirit of the new vision for heritage.

Heritage has an incredible identity and diversity. Cultural integrity, given to a certain area, has historical roots that have formed as a complete macrostructure.

The idea to build the authentic image of a region starts from culture, showing this rich culture in its entirety and simultaneously highlighting national specificities, and contains a bright positive message.

Future prices will "deep" environment having memory layers. Create a new vision and new ideas about the role and approach to cultural heritage. It is a message of past generations fallen temporarily in our hands, which we must pre-serve in its original form for future generations (the philosophy of the Venice Charter of ICOMOS of 1964—Cultural heritage should be seen as a resource and stimulus for economic and social development that not only should be protected but also be used rationally and efficiently).

Real evolution in recent years occurred in notions of cultural heritage. The vision for heritage already seen as testimony—tangible and intangible, testimony for values, beliefs, skills and traditions, resource for sustainable development and quality of life, a means of intellectual dialogue, incentive for exchanges and con-tacts, understanding and consent.

In this case, it can be said that the leisure time extends the spectrum of its components, as given above. Free time can be also resources of regional devel-opment with sustainable character depending on the status, identity, and diversity of cultural heritage. Leisure falls in a competitive medium of cultural corridors, leading to improve its essence and balance.

13.2.2 A New Vision of Cultural Heritage

The new vision draws attention to the element "time" of the human environment—a historical symbol of the exchange, the dynamics of relationships and dialogue between communities and nations, taking place through:

- "cultural routes" (cultural itinerary)—refer the concrete, historical roads/paths with a particular historical feature, theme associated with particular landscapes and values—tangible and intangible;

- "cultural corridors"—including an routes that have preserved their historical, economic, and cultural importance over the centuries, passing through different countries and continents and unifying values, ideas, and innovations of international and global significance (Shishmanova 2015: 246–254).

These corridors can be "overlaid" thematic space to recover intangible objects (Silk Road, wine, silver, amber, etc.). Legend/fairy tale, literature can transform physical space and tourist site in a new cultural tourist space.

For example, Southeast Europe is the right space for the expression of the new vision for Heritage—a true crossroads of civilizations and religions over the centuries, a mediator between East and West, North and South, in which there are multiple relationships, influences with common historical roots.

Preservation of cultural heritage becomes a collective project linking more and more partners. Normally, the state has the priority in conservation, with the assistance of local authorities. The legal protection of cultural monuments is a matter of national interest and must be a national priority. It is not possible functions to be concentrated in one institution, which requires optimal decentralization of preservation activity. It is possible to introduce a partnership between central and local government, NGOs, private, and voluntary sectors in the field of heritage and so on. It should create conditions for a better coordination between all partners and activities—between archaeological research, conservation, spatial planning, urbanism and others. (Convention on the archaeological heritage of Europe, ratified by Bulgaria, introduced the concept of "integrated conservation," meaning just such coordination.) This suggests the relevant legal framework and subsequent documents such as rules, regulations, for each partner to regulate its functions.

13.3 Cultural Tourism

13.3.1 Essence of Cultural Tourism

The affirmation of cultural tourism as a means of mutual knowledge of the various communities, for expression of regional identity and diversity, and integration in the common European cultural space, contributes to the enrichment of the spiritual realm of society.

Cultural tourism can only exist in the presence of cultural and historical heritage. In cultural tourism should be assessed not only the individual object and environment where exposed, but the combination of composite interactions and the interactions human–environment or human–cultural landscape (Bulev 2005: 31).

These trends are particularly relevant for Bulgaria, which has a huge but underused potential for intense and very attractive cultural tourism.

The development of cultural tourism has for recovery extraordinary potential of its heritage, and it can manifest its specificity by common roots, strong mutual influences and remarkable cultural and historical values. Besides, cultural tourism can contribute significantly to the dissolution, mutual understanding, and cultural integration between countries and regions.

13.3.2   Cultural Corridors and Cultural Routes (Cultural Itinerary)

Cultural routes are considered to be promoting a sustainable cultural tourism—in close partnership with the tourism sector. They are able to express the identity and diversity of cultural heritage in the region and contribute to its European integration.

If traced, the cultural routes of South Eastern Europe would be of great interest at the moment for Europe as this area offers tremendous cultural resource. As a consequence is formed in time cultural corridors—axes of ancient interactions—living memory of civilizations. This region forms its remarkable cultural integrity and common cultural phenomena with unique local varieties. Such wealth requires coordinated efforts. A unified and coordinated management of regional tourism resources in the network of regional cultural corridors would increase the competitiveness of this type of tourism in the region and the country, revealing their unsuspected riches of objects and phenomena.

To assess the role of cultural corridors opening up to European cultural space should be given the current network of European cultural routes.

The entry of the cultural space of Bulgaria in the general treasury of the world is a unit of the overall network of sites and streams.

Bulgaria is an attractive hub for leisure of people of European and global space —space for culture and leisure, space for integration, and enrichment of cultures from ancient times until now.

It is necessary to promote in our country innovative cultural tourism, activating cultural exchanges within the region and beyond and contributing to the preservation of heritage. This means creating a chain of connected packages for cultural tourism along those corridors in European network for cultural tourism.

Between culture and tourism, there should be a good bilateral relationship. Sometimes tourism threatens heritage. There are instances of degradation and even rough commercialization. The state must take reasonable system of tax incentives in the field of cultural heritage. The sometimes inefficient use of cultural monuments can be added.

13.4 Cultural Tourism—Sub-sector of the Economy

13.4.1 Cultural Tourism Revives Settlements

Cultural tourism is analyzed also as a factor in synergistic effect on reanimation of certain activities and revival of settlements. This tourism is sub-sector of the economy contributing to the sustainable development of natural and anthropogenic environment with a balanced use of natural and cultural resources. Cultural tourism in the market environment with the correct parameters for its development would have weathered the "mummification" of cultural values.

Cultural tourism is growing year-round, which is of great importance. The adopted public model is the creation of a human society that actively rests in different places. It is believed that the actual visit conducted by tourism cannot substitute virtual reality and achieved through new technologies. Trips enrich culture (Dickens and Carole 2000).

The municipality—the city cannot develop only as a tourist site. It is necessary to give priority to the "fabric" of the city—"tangle" of different activities and functions, of different use of a city and in it to have functional relatedness. Cities respectively settlements should not become models. When a village is becoming a tourist destination, priority is to its inhabitants. There is no other business that so hard to transform a village as tourism.

Besides the direct economic impact, the development of cultural tourism also has a multiplier spiritual effect. With the construction of cultural values, the individuals would include in their daily lives and in the budget of their leisure time, the cultural tourism is important in globalization and opening to the world. By focusing on spiritual values and the richness of the land and our people, all efforts should be directed to the realization of cultural and national identity so develop both intellect of the nation and awareness of the contribution and place of the people and our country in European and world civilization.

13.4.2 Tourist Destination and Tourism Product

Tourist destination must be a multifunctional model that stores identity and the wide range of cultural events provides employment 24 h.

Consideration of the tourism product can be done from two perspectives—of its customers and of its suppliers. On the one hand, it is a comprehensive service that includes a set of services sold to tourists in one package. In this sense, tourism product represents each component of the total package of services. Moreover, the tourism product has atomic type consisting of a core of natural climatic, cultural, historical, and other resources around which gravitate developed and offered by tourism, transportation, entertainment and more businesses, tourist goods and services. One of the most important gravitating elements is transport and transfer of tourists, providing shelter and food, entertainment and other services related to securing the earmarking of tourism, utilities and provision of various consumer goods, incl. souvenirs. The core of product in tourism is services ensuring the realization of the purpose of the journey. The tourism product refers to anything that tourists buy, see, experience and feel throughout their journey or tourist product incorporates various services aimed at fulfilling the needs of tourists during their travel and leisure.

The tourism product has an intangible and integral character because of its transience and to be stored is regarded as manufacturing services for tourism. It is formed by components time, space, and personality, i.e., this product is composed of many different elements, often intertwined and therefore difficult to be differentiated. In this, production of the tourism product is engaged many people and thus increasing employment of the population.

13.4.3 The Tourism Cluster

The cluster is a self-organizing network, an association of companies linked by technology or supplies that produce complementary products, use in conjunction given production factors and technology, collaborate or cooperate voluntarily in vertical or horizontal "chains." The term cluster can be understood as networks of small and medium enterprises in limited geographical area, so the mega-clusters too. Clusters are the most intelligent form of increasing the competitiveness of a country.

The term "competitive cluster" comprises a whole set of different actions and services, created for more attractive tourist offering. At the core of the cluster is the relative advantage consisting of natural attractions and biodiversity of a protected area. The competitive cluster is supposed to enlarge and support the very important relations between the business, the state institutions, and the dopant entities. They must aim to encourage the utilization of cultural tourism (www.slideshare.net).

The practice of creating and maintaining a "competitive clusters" is currently endorsed in some Third World countries and countries in transition. It brings together a number of travel companies, institutions, and other entities involved in the marketing of a comprehensive tourism product united in a particular territory.

Sustainable tourism is the one that, including all types of tourism, provides continuous maintenance of natural, demographic, and economic prosperity of the country and takes care of maintenance in excellent condition of all natural and cultural resources. In this type of organization, the natural, cultural, financial, and social resources are treated carefully with a view to sustainable use in the future by ensuring equality and self-renewal. So tourists are offered unique new experiences. Quality of life of the local population is improved by the additional opportunities the partnership between governmental institutions, the private sector, and human societies (www.slideshare.net).

   The tourism cluster is a grouping of related industries and institutions on a given area. Companies are linked in a variety of ways. Some operate in the cluster of other providers; some are buyers, other sellers, third use total human and other resources. The most important in cluster is that participating companies are economically linked. They both cooperate and compete with each other and to some extent depend on each other. Moreover, the tourism cluster should look for complementarity, cooperation, competition, closing the full cycle of activities, and receiving complete tourist product and economic effect. The actions at regional level are to support for building clusters.

   In developing the tourism cluster must clearly define segments and niches in the market through multiple marketing research on the basis of which can be promoted services satisfying consumers. Marketing research must attend the entire leg of the journey pertinent to the cluster. Planning takes into account the time span of planning, what is planned in advance, sources of information, the role of tour operator, reasons for travel and group travelers. The selection of the destination encompasses the model of decision as a value, the final selection criteria, the preferences package, and the method of ordering. For the place of visit is taken into account preferred general attributes, specific demands and needs such as accommodation, dining, shopping, entertainment, transport, and other activities. Subsequent trips are planned by determining the frequency of visits to the same destination. Other important elements of consumer demand are income, marital status, age, travel time, operating costs per person per day, the types of previous destinations, accommodation during the previous trip, number, and types of vacations lately.

13.5   The Creative and Cultural Industries and Their Interrelations with Cultural Tourism

The boundary between the creative industries and cultural industries is much discussed. Cultural industries as economic activities are best defined as complementary activities to the creative industries. They include focusing on cultural heritage (incl. museums, libraries, exhibitions, and reenactments), but also sport outdoor activities. Overall, they are activities that diversify the people's way of life. In the limelight of cultural industries is providing other types of activities and the inclusion of the value of cultural heritage and social well-being rather than providing mainly financial benefit (http://en.wikipedia.org/wiki/Creative_industries) (http://innova.eszak-alfold.hu/).

   According to international organizations, such as the General Agreement on Tariffs and Trade (GATT), UNESCO cultural industries (sometimes also known as "creative industries") combine the creation, production and distribution of goods and services that are of cultural nature and usually protected by rights of intellectual property (http://www.theinfolist.com/php/SummaryGet.php?FindGo=Cultural%20industry).

The UN report "Creative Economy-Report 2010" states that the successful coordination of actions among sectors is the key to a long-term strategy for the creative economy.

Creative economy is the intersection and integration of art, business, innovation, and new business models. In the development of creative economy, policy must take into account not only economic need, but also special requirements, such as social education, cultural identity, social inequality, environmental factors. Each country must identify its key sectors in the creative economy that still is not fully controlled (http://russian.cri.cn/841/2011/03/31/1s376542.htm).

The actual production of creative products and services forms the creative industries. The entire production chain of creative industries does not include common services. It forms a chain of production, reproduction, delivery, and logistics for all sectors of the creative industry. When we identify and evaluate the features of the numerous sectors within the creative industry, we generally recognize these fourteen sectors: editors and publishing, software development, radio and television, advertisement, cinematography, photography (photography as a souvenir), toys production, music, fashion and design (making costumes, national embroidery), arts, crafts, literature (folklore—legends, tales, proverbs), theater and dance, architecture.

Cultural tourism has an organic connection with the activities of the creative industry.

Three sports activities, dining and catering and accommodation, which are mentioned in some other definitions of creative industries, are not included. It is necessary also to know that the creative industry is closely related with the tourism industry and the sectors covered by it largely.

Creative industries are of great importance for all regions. It is an important economic sector, which includes a large number of employees and whose turnovers are very large. In a study, it is revealed that this industry has been developing at a rate higher than the average for the economy of each country. During this study is revealed that among different regions there are many common features. One of the common features reveals that creative activities and culture are at the heart of an important economic sector that is growing rapidly. Other conclusion is that this branch is operated predominantly by small companies (http://www.creative-growth. eu/Portals/10/Ostsam%20Creative%20report-BG_highres.pdf).

Relatively similar activities prevail in almost all surveyed regions, with design and architecture among them. But still, there are some existing distinctions. Regions have special or unique activities, and they identified as prior to the visibility, recognition, and popularity of the region. Individualization of the activity of creative industries is beneficial for the region because it allows creating a brand for the area. The potential must be examined and developed in the future and to be linked to the development of cultural tourism.

An important step in the development of creative industries, on which depends its growth, is to start work on four themes: fund-raising, build incubators, cluster cooperation among partners, and/or competitors, business collaboration within the creative sector.

Cultural and creative industries usually involve in some countries architecture, visual and performing arts, sports, advertising, and cultural tourism, which can increase the added value and create new jobs. By promoting creativity and innovation, communities will retain their cultural diversity and will enhance economic performance.

The program "Creative Europe," which has been functioning since 2011 will allow better protection of cultural and historical heritage and intensify the transport and exhibitions of works of art both within the EU and beyond. Its importance will express in encouraging international cooperation and professional development of related sectors. European Commission provides funds' managed by the European Investment Bank to ensure capital funding for cultural and creative industries.

EU plans to develop clusters, financial instruments, and pre-emptive actions to stimulate and develop this sector. The European Commission wants to help European artists and creative businesses to develop new markets through the use of electronic and computer technologies and looking for a way for best contribution through its policies. Culture of entrepreneurship will have to take more risks, to invest potential for innovation, forecasting future tendencies. When it comes to creative and artistic potential of the country, creativity plays a very important role because it involves creating new jobs for people with specific skills. It is expected that the post-crisis economy will support the mobility of labor resources to guarantee or confirm that people are engaged in relevant areas that require their skills (http://innova.eszak-alfold.hu/).

Cultural and creative industries including cultural tourism increase the added value and create new jobs. By promoting creativity and innovation, communities will retain their cultural diversity and will enhance economic performance. All activities in the creative industries could develop much more successfully if are bound and incorporated into a single mechanism which can set up and work creatively in tourist cluster.

From the examination and analysis of various papers cited in the study and the literature, I can summarize the following:

Similarities:

- Cultural tourism is part of the creative industry;
- Cultural tourism could revive settlements;
- The cultural corridors and cultural routes improve the competitiveness of cultural tourism in a certain area, region, or country;
- The innovative cultural tourism creates a network of cultural—tourist products established along these corridors;
- Cultural tourism can lead to sustainable growth;
- Differences and new suggestions in the current study:
- The entry of the cultural space of a given area a party in the general treasury of the world represents a unit of the total network of cultural values and streams;
- This node of the general network leads to social and economic revitalization;

- In the development of tourist cluster segments and niches in the market must be clearly defined through multiple marketing research upon which can be promoted cultural and creative services satisfying the consumers;
- In the marketing, researches for the compilation of the cluster the entire leg of the journey having regard to the cluster itself must be present;
- Creative industry must accurately be incorporated into a single mechanism to cultural tourism in order to form and act creatively in a tourist cluster.

13.6 Conclusion

The creative industries are a forerunner and an important tool for regional revitalization. Cultural tourism is a major sector of the creative industries. The economy is always influenced by consumption and "production" in the cultural sphere, creating cultural heritage—tangible and intangible, and creative products. Development of cultural tourism should be linked, synchronized with the other activities of the creative industries in the municipality and functions complement each other so as to obtain a synergistic effect. Best solution would be to create and develop clusters of creative industries and cultural tourism, building incubators to help them.

Development of a clear policy for the revival of creative activities in the settlements and territories which have the potential for development and their inclusion in the chain of cultural routes would create new attractive jobs for the population and mostly for young people and would attract new young contingents.

References

Bulev, T. (2005). Dialogue with society at all levels. In *Preserving the cultural identity of Bulgarian landscape should grow into a national priority, architecture* (№ 3, p. 31).

Creative Growth—Policy Recommendations. http://www.creative-growth.eu/Portals/10/Ostsam%20Creative%20report-BG_highres.pdf.

Dickens, R. S., & Carole, E. (2000). *Cultural resources—Planning and management.* Social Impact Assessment Series, № 2.

Exploring The Cultural and Creative Industries Debate. (2013). *Culture action Europe.* Retrieved July 7, 2013. http://www.theinfolist.com/php/SummaryGet.php?FindGo=Cultural%20industry.

Kostov, E. (2001). *Cultural tourism.* Sofia: Economy.

Krastev, T. (2005). A real evolution in the perception of cultural heritage. *Arhitekture* (3), 20–23.

Shishmanova, M. (2015). Cultural tourism in cultural corridors, itineraries, areas and cores networked. *Procedia—Social and Behavioral Sciences, 188,* 246–254.

Tourism-Concept & Perspectives, www.slideshare.net.

Vallalatok K+F+I televekenysegenek tamogatasa, http://innova.eszak-alfold.hu/.

UN: Creative industry plays a special role in the process of economic recovery. http://russian.cri.cn/841/2011/03/31/1s376542.htm.

Chapter 14
Design and Delivery of Experience-Based Tourism Products and Services in Heritage Settings: The PEGA Training Programme

Theodoros Stavrinoudis and Dorothea Papathanasiou-Zuhrt

Abstract PEGA is an intensive training programme for tourism professionals funded by the ESF 20017–2013 Programme. In 2015, it was commonly undertaken by the University of the Aegean, the Panteion University of Athens and the University of Thessaly aiming to update the knowledge of tourism professionals. A Cultural Heritage Module has specifically instructed tourism professionals into the design and delivery of cognitive–emotional experiences for visitors at heritage places, addressing three main challenges: A. the discontinuity of supply and demand in the production of smart heritage that is disabling the consumption of quality and highly customized heritage products and services at local level; B. the need for multilateral and transparent collaborations and the creation of an effective stakeholder network; and C. the need for real-time accessibility of the cultural product per se servicing the connected consumer market. The training has demonstrated that interconnected professional networks and enhanced skills to exploit the local heritage potential with new heritage consumption models is a sine qua non condition for the future of tourism professionals while at the same time it is pointing towards new opportunities for structural changes in the heritage sector.

Keywords Cultural heritage experience · Tourism education · Tourism planning

14.1 Introduction

The PEGA Training Programme updating the knowledge of 3rd Grade Tourism Professionals in the organization and management of tourism businesses and the promotion of tourism destinations (PEGA) has been implemented in 2015 within the Priority 07 Support for Lifelong Learning and Adult Education in the 8

T. Stavrinoudis · D. Papathanasiou-Zuhrt (✉)
University of the Aegean, The Wave Lab, 10 Blessa Street,
15669 Athens, Greece
e-mail: dorothea.papathanasiou@aegean.gr

© Springer International Publishing AG, part of Springer Nature 2019
V. Vasile (ed.), *Caring and Sharing: The Cultural Heritage Environment as an Agent for Change*, Springer Proceedings in Business and Economics,
https://doi.org/10.1007/978-3-319-89468-3_14

Convergence Regions of the Operational Programme Training and Lifelong Learning of the National Strategic Reference Framework Greece 2007–2013 (EPDMB). PEGA has been funded by the European Union (European Social Fund) and national funds. The University of the Aegean, Faculty of Management Sciences, Department of Business Administration, has operated as coordinator in partnership with the University of Thessaly, Department of Planning and Regional Development, School of Engineering and the Panteion University of Social and Political Sciences, Department of Economic and Regional Development. PEGA aims to deliver an integrative educational intervention in terms of processes, quality of contents and updating of knowledge of third-grade graduates in the organization and management of tourism businesses and the promotion of tourism destinations. Within this framework, the PEGA actions include: coordination, organization and programme support; preparation of study materials; teaching and training activities; communication and dissemination of achieved results; internal and external programme evaluation.

14.2 Structuring the PEGA Training Programme

Due to the wide spatial distribution of the three (3) educational cycles with six (6) training activities in Athens, Chios and Volos run by three institutions, a series of teleconferences between the universities of the Aegean, Panteion and Thessaly have facilitated information, organization and coordination for the staff involved in the PEGA actions, resulting in the conclusion of the study programme. In October 2014, the Programme website has been launched at http://tourism-pega.aegean.gr. During the operation phase, the Platform has managed all available information for students and teaching staff: title and main features of PEGA; the identity of the scientific supervisor; aims and goals; course descriptions and thematic units; duration and implementation of the educational cycles in Athens, Chios and Volos; teaching methodology and study materials; news and announcements (calls for the selection of expert trainers; calls for the selection of trainees, organization of events, etc.); communication with ICT staff to ensure user assistance. The website has become a nodal point for the meeting of teaching staff and trainees facilitating communication for all actors involved. The ICT staff at the University of the Aegean has developed the Platform Manual to support trainees and teaching staff in the use of the Platform. During the operation phase, continuous support was offered to all users by the ICT expert staff including assistance for software set-up in personal computers which enabled individual participation in lectures via the selected video conferencing software (BBB) and resolution of technical problems. Prior to the kick-off of PEGA, experimental teleconferences have been conducted for both trainers and trainees to enable users to familiarize with the selected software, to use the e-Platform, access the study materials and understand the software used for the tele-education. Communication was further supported through chat, stable phone, Skype and remote access to PCs. Finally, the Platform for the

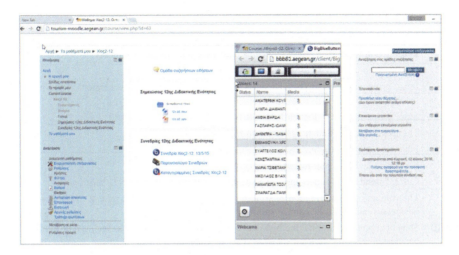

Fig. 14.1 PEGA Training Programme, Big Blue Button conferencing system with attendance list. *Source* Papathanasiou-Zuhrt (2016), the PEGA Project Record

Management of e-Classes has been activated, whereas access has been ensured through the creation of personal accounts for all users. The Platform has hosted all study materials and enabled the full tele-education modality planned for the six training activities in Athens, Chios and Volos (Fig. 14.1).

14.2.1   The PEGA Training Modules

PEGA includes 15 training modules, effectively supporting the learning process and the scientific knowledge to improve the management of tourism businesses and the promotion of tourism destinations (Table 14.1).

The PEGA trainers' pool has been created by employing permanent academic staff of the cooperating institutions (universities of the Aegean, Panteion and Thessaly) with domain-specific topics and research interests close to the 15 selected thematic contents of PEGA. Additionally, thematic experts from other third-grade institutions were selected through a special call for experts to recruit PEGA as external experts. The pool of the external experts was of crucial importance for the overall success of PEGA as their expertise was tailored to the 15 thematic poles of the educational cycles. The development of an Expert Registry in adult education was dictated by two main conditions:

- Permanent academic staff in the three cooperating institutions could not numerically cover the intensive needs of PEGA.
- The three cooperating institutions lack permanent staff with expertise in tourism as tourism studies per se do not make part of an autonomous third-grade curriculum in Greece.

Table 14.1 PEGA Training Programme

PEGA training modules	
1	Introduction to tourism. Basic concepts and contemporary developments
2	Contribution of tourism to the local and regional development
3	Basic principles and current tendencies in the organization and management of tourism businesses
4	Strategic management for the competitiveness of tourism businesses
5	The importance of human resources in tourism businesses
6	Financing tourism businesses
7	Economic and financial management of tourism businesses
8	Current trends in the marketing of tourism businesses and tourism destinations
9	The role and the contribution of ICT in the organization and management of tourism businesses and the management of tourism destinations
10	Statistical and quantitative methodology in the organization and management of tourism businesses and the management of tourism destinations
11	Contemporary cultural heritage products, the use of cultural heritage and tradition and the production of genius loci as a means to support the competitiveness of Greek tourism destinations
12	Challenging the experienced tourist: cultural heritage itineraries as an innovative tourism business
13	Sustainable development of tourism destinations and the role of tourism entrepreneurship
14	Current models for developing tourism destinations, special and alternative tourism forms
15	Organization and management of tourism businesses offering special and alternative tourism forms

Source Papathanasiou-Zuhrt (2016), the PEGA Project Record

Prior to the start of the educational operation, intensive communication has taken places and meetings have been conducted between the scientific supervisor and the trainers aiming to achieve the best possible organization of PEGA, to timely resolve any difficulties that may appear during implementation and to consolidate the pool of trainers. The scientific supervisor has coordinated the summative information flow to the trainers' pool analytically informing on: standards for study materials; deadlines for the delivery of the study materials; expert trainers in charge of the study materials for each didactical unit; coordinators for each didactical unit, etc. Additionally and in order to support authors to complete their tasks on time, templates have been adopted for the production of the study materials and made accessible to authors in the Platform.

14.3   Implementing the PEGA Training Programme

PEGA has been implemented through three didactical cycles with six (6) training activities of 150 training hours each, 19 ECTS in total, of which 50 h in the teaching classroom and 100 h through the Platform. To satisfy the training needs, a blended learning methodology has been adopted, flexible enough to include different learning styles and augment the active participation rate among trainees at distance and e-learning, synchronous and asynchronous learning level. The distance and e-learning modus have been implemented via the BigBlueButton Programme (BBB). The BBB tele-education modus has become a major learning pillar of PEGA, successfully servicing the particularities of the inter-institutional and interdepartmental character of the learning process in the PEGA framework. To ensure active participation, trainees have been involved in written assignments and a final exam, which has taken place in each institution involved in the PEGA Training Programme. The written assignments were strictly connected to the fifteen (15) training modules aforementioned and were meant to prove that domain-specific knowledge has been successfully acquired. Upon conclusion, trainees have received the Certificate of Attendance issued by the University of the Aegean in the spirit of the European Qualifications Framework (EQF).

14.4   Design and Delivery of Experience-Based Tourism Products

PEGA defends the access to cultural heritage for all and is oriented towards the inclusion of multicultural and multigenerational audiences with different conceptions of heritage and culture. Modules 11: Contemporary cultural heritage products, the use of cultural heritage and tradition and the production of genius loci as a means to support the competitiveness of Greek tourism destinations and Module 12: Challenging the experienced tourist: cultural heritage itineraries as an innovative tourism business are therefore concerned with the design and delivery of quality tourism experiences (European Union 2015b: 8). Although it is common knowledge that cognitive–emotional experiences are crucial significance for the convergence of supply and demand in the heritage domain, especially because users attach personal meanings to heritage assets, there is not a methodological reference framework at EU level for the (co) creation of validated contents that can ensure cognitive emotional access to the values of heritage avoiding standardized views (European Commission 2015a: 10–11; Prutsch 2015: 9). The missed opportunity is that the added value generation is not noticed and the turnover as indication of significance because the main outputs are intellectual and intangible and only very recently this view is starting to change (Belfiore and Holdaway 2014: 1; Prutsch 2015: 16; Houmbouri and Boizesson 2015: 9; the 1014 Manifesto of the New

Narrative for Europe).[1] Modules 11 and 12 are focused to explore (a) the conditions under which immersive experiences take place in heritage settings from a cognitive point of view and (b) the communication gap between validated content carriers of the supply side, e.g. museum curators, archaeological authorities and non-validated content carriers of the demand side; e.g. individual visitors in order to assist trainees formulate a value-driven communication framework with the public and a progressive convergence of supply and demand towards a sustainable quality experience with territorial benefits and new skills for new jobs in the heritage sector. Further important considerations are how new services are generated in the creative economy through the co-creation of contents by individual prosumers and how the social media are affecting the cognitive paradigm. Should the heritage sector be interested in the diversification of new jobs that require new skills, it should be directly addressing these challenges for its own sustainability and regeneration. The inclusion of the technological condition into the onsite heritage experience is producing an emotional impact on young visitors that may define a new production–consumption process in heritage settings. Modules 11 and 12 are dedicated to assist trainees perceive the nature-size of the problem with praxis validated tools and methods, so that they can identify remedies, frameworks and models for new heritage experiences and develop methods/ processes to put the remedies, the frameworks and the methods to work. It is imperative to understand the supply–demand interactions and help transform results to products and services towards the creation of new business opportunities that will sustain and regenerate the heritage sector.

14.4.1 Heritage Experiences

'Experience' is a term often used with little attention to meaning, often interpreted as a sensation; however, humans 'constantly give meaning to everything they feel, see, hear or experience' (European Union 2016: 1). Therefore, experience generally indicates a distinctively human complexity and stands at the centre of educational endeavour, as education can be understood as an emancipation and enlargement of the experience. Experience implies process and content: it includes what we do, and also how we act and are acted upon, the ways in which we do and suffer, desire and enjoy, see, believe, imagine, love. The process of experiencing has two meanings: 'having an experience' and 'knowing an experience'. Primary experience is what occurs as through a minimum of incidental reflection, and secondary reflective experience through the intervention of systematic thinking. Experience has within it

---

[1]The New Narrative for Europe is an EU pilot project, initiated by the European Parliament and implemented by the European Commission. It is accessible at: http://ec.europa.eu/culture/policy/new-narrative/index_en.htm.

judgment, thought and connectedness with other experiences. Also 'experiencing' and 'what is experienced' stand to one another in the most complete interdependence, comprising a whole (Dewey 1963, 1966). Following Dewey, we can define experiences as interactions of humans with tangibles and intangibles: with objects, products, services, time, space, notions, concepts and skills. The rise of skilled consumption, hallmark of the twenty-first century, demands special skills for pretty much every hour of the day (Ury 1990; Florida 2002; Jenkins 2006; A.M.I. 2014: 21). Sophistication, social status and connoisseurship are not anymore associated with a higher social class or income. The consumption of culture is a universal right, rather than a privilege of the elite, and heritage consumption is highly reputable (Chan and Goldthorpe 2007: 374; Abeledo and Rausell 2011: 7–8). In the last decade, highly skilled workers, innate to the digital world, are looking for the technology intense experience (Benghozi et al. 2015: 90). The heritage sector is facing a new reality: cultural heritage consumers share their experiences in the social networks, whether positive or negative, influencing the decisions of others and regulate supply and demand to a certain extend. Traditional heritage management in sites and museums and outdated organizational structures depending on individuals with outdated skill sets cannot deliver the desired experience. Specific job-related competences learned throughout education and training must be now underpinned by transversal competences, especially digital and entrepreneurial competences, in order to better adapt to the emerging market. There is a need for a value-driven knowledge acquisition pattern in heritage places, capable of integrating both new technologies and quality contents into the heritage experience.

Heritage is consumed for very different reasons: therefore, heritage visitors wish to select, co-create and customize their own experiences. Planning for experience diversity helps to avoid the conflicts that often occur among visitors who want different things from their visits. This means that heritage places shall provide for a variety of experiences and activities of interest to families, children, women, couples, older people, specific interest visitors and enthusiasts, the list is long. This audience may then create the own sense of place: it can select a place to stay, taste local products and cuisine, find and walk along historic pathways, decide between indoor and outdoor activities, escape in nature, indulge in shopping, participate in activities and events, visit theatres, sites, museums and places of personal interest, stroll around attend cooking classes or festivals. Planners shall take into consideration that visitors are sovereign, today more than ever—and make their own choices following their own motivations and not those of the supply side.

14.4.2 Cultural Communication

Cultural growth is linked to the existence of particular tangible and intangible assets, such as monuments, museums, heritage sites and historic cities, natural attractions and landscape (Houmbouri and Boizesson 2015: 6). Tourism operators try to sell a destination, merely focusing on the fame of heritage assets, exploiting at the maximum their visibility in the landscape, while the intangible dimension, the meaning hidden in the tangible form, is neglected. On the other hand, cultural heritage authorities hold the monopoly of information and often reject the individual expressions and aspects about heritage as untrue. There is an urgent need to establish a new learning paradigm in heritage settings and a value-driven cultural communication framework. The use of culture as a permanent education source is a constant value in citizen education because it uses the vast treasure of stories that makes Europe. Communicating culture is, however, a very complex activity that integrates many different disciplines and many talents within the heritage, creative industries, tourism and AV sector to name but a few prevailing domains—in order to meet visitor expectations and realize opportunities for mindful visitors at heritage places (Di Russo 2005). It goes beyond the 'find and show', means to interpret and provide elements that, while emotional, retain a clear trace of a rational path precisely. When a historian presents theses, h/she communicates facts. H/she generally does so by showing letters, newspapers, pictures, reports in support of the thesis itself. This is a typical structure of a lesson. But over the document analysis, cultural communication presents a *story as set of relationships between documents*, which are the bridges between one event and another, between a letter and an article, between a static image and its moving counterpart, and argumentative connections between the story elements (Di Russo 2006). Static documents and reports become in the AV language, transitions between shots, and the very dynamics of the passage of time in an AV format. In this way, a new visual expression emerges that exploits the infinite possibilities of digital systems for production, reproduction and distribution. The production of quality cultural communication including AV programs and projects relies on expertise that has its roots in the immense European heritage repository, available as a testing ground and therefore extremely attractive in the overseas market. European archives are keepers and providers of a vast quantity of immovable data: photographs, documents, books, newspapers, etc. Multivision technologies can exploit this vast potential to enrich the market with new elements of rich media, which would have been otherwise limited only to film archives and movies. Given the fact that film materials are newly born, such documents are rare to find, low in numbers and very expensive. The transformation of still images and frozen data to speaking objects builds a tremendous opportunity for the media market and is an opportunity to revive the media market using contents coming from peripheral centres of production.

14.5 Instructional Strategy

Modules 11 and 12 employ hermeneutics to establish a paradigm that heritage settings may operate as an informal learning space, where multiple views and different interpretations are openly dealt within a collaborative process (Lowenthal 1985; Gadamer 1990). On the other hand, modern neuroscience is yielding insights which can give valuable tools for the design and delivery of effective instructional design. Modules 11 and 12 strive to reduce extraneous cognitive loads and to redirect attention to cognitive processes that are directly relevant to schema construction. Both modules strive to present information effectively, facilitate domain-specific knowledge acquisition and direct learners' attention to the relevant learning processing. Following the EU guideline to reconsider the crucial roles of teacher and curricula to support cultural awareness and expression (European Union 2016: 43). Modules 11 and 12 have been analyzed from a working memory limitation perspective, a defining aspect of human cognitive architecture expression. Design procedures are based on the reduction of working memory load, reinforcing the association chain by provocative use of schema construction and automation (Sweller 2008). Both modules strive to facilitate presentation of information in a manner to optimize intellectual performance and knowledge transfer, encourage learner activities and reduce unnecessary cognitive loads and free working memory capacity (Baddeley and Hitch 1974; Berninger and Corinna 1998; Baddeley et al. 2014).

14.5.1 Module 11: Learning Objectives

Within Module 11, trainees are offered a methodology to classify a place's assets to heritage classes in order to further select distinctive and visit-worthy features and to produce a place's identity. Learners familiarize with the Significance Assessment Process, a methodological approach based on criteria for the assessment of cultural heritage assets from natural and man-made environment. At practical level, an assessment was undertaken during the onsite Study Visit at the Benaki Museum in Athens on 14 February 2016 to demonstrate multiple asset identities at spatial (global, national, regional, local), scientific (research, technical), historic, aesthetic, social (national, community, group, family personal) and spiritual (tradition, religion, rites and beliefs, lifestyles) level and assess the interpretive potential of selected exhibits from the Museum's permanent collections. Module 11 introduces trainees to the genius loci, a place's identity and spirit, placing heritage into its broad cultural context and emphasizing the importance of interpretation and communication in the understanding and valuation of heritage. The digital Study Visit in the Narrative Museum: The World of Frederick II Hohenstaufen, at Castel Lagopesole, Italy, has demonstrated that heritage tourism may offer even small communities economic growth and employment diversification and improve the residents' income, enabling young people to stay in their local communities (Di Russo and Papathanasiou 2015 forthcoming). Trainees have acquired knowledge about how to plan and manage tourism attractions and how to promote experience-based tourism products and services. Aldo Di Russo, the creator of the Narrative Museum, has participated one BBB session per training cycle answering questions of the trainees transferring at the same time first-hand experiences from the domain of digital cultural heritage and global emblematic producers like Hollywood and Cinecittà (Table 14.2).

Table 14.2 PEGA Training Programme. Module 11: e-Lib sections

Heritage library	
1	Heritage charter library (UNESCO; ICOMOS; COE; English heritage; WWF; NSW)
2	Authenticity
3	Integrity
4	Capturing the value of heritage
5	Cultural consumption
6	Natural heritage
7	Man-made heritage
8	Heritage interpretation
9	Capturing the value of heritage
10	Cultural marketing
11	Heritage management glossaries
12	EU culture and cultural industries
13	Methodologies

Source PEGA Training Programme, Module 11

Accordingly, learning objectives for Module 11 have been set as follows (Table 14.3).

Prior to the Study Visit, trainees have been introduced to a series of international charters, treaties, conventions, guidelines and recommendations for the protection conservation management and interpretation of heritage such as the COE Conventions 018/1954, 066/1959,119/1985, 121/1987, 143/1992, and especially 199/2005 'Value of Cultural Heritage for Society', European Landscape Convention 2000, Venice 1966, Florence 1982, Washington 1987, Charter for the Protection and Management of the Archaeological Heritage 1990, ICOMOS International Cultural Tourism Charter 2002, Burra 1981, Appleton 1983, Charter for the Conservation of Places of Cultural Heritage Value 1992, ICOMOS Charter for the Built Vernacular Heritage 1999, UNESCO Operational Guidelines for the Implementation of the World Heritage Convention 2005, Resolution on the Conservation of Smaller Towns 1975, Amsterdam Declaration 1975, Tlaxcala 1992.

However, these standards are viewed as providing guiding principles towards defining an appropriate response to particular value issues, not as the instant and all-inclusive prescription.

14.5.2   Module 12: Learning Objectives

Module 12 teaches heritage communication medium in recreational and leisure settings. It exploits the different ways of communicating as a means to bridge the spatiotemporal distance between visitors and heritage assets (Di Russo and Papathanasiou 2015). Accordingly, learning objectives have been set as follows (Table 14.4).

Table 14.3 PEGA Training Programme. Module 11: learning objectives

Objective	Process	Skills
1A	Knowledge acquisition	Understand basic concepts of contemporary heritage management (protection, conservation, management, interpretation, significance assessment, use of cultural values, international treaties and conventions, heritage economics, the historic environment); a unified heritage management system with praxis-validated tools to be employed during the planned Study Visit
1B	Skills development	Be able to perceive the protection-use conflict and find solutions to mitigate it; classify heritage resources; analyse and synthesize different heritage classes; know and employ regulations deriving from international treaties and conventions
1C	Professional performance	Complete statement of significance for natural and cultural heritage assets; produce heritage typology; advice multilevel actors (local authorities, development agencies, private investors, associations, etc.) on the importance and economic usability of heritage assets
2A	Knowledge acquisition	Understand the tourism industry (differences between consumers, users, visitors, tourists, the intangible nature of the tourism product, tourism construction and distribution channels, tourism forms, tourism production and consumption); the heritage tourism industry and its particularities; sustainable tourism development; territorial and resources' carrying capacity; service capacity; human resources; familiarize with the five principles of tourism planning (assets, benefits, needs, audiences, uses)
2B	Skills development	Be able to manage assets and track down market trends and needs of audiences; create a destination management and marketing plan; employ heritage tourism products and services for different audiences; structure and disseminate information with tourism value; develop and sell holistic products; employ accessibility of tourism products and services; develop a destination branding concept
2C	Professional performance	Carry out heritage attractions plans; create quality user and visitor experiences; consult multilevel actors on the development of place-centric products and services in relation to tourism and cultural consumption; sell destinations and material cultural heritage

Source PEGA Training Programme, Module 11

Table 14.4 PEGA Training Programme. Module 12: learning objectives

Objective	Process	Skills
3A	Knowledge acquisition	Understand the leisure environment (recreational and in situ) and the particularities of multicultural and multigenerational audiences; understand the particularities and the learning behaviour of non-captives audiences at heritage places
3B	Skills development	Be able to develop leisure time concepts; accessibility plans; a place-centric typology of leisure products and services
3C	Professional development	Consult cultural heritage operators on leisure concepts; design and deliver destination accessibility plans; design and deliver a visitor experienced opportunity plan
4A	Knowledge acquisition	Understand basic notions in heritage interpretation (provoke, relate, reveal a resource's values); spatiotemporal distance; categories of interpretive products and services
4B	Skills development	Be able to develop topics, themes and interpretive messages; attract and retain the attraction of different target publics; create cognitive and emotional bridges among audiences and phenomena (tangible or/and intangible cultural resources; associate resources' values to the visitors' everyday life; fabricate compelling stories and narrative structures
4C	Professional development	Carry out structure layered information; design and deliver a series of basic interpretive products (an informal contact, guided visit, a self-guided trail, directional and interpretive signage); design and develop personal- and media-aided interpretive products and services

Source PEGA Training Programme, Module 12

14.5.3 The Study Visit

An extra-curricular onsite Study Visit has been designed and implemented within Module 12. The onsite Study Visit has taken place within Module 12 on 14 February 2015 at the Benaki Museum, 1 Koumbari Street and Vassilissis Sofias Street in Athens. The Museum has been selected among other institutions for two main reasons:

(a) Its permanent collections offer the most comprehensive view of the Greek history from prehistoric to modern times, with a clear and smooth transition between the interchanging historic eras.
(b) It incorporates a business model with selling facilities, extended public hours (Wednesday, Friday: 9:00–17:00; Thursday, Saturday: 9.00–24.00; Sunday: 9:00–15:00) and a roof garden café restaurant.

The learner community has gathered on St. Valentine's Day, Saturday, the 14th of February 2015 at 190.00 hours at the Museum fully equipped with recording, photograph and smart devices to document the Study Visit across the permanent collections of the Museum, which ended at 22.00 h. A Workshop started at 22.00 h until 12.00 precisely, when the Museum closes for the public on Saturdays.

Table 14.5 PEGA Training Programme. Study Visit segments

Benaki Museum. The permanent collections	
1	Prehistoric, Greek and Roman Art
2	Post-Byzantine and Neo-Hellenic Art
3	Byzantine Art
4	The historic heirlooms collection
5	The collection of painting, drawings and prints

Source PEGA Training Programme, Module 12

Fig. 14.2 PEGA Training Programme, success story, Module 12. Video recordings at the Benaki Museum, Athens, Greece. *Source* PEGA Project Record

The exploration of the Museum's silent objects and the formulation of a potential business model to transform the silent visit into a memorable experience were the main task of the learner community. A Socratic style of inquiry has replaced the frontally developing guided visit provoking interactivity among trainees. The PEGA Study Visit at the Benaki Museum has inspired discussions with background information, while trainees vide-recorded exhibits and emotions of visitors as well as interviews among the individual members of the learning community (Table 14.5).

The Study Visit is capitalizing on the 2013-1-BG1-LEO05-08769 HeriQ: 'Heritage Story Telling—Quality Interpretation' (Papathanasiou-Zuhrt 2014). It aimed to explore how new cultural consumption types are generated in the creative economy and how these changes are affecting the heritage consumption pattern (Fig. 14.2).

14.6 Conclusions

Striving to make its way out of the financial crisis, Greece, a heritage tourism destination per definition, cannot possibly neglect the potential of cultural heritage as a driver for development, real growth and jobs. However, heritage products and services are viable only if they possess widely recognized values and are accessible in real time. Moreover, heritage values depend directly on the capacity of human capital to interpret and use them for public benefit. Real-time accessibility to products and services is one major factor, which makes the difference in the market producing a destination's competitive advantage. Cultural consumption is a knowledge-based activity; therefore, heritage assets are important, only if they possess widely recognized values. The heritage sector shall perceive the Grand Societal Challenges as the new force for reshaping, perceiving, expressing, organizing the participatory public space. As the heritage sector in Greece is entirely subsidized, it has not yet developed feasible value propositions adapting with new business models to the rising demands of emerging markets. Without technological innovations, the heritage sector fails to attract audience innate to the digital world, cannot offer experience-based products and services, cannot inspire new (digital) heritage artworks and skips the opportunity for meta-cognition and critical thinking among visitors. The investigation of entrepreneurial needs and skill needs shall assist the supply side become responsive to the labour market demands and identify a new generation of smart services following the trends of global transformations in society and economy. While the demand side strives to co-create contextual information in the era of mobile telephony, exploit learning opportunities in the participatory heritage space, promote aptitude and skills that forge the continuity of the aesthetic experience with normal processes of living and other relations in the world integrating strengthened personalities into collective identities, the supply side blocks the demand on the basis of authority and expertise in a non-shared, non-explorative, non-dialogical, ex cathedra and top-down attitude. The challenges Greece is facing nowadays are also connected with a lack of collaboration culture among stakeholders in the heritage sector. It is therefore impossible to promote the capacity of shared exploration, mastery and autonomy of the audience. In any heritage setting whatsoever, knowledge results cannot be predicted and must be each time achieved with multiple users in an intense cognitive and emotional interaction. In the era of mobile telephony, the constantly rising tendency to create and disseminate the individuals points of enthusiasm and reference values, the capacity to demonstrate originality and construct singular viewpoints, the need of the demand side to cope with novel content and resulting tensions, the need to co-create historically and culturally validated contents and discharge the falsification of history supported by ignorance, the need to generate multiple views and intercultural interpretations cannot be simply ignored by the supply side. The onsite Study Visit at the Benaki Museum in Athens has revealed that only by mapping entrepreneurial and skill needs in the heritage sector, a wide range of different actors will be enabled to create the experienced environment for the development of smart products and services with visitor affinity and thus address the shifts in global transformations in the production and consumption of cultural heritage. It is imperative to inspire decision-makers and tourism stakeholders towards a new vision for higher quality services where highly skilled workers implement and sell new customized services at (g)local level and where identified experience-based products and services help connect new skills and new jobs forging permanent connections within the broader Public–Private–Third Sector (PPT) and to ensure stronger partnerships and cooperation in regard to better job performance in tourism through a renewed focus on cultural heritage. During the onsite workshop at the Benaki Museum, three main conclusions have been formulated by the trainee community.

Heritage Education: It is necessary to establish a transdisciplinarity research framework both in the cultural and tourism sector to advance heritage education. Especially third-grade education in Greece shall consider to provide for a trans-disciplinarity, heritage education and media literacy research framework for the transformation of heritage settings into a participatory value-generating public space. Heritage education feeds and transforms the relationships we develop with ourselves, others and the world. It must therefore escape compartmentalization in disciplines and to encourage the transdisciplinarity approach. Heritage education shall be organized in terms of three complementary approaches: (a) a direct rela-tionship with tangible–intangible aspects of heritage assets through an analytical, cognitive approach to each entity to the other fields of knowledge, which constitutes the cultural dimension and shall distil the asset value and its recognition by the multicultural and multigenerational audience; (b) presentation and communication of asset values for non-captive audiences in conformity with human cognitive architecture; (c) creation of validated contents and expressions in a participatory public space. Heritage education shall further employ transdisciplinarity, intellec-tual position to understand complexity and to connect different methods and bodies of knowledge in order to foster a holistic approach to thinking and problem-solving. The approach differs from interdisciplinarity in that it goes beyond discipline, involving mastery of disciplines needed to produce the remedies and open disci-plines to themes which pass through and beyond them. Transdisciplinarity is supported by pluridisciplinarity and interdisciplinarity, but goes beyond them to encourage an integrated view of a subject, leaving discipline-based approaches behind. Transdisciplinarity shall facilitate the audiences at heritage places to think contextually and globally and to express their views in concrete terms through validated contents. Going beyond structured forms of knowledge (disciplines), transdisciplinarity heritage education re-evaluates the role of intuition, imagination, sensibility and the body in the transmission of knowledge.

The technology intense experience: Acknowledging the fact the deployment of ICT alone cannot ensure the quality experience, both the heritage and tourism sector shall cooperate to deliver a technology intense experience; however, the latter shall allow for cognitive and emotional accessibility about heritage places and objects. There is a dearth regarding the analysis of technology types used by both the supply and demand at heritage places, usually with the demand side (audience) being equipped with substantially advanced devices on 4G connections against a supply side that relies on coded language labels to communicate the value of items. Another major obstacle is the connectivity issue which determines how ICT technologies can contribute to a holistic quality experience in conjunction with the role of cognitive accessible value content. Acknowledging the fact that heritage settings are frequented by multigenerational and multicultural audiences with usually minimal prior knowledge about heritage values, an experienced typology connected to motivation, expectation and use of ICT shall be explored and formulated. The tourism sector shall explore the contextual co-creation possibilities and reshape the setting, where citizens become self-providers and distributors of knowledge.

Visitor-driven cultural communication: Acknowledging the fact that any information presentation that disregards human cognitive architecture (HCA) is ex principio deficient, even the most sophisticated smart device application, while operationally advanced, in terms of delivering heritage experiences could remain ineffective. Heritage and the tourism professionals need to understand the conditions prevailing in heritage settings and that the audience at heritage places is usually multigenerational and multicultural with very different backgrounds and beliefs and not always familiar with the heritage presented to them. Both sectors need to formulate a methodological framework, where proactive experiences and the participatory cultural space are fostered and promoted. The use of culture as a permanent education source is a constant value in citizen education because it uses the vast treasure of stories that makes the heritage of Greece to be the cradle of European and Western civilization. Communicating culture is, however, a very complex activity that integrates many different disciplines and many talents. The heritage sector shall adopt an audience-driven communication policy interpreting heritage for international visitors with elements that, while emotional, retain a clear trait of rationality.

References

A.M.I.—Aide aux Musiques Innovatrices. (2014). *Cultural and creative sector: Something to stand for*. Roma: 3C 4 Incubators. Co-financed by: MED Programme—European Regional Development Fund.

Abeledo-Sanchis, R., & Rausell-Köster, R. (Eds.). (2011). *Culture as a factor of economic and social innovation*. Marseille: Creative Commons.

Baddeley, A. D., Eysenck, M., & Anderson, M. C. (2014). *Memory*. Hove: Psychology Press.

Baddeley, A., & Hitch, G. J. (1974). Working memory. In G. Bower (Ed.), *Recent advances in learning and motivation* (pp. 47–90). New York: Academic Press.

Belfiore, E., & Holdaway, D. (2014). *The future of cultural value. How do we invest in our cultural life?*. Coventry: University of Warwick.

Benghozi, P.-J., Salvador, E., & Simon, J.-P. (2015). Models of ICT innovation. A focus on the cinema sector. In M. Bogdanowicz (Ed.), *JRC science and policy report*. Luxembourg: Publications Office of the European Union.

Berninger, V., & Corina, D. (1998). Making cognitive Neuroscience educationally relevant. *Educational Psychology Review, 10*(3), 343–354.

Chan, T., & Goldthorpe, J. H. (2007). The social stratification of cultural consumption: Some policy implications of a research project. *Cultural Trends, 16*(4), 373–384.

Dewey, J. (1966). *Democracy and education: An introduction to the philosophy of education*. New York: Free Press.

Dewey, J. (1963). *Experience and education*. New York: Mc Millan.

di Russo, A. (2005). Nuove opportunita a vecchi preguidizi per l'audiovisivo italiano. *Arts and Artifacts in Movie. Technology, Aesthetics Communication (AAM TAC), 2*, 175–187.

di Russo, A. (2006). *Voices of the constitution. Storyboard and direction notes*. Rome: Fondazione della Camera dei Deputati.

di Russo, A., & Papathanassiou, D. (2015 forthcoming). *An emerging market and the query of how-to-do: Culture as a driver for development and socio-economic cohesion*. Paper presented at the Procedia—Financing sustainable economic growth for security and well being. 4th edition of Emerging Markets Queries in Finance and Business.

European Commission. (2015a). *Culture and Tourism. Ex post evaluation of Cohesion Policy programmes 2007–2013, focusing on the European Regional Development Fund (ERDF) and the Cohesion Fund (CF)*. Brussels: Directorate-General for Regional and Urban Policy.

European Commission. (2015b). *European capitals of culture, 30 years*. Luxembourg: Publications Office of the European Union, Directorate-General for Education and Culture.

European Commission. (2016). *Cultural awareness and expression handbook*. Luxembourg: Publications Office of the European Union, European Union.

Florida, R. (2002). *The rise of the creative class*. New York: Basic Books.

Gadamer, H. G. (1990). *Hermeneutik I. Wahrheit und Methode. Grundzuege einer philosophischen Hermeneutik*. Tübingen: J.C.B. Mohr.

Houmbouri, E., & de Boissezon, B. (2015). *Getting cultural heritage to work for Europe*. Luxembourg: European Commission, Directorate-General for Research and Innovation.

Jenkins, H. (2006). *Convergence culture: Where old and new media collide*. New York: New York University Press.

Lowenthal, D. (1985). *The past is a foreign country*. Cambridge: Cambridge University Press.

Papathanasiou, D. (2014). *HERIQ: The online e-course assistance for interpretive skills*, from https://www.facebook.com/pages/First-Step/1506373086288105.

Papathanasiou-Zuhrt, D. (2016). *Tourism accessibility handbook*. Bucharest: National Authority of Tourism, Romania.

Prutsch, M. (2015). *European historical memory: Policies, challenges and perspectives*. Brussels: Policy Department B: Structural and Cohesion Policies European Parliament.

Sweller, J. (2008). Human cognitive architecture. In J. Spector, M. D. Merill, J. van Merrienboer, & M. P. Driscol (Eds.), *Handbook of research on educational communications and technology: A project of the association for educational communications and technology* (pp. 370–381). New York and London: Taylor & Francis.

Ury, J. (1990). *The tourist gaze*. London: Sage.

Chapter 15
The Global Heritage: Knowledge and Innovations

Liliya Sarach

Abstract Today when the situation in the world is changing at an accelerated rate, there is an actual question of the global heritage management. The global heritage management is a condition of sustainable civilization development. It is known there are a lot of different types and levels of heritage. Therefore, this paper pays attention to the knowledge and innovations management problems as a part of global heritage. It is suggested an author's approach to the global heritage management and its model in this paper.

Keywords Global heritage · Knowledge management · Innovations
Clusters · Cooperation · Competition · Triple helix model

15.1 Introduction

The rapid-fire development of the world conjuncture dictates that the heritage may refer to the different life spheres, such as history, culture, and economics.

Today there is an interesting question about the problems and prospects of not only the preservation of the heritage, but also usage of it as a resource for economic development. In this case, the socioeconomic aspect of heritage involves the study of heritage as a resource for the development of society as a whole, including a wide range of social aspects, including education, the fight against poverty, quality of life and sustainable development. In this regard, it is important to take into account tangible and intangible forms of heritage. In this article, we will stop at the intangible forms of heritage expressed as knowledge and innovation in a global context.

Nowadays, when situation in the world is changing at an accelerated rate there is an actual question of the global heritage management. The global heritage management is a condition of the sustainable civilization development. It is known that there are many different types and levels of heritage. Therefore, this paper pays

L. Sarach (✉)
Kazan Federal University, Kremslevkaya 18, Kazan, Russia
e-mail: liliache@mail.ru

© Springer International Publishing AG, part of Springer Nature 2019   183
V. Vasile (ed.), *Caring and Sharing: The Cultural Heritage Environment as an Agent for Change*, Springer Proceedings in Business and Economics,
https://doi.org/10.1007/978-3-319-89468-3_15

Fig. 15.1 Structure of the global heritage. *Source* Author

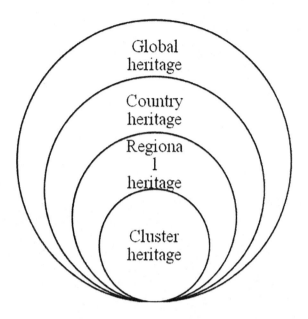

attention to the knowledge and innovations management problems as a part of global heritage. In the author's opinion, the global heritage in the knowledge and innovation context includes three key types of heritage (Fig. 15.1).

These types of heritage have a strong link between each other and the global heritage. The global heritage evaluation can be represented as a function, which can be expressed by Eq. 15.1.

$$GH = f(CH, RH, ClH) \tag{15.1}$$

where

CH   country heritage;
RH   regional heritage;
ClH   cluster heritage.

At the cluster level heritage can be described as a network of interactions, which includes knowledge, innovations, people, and infrastructure (Sarach 2015). Every organization in the cluster has their own policies, values, traditions, behaviors. Thereby, the cluster heritage represents the result of the synergy and emergence effects from interconnected organizations. In the same way at the regional and country levels, the heritage concentrates knowledge and innovations from all clusters in the region and country, respectively.

It stands to mention that the global heritage can be differing from initial knowledge and innovations. For clear understanding of the global heritage development process, it is recommended to examine every key type of heritage using two different models: the SECI model of knowledge dimensions (Nonaka and Takeuchi 1995) and the triple helix model (Etzkowitz and Leydesdorff 1995).

15.2 Methodological Support

Before proceeding to the description of the author's heritage management model, let's consider the SECI model of knowledge dimensions (Nonaka and Takeuchi 1995) and the triple helix model (Etzkowitz and Leydesdorff 1995).

Prior to the twentieth century, business and other organizations functioned in a less complex environment than that of today. Under these conditions, the heritage can become global in case of tacit and explicit knowledge dimensions (Fig. 15.2).

As shown in Fig. 15.2, the model of the process of creating knowledge is the interconnection and combination of tacit and explicit knowledge. As a result of the combination, there are four ways to create knowledge (socialization, externalization, combination, and internalization). This model has gained wide popularity, and many researchers specialized in the knowledge management often use it as the universal scientific instrument.

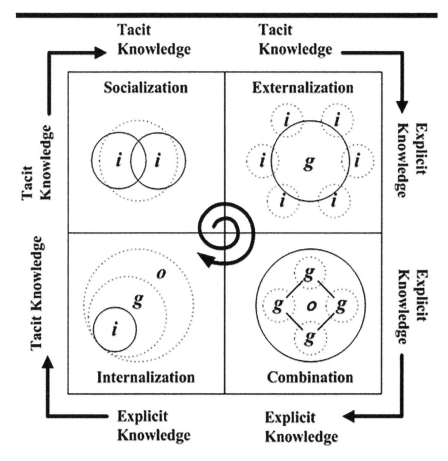

Fig. 15.2 SECI model of knowledge dimensions. *Source* Nonaka and Takeuchi 1995

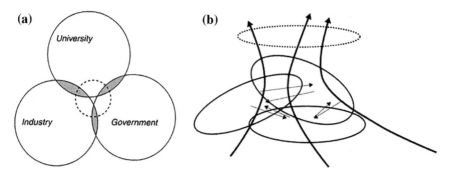

Fig. 15.3 Triple helix model. *Source* Etzkowitz and Leydesdorff 1995

One more model, which can help to analyze the global heritage development process, is the triple helix model (Fig. 15.3).

The main idea of it has been described in detail in the paper "The Triple Helix of University-Industry-Government Relations" (Leydesdorff 2012). According to this paper, the close interactions between university, industry, and government are a necessary condition for new quality of economic growth.

15.3 Results and Discussion

As follows from the analysis above, the global heritage management is perhaps the most important aspect of heritage. In the author's opinion, functions of the global heritage management are not only accumulation and conservation of knowledge and innovations, but also applying them for solving the global problems of dynamic world of increased population, migrations problems, global warming, water scarcity, air pollution.

In this connection, it was decided to suggest the model of the global heritage management (Fig. 15.4). The global heritage management model has three critical components: initial knowledge and innovations, "lens" of the global heritage, and focus of the global heritage (Fig. 15.5).

According to the author's model, the heritage management process has some phases. The knowledge and innovations flow passing through the "lens" of micro-, meso-, and macro-levels. The "lens" represents the combination of two models: the SECI model of knowledge dimensions and the triple helix model. Therefore, some initial information about knowledge and innovations becomes misconstrued, forming particular focus of global heritage.

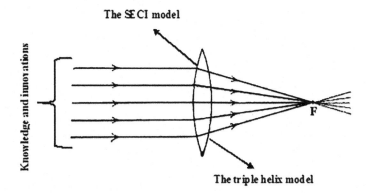

Fig. 15.4 Model of the global heritage management. *Source* Author

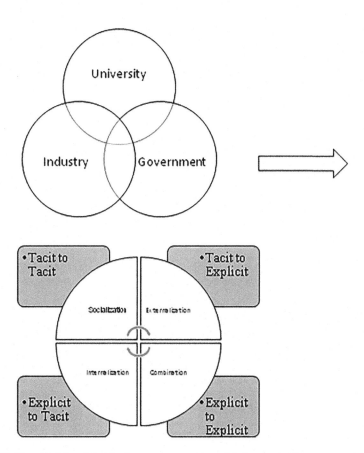

Fig. 15.5 "Lens" of the global heritage management model. *Source* Author

15.4 Conclusions

The study results show the meaning and importance of global heritage management. It is worthwhile to say that the suggested model of the global heritage management is a universal model. It can be used not only in economics, but also in cultural and historical branches.

References

Etzkowitz, H., & Leydesdorff, L. (1995). The Triple Helix of University-Industry-Government relations: A laboratory for knowledge-based economic development. *EASST Review, 14,* 14–19.

Leydesdorff, L. (February 2012). *The Triple Helix of University-Industry-government relations* (p. 4), https://core.ac.uk/download/files/418/11888706.pdf.

Nonaka, I., & Takeuchi, H. (1995). *The knowledge creating company: How Japanese companies create the dynamics of innovation* (pp. 62–71). New York: Oxford University Press.

Sarach, L. (2015). Innovative interpretation of heritage management in industrial clusters. *Procedia—Social and Behavioral Sciences, 188,* 170–173.

Chapter 16
Smart Specialization in Supporting SMES in the Tourism Sector Through Innovative Clusters

Liliana Scutaru, Gabriela Prelipcean and Angela-Nicoleta Cozorici

Abstract The paper aims to identify the competitive advantages of the tourism sector in Romania and to conduct radiography of the SMEs in this sector, including their concern in which regards the R&D activities, as part of smart specialization strategies promoted by the EU. There are also studied the opportunities in exploiting the Romania's competitive advantages by the SMEs in the tourism sector through development of innovative clusters in the area, which enhance the performance of R&D activities and increase the competitiveness of companies. There are also analysed the sources of funding from EU programs for the 2014–2020 financial framework as support for increasing competitiveness and regional development through support and intelligent promotion of tourism sector. At the end of the paper, solutions and courses of action (policies) in this area are offered, leading to national and regional sustainable economic development.

Keywords Smart specialization · Tourism · SMEs · Innovative clusters
Competitive advantages · R&D

16.1 Introduction

The smart specialization strategy promoted by the European Union for the 2014–2020 financial framework represents a new vision of economic development seen as an innovative strategy that offers the possibility of a beneficial economic change at regional and local levels.

The main idea around which the strategy is built does not consist in an even recipe that can be applied to all countries or regions of a country, but consists in developing finding development solutions specific to each territory in accordance to its characteristics. Essentially, it comes to the initial endowment with production

L. Scutaru (✉) · G. Prelipcean · A.-N. Cozorici
Stefancel Mare University of Suceava, Universitatii 13,
720229 Suceava, Romania
e-mail: lilianas@seap.usv.ro

© Springer International Publishing AG, part of Springer Nature 2019
V. Vasile (ed.), *Caring and Sharing: The Cultural Heritage Environment as an Agent for Change*, Springer Proceedings in Business and Economics,
https://doi.org/10.1007/978-3-319-89468-3_16

factors, climate, natural resources, human resources and even created resources. In other words, it is necessary to identify the strengths and the potential held by a region or a country that have comparative advantages, and to focus on their amplification so that they can be transformed into competitive advantage at national and international levels.

This aims to identify those areas or sectors for which the regions have the greatest development opportunities through the potential which they hold and also to direct the national or the EU funding allocation to those economic sectors. At the same time, the smart specialization aims the conveyance of these funds towards those economic sectors that can generate high and very high added value that are capable of international competitiveness (European Commission 2015a). Basically, this strategy, from our point of view, has as a starting point the idea of international labour division, but amplified and applied specifically on several levels: national, regional and even local levels.

The key priority of the smart specialization strategy consists in stimulating and supporting research and development activities (R&D) as the key competitive factor, aspect that fosters cooperation, inter- and intra-sectorial connections and knowledge outsourcing. The investments in innovation, one of the priorities of Europe 2020 strategy (European Commission 2010) are offering support for strengthening partnerships between universities, research centres and business environment and, at the same time, they create jobs and represent a main instrument of the cohesion policy at the EU regions level.

16.2 Smart Specialization and Directions of Industrial Policy

In March 2014, the European Council concluded that, both at European and national level, it is necessary to create a framework conducive to innovation and sustainability, stating that smart specialization should be supported in order to facilitate contacts between enterprises and groups and to improve the access to the innovative technologies (European Commission 2014). This issue can be supported by a Europe-wide reform based mainly on policy consolidation for creating and supporting the innovative clusters. It is envisaged, however, the implementation of a process which will facilitate the cooperation between public research institutions and private companies in order to develop common research agenda focused on long term.

In Romania, for the 2014–2020 strategic cycle, there have been identified several areas of smart specialization based on their natural, scientific and commercial potential, and also there have been established the directions for the industrial policy. The tourism is among them a priority of the Romania's development policy, being mentioned among the industrial policy directions in three of the five areas of smart specialization. This aspect highlights the enormous potential that the tourism and ecotourism in Romania own, currently untapped to its full potential.

It is acknowledged that Romania has many unique historical and geographical objectives in the world, from the Danube Delta to the Dacian fortresses or to the monasteries from Moldova and Maramures, included in the UNESCO World Heritage, together with its various and rich cultural, religious and spiritual resources. All these elements constitute the competitive advantages of the Romanian tourism sector. However, in Romania there are 5 of the 11 bio-geographic regions of Europe that are in compliance with the ecotourism requirements at EU level, an aspect that confers Romania multiple regional comparative advantages.

A detailed presentation of the indicators revealing information on the current situation of the tourism sector in Romania can be observed in Table 16.1.

Table 16.1 provides information on SMEs and labour force employed in the Romanian tourism sector. For the entire analysed period, the share of SMEs is about 99,9% of all enterprises operating in the tourism field, aspect that is representative across Europe. In contrast, the percentage of employees is reduced, less than 3%, aspect which highlights an under dimension of the real absorption capacity of the sector. Regarding the evolution of data for the period analysed, the years 2010–2011 recorded the lowest values, both in terms of number of SMEs and their employees, fact which is explained by the effects of the financial crisis traversed by Romania. Starting with 2012, the number of employees increases, reflecting a positive situation.

The country's economic development through tourism can be achieved by improving the infrastructure of the existing tourist resorts and by creating new ones, as the potential exists all over the country, by increasing employability of the workforce in this sector, by enhancement of natural heritage and a more effective policy of promoting tourist destinations and products and including them in the tourist circuit at European level and worldwide. Tourism holds a share of about 3% of all employees at country level, and the proportion is almost double, if we add the related sectors. Even if currently the share of tourism to GDP is modest,

Table 16.1 Tourism sector indicators

Indicators	2008	2009	2010	2011	2012	2013	2014
Enterprises active in the tourism sector (total)	23.653	26.170	24.402	22.210	23.499	24.297	25.111
SMEs active in the tourism sector	23.631	26.151	24.379	22.186	23.473	24.272	25.083
SMEs active in the tourism sector (%)	99,90	99,92	99,90	99,89	99,88	99,89	99,88
Total employees in the economy sector (thou.)	5.233	4.879	4.581	4.660	4.777	4.801	4.901
Employees in tourism sector (thou.)	122	121	112	119	131	138	145
Employees in tourism sector (%)	2,33	2,48	2,44	2,55	2,74	2,87	2,95

Source Adaptation from Romanian Statistical Yearbook, 2009–2015

approximately 1,6–1,9%, the estimates are predicting a growth of the percentage of about 4% by 2025 (Travel & Tourism Economic Impact 2015 Romania).

The research & development and innovation activities are the essence of the smart specialization strategy for the current financial framework of the EU—and they support the regional development and the global competitiveness. The research & development and innovation in Romania hold low levels of approximately 0,37–0,40% of GDP, issue that requires a reorientation of the state policies and priority ranking in the immediate future. The situation of innovation activities in the Romanian tourism companies can be assessed following Table 16.2, respectively, Fig. 16.1.

The data presented reveal that innovation activities of SMEs in the tourism sector are largely oriented towards developing new products, especially new market services and introducing new management and marketing approaches. In return, it is noted that many of the companies belonging to the tourism sector are not interested and do not consider as a priority the concerns for innovation.

Table 16.2 Innovation in SMEs from the tourism sector (%)

Innovation efforts have focused on the development of:	2008	2009	2010	2011	2012	2013	2014	2015
New products	52,63	36,0	14,29	46,36	32,59	50,00	27,78	13,51
New technologies	34,21	32,0	3,90	11,82	9,63	7,89	13,89	0,00
New managerial and marketing approaches	15,79	24,0	14,29	33,64	2,96	43,42	47,22	21,62
Upgrading IT system	2,63	24,0	9,09	6,36	15,56	7,89	2,78	10,81
Human Resources Training	23,68	20,0	6,49	6,36	12,59	6,58	8,33	8,11
Not the case	15,79	20,0	57,14	23,64	37,04	25,00	22,22	59,46

Source The White Charter of SMEs in Romania, 2009–2015

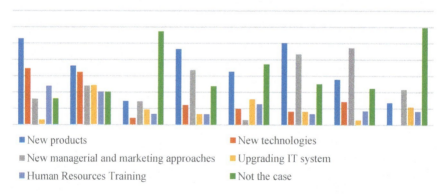

■ New products   ■ New technologies
■ New managerial and marketing approaches   ■ Upgrading IT system
■ Human Resources Training   ■ Not the case

Fig. 16.1 Innovation in SMEs from the tourism sector

This issue have as a main cause the lack of funds for financing the activities conducted by companies or the difficulty of accessing funding, along with a wide range of other causes, such as the size of companies, knowing that the vast majority of them are small in size, being a family business; another reason may be that SMEs are more oriented towards the domestic market which has as main actors local customers, less demanding and not on the external ones; some companies have seasonal character meaning a lack of priority for investment in innovation; many of the SMEs come from related fields such as food industry wood exploitation and do not represent the main form of insurance for the daily living.

The conclusion consists of Romanian tourism sector need to be reoriented towards adding value through activities of R&D and innovation, market development, expansion and diversification of the tourism offer and increase its quality, and that, finally, lead to increased sector competitiveness.

Furthermore, the SMEs of the Romanian tourism sector need support for from local, regional and also national authorities for understanding the need to increase the concerns for innovation, facilitating access to finance by offering a wide range of financing instruments, including non-reimbursable funds EU (Scutaru et al. 2014). This measure meets the requirements of the smart development strategy in which Romania has committed in order to respond to the criteria of competitiveness and economic growth.

16.3 Smart Specialization and Innovative Clusters

The EU regional development policy, and at the same time, of competitiveness and supporting R&D and innovation policies, is based primarily on the creation and development of innovative clusters that support smart specialization, designed to support regional development and reducing disparities between countries and regions, growth and economic development of all EU states. It is also widely accepted the idea that, both at European and international level, the clusters represent, in the current stage of the economic development, the most effective solution for recovery and efficiency of economic activities at the level of the economic factors, are jobs generators, create added value and represent R&D incentives, and are generating GDP regionally, and therefore nationally.

The importance of clusters consists in the economic benefits created, benefits that could extend on several levels. Thus, it has been found (Porter 1998) that the efficiency of the companies constituting a cluster is clearly superior compared to the case where it acted in isolation. This matter is explained by far more efficient use of assets and more specialized suppliers with shorter reaction times. Another benefit arises from the increased capacity for innovation. When working together, the firms and the research organizations can obtain better results in creativity and research activity, being stimulated in the innovation process of the permanent connection with customers and other companies. The permanent concern for innovation has led to the concept of innovative cluster (Porter 2001), a theme to who are dedicated new studies constantly. Finally, last but not least, the companies within the clusters are less susceptible to failure and the level of business development tends to be higher in clusters.

Cluster-based economic development can be seen as a new development model through microeconomic policies, widely extended, because the clusters are "essential engines for the economic ensemble of a region or a nation", playing a key role in this process (Ketels 2003, p. 19). Successively, clusters can help create a new vision on economic policymaking by the public and private sectors characterized by collaboration and consensus of all stakeholders, creating thus a two-way relationship between the two sides.

The tourism clusters exist in many European countries, most of them with a highly efficient activity. For example, Italian clusters are structured in different categories, such as clusters in the food and wine industry, health and tourism, tourism contributing with 10,3% in GDP in 2013 (Ali et al. 2014). In Spain, tourism clusters are mature, and firms belonging to clusters generate a higher profit than the other companies (Segarra-Oña et al. 2011). In contrast, in Greece tourism clustering occurs after 2000, based on national strategies in this domain. They still need support through local policies, particularly in rural areas, and to increase trust between cluster members (Partalidou and Koutsou 2012). Tourism in Greece has a contribution of about 17% in annual GDP, and the government is very interested in supporting this sector.

In Romania, there are currently (March 2016) seven clusters operating in tourism that began to emerge since 2008. Some of them have structures under consolidation being not yet specified the number of members or the composition of SMEs since the accession of SMEs in the cluster is in full swing, as shown in Table 16.3.

The clustering process in Romania is underway as a result of smart specialization strategy requirements, as a condition of access to the funds that EU provides for SMEs for the 2014–2020 financial framework. Regarding this process, we can say that it produces fairly slowly, due to the fact that it was found that companies are reluctant to join an association, to work and develop strategies together, to create partnerships, to trust the partners cluster because these are considered on the contrary competitors. The psychological explanation of this phenomenon consist in the mandatory methods of association in the communist period that many of the current SMEs managers, as well as the employees, still remember.

For that reason, it has been found that in Romania does not work the traditional model "triple helix" (Etzkowitz and Leydesdorff 1995) which brings together business environment universities and/or research centres and public authorities, but it works the pattern "four clover" (Guth and Cosnita 2010), in which case the initial model is complemented by catalysts organizations, such as chambers of commerce and industry, innovation and technology transfer centres, consultancy companies. However, in both cases the existence of successful clusters is based on innovation activities, an aspect that contributes to the economic success of a country or region (Porter 1990).

The layout in a territorial plan of the tourism sector clusters from Romania is shown in Fig. 16.2.

Table 16.3 Clusters from tourism sector

No.	Cluster name	Year founded	No of members/ companies	Location
1	Turinn Cluster	2010	20/10	South-West Oltenia Region
2	Tourism Oltenia Cluster	2012	66/26	South-West Oltenia Region
3	Tourism Regional Cluster	2008	39/32	North East Region
4	Bio-Danubius Cluster	2015	na	South-East Region
5	Touristic Danube Cluster	2014	64/na	Interregional: West, South-West, South-Muntenia and South-East Regions
6	Carpathian Tourism Cluster Romania	2010	na	Interregional: South-East Region, South-Muntenia Region and Centre
7	Youth Tourism Cluster	2014	na	Bucharest-Ilfov Region

Source www.clustero.eu and the clusters sites

The map reveals that, in their vast majority, the clusters from the tourism sector in Romania are located in the southern half part of the country. Some of the clusters have several particularities:

Fig. 16.2 Clusters from the tourism sector in Romania in March 2016

- A first peculiarity is represented by the interregional cluster from the centre of the country, Carpathian Tourism Cluster, consisting of tourist SMEs belonging to three regions: South-East, South-Muntenia and Centre. We can say that this cluster capitalizes the tourist potential of an area with many natural, cultural, historical, religious and spiritual valences which constitute, at the same time, in competitive and comparative advantages. This aspect enables the clusters SMEs to overcome the seasonal nature of activities, this representing a great advantage in their favour.
- The Touristic Danube Cluster presents the second peculiarity, as it does not comply with a typical arrangement at a regional level in terms of regional concentration of SMEs from its composition, but it extends along the whole Danube River route in Romania, from Baziaş to Sulina. Thereby, we can say that this cluster is interregional, including the West, South-West, South-Muntenia and South–East Regions. In the case of this atypical cluster, the question is the seasonality for SMEs from its composition, which forces them to continue finding innovative solutions for tourism activities during the cold season.
- Bio-Danubius Cluster owns also a peculiarity among the country's tourist clusters, being characterized by multi-sectorial activities, being situated at the confluence between biological agriculture, tourism industry and capitalization of the natural bio-resources from the Danube Delta Natural Reservation, notably the renewable energies in the region. We believe that, as SMEs in the composition of this cluster will strengthen their cooperation and mutual trust, they will form several distinct clusters differentiated on several economic sectors in order to enhance their competitiveness.
- Finally, the Youth Tourism Cluster is the first cluster constituted at a global level, being dedicated to young people, which brings together tourism SMEs from the area of the country capital, the city of Bucharest. The idea is totally innovative and presents both comparative and competitive advantages of the area, offering a very tourist services to a well-defined segment of elderly tourists, both local and foreign tourists. Tourism for Youth is an opportunity for Romania and is seen as a niche that deserves to be fully valued, given the fact that young people represent over one-third of the total worldwide tourists, are less demanding and less affected by the weaknesses of Romania, such as infrastructure.

Romanian authorities expect that in the next 1–2 years the number of clusters in tourism area to increase up to at least 50, in each county of the country to be at least one cluster contributing to the development of the area and having its own tourism products and strategy, aspect that will improve the performance of R&D activities and will increase the competitiveness of SMEs from tourism sector.

16.4 Non-Reimbursable Financing Methods for SMEs in the Tourism Sector in the 2014–2020 Financial Framework

Given that tourism is one of the strategic sectors of Romania's development, which presents multiple comparative and competitive advantages at the regional level, for the 2014–2020 financial framework there are available through the European Regional Development Fund (ERDF) numerous sources of financing, both through the Regional Operational Programme (ROP), entirely dedicated to SMEs from the tourism sector and through the Competitiveness Operational Programme (COP) targeted to productivity growth of SMEs by supporting the competitiveness of companies, including the creation and development of innovative clusters.

For the previous period 2007–2013, the total budget allocated to ROP was of 4,4 billion Euros and the distribution of financing was conducted on 6 priority axes, in the current financial framework, the allocated funds are of 8,25 billion Euros, of which 6,7% billion represents EU support, respectively, 1,5 billion Euros from national contribution (state budget, local budgets) (MRDPA 2015), their distribution being operational on 12 priority axes, as shown in Table 16.4.

Therefore, the corresponding financing allocations of the priority axes 2, 5 and 7 are assigned to sustainable development and tourism promotion in Romania as well as to supporting SMEs from the tourism sector. If in the previous financial framework, the ROP allocations that financed the tourism were of 663,3 million Euros (MCROP 2013), from Table 16.5 it can be observed that the total amount is of 1240,24 million Euros, a sum twice as high.

In addition to these funds, there are provided 10,75 million Euros for implementing the EU Strategy for the Danube Region (European Commission 2011) for Axis 7 of the project. In addition, for continuing in the current financial framework the implementation of the project "Integrated Strategy for Sustainable Development of the Danube Delta 2030" through Integrated Territorial Investment mechanisms, known as ITI Delta (MRDPA 2013) there are provided 63,83 million Euros for Axis 2 of the project, 44,88 million Euros for Axis 5 and for Axis 7 there are allocated 5,19 million Euros. Furthermore, the European Agricultural Fund for Rural Development (EAFRD) provides sources of funding for local tourism in rural areas allocated through the National Rural Development Programme (NRDP) for the period 2014–2020, as is shown Table 16.5.

NRDP provides support for micro and small enterprises for creating non-agricultural activities in rural areas. This measure aims at diversifying the rural economy through the development of services and creating jobs. The amount of support is 50.000 Euros/project, with the possibility of increasing to 70.000 Euros/project for the activities in agricultural tourism. In addition, the financial support is granted for the creation and development of non-agricultural activities in order to diversify the economic activities, increasing incomes and creating occupational alternatives for the rural population.

Table 16.4 Priority axis of ROP for Romania and EU financial allocations

No.	Priority axis of ROP	Financial allocations 2014–2020 (mil. Euros)
1	Promotion of technology transfer	175,53
2	Improving the competitiveness of SMEs	744,68
3	Supporting the transition to a low carbon economy	2003,38
4	Supporting sustainable urban development	1178,83
5	Improving the urban environment and conservation, protection and sustainable valorization of the cultural heritage	394,50
6	Improvement of road infrastructure of local and regional importance	907,45
7	Diversification of local economies through sustainable tourism development	101,06
8	Health and social infrastructure development	425,53
9	Supporting the economic and social regeneration of disadvantaged urban communities	95,74
10	Improving the educational infrastructure	296,70
11	Geographical expansion of the system of property registration in cadastre and land registry	265,96
12	Technical assistance	110,64

Source The Regional Operational Programme 2014–2020, May 2015

Table 16.5 Financial allocation through NRDP

Priority areas for intervention	Financial allocation 2014–2020
Support for the creation of non-agricultural activities in rural areas	50.000–70.000 Euros/project
Investments in the creation and development of non-agricultural activities	Maximum 200.000 Euros/beneficiary
Investments associated with the cultural heritage protection	Maximum 500.000 Euros (for public utility projects that do not generate income)
	Maximum 200.000 Euros (for public utility projects that generate income)

Source Adaptation from EAFRD, National Rural Development Programme (NRDP) for the period 2014–2020

The local heritage protection is also a concern of the authorities, a measure which grants financial support for the restoration, maintenance and upgrading of cultural and monastic establishments, preserving traditions and spiritual heritage. This aspect has a positive impact on the local tourism and stimulates the local business development.

Regarding the financing of SMEs that are part of innovative clusters, this can be achieved through the Competitiveness Operational Programme (COP) which has allocated a budget of 620 million Euros for the period 2015–2020 and is designed primarily for start-ups. In this case, beneficiaries of the funds are the cluster management organizations.

Through these funds, there are financed various projects, such as research and innovation projects related to tourism, creation of incubators for tourist services, development of innovative tourism services development of niche tourism (eco-tourism, cultural tourism, spa tourism, sports tourism, gastronomic tourism, etc.), protection and rehabilitation of cultural and heritage objectives, increasing the employability and skills of human resources in tourism, projects for the creation and support for SMEs, including through the creation and development of clusters between the tourism sector and related industries in order to extend the tourist season and the regional tourism product diversification, etc. (European Commission 2015b).

The conclusion that can be drawn from this analysis of the funds available to SMEs in the tourism sector for the 2014–2020 financial framework is that the range of grants is broader and also more focused on a few strategic priorities that support the actions of R&D and innovation for the regional development through smart promoting and growth of the competitiveness of the tourism sector in Romania.

16.5 Conclusions and Proposals

For the 2014–2020 financial framework in Romania, there have identified several areas of smart specialization based on natural, scientific and commercial potential and also there have been established directions for industrial policy. The tourism sector is a priority of Romania's development, being found among the directions for industrial policy in three of the five areas of smart specialization.

SMEs in the Romanian tourism sector have a share of about 99,90% of all enterprises operating in tourism, a situation similar at European level, still, the percentage of employees is reduced, less than 3%, which emphasizes an under dimension of the actual absorption capacity of the sector.

The analysis of the innovation activities from SMEs in Romanian tourism sector shows that concerns are largely concentrated on new product development, particularly on the new services provided on the market on introducing new management and marketing approaches. However, it is noted that a significant proportion of firms are not interested and do not consider as a priority the concerns for innovation. We conclude that it is necessary that the Romanian tourism sector to be refocused towards adding value through R&D activities and innovation, market development, expanding and diversifying the tourist offer and improving its quality, aspects that lead to greater competitiveness of the sector.

In the 2014–2020 financial framework, the Romanian tourism sector has a wide range of funding opportunities through the European Regional Development Fund, both through the Regional Operational Programme, targeted for SMEs in tourism, as well as through the Competitiveness Operational Programme, aimed to increase the productivity and competitiveness of the companies, including the creation and development of innovative clusters. Also there are provided funds for the implementation of the EU Strategy for the Danube Region and for the project Integrated Strategy for sustainable development of the Danube Delta 2030. The third source of funding comes from the National Programme for Rural Development for the financing of local rural tourism and for the restoration and protection of local cultural heritage.

In Romania, there are currently seven clusters in the tourism sector, but in the coming years it is expected that their number to reach at least 50, given the fact that there is tourism potential in every county.

This paper proposes policies in this field, in order to increase the competitiveness of the Romanian tourism sector and to meet the smart development strategy, that are primarily based on good cooperation between local, regional and national authorities. Thus, it is necessary to continue the SMEs clustering policy in tourism sector as it constitutes an efficient way of access to EU funds and to support the growth of R&D and innovation, aspects that lead to an enhanced productivity and company's competitiveness. Also, the Regional Development Agencies (ADR) can create IT platforms in order to facilitate the communication and good practices between Romanian tourism SMEs. It is necessary, as well, the creation of relational networks within each clusters; all members should have access to the good practices, that fosters creativity and innovation and help SMEs to overcome the current barrier of non-cooperation. At the same time, it is necessary to create, at the regional and local level, an efficient system of training and retraining of the human capital of the companies, considering that the tourism sector in Romania has a high percentage of low qualified workforce. Providing the national financial support for those SMEs that adheres to the clusters through a soft loan granted through a bank designated by the government would be a complementary measure for EU funds. Also, it is required the internationalization of Romanian tourism clusters by establishing partnerships with tourism clusters from other countries, in order to have specialized human capital, networking communication and international good practices. There can be involved both the state and RDAs or the local authorities.

All the aspects presented as policies proposals, such as clustering in tourism, the financing sources, private or mixed, the human resource development in tourism, respectively, the internationalization of this domain can be themselves subjects of research in the future and would require closer analysis, thereby constituting for us directions for future research.

References

Ali, Y., Ciaschini, M., Pretaroli, R., Severini, F., & Socci, C. (2014). *Economic relevance of Tourism industry: The Italian case*. Università degli Studi di Macerata, Dipartimento di Economia e Diritto, Quaderno di Dipartimento n. 72, June, available at http://economiaediritto. unimc.it/it/ricerca/pubblicazioni/quaderni/QDed722014.pdf.

Etzkowitz, H., & Leydesdorff, L. (1995). The Triple Helix -University-Industry-government relations: A laboratory for knowledge based economic development. *EASST Review, 14,* 14–19.

European Commission. (2010). *Europe 2020 strategy, communication from the commission Europe 2020, A strategy for smart, sustainable and inclusive growth.* Brussels, 3.3.2010, COM (2010)2020 final.

European Commission. (2011). *EU strategy for the Danube region.*

European Commission. (2014). *Reindustrialising Europe.*

European Commission. (2015a). *Perspectives for research and innovation strategies for smart specialization (RIS 3) in the wider context of the Europe 2020 growth strategy.*

European Commission. (2015b). *Guide on EU funding 2014–2020 for the tourism sector.*

Guth, M., & Cosnita, D. (2010). *Clusters and potential clusters in Romania—A mapping exercise,* February.

Ketels, C. (2003). *Clusters of innovation in Europe, in structural change in Europe 3—Innovative city and business regions.* Bollschweil: Hagbarth Publications.

Ministry of Regional Development and Public Administration (MRDPA). (2013). *Integrated strategy for sustainable development of the Danube delta 2030.*

Ministry of Regional Development and Public Administration (MRDPA). (2015). *The regional operational programme 2014–2020,* May.

Partalidou, M., & Koutsou, S. (2012). Locally and socially embedded tourism clusters in rural Greece. *Tourismos: An International Multidisciplinary Journal of Tourism, 7*(1), 99–116, Spring-Summer, UDC: 338.48 + 640(050).

Porter, M. E. (1990). The competitive advantage of nations. *Harvard Business Review,* 73–91.

Porter, M. E. (1998). Clusters and the new economics of competition. *Harvard Business Review, 76*(6), 77–90.

Porter, M. E. (2001). *Council on competitiveness and monitor group, clusters of innovation initiative: Regional foundations of U.S. competitiveness.* Washington, DC: Council on Competitiveness.

Scutaru, L., Prelipcean, G. & Cozorici, A.-N. (2014). *Financing SMEs from the tourism sector and valorization of local cultural heritage.* Paper presented at the International Conference "Heritage as an alternative driver for sustainable development and economic recovery in South East Europe", Basilicata, Italy, 11–14th April 2014.

Segarra-Oña, M., Miret-Pastor, L. G., Peiro-Signes, A., & Verma, R. (2011). The effects of localization on economic performance: Analysis of Spanish tourism clusters. *European Planning Studies, 20*(8), 1319–1334.

The Authority on World Travel & Tourism. (2015). *Travel and tourism economic impact, 2015, Romania.*

The Monitoring Committee of the Regional Operational Programme (MCROP). (2013). *The implementation status of the Regional Operational Programme 2007–2013,* 28–29 May.

The National Rural Development Programme for the period 2014–2020.

The Regional Operational Programme 2007–2013. (2013). *The annual implementation report, version 3,* May.

Chapter 17
Challenges and Innovations to Sustainable Forest Management in Romania: Virgin Forests as Heritage

Victor Platon, Simona Frone and Andreea Constantinescu

Abstract Protection of forest cover has a primary importance in conserving natural heritage, as well as sustaining other forms of life and land use. As argued in our previous research, sustainable forest management (SFM) is therefore supported by the necessity to preserve, value, and develop forest ecosystem services and the total economic value of forests, as part of a country's natural heritage. This chapter will emphasize the role of virgin forests in Romania, as a part of cultural heritage. Our approach is motivated by the need to protect and increase awareness of the significant heritage represented by the virgin forest in Romania. We start by highlighting some of the most important current developments concerning forests in the European Union (EU) and Romania. In this respect, we analyze the ranking of European countries, including Romania, with regard to their share of forestry areas across Europe. In Romania, what stands out is the peculiar increase of forest areas in the last decade, which can be explained by the changes in methodology used for classification and data gathering, due to the new Forestry Code. The next section of our chapter is dedicated to the importance of virgin forests as natural heritage sites. These are mostly represented by natural beech forests located in several remote counties. The value of Romanian virgin forest is proven by the current ongoing nomination process to include them in the United Nations Educational, Scientific and Cultural Organization (UNESCO) World Heritage List. Romania's virgin forests are a national, European and global heritage—so the task of protecting this natural heritage should not be left solely to the private forest owners. It is required to have the intervention of the state and efforts by public authorities to continue having and sustainably manage these forests. The impulse for protection of such forests came from NGO and activists in biodiversity protection, foresters etc.

Keywords Natural heritage · Virgin forest · Sustainable forest management instruments · Forest ecosystem services

V. Platon · S. Frone (✉) · A. Constantinescu
Institute of National Economy-Romanian Academy, 050711 Bucharest, Romania
e-mail: simona.frone@yahoo.com

© Springer International Publishing AG, part of Springer Nature 2019   203
V. Vasile (ed.), *Caring and Sharing: The Cultural Heritage Environment
as an Agent for Change*, Springer Proceedings in Business and Economics,
https://doi.org/10.1007/978-3-319-89468-3_17

17.1 Introduction

This chapter aims to show the main challenges facing, and innovations adopted by, Romania with regard to forest management with a special focus on virgin forests that are an important heritage asset. As is already known, forests support life and biodiversity; stabilize our climate; reduce high wind speeds thus preventing soil erosion; contribute to carbon sequestration; provide us with smart, natural, and sustainable materials and energy; and offer a better environment for tourism. Currently, forests are under significant danger from fires, pests, floods and diseases, climate change, etc. In addition, people are a significant threat to forests either through overexploitation or by failing to protect them.

The virgin forests that still exist in Romania have a significant value from the point of view of heritage, so it is important to protect them. In this respect, sustainable forest management instruments and practices are required.

17.2 European Union Approach to Forest Protection

The new European Union (EU) strategy for forests and the forestry sector (COM (2013) 659 final) specifies that although the socioeconomic importance of forests in the EU is high, it is often underestimated.

Of equal importance to natural heritage conservation is maintenance of forests, which is the key to sustaining biodiversity and life forms. It is well known that forests provide a large range of services to society, including: protection against soil erosion, desertification, and avalanches; water retention and flood prevention; reduction of wind intensity; reduction of temperatures in urban areas; carbon sequestration; enhancement of tourism activities and biodiversity, etc. (European Communities 2003).

As stressed by Platon et al. (2015), all these services need to be given a value and included in the price of timber or other goods provided by exploiting forests. It should be mentioned that besides the economic functions of forests, all other ecological, social, and bequest functions are interrelated and integrated. These increase the value of forest ecosystem services.

The importance of sustainable forest management (SFM) is supported by the necessity to preserve value and develop forest ecosystem services, and the total economic value of forests, as part of member states natural heritage. Therefore, it is considered that ensuring the sustainable management of forests is essential if we want to enjoy a balanced development of resources and the benefits from EU forests.

Some facts about EU forests are given here:

- Forests contribute to rural development providing approximately three million jobs across the EU.

- Wood is still the main source of financial income from forests. So, a strategy needs to take into account the EU's forest-based industries, which fall within the EU's industrial policy.
- Wood is also considered an important source of raw materials for bio-emerging industries.
- According to the latest data, forests and other wooded land covers more than 40% of Europe's land area, having varied character from one region to another.
- Afforestation and natural evolution have contributed to an increase in forest area in the EU by about 0.4% per year in recent decades.

However, global forested areas continue to decline (mainly in the Amazon area, Indonesia, Southeast Asia, and Africa). Currently, in the EU, only 60–70% of annual forestry growth is cut, leading to an increasing forested area. However, member states, with regard to land use, land-use change, and forestry (LULUCF), expect the operating ratio to increase by about 30% by the year 2020, compared to 2010.

About 60% of EU forests belong to several million private owners and their numbers have tended to increase, given that some member states continue the process of restitution of land to former forest owners. The remainder of forests belong to the state and other public owners.

17.3 Forests in Romania

Eurostat data shows that in 2000–2010 the Romanian State (the biggest owner of public forests) recorded the largest loss of forestry funding in Europe. In Romania and other new EU countries, forests in public property came out in the red while public sector in countries such as Bulgaria or Spain went on to increase forest areas.

The area actually covered by forest in Romania is 6373 million ha, accounting for 97.6% of Romania's national forests. The difference represents 156 ha which is land intended for cultivation, production, forest administration, forest roads, land destined to some unproductive occupation and litigation, other surfaces, etc.

By comparison with the situation in Europe (average), Romania has a surface area of which 29% is forest, well below the European average of 45%. This European average value (45%) is greatly affected by Russia with a huge forested area (809 million ha). If we calculate the European average without including the Russia Federation the average is 33%. The countries with the next largest percentages of forest cover are the 28.2 million ha of Sweden and Finland's 21.15 million ha. With 6.5 million ha of forest, Romania ranks 12th in Europe (Table 17.1).

In terms of shares of surfaces covered with forests, Finland is first with 73% and Sweden is second with 69%. From this perspective, Romania ranks 29th in Europe. According to official data, Romania's forests cover an area of 6529 million ha. An area of 3228 million ha or 49.53% (as of 31 December 2013) of the 6.5 million ha

Table 17.1 Forested areas in European countries

Country	Forests areas (thou. ha)	Share of forestry areas in total (%)
Albania	776	28
Andorra	16	36
Austria	3887	47
Belarus	8630	42
Belgium	678	22
Bosnia & Herzegovina	2185	43
Bulgaria	3927	36
Croatia	1920	34
Czech Rep.	2657	34
Estonia	2217	52
Finland	22157	73
France	15954	29
Germany	11076	32
Italy	9149	31
Norway	10065	33
Poland	9337	30
Portugal	3456	38
Romania	6573	29
Russian Federation	809090	49
Serbia	2713	31
Slovakia	1933	40
Slovenia	1253	62
Spain	18173	36
Sweden	28203	69
Ukraine	9705	17
United Kingdom	2881	12
Europe	1005000	45

Source Global Forest Resources Assessment, 2010

Note The top 10 countries in terms of area covered by forests are colored red; countries that have higher rates than the European average are colored green

of forest, is owned by the state, which administers the land through the National Forest Administration, Romsilva.

The total area of forest which is public property is managed by Romsilva through 41 silvic directorates and the Institute for Silvic Research. Public forest represents 3,227,907 ha, about half Romania's national forest (Drăgoi 2008).

Romanian forests have the following structure:

- Coniferous trees: 815,643 ha (26.2%).
- Beech trees: 1,000,697 ha (32.1%).

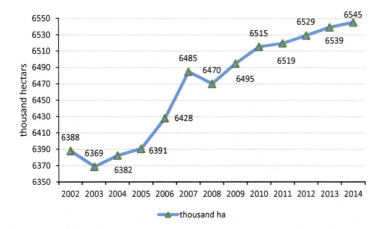

Fig. 17.1 Evolution of forestry area in Romania (ha). *Source* Romanian Statistical Yearbook 2015 and www.insse.ro

- Oak trees: 563,338 ha (18.1%).
- Various other hardwood trees: 525,480 ha (16.8%).
- Various redwood trees: 213,684 ha (6.8%).

As can be seen from Fig. 17.1, and the data from the National Forest Inventory, forest areas in Romania increased in area to 6.5 million ha in 2011. The explanation for this increase in forested surfaces lies with the new methodology used in gathering data and the provisions of the new Forestry Code.

17.4   Virgin Forest as Romania's Natural Heritage

The area covered by forests in Romania is less than the European average but there are some important peculiar forests. We should mention that Romania holds significant areas covered by virgin forests. Virgin forests are the remaining parts of the immense primeval forest that once stretched across the European Plain, and now is gone. In the Carpathian ecoregion, the estimate is that there are 322,000 ha of such virgin forest, of which 77.6% (250,000 ha) are in Romania.

The development of these forest ecosystems took place without human intervention. They are an exceptional example of complex, undisturbed woodlands that sustain high biological diversity (Bősze and Mayer 2014).

As has been shown in numerous articles, Romania features exceptional samples of natural beech forests. These forests have not yet had any human intervention and, from a biodiversity protection point of view, represent true heritage. This is very important in the framework of improving the management of forests and protecting biodiversity.

In the context of virgin forests it should be mentioned that beech trees are still predominant in Romanian forests. These natural beech forests represent Romania's heritage and are not only well-known, but also appreciated by the general public in addition to specialists who have observed and emphasized their importance and significance over the years. Also, it is important to mention that the World Wildlife Fund (WWF) played a substantial role in saving two forest areas: Strâmbu Băiuț–Groșii Țibleșului in Maramureș county and Șinca in the Făgăraș highlands.

Virgin forests represent the few remaining areas in which nature continues to survive in its pristine form, without the intervention of humans. So, evolving without human intervention, these ecosystems are very stable, providing habitats for more than 13,000 species of plants, animals, and insects. Many specialists and organizations that have made significant contributions to preserving biodiversity (such as the WWF) have confidence that these forests, which represent 65% of the remaining virgin forests in Europe (excluding Russian forests), have a vital inheritance value for Romania, Europe, and the world.

As recognition of the value of the virgin forests, in 2012, the Romanian authorities started the nomination process to include the virgin beech forests of Romania in the United Nations Educational, Scientific and Cultural Organization (UNESCO) World Heritage List.

As is known, the UNESCO World Heritage List already contains some European virgin beech forests. We should mention that these virgin forests are located mostly in Germany and in the Carpathian Mountains (in Slovakia and Ukraine). To these existing forest areas would be added the nominated primordial Romanian forests (Strâmbu Băiuț–Groșii Țibleșului in Maramureș county, and Șinca forest in the Fagăraș mountains). The direct effect would be to increase the representation of this type of ecosystem in the UNESCO World Heritage List.

Over 20,000 ha of quasi-virgin forests have been identified in the following areas:

- 2013: In Maramureș—over 4700 ha.
- 2014: In Covasna—over 400 ha and in Brasov—over 4300 ha.
- 2015: In Sibiu—over 2800 ha.
- 2016, at the end of February: In Gorj—4000 ha; in Mehedinți—over 2100 ha; and in Caraș-Severin—more than 800 ha.

For those counties where the identification process of quasi-virgin forests is not fully complete, assessments may continue into the future.

17.5 Instruments Used in Romania for Preserving Forests

In recent years in Romania, the need for effective and sustainable forest management has become a priority. The main challenge to be overcome is potential forest destruction through illegal logging and unsustainable exploitation. A recent study published by Greenpeace (Greenpeace 2015) shows that total forest area deforested and damaged, during the period 2000–2010, was 280,108 ha—approximately 28,000 ha per year. The counties most affected are Harghita Suceava, Cluj, and Maramureș.

The Greenpeace study revealed that almost half, specifically 48.95%, of deforested areas during the period 2000–2011 were found in protected areas. Even more serious is the fact that virgin forests were affected, even those considered the most valuable.

In Romania, there are several economic and administrative instruments which can be used to protection forests, some of which may be considered innovative. The most significant instruments are: forests radar, long-term contracts for the exploitation of forests, transparent forest management decisions, limiting logging, etc.

17.5.1 The Forests Radar

A new tracking system called the "traceability of wood," also known as "the forests radar," represents a big step forward in addressing illegal logging in Romania. It was recently introduced in 2014 by Governmental Decision 470/2014.

This new instrument proposes the following:

- Traceability of timber tracking in real time.
- Creating a cross-checking system between what the seller and purchaser (registered) reports online.
- Mandatory verification by the buyer of origin document veracity; this is an essential preventive measure proposed in 2012 by the WWF.
- Wooden materials with documents not verified by the buyer should be regarded as having an illegal origin and could be confiscated.
- Using a system to signal alerts to the authorities.
- Operating a system which cannot record a larger volume of wooden materials than originally purchased and registered.
- Connection to the 112 emergency system allowing involvement of civil society/citizens to monitor timber transport.
- Supporting economic agents, since they may receive internal reports which can be used by companies for management and tracking/traceability of timber.

The implementation of the forests radar mechanism is linked to the proper implementation of the European Regulation regarding the timber trade. Thus, it will transpose into national legislation the provisions of Regulation (EU) 995/2010. This regulation mandates operators to implement preventive procedures to reduce illegal logging. As a result of this mechanism, which started on 1 January 2015, operators' participation in tenders is conditional on implementing a system of preventive procedures concerning the marketing of illegally harvested timber.

17.5.2   Long-Term Contracts for Forestry

An important legal instrument for sustainable forest management and dynamic economic regions, is the long-term contract (10 years). Thus, the National Forest Administration, Romsilva, has signed contracts for the sale of timber for long periods of time with a number of multinationals.

Short-term contracts do not allow significant investment which contributes to sustainable economic development and growth and maintains jobs. In practice, a number of foreign companies (mentioned above) have conducted large economic activities involving the uncontrolled exploitation of timber and even illegal logging.

17.5.3   The National Catalogue of Virgin and Quasi-virgin Forests

The main problem with the protection of virgin forests is that only 18% have some sort of protected status by their inclusion in protected areas. A smaller percentage enjoys full protection. The rest, which constitute more than 80% of all virgin forests in Romania, have no form of protection and are in danger of being legally destroyed.

In this context, the Order of the Minister of Environment 3397/2016 defined quasi-pristine forests and the criteria and indicators for their identification and designation.

Unfortunately, the legal procedures for the protection of virgin forests have proved to be less effective for several reasons:

- The establishment of such a strict protection regime is a lengthy process since the identified virgin forests can be classified into categories with different role which are updated every 10 years.
- Such a participatory process is not always transparent.
- Maintenance status does not guarantee long-term protection.
- The protection established while awaiting the completion of identification of forests was inefficient, being applied in less than 80% of cases (procedures refer basically only to forests included in decennial harvesting plans for main products—it does not refer to conservation, cleaning, or accidental cuts).

Under such circumstances, it was important to build the National Catalogue for Virgin and Quasi-virgin Forests, to be used as an innovative tool for the sustainable management of virgin and quasi-virgin forests in Romania. There remains one last step to complete the legislative regulatory framework, that is, to await an order from the head of the legislative authority responsible for forestry. It is important to mention that many effective solutions would be obtained by completing the catalogue.

The National Catalogue of Virgin and Quasi-virgin Forests is not just an online database with the purpose of maintaining records and ensuring the strict protection of these forests. It should also regulate procedures which record these land surfaces and provide them with prompt protection. Thus, the National Catalogue of Virgin and Quasi-virgin Forests should address the following issues:

- Establishing procedures for effective prevention objectives in areas included in the PIN-MATRA/2001/018 study or the management plans for protected areas (Biris and Veen 2005).
- Specifying the minimum requirements for studies/proposals submitted by stakeholders to be considered by a competent authority for the purposes of gradually completing gradually catalogue.
- Providing objective regulations and procedures (clear responsibilities and deadlines for stakeholders) for received field studies/proposals submitted for approval by the authorities involved.
- Providing effective procedures (clear responsibilities and deadlines for stakeholders) for the designation and inclusion of areas in the "catalogue," namely the establishment of strict, long-term protection.
- Designating an authority responsible for managing the catalogue.
- Supporting additional efforts to identify virgin forests in Romania.

17.5.4 Other Tools

There are other tools used in Romania for the administration/management of forests:

- Grants issued for the management of small forest (below 30 ha).
- Free plans of forest management drafted for small properties, with measures stipulated by Law 46/2008 amended and supplemented.
- New regulations attesting to the economic activity of logging and recording saw mills (under development).
- Compensation to forest owners not illegally logging.

17.6 Conclusions

From this research we can draw some conclusions regarding the role of forests as heritage sites, in particular the role of virgin forests. In Romania, forests represent 29% of the land cover, a figure which is below the average of other European countries. With 6.5 million ha of forest, Romania ranks 12th in Europe in terms of forested area.

Of this forested area, of particular importance, from heritage point of view, is virgin forest. In Romania, virgin forest is a new concept and deserves more detailed attention and special effort to preserve it. There are several reasons for this:

- Romania's virgin forests represent national, European, and global heritage—the task of protecting this natural heritage should not be left solely to private forest owners. State intervention is required along with efforts by public authorities to ensure sustainable management of these forests. The impulse for the protection of such forests came from non-governmental organizations (NGOs) and activists in the fields of biodiversity protection, forestry, etc.

- In the last 25 years, public forests have been reduced through retroceding forests to their former owners or their successors, corruption, illegal logging, etc. Under these circumstances, existing virgin forests and quasi-virgin forests cannot be safeguarded fully. Therefore, special efforts to ensure their safeguarding must be undertaken. Here, we have identified and analyzed two innovative tools: the National Catalogue of Virgin and Quasi-virgin Forests and the system of compensation given to all forest owners throughout the country who do not damage or undertake logging on their land.

References

Biris, A. I., & Veen, P. (2005). *Project PIN-MATRA/2001/018—Inventory and strategy for sustainable management and protection of virgin forests in Romania.*

Bősze, S., Mayer, H., (2014). Oportunități de dezvoltare regională a ariilor ocrotite și a patrimoniului natural din Carpați. Pachet de lucru 4. Management integrat al diversității ecologice și peisagistice pentru dezvoltarea regională durabilă și conectivitate ecologică în Carpați. WWF—Fondul internațional pentru viață sălbatică—Programul Dunăre-Carpați, Viena, Austria.

COM (2013) 659 final. Communication from the Commission to the European Parliament, the Council, the European Economic and Social Committee and the Committee of the Regions. A New EU Forest Strategy: For Forests and the Forest-Based Sector, https://ec.europa.eu/agriculture/forest/strategy/communication_en.pdf.

Drăgoi, M. (2008). Analiza cost-beneficiu a conversiei pădurilor naturale în plantații de plop, programul LIFE 2008.

European Communities. (2003). *Sustainable forestry and the European Union Initiatives of the European Commission*, EC 2003.

Greenpeace. (2015). *Raport taieri ilegale 2013–2014*, http://www.greenpeace.org/romania/ro/campanii/paduri/publicatii/Tierile-ilegale-de-arbori-din-Romania-2013-2014/.

Platon, V., Frone, S., & Constantinescu, A. (2015). New developments in assessing forest ecosystem services in Romania. *Procedia Economics and Finance, 22*, 45–54 https://doi.org/10.1016/s2212-5671(15)00225-7, http://www.sciencedirect.com/science/article/pii/S2212567115002257.

Chapter 18
Public Cultural Heritage and Private Property Rights: Building Sustainable Community Through Individuality

Octavian-Dragomir Jora, Mihaela Iacob
and Matei-Alexandru Apăvăloaei

Abstract Material and immaterial culture and both economy and economics are part of one and only reality, contrary to views placing the "priceless" things out of the scope of mundane calculi. What keeps together any community are not only the aesthetic joys or sober rituals, but productive relations within the framework of cooperative division of labour, for culture is not floating into nothingness, but overwrites the material world of scarce resources which is either governed by a critical infrastructure of property rights or gets ungovernable at all. In order to culturally thrive, communities are obliged to discover those very institutions responsible for peace and prosperity which culture (in the "anthropological" sense) prepares, following époques of social selection, and on which culture (in the "artefactual" sense) roots its desired sustainability. Our thesis, all the more acute in a post-socialist society, is that private property rights link individuals in communities, by giving them sound incentives, information and instruments to create, share and bequeath tangible and intangible culture, that is the offshoot of the freedom of expression, of the freedom to produce and of the freedom to trade.

Keywords Culture · Heritage · Property rights · Sustainability
Community · Individuality

18.1 Introduction

There is a question not so often thought of and even more rarely asked: is culture a product of free markets or, on the contrary, is it, "par excellence", a public good to be provided by the state, allegedly the only social institution able to grant individuals the collective framework for reviewing the cultural values, for the

O.-D. Jora · M. Iacob (✉) · M.-A. Apăvăloaei
Bucharest University of Economics, Roman Square 6,
Bucharest 010374, Romania
e-mail: mihaela.iacob@fin.ase.ro

© Springer International Publishing AG, part of Springer Nature 2019   213
V. Vasile (ed.), *Caring and Sharing: The Cultural Heritage Environment
as an Agent for Change*, Springer Proceedings in Business and Economics,
https://doi.org/10.1007/978-3-319-89468-3_18

rationalization of cultural capital and for the sustainable cultural refill? The economists acknowledged the double dimension of culture: anthropological ("shared attitudes, beliefs, customs, traditions, values and practices") and artefactual ("cultural goods/institutions/industries/sector"). They understood that both economy (the reality of scarcity) and economics (the science of scarcity) impregnate (and are impregnated) with culture—since the material substance upon which the cultural symbols are overridden is basically scarce.

Economists, though unevenly within the profession, understood also that the economic ideas themselves are dependent to a certain way of the sociocultural (or political and ideological) representation of the economic reality, applying, of course, a certain "discount" to the "scientific truth" based on its "social acceptability". Whatever the moral serfdoms and material privileges, it has been understood that scarcity cannot be socially managed absent a well-defined property rights framework. Still, here too the "water springs" of economic science were separated between those that derive the assignment of property rights from general equilibrium or efficiency maximization and those who a priori place them at the foundation of order, as ethical precondition from which the legitimacy of the economic problem derives, not the other way around.

Hereinafter, the philosophy is to give a property rights-based representation of the cultural space which strives for its sustainability both in its high, elitist, Humboldtian dimension and in the common, popular, Herderian one. Caught between survival and thriving, culture declaims value, claims resources and reclaims duration. It has no mystical collective consciousness, but lives in its individual members, depending on the strength with which "sense" disciplines "sensibility". Culture cannot escape the basics of the "value—capital—sustainability" dialectic of economic development; it can make a difference between "eternities" and "ephemerides". "Culture is wealth. Without well-being, without wealth, there never has been culture", said von Mises (1983: 74). Cultural heritage is an avatar of wealth, standing and falling with pro-wealth institutions.

Our aim is to reveal the link between private property and private property-based society, on the one hand, and cultural heritage and its flourishing, on the other. We argue that this relation is organic and any attempt to instil coercion into this natural order necessarily leads to consequences endangering the harmonious and sustainable development of shared cultural heritage. This plea is set upon the following routes of reasoning: (1) we'll first define culture and sustainability, as they rely on freedom of expression and on proper(ty) tools; (2) then, we'll present some essential dichotomies with respect to property rights settings with cultural impact; (3) after that, some notes on the relationship between creators, entrepreneurs and bureaucrats will be exposed; (4) finally, we'll sketch the essential lines of the "property economics" analysis of culture and cultural heritage.

18.2 Culture and Sustainability—Some Proper(ty) Notes

18.2.1 Is (Cultural) Heritage Coherent Without Ownership?

The very word culture, as well as its competitor/complement, civilization, is one of the semantically richest in each and every language of the world. Common in defining culture is to observe both its immaterial and material dimensions, meaning both sharing and bonding thoughts and facts, on the one hand, and the artefacts embodying them and resources involved in their making, on the other. Perceived either as a warm spiritual "software" of the cold "hardware" civilization or as a shared identity differentia specification alongside the genus proximum that is the human civilization, culture began since (post-Industrial Revolution) Romanticism to express the superior and steadfast support of collective identities, as opposed both to the outer-West "barbarities" and the inner-West "alienation", both in values and (arte)facts.

Culture equally refers to (Williams 1976: 80): the intellectual, spiritual and aesthetic development of an individual, group or society; the intellectual and artistic activities and results (i.e. visual, performing arts); the whole way of life, activities, beliefs and customs of a community of every kind. Culture spreads both "synchronically" (intra-generation ties) and "diachronically" (bequeathed and inherited).

The cultural heritage of any human society plays a crucial role for its members; it allows them to gain a sense of identity by choosing to adhere, with their persons and properties, to a set of common values and by adopting a single historical interpretation of their past. Due to this common identity, the individuals that are part of society can better tackle uncertainty and potential conflicts by simply taking the shared ground represented by their cultural heritage as core referential. For example, the Western custom of allowing females to enter a room first, before the males, is a mundane case of spontaneously evolved norms, as the performance of a ritual folk song or dance in a certain place owned by (a member of) a community. Grosso modo, these are part of a society's cultural heritage, acting as means of creating bonds from mine to ours.

The cultural heritage of a society allows the individuals that form it to minimize the chance of engaging in open conflict, while maximizing the chances of reaching an agreement on what form of governance will be accepted. In this sense, the cultural heritage of society is just another institution that complements and perfects the institution of private property, the rational relational tamer of scarcity-driven clashes.

18.2.2 Is Sustainability a Property Rights-Neutral Concept?

One of the fanciest words in nowadays economics is sustainability, though its consonance with logic of private property rights is if not missed then severely misinterpreted. This laxity of reasoning is equally deplorable no matter if we have in mind "environmental sustainable development" or relatively recently extrapolated idea of "sustainable cultural development" (Throsby 1995). It is unquestionably that (also) with the work of man, the natural climate is ever changing and not necessarily for the better, as well as the fact that the digestion of these changes remains a function (also) of the intellectual climate out of which they sprung. The theory of sustainability is the offshoot of neoclassical paradigm, starting from the premise that "current generations" (a time-invariant sense) are experiencing a "market failure" in maintaining a "capital stock", which is defined in a "broad sense", at the disposal of "future generations". We argue that the image is fundamentally macro-biased, in the positive sense, and state-biased, in the normative sense; therefore, a micro- and market-oriented perspective, based on private incentives and instruments, is sounder (Jora 2015: 44–49).

Briefly stated, the mainstream sustainability theory is, in the most part, rather metaphorical and unworkable (Brätland 2006). Its weakness stems from several facts: it assumes value(s) (of capital and corresponding revenues) as being objective, stable and able to be easily extracted from the minds of the individuals by the gurus of societal knowledge (public experts/technocrats), and not (as it really is) subjective, ever changing and revealed only within the course of action, through free exchanges, intermediated by money and effectively undertaken by the private owners of the capital resources; natural capital, put out of the context of monetary valuation, absent free markets, is void of economic sense; private property and monetary exchange provide an incentivized, informational and instrumental framework for the entrepreneurial appraisal of depreciation, depletion, destruction, as well as maintenance and replacement of (natural) capital, unparalleled by bureaucratic practices (though they claim to be scientific). The nowadays captive paradigm of "public goods" and of "negative externalities", as opposed to "private provision" and "property conflicts", is responsible for the contemporary sterile legal and inefficient economical mainstream resolutions (Anderson and Leal 2001).

18.2.3   Is Culture Sustainable Absent Private Property?

In his influential works on the economics of culture, Throsby (1995, 2001) proposes to address the problem of cultural sustainability, built on some (disputable) pillars: integration of material and non-material well-being by including the cultural factor in the assessment of communities' development, by means of "proper indicators" and involving, ultimately, a "political judgment"; inter-generational equity and the maintenance of the cultural capital by operationalizing the (economic) notion of "cultural capital", as well as the (ethical) idea of "social responsibility" towards the generations to come; intra-generational equity by understanding that market is a good wealth creator, but poor wealth distributor, the provision of cultural services being the most prone to be sacrificed in the less fortunate social categories; interdependence between cultural and economic systems by adopting some "eco-"type "whole systems approach", this is because the conservation of cultural mechanism is as crucial for the economic thrive as it is that of those of biological nature.

Just as in the case of economic and ecological sustainability, the cultural adaptation suggests the idea that unsustainability is a freedom-failure, not some unintended consequence of public policy.

In Jora and Iacob (2014), we summed up some reasons for which the entire concept of cultural sustainability, assessed as a mimic of ecological sustainability, is both a priori and empirically unsustainable: not only that there is no solid theoretical link between equity and sustainability, the entire history of Western Civilization is a living proof of the compatibility of certain degree of inequality with the societal regeneration; leaving the present generation at the mercy of future generations verdicts is either absurd, annulling present choices, or hypocritical, setting arbitrarily the political spokespersons of the unborn. In the following parts of our analysis, we will re-evaluate the capacity of private property arrangements to sustain precisely that kind of culture that communities feel comfortable with, as well as in a lasting perspective, because propensity to moral degradation, to short-termism and to community dissolution is not alien to property rights alteration and to usurpation of the works of the social characters responsible for true sustainability.

Bellow some theoretical thoughts will be dedicated to the presentation and explanation of a synthetic diagram of conceptual dichotomies around property rights, relevant in the cultural realm.

18.3 Property Rights, a Diagram of Cultural Dichotomies

Property rights represent the rational and relational answer the members of human societies historically found as being able to discipline the use of socially scarce economic resources, whose allocation is in peril of being both conflictual and wasteful absent a proper institutional framework. Political philosophers, jurists, sociologists, economists analysed property rights role in human action(s). The way property rights are assigned determines the performance of society/communities/ organizations in ethical terms, defined as non-conflictual orderly behaviour (Rothbard 1982), as well as in economic terms, wealth creation being dependent on the soundness of incentives (Smith 1994), on the access to dispersed social information (Hayek 2011) and on the profit-seeking economic calculation (von Mises 2008a). The cultural scenery, however prone to transcendental issues, lives in the immanent of scarcity of the means of cultural expression, and the production of tangible and intangible culture, as proper means of lastingly answering to the spiritual ends of the members of communities (not to the whims of impostors or dictators), depends on the way in which the definition, defence and disposition of property are realized. Fig. 18.1 summarizes dichotomies alongside which property rights competing perspectives can be mapped: natural law versus positive law, private (personal) versus public (state), individual versus collective, material

| Natural (Legitimate) | Positive (Legal) | Private (Personal) | Public (State) | Individual (Single) | Collective (Common) | Material (Tangible) | Intellectual (Intangible) |

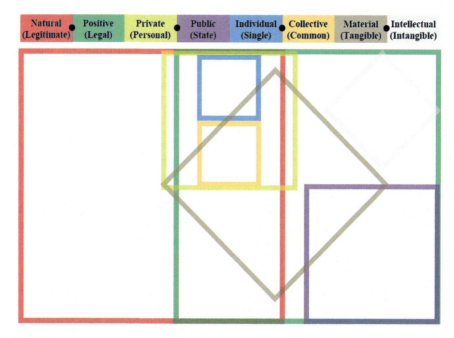

Fig. 18.1 Some conceptual dichotomies on property rights. *Source* Authors' representation

(tangible) versus intellectual (intangible). We will argue, in the next sections, that the "Lockean property, laissez-faire cultural capitalism" is the superior social option.

I. Natural law property versus positive legislation property. The jus naturalist, Lockean perspective, sees self-ownership, homesteading, voluntary production and contractual transfers as the only logic and legitimate ways of acquiring property. The law, as produced by law-making bodies, may not follow the natural rule, case in which it uses ethically and epistemically invalid social efficiency allegations (Rothbard 2009; Hoppe 2010).

II. Private (personal) property versus public (state) property. Private property is arguably the best incentivized, informational and instrumental solution to the problem of governing scarcity, while "expropriated state property" is prone to capital malinvestments and depletion due to poorly done economic calculation and to corruption and fraud, for resources are not in the range of control of their rightful creators (von Mises 2008a, b).

III. Individual property versus collective property. Free markets, defined as the absence of governmental interventionism in the natural, legitimate course of property creation and circulation, provide individuals with tools for administering resources owned in common. There is no tragedy of the commons (i.e. in corporate ownership) if laws do not create imbalances of rights among owners or between owners and administrators.

IV. Material (tangible) property versus intellectual (intangible) property. The case of intellectual property is by far the most sensitive one. Some argue that since information, once shared, is free floating and thus not scarce, it cannot be subjected to the same considerations as material things. Creators have free market tools for protection from imposture (i.e. plagiarism) without blocking others' freedom of expression (Kinsella 2001).

18.4   Creatorship, Entrepreneurship and Statesmanship

The origins of society, of human communities that are based on private property (not only atomistic, but also common) and ("private", natural) governance—differing from mere "government" by its anchorage on voluntarily accepted rules and social elites emerged from the bottom up, while the state is based on coercion, depredation and hierarchical edicts (Hoppe 2014)—stem from human reason and sound incentives which make the curtailment of basic, primitive instincts, cooperation and exchange attractive to individuals. In the tradition of spontaneous order à la von Mises (2008a) and Hayek (1982), the cultural heritage of society is the product of reason and of interaction between individuals acting on a level playing field. The very fact that the cultural heritage is shared, in the absence of coercion, makes it voluntary, ever changing and genuinely "public": for it is not owned, managed or thought of by any single individual or entity. The cultural heritage of a society is organic; it unites individuals and their property into a (relatively) smoother functioning whole.

The economist, qua scientist, approaches and investigates social phenomena from a wertfrei perspective (Rothbard 2011a). Therefore, he finds himself in a difficult position when called upon to analyse the cultural heritage of a given society. Such an approach entails abandoning all aspects pertaining to aesthetics. In this sense, the economic analysis of culture is going to be different from that proposed by Ruskin (1912), who criticized the detrimental impact capitalism supposedly has on art and architecture. Also, a purely scientific analysis is different from what we may call, following Robbins (1981), "political economy", an approach that introduces implicit value judgments when economists make supposedly scientific policy recommendations in the name of a certain widely held belief (Rothbard 2011b). The stake of an economic discussion on this particular and delicate subject as the cultural markets and policies (Cowen 2000; Scott 1998) is to deduce the transformation effects that the different ways of organizing social interaction have upon the cultural heritage.

18.4.1   Laissez-Faire Cultural Capitalism

Capitalism is the system that made the mass production of the Bible possible (Rockwell 1995), but it is precisely this ever-increasing material wealth made possible by capitalism that its detractors consider to be inopportune—"capitalism may produce more, but the issue is one pertaining to quality, not quantity!". Crux for this argument is that laissez-faire capitalism tends to make available a more plentiful supply of high-quality cultural artefacts by the simple fact that it can outcompete, by far, all other economic systems. Such conclusion is a priori valid, and it does not require any value judgment on part of the economist as to what should be considered "good quality" and who is in the position to make "competent" pronouncements. Also, decrying that not all cultural products are of the best quality possible is tantamount to raising an objection against the market that it does not produce only five-star restaurants (fit only for the gourmet-rich elite). One must also take into account that tastes and opinions are in constant flux, subject to turns and twists. In a lecture on Shakespeare's works, Cantor (2012) mentions that during the playwright's life, theatre was seen as a rather marginal profession, and theatre productions were popular mainly among members of the vulg.

Without entering the field of aesthetics, we may add that a free market in art/ cultural products has a tendency to "separate the wheat from the chaff" when it comes to the issues of "intertemporal conservation". If one were to consider the Greek tragedies, of all the texts that are known to have existed, only three full-length materials survived. "Coincidently", these texts, authored by Aeschylus, Sophocles and Euripides, were also considered the most noteworthy during their age. Their commercial success with the public precisely insured their preservation. Sustainability came along with free choice from the (of course, educated) public. Moreover, under laissez-faire capitalism, each community is going to adopt and develop its own set of cultural values and core artefacts. Instead of a state-accepted or influenced heritage, a number of potential cultural heritages may spur, out of which individuals can opt for. Therefore, laissez-faire capitalism offers both greater output and cultural diversity within the tradition of one particular cultural heritage, while at the same time it is compatible with the preservation, coexistence and flourishing of a great number of cultural heritages. Material wealth and spiritual welfare are sides of the same coin, that of freedoms of expression, production and trade.

18.4.2   State Cultural Interventionism

According to Oppenheimer's dichotomy (1922), an individual can acquire wealth either by employing the economic means, i.e. voluntary cooperation through appropriation, production, exchange or gift, or by employing the political means, i.e. using coercion in order to extract resources. By its very nature, political action does not create any resources; it must first of all extract resources and only then attempt to redistribute them and, therefore, any decision to alter the natural output level of cultural products can only come at the expense of extracting those scarce resources from other sectors of the economy. And this kind of choices set into motion a set of consequences (Apăvăloaei 2015a, b). Adding the "cultural" epithet to "resources" only brings particular colour to the theoretical judgment concerning the socio-economic effects of public policies.

For instance, if we analyse taxation, we will understand prior to any econometrical verification that this is associated with a relative tendency towards a slower economic growth coupled with a tendency of the taxed subjects to turn towards more short-term and materialistic problems, or to evading law and corrupting state officials. These are prerequisites for the moral dissolution of a community and an assault on the structural cultural backbones. At the other end of redistribution, the subsidy recipients are experiencing behaviour distortions: granted to consumers or to producers, subsidies lead to the mal-supply of the cultural products. The "assisted cultural goods production" comes with greater quantities at the expense of quality or originality, and "assisted cultural heritage maintenance" comes with conflicts between destination communities of funds.

18.5   A Property Economics Analysis of Cultural Heritage

In this paper, we insisted that there is a way of deducing, beyond common-sense intuition and without the need of sophisticated "metric" instruments, that there is a solid and sound scientific way of assessing and addressing the role of property rights in the perimeter of cultural sustainability. Finally, we came to the point where we can "reveal" it in a straightforward synthesis: property economics. The counterfactual economic analysis based on property rights relies on the a priori comparisons of the effects on social wealth and welfare coming from interactions, which are, essentially, appropriations of resources via interpersonal transfers. The appropriations of resources can be done either with the consent of the legitimate owners or by aggression, tertium non datur. This reveals a special category of economic laws, rooted in the logic of human action and the universality of human nature, being both time and place invariant. Hülsmann (2004: 41) calls them "counterfactual laws of appropriation" and the basic decoding tool in the analysis of economic systems.

Property economics enables very strong pieces of a priori theorizing. The reasons for which the institution of private property leads to the highest possible production of cultural wealth (the most efficient allocation of resources) are obvious: any abdication from this set of rules implies, by definition, a redistribution of property titles and, accordingly, of revenues from users/producers/contractors of needed cultural goods to non-users/non-producers/non-contractors. As a result, any such abdication implies that there will be relatively less culture-devoted resource homesteading, less production of new cultural goods, less preservation of existing cultural goods and fewer mutually beneficial voluntary exchanges of cultural artefacts, thus an inefficient resource allocation of creatorship and cultural entrepreneurship spirit. And this, absolutely logically and naturally, involves a lower standard of living in terms of cultural goods. Instead, a cohabitation of pseudo-culture (waste) and penuries of authentic cultural infrastructures and artefacts will be delivered.

Any policy decision is never value-neutral. It always implies policymakers making decisions on what they or a commission, delegated by them because it is deemed representative, considers important for the cultural heritage of the polity. This means that only what is deemed acceptable output is going to be eligible for benefiting from subsidies. Anything that does not pass the bureaucratic criteria imposed by the scheme is going to be left to fare for itself in a world in which individuals are already left poorer by the tax and also live under the impression that they have already contributed to the flourishing and conservation of the cultural heritage. A similar perverse initiative is created by the modern state-funded "welfare" systems when it comes to the erosion of family values and private charitable initiatives.

When explicitly acting as a cultural heritage custodian, the state acts in fact as the great equalizer. It tirelessly worked towards eliminating local measuring units, it combated regional customs by legislation, it decreed what is the literary language to be used in institutions and taught in schools, it built roads for armies and fences for civilians, and it discriminated among races, nationalities and classes. All these were adopted in the name of creating a culturally unified political entity. Unlike the polycentric world that would develop under laissez-faire capitalism, with a variety of coexisting cultural heritages, a society living under the hegemony of the state will tend to have a uniform and carefully selected cultural heritage that will tend to forget anything that might challenge the monopoly position(s) of the "centrum".

18.6 Conclusion

In this brief essay, we argued that the sustainable development of cultural heritage, defined in its broadest sense (both with respect to tangible and intangible dimensions), is theoretically inappropriate to be severed from the property rights settings of a community, for the culture-devoted and culturally endowed capital cannot regenerate itself, in a meaningful way, absent proper incentives, information and economic instruments assorted only with legitimate private property rights-free markets. The sense we accepted for the word culture—socially shared set of subjectively valued "things"—is unsuitable to match with coercive, expropriating, fraudulent political measures (even if "legally" enforced) because culture is either voluntary acquis or is a sad parody. The market is by no means the archetypal enemy of culture, since culture has both pop and high faces.

The cultural heritage of a nation (be it composed of old folkloric customs and modern artistic performances or paintings, sculptures and architectural sites) stays and falls with its voluntary perpetuation within a community with all the resources needed to do it. State-undertaken interferences motivated by egalitarian access to culture of superior credential for artists alienate communities from their symbolic coexistences, exposing them to moral bankruptcy (i.e. that experienced in socialist Romania's "cultural revolution") and/or conflicting cohabitation of the Übermenschen and Untermenschen of the culturally biased "planned market". The principles and practices in fashion nowadays in the core of modern democratic world, with its state-driven cultural industries, are differing only in "shades" from the extreme "communist" cultural heritage perversions.

References

Anderson, T., & Leal, D. (2001). *Free market environmentalism* (rev ed.). New York: Palgrave.

Apăvăloaei, M. A. (2015a). Interventionism: An economic analysis of priceless resource allocation. *Scientific Bulletin—Economic Sciences, 4*(1), 11–19.

Apăvăloaei, M. A. (2015b). An outline of a praxeological theory of politics. *The Quarterly Journal of Austrian Economics, 18*(2), 91–125.

Brätland, J. (2006). Toward a calculational theory and policy of intergenerational sustainability. *The Quarterly Journal of Austrian Economics, 9*(2), 13–45.

Cantor, P. A. (2012). *The invisible hand in popular culture: Liberty versus authority in American film and TV.* Lexington, Kentucky: University Press of Kentucky.

Cowen, T. (2000). *In praise of commercial culture.* Cambridge, Massachusetts: Harvard University Press.

Hayek, F. A. (1982). *Law, legislation and liberty. A new statement of the liberal principles of justice and political economy.* London: Routledge & Kegan Paul Ltd.

Hayek, F. A. (2011). The use of knowledge in society. *The American Economic Review, 35*(4), 519–530.

Hoppe, H. H. (2010). *A theory of socialism and capitalism.* Auburn, Alabama: Ludwig von Mises Institute.

Hoppe, H. H. (2014). *From aristocracy to monarchy to democracy, a tale of moral and economic folly and decay.* Auburn, Alabama: Ludwig von Mises Institute.

Hülsmann, J. G. (2004). The a priori foundations of property economics. *The Quarterly Journal of Austrian Economics, 7*(4), 41–68.

Jora, O. D. (2015). *Durabilitatea culturii şi logica economiei drepturilor de proprietate: natural-pozitiv, privat-public, individual-colectiv, material-intelectual.* Post-doctoral thesis, The Romanian Academy.

Jora, O. D., & Iacob, M. (2014) The economics of culture and the cultural economy: Praxeological account on material wealth and spiritual welfare. In *Proceedings of the 5th Biennial International Conference "The Future of Europe".* Bucharest: ASE Publishing House.

Kinsella, S. (2001). Against intellectual property rights. *Journal of Libertarian Studies, 15*(2), 1–53.

Oppenheimer, F. (1922). *The state: Its history and development viewed sociologically.* New York, NY: B. W. Huebsch Inc.

Robbins, L. (1981). Economics and political economy. *American Economic Association, 71*(2), 1–10.

Rockwell, L. (1995). Capitalism and culture. *The Free Market, 10,* 1–4.

Rothbard, M. N. (1982). *Ethics of liberty, Atlantic highlands.* New Jersey: Humanities Press.

Rothbard, M. N. (2009a). *Man, economy, and state (with power and market)* (2nd ed.). Auburn, Alabama: Ludwig von Mises Institute.

Rothbard, M. N. (2009b). *The mantel of science, economic controversies* (pp. 3–25). Auburn, Alabama: Ludwig von Mises Institute.

Rothbard, M. N. (2009c). *Praxeology, value judgments, and public policy", economic controversies* (pp. 81–102). Auburn, Alabama: Ludwig von Mises Institute.

Ruskin, J. (1912). *Unto this last and other essays on political economy London.* United Kingdom: Ward Lock & Co Limited.

Scott, J. C. (1998). *Seeing like a state: How certain schemes to improve the human condition have failed.* New Haven, Kentucky: Yale University Press.

Smith, A. (1994). *An inquiry into the nature and causes of the wealth of nations.* New York, NY: Modern Library.

Throsby, D. (1995). Culture, economics and sustainability. *Journal of Cultural Economics, 19*(3), 199–206.

Throsby, D. (2001). *Economics and culture.* Cambridge, Massachusetts: Cambridge University Press.

von Mises, L. (1983). *Nation, state, and economy. Contributions to the politics and history of our time.* New York: New York University Press.

von Mises, L. (2008a). *Human action: A treatise on economics* (1st ed.) (J. M. Herbener, H. H. Hoppe, & J. T. Salerno Eds.). Auburn, Alabama: Ludwig von Mises Institute.

von Mises, L. (2008b). *The anti capitalistic mentality.* Auburn, Alabama: Ludwig von Mises Institute.

Williams, R. (1976). *Keywords: A vocabulary of culture and society.* New York, NY: Oxford University Press.

Chapter 19
Protection of Natural Heritage: A Conservation Criminology Perspective

Radu Tudor Petre

Abstract Conservation criminology is an emerging interdisciplinary field which integrates elements of criminology, environmental science, and risk management in order to provide a realistic framework for the analysis of the problems related to conservation of natural resources and biodiversity. It comprises broad categories of environmental crimes and risks, including, but not limited to illegal lodging, illicit wildlife trade, corruption in environmental matters and ecoterrorism. The new international and regional developments indicate an increasing threat to natural resources conservation from criminal networks which seek to increase their profits through hard to detect and reduced penal liability activities, resorting to environmental crimes in order to complement their illicit activities or even as a main operation. The impact of such crimes is cumulative and persistent, having a twofold negative effect, on environment, mostly reflected in depletion or contamination of resources, and on local sustainable development, reducing opportunities for tourism, eco-agriculture, or other environmental low-impact activities. This paper argues that conservation criminology is well suited and could provide valuable insights in the analysis of the risks to safeguarding natural heritage, through integration into environmental governance, specifically for the regions which are confronted with threats generated by criminal networks.

Keywords Conservation criminology · Environmental crime · Natural heritage · Risk

19.1 Introduction

The protection of natural heritage is a regular subject of analysis for natural and environmental sciences, the emphasis being placed on natural hazards assessment and environmental risk management. What could be characterized as an emerging

R. T. Petre (✉)
Institute of National Economy-Romanian Academy,
Calea 13 Septembrie, 050711 Bucharest, Romania
e-mail: p.r.tudor@alumnus.rug.nl

© Springer International Publishing AG, part of Springer Nature 2019
V. Vasile (ed.), *Caring and Sharing: The Cultural Heritage Environment as an Agent for Change*, Springer Proceedings in Business and Economics,
https://doi.org/10.1007/978-3-319-89468-3_19

225

phenomenon and a threat to natural heritage are environmental crimes, which can take complex forms and can have transnational impact (White 2013; Dutu 2013). The cross-border criminal networks, interested in increasing their illicit profits, have identified a very lucrative niche in the field of illegal exploitation of natural resources or performing activities which can irreversibly damage it, such as toxic waste trafficking or dumping (Lynch and Stretesky 2007; Ionita-Burda 2012). Due to the low rate of detection and prosecution, as well as reduced judicial and administrative penalties, environmental crime is becoming, increasingly, more present both as an illicit activity and threat to sustainable development.

Even though there are serious concerns of specialized international organizations (Faure et al. 2015) with regard to the development of the phenomenon, the lack of national capacities, coordinated transnational enforcing activities, coherent international legal framework, and early warning signals impedes on the effort of tackling crimes against natural heritage (Interpol 2014).

What is still needed, before initiating and implementing national and international institutional capacity building programs, is embedding a new approach into the policy-making process, as well as actively acknowledging the contribution that criminology, integrated into a multidisciplinary framework with natural sciences and risk management, could bring with regard to anchoring natural heritage protection policies into local realities and prioritizing the efforts to address the causes of environmental crimes.

19.2 Conservation Criminology: Crime as Environmental Risk

Conservation criminology, refined from green criminology, fuses criminology and environmental science together with decision, risk and management sciences into a multidisciplinary structure for the analysis of environmental crimes and risks (Gibbs et al. 2010, p. 138). Due to the characteristics of environmental risks which cannot be analyzed within one discipline, there is a need of integrating various theories across research fields and considering the social dynamics created by the criminalization of various activities.

Criminology contribution could improve the policy design and evaluation through introducing a critical approach on crime phenomenon considered, specifically for some type of crimes—environmental included, as a subcultural response. Starting with the criminalization of certain activities, some of them related to exploiting natural resources, and continuing with the relative deprivation in an increasingly exclusive society (Runciman 1993; Young 1999), local communities build resentment on perceived unfair advantages established by law for other economic interest groups and one of the response could be crime, either poaching, illegal lodging or other crime against environment.

The change of perspective to which conservation criminology contributes, given its emphasis on prevention, could support environmental governance through facilitating a more inclusive dialogue with local communities. Giving a voice to minority groups and striving to incorporate solutions to ensure the sustainability of their livelihood contributes significantly to reducing environmental risk. What should be avoided is the misdirected efforts to police the problematic territory, where environmental crimes have a high frequency, but low detection rate. The effectiveness of such intervention is low, and the potential social side effects are long lasting, in the form of estrangement of communities from authorities and building cohesion around criminal groups and values. Over-policing such areas by employing offensive or intrusive means, such as *stop and search* or police raids, can produce opposite results in the form of increasing crime, civil disobedience, and even revolts (Box 1987).

Robust policing or environmental enforcing is not efficient under such circumstances and involving the relevant stakeholders in the decision-making process could reverse a spiral of aggression between different parties, which also impacts irreversibly on environment directly, as a crime, or indirectly, as inaction from the authorities which are focusing their efforts only on detection and prosecution, giving little consideration to the prevention approach. Not only robust policing produces irrelevant results, but it might act as a catalyst to previous social discontent, fueled mainly to the behavior of the elite groups which monopolize the exploitation of environmental or other type of resources and marginalize other groups.

Methodologies to ensure participation and local ownership of strategies or action plans can build upon community planning (Grobe and Hendriks 2014, p. 16–17) and can be further refined and adapted to provide local environmental management strategies. Leveraging local capacities of participation and learning, as shown in Fig. 19.1 cycle, local environmental governance can better support sustainable development through integration of the conservation criminology perspective. Various strategies, including for crime control, can be integrated into a coherent manner with the purpose of enhancing the prevention measures through stimulating economic growth and development which offers meaningful labor and education opportunities for the local communities, as well as supporting provision of adequate social and health services for the groups at risk of poverty and social exclusion.

The benefits for the environmental governance with regard to integration of conservation criminology reflect mostly in balancing the local and regional relationships with corporations, due to the corporate criminal liability. It outweighs the "polluter pays" principle and, given the severity of criminal sentences, increases the responsibility of the corporate top management toward environment and local communities. Such integration should be approached with care, in order not to produce a punitive response toward the business community, and more research is needed to collect and analyze data regarding different types of approaches, responses, and impact with regard to the environmental protection in order to identify good practices which can be locally adapted and implemented.

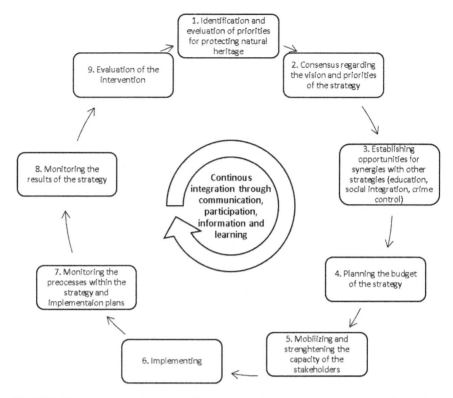

Fig. 19.1 Environmental governance with integration of conservation criminology (adapted from Grobe and Hendriks 2014, p. 19)

19.3 Conservation Criminology and Environmental Risk Management

Risk management, as a coordinated activity with the purpose of directing and controlling an organization with regard to risk, has as its main goal to increase both the likelihood and impact of positive events, while decreasing them for negative events (Raz and Hillson 2005). Under such framework of uttermost importance is the iterative risk identification (Verzuh 2011, p. 106), as well as focusing on the assessment of the unknown unknowns.

The outlier event, the unknown of which magnitude changes severely and irreversibly the environmental equilibrium, must not be dismissed as having a low probability or addressed through the pre-conditionality framework, but considered as possibility and valued as a constant reminder for focusing proactively on environmental risk management. Along the same lines, but from a different perspective, there are consistent appeals for placing institutional checks and controls for mitigating not only the external outlier risks produced by external factors, but also the internal outlier, which frequently refers to the planning fallacy that, due to over-optimism, systematically and consistently underestimates the cost and time budgets of the projects and cumulatively amplifies the overall risk (Flyvbjerg et al. 2012, p. 494), especially for the final phases (Chapman 2014, p. 448) of projects or action plans.

Environmental crime can have a devastating impact on natural heritage and environmental risk management must consider the associated risks, as well as appropriate risk mitigation strategies. The segment of corporate crime is particularly challenging to address, due to the complexity of the phenomenon, association with corruption, and access to important resources for dissimulating the illicit activities. Punctual events, caused by corporate criminal negligence in ensuring the environmental safety, motivated by reducing costs and increasing profits, specifically in the industrial fields or oil and gas, naval transportation or chemical engineering, have produced catastrophic events with long-lasting impact on environment and local communities. When such activities are coordinated by criminal networks, the risks are amplified also by additional diversion of resources from economic growth to private illegitimate channels.

Therefore, regarding environmental crimes, not only harms caused by individuals should be considered, but also and foremost the corporate environmental harms which effect is amplified by the use of legitimate activities or official permits simulating legality in covering their actions. Under such circumstances, the awareness of the different stakeholders is critical in identifying the risks associated with corporate criminal behavior and planning for mitigation strategies, including, if necessary, investigation, prosecution, and reparatory measures.

Validated environmental risk assessment methodologies are critical for the risk management of natural heritage areas, but also the existence of a suitable organizational and behavioral environment for their implementation (Krezner 2013, p. 788), as well as anchoring environmental protection programs into their local and institutional context. This means a heavy involvement of the local stakeholders and emphasis on educating legislators and regulatory authorities, and through this, it is ensured the coevolution of the natural heritage protection projects and the legislative and regulatory framework that makes it viable (Miller and Hobbs 2006, p. 9–12).

19.4 Conclusions

Risks associated with both criminal cross-border networks and corporate criminal activities, in some instances even a combination of the two, can be adequately identified and managed through incorporation of conservation criminology framework into environmental governance. Due to its cross-disciplinary approach and focus on building knowledge about environmental risks and crime by means of inductive reasoning, transferring and adapting methodologies from criminology, environmental, and decision sciences (Gibbs et al. 2010, p. 139), conservation criminology could inform the policy-making process and facilitate the synergy between different strategies in the field of natural heritage protection, economic development, social integration, and crime control. More effort is needed to develop an inter-, trans-, and pluri-disciplinary frameworks for an integrated analysis of environmental threats, especially with reference to collection and interpreting data regarding existing models in which the emphasis is placed on preventing, detecting, investigating, and prosecuting crimes against environment with the purpose of analyzing comparatively the results and the medium- to long-term impact.

Integrating conservation criminology analysis into environmental governance could contribute toward an increased corporate responsibility regarding natural heritage and, in the same time, provide valuable inputs regarding relevant environmental risks and crimes, for their assessment and management.

Acknowledgments This paper is made and published under the aegis of the Research Institute for Quality of Life, Romanian Academy as a part of program co-funded by the European Union within the Operational Sectorial Programme for Human Resources Development through the project for pluri- and interdisciplinarity in doctoral and postdoctoral programs Project Code: POSDRU/159/1.5/S/141,086.

References

Box, S. (1987). *Recession, crime and punishment*. London: Macmillan Education.

Chapman, M. R. (2014). *The rules of project risk management: Implementation guidelines for major projects*. Surrey: Ashgate Publishing Ltd.

Dutu, M. (2013). Criminologiamediului. *Dreptul, 6,* 220–233.

Faure, M., Gerstetter, C., Sina, S., & Vagliasindi, G. M. (2015). Instruments, actors and institutions in the fight against environmental crime. EFFACE. Available at www.efface.eu on 12.10.2015.

Flyvbjerg, B., Holm, M. S., & Buhl, S. (2012). Underestimating costs in public works projects: Error or lie? *Journal of the American planning association, 68*(3), 279–295.

Gibbs, C., Gore, M. L., McGarrell, E. F., & Rivers, L. (2010). Introducing conservation criminology towards interdisciplinary scholarship on environmental crimes and risks. *British Journal of Criminology, 50*(1), 124–144.

Grobe, F., & Hendriks, J. (2014). *Community planning: A multi road map*. București: AO Foundation for Organisation Development.

Ionita-Burda, S. D. (2012). Forme de manifestare a criminalitățiiecologice. Pro Patria Lex10 (1), 273–280.

Interpol. (2014). National environmental security task force: Bringing compliance and enforcement agencies together to maintain environmental security. Available at http://www.interpol. int/content/download/18678/166703/version/9/file/NEST%20Manual%20-%20English%20-%202014%20Feb%202014.pdf on 9.10.2015.

Kerzner, H. R. (2013). *Project management: A systems approach to planning, scheduling, and controlling*. New Jersey: Wiley & Sons.

Lynch, M.J., & Stretesky, P. (2007). Green criminology in the United States. In Beirne, P., & South, N. (Eds.), (2007). *Issues in green criminology*. New York: Routledge.

Miller, R., & Hobbs, B. (2006). Managing risks and uncertainty in major projects in the new global environment. In Cleland, D., & Gareis, R. (Eds.), *Global project management handbook: Planning, organizing and controlling international projects*. London: McGraw Hill Professional.

Raz, T., & Hillson, D. (2005). A comparative review of risk management standards. *Risk Management, 7*(4), 53–66.

Runciman, W. G. (1993). *Relative deprivation & social justice: Study attitudes social inequality in 20th century England (Republished)*. Hampshire: Gregg Revivals.

Verzuh, E. (2011). *The fast forward MBA in project management*. London: Wiley & Sons.

White, R. (2013). *Crimes against nature: Environmental criminology and ecological justice*. New York: Routledge.

Young, J. (1999). *The exclusive society*. London: Sage Publications.

Chapter 20
Development of Romanian Corporate Governance in Hospitality Industry: Necessity and Favorable Factors

Florin Boghean and Carmen Boghean

Abstract The risk derives from people's incapacity to foresee the future, and it is acknowledged only when the possible outcomes have a fairly significant degree of uncertainty. Risk cannot be completely eliminated by man when future results are influenced by random factors. However, it lies in its power to reduce the risk to a level that makes it acceptable. Never, in the history of mankind, larger monetary losses have existed. In this case, two external elements influence the process of making economic decisions, with contrasting effects. The first element is an external one and refers to the accuracy of the obtained results, which of course needs to be maximized, because with increasing precision of the results, the probability of an error decreases. The latter factor relates to the timeframe in which economic decision has to be made, which is increasingly transforming into a luxury characteristic afforded by few entities. This scientific approach aims to identify the corporate governance development favorable factors, and it is based on a specific research methodology, consisting of techniques and methods used to achieve the proposed objective. The paper approaches, from an interdisciplinary perspective, the corporate governance efficiency, a relatively new theme compared to other fields, but which presents an ever-increasing interest. The research falls within a positivist scientific endeavor, which is not deprived of some critical and interpretative approaches that aim at explaining different concepts, as well as highlighting the possible solutions for the identified problems.

Keywords Corporate governance · Management systems · Decision-making process

F. Boghean (✉) · C. Boghean
Faculty of Economics and Public Administration,
Ştefan cel Mare University of Suceava, Suceava, Romania
e-mail: florinb@seap.usv.ro

20.1   The Current Stage of Knowledge in the Field

The global economic prosperity forecasts are facing the huge repercussions of the economic crisis. In this framework, the financial flexibility in case of risk for most companies from hospitality industry becomes ever smaller due to the fact that the insolvency menace becomes more real and the economic success of most companies is increasingly shaky (Hoag 2010). In our opinion, we believe that the accumulation of a rising risk was due to the deficiencies in the global financial system, the failure to implement the principles of corporate governance, and especially the lack of financial supervision of credit institutions of systemic importance. Even if we cannot attribute the triggering of the crisis to corporate governance in hospitality industry, the absence or inadequacy of effective control mechanisms ultimately determined most institutions to assume excessive risk.

Since the outbreak of the financial crisis, a pronounced concern was manifested toward the credibility and accuracy of accounting data. The entities with a poor corporate governance system are more inclined to have a fraudulent reporting than the entities with a developed corporate governance system (Farber 2005). Moreover, the entities from hospitality industry with a weak corporate governance system have many issues related to agent theory, because it provides low protection to minority shareholders (Core et al. 1999).

The role of corporate governance within an entity in decisions substantiation has been approached in the literature, in many books and articles.

20.2   The Research Methodology

This scientific approach aims to identify the corporate governance development favorable factors, and it is based on a specific research methodology, consisting of techniques and methods used to achieve the proposed objective. The bibliographical reference, which is a significant component of the scientific documentation process, is crucially important because through the literature it enables us to acknowledge the scientific heritage. The paper approaches, from an interdisciplinary perspective, the corporate governance efficiency, a relatively new theme compared to other fields, but which presents an ever-increasing interest. The research falls within a positivist scientific endeavor, which is not deprived of some critical and interpretative approaches that aim at explaining different concepts, as well as highlighting the possible solutions for the identified problems.

In order to achieve the proposed objective in this scientific approach, a methodology based on an approach that combined qualitative with quantitative research was used. This way, we attempted to identify both the theoretical valences and the practical challenges posed by corporate governance in hospitality industry too.

The extent to which companies from tourism industry respect the principles of corporate governance becomes an increasingly important factor in the investment-related decision-making process. The relation between corporate governance practices and the increasingly international character of investments receives a special relevance. Listed companies that are well managed and have a strong corporate governance structure and suitable environmental and social programs experience a better market performance against the competitors; the institutional investors are willing—according to a 2013 PWC report—to pay with 16% more for their shares in the developed markets and 27–28% in emerging countries.

20.3 Corporate Governance in Hospitality Industry— Between Globalization and Regulation

Corporate governance occupies more and more debate space in nowadays business world. The reason seems to be related to the globalization of business and to the fact that their owners become increasingly distanced from their actual management. In most cases, the owners of big business cannot get personally involved in the management of their business. The reasons may vary and of these there can be mentioned:

- tourism business expansion beyond traditional borders;
- the rapid evolution rate and business complexity increase;
- the necessary technical knowledge in order to ensure an effective governance;
- the inability to simultaneously know and assimilate local particularities of the environment in which the business evolves: culture, legislation, regulations, customs, etc.

The papers wrote about the failure of risk management in large enterprises: environmental disasters like Fukushima, bribery (e.g., EADS, Siemens) or financial engineering (for instance, Satyam, Parmalat, Xerox, Enron). The failure of risk management was one of the financial crisis's complete surprises. Often, companies did not manage risk efficiently due to the separation of the risk management from the other governance structures and not considering an important part of it (Fig. 20.1).

In spite of some considerable progress, significant lacuna remains in various fields, especially concerning the risk management feature; therefore, the following recommendations are necessary (Financial Stability Board (FSB) 2013):

- National authorities should focus on regulating and overseeing financial investments in tourism, and also managers to allocate adequate resources for effective risk management in the entities they manage;
- Standardization organizations should revise their governance principles, taking also into account the risk governance practices;

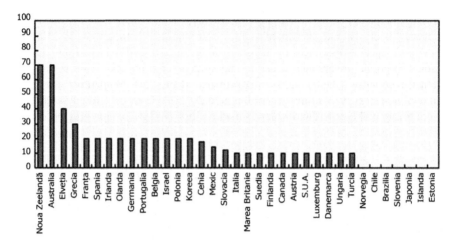

Fig. 20.1 Companies that have implemented standard no. 11—Risk management (2010). *Source* OECD (2010)

- Risk culture in financial institutions should be officially assessed;
- General instructions regarding key elements should be provided for their inclusion in the risk appetite assessment;

In Romania, the issuers that decide the total or partial adoption of the recommendations of the Corporate Governance Code (CGC) will annually send to the Bucharest Stock Exchange (BVB) a statement of compliance or non-compliance with the provisions of CGC (*The Comply or Explain Statement*) that contains information regarding the CGC recommendations that are effectively implemented by them and the implementation manner. *The comply or explain statement* provides information regarding the application of corporate governance recommendations. The assessment of the application mode of the corporate governance recommendations by the companies listed on BVB is achieved through the 51 affirmative or negative answers.

20.4   Best Corporate Governance Policies

The incentive schemes for the managers were not in the best interest of the shareholders. First of all, they were to the benefit of directors who, despite the losses suffered by companies, have become richer. Nothing happened to the directors because of the corporate governance faulty implementation. Generally, corporations are, in theory, formally managed by the shareholders. In reality, in a very large extent, these are run by the management teams in their own benefit. There are certain boundaries to which the management team can abusively use its position, as it can be seen from the battles between shareholders and the company's takeovers.

Where the property is widely diversified among many scattered shareholders, the majority of the members of the board of directors are practically appointed by the management team, which of course will appoint those able to best serve their interests. The board is the one that ultimately decides the manager's wages, and the company provides substantial rewards to the board members. It is a close and comfortable relationship for both parties.

The American capitalist system also defined as *managerial capitalism* is characterized by a clear separation between property and economic additional spectrum, the interest being represented exclusively by the action's benefits, known as dividends. In this market system, the high level of transparency and facilitation in obtaining information represents the main manner of establishing financial resources, as well as the most important controller of all economic and financial operations.

In the USA, the management structure is characterized by the existence of a single organ, both with directive and control responsibilities. From a formal point of view, the fundamental organ of the American corporate governance is represented by the *shareholders*, while substantially is represented by the *board of directors*, which has the main role in running the business. Therefore, all the shareholders, especially in the US economy, have neither a control role nor a management one; to a certain extent, the shareholder rights protection falls under the responsibility of the pension funds, these funds having available large resources and holding investments in the most important national and international companies.

In the American corporate system, contrary to the tendencies, the role played by the banks is currently limited, as compared to what happened not very long ago. Therefore, the banking sector, its decline, and the bankruptcies represented the engines that generated the economic and financial crisis of 1930 and 2008. As a result of these recessions, the banking sector has been the subject of a series of legislative interventions that have significantly postponed and limited the field of action and the power levers within banks reach. An exception to this situation is represented by the *investment banks*—which occupy a central role in the American banking system (Stiglitz 2010).

After analyzing a series of reports of various institutions from the risk management and corporate governance fields, we propose a series of policies for efficient corporate governance in hospitality industry presented in Table 20.1.

Table 20.1 Policies for efficient corporate governance in hospitality industry

Governance elements	Proposal
The board of directors	• The board must include independent directors, with a clear distinction among external (non-executive) directors and independent directors • Clear indications, reference ones, will be established for the board and subcommittees (including the mandate). The communication mechanisms will be established regularly and transparently in order to ensure dialog, a continuous information, an exchange of information between the board and subcommittees
	• A periodic evaluation of the board members and subcommittees members performance will be accomplished (the nominating board or supervisory board). This includes at least an annual revision of the managers' qualifications as well as of their combined skills (this includes expertise in the financial and risk fields), of their time commitment and ability to evaluate the given information and understand the business model of the company, their specialty background necessary for the demanded skills, wishing to highlight that there exists a directly proportional ratio between remuneration and long-term results • The board of directors must efficiently impose an adequate risk culture in the entire entity • The board is responsible for the supervision of the efficient implementation of risk management for the entire entity • The board is responsible for the supervision of the efficient implementation of risk management for the entire entity
	• On a quarterly basis, the board receives and has access to any information it requires, from the committees
The risk board	• Is necessary to have a freestanding committee, other than the audit committee • Is an independent actor and it avoids the "double subordination" with the chairman of the board of directors—B Of D or any other trustees • Consists of independent members • Comprises members which have risk management issues experience • Debates all the risk strategies depending on the risk type • Has the obligation to examine and approve, at least annually, the company's risk policy
The audit committee	• Has to be a freestanding committee, other than the risk board • Is an independent actor and it avoids the "double subordination" with the chairman of B Of D or any other representatives • Independent members are included • Includes members that have experience related to the internal audit and financial practices • Evaluates the audits concerning the internal management control system in the annual audit plan, set by the management to confirm that it functions according to the standards
The risk management position	• Is independent (e.g., it is not involved in income generation) • Has the authority to make decisions that influence the risk exposures the company has

(continued)

Table 20.1 (continued)

Governance elements	Proposal
	• Is responsible for the establishment and periodic revision of risk management at company level; framework that also comprises the appetite for risk • Has access to relevant data • Provides, accurate and relevant, information that is risk related to the board of directors and to senior management, which is frequently reviewed by a third party (the internal auditor), in order to ensure its comprehensiveness and integrity • Periodically and upon request, it performs stress tests (including reverse crisis tests). In the budget revisions, in the establishment of the risk appetite, and in the settling of the urgency plans against the crisis conditions are included the results of the stress tests
The internal audit	• The internal audit will establish its obligations toward the supervisory board, as follows • It annually provides a general opinion related to the audit committee risk management efficiency • It performs a qualitative assessment of risk and of the internal control system • To provide feedback on the company's risk management, the identification of best practices as a way to influence risks • To provide feedback about the internal controls during the planning and implementation processes of the system and data for risk assessment • Is informed about the trends in the field and the best practices • At least quarterly, it has meetings with the supervisory committee

20.5   Conclusion

Considering the trends encountered in the international tourism market, a natural conclusion is that corporate governance in hospitality industry will linger on the list of companies' top management for a long time from now on. All is reduced to a simple reality: Companies which refuse to adopt a transparent culture and an efficient model of corporate governance will perform much worse than the ones that do, and nowadays, they will even record poorer results. It is obvious that the market volatility, combined with economic uncertainty and the pressure from shareholders, will create the risk premises for the top management to act ethically incorrect. Therefore, the importance of an effective corporate governance model which controls and evaluates the company's performance will increase even more, while meeting the needs of all stakeholders, thus creating added value. And indeed, under these circumstances, corporate governance in tourism industry is still far from being another bureaucratic layer. It resembles more to an instrument that contributes to the company's value maximization. The entities must act extremely aggressive on various international tourism markets and use more than just one risk management tool, more exactly a mix of such instruments, in order to withstand in a global economic climate that is highly complex and aggravated from the financial crisis. This department's activity is very important, because it becomes a vital one in the society.

References

Core, et al. (1999). Corporate governance, chief executive officer compensation, and firm performance. *Journal of Financial Economics, 51*, 371–406.

Farber, D. B. (2005). Restoring trust after fraud: Does corporate governance matter? *The Accounting Review, 80*(2), 539–561.

Financial Stability Board (FSB). (2013). Thematic review on risk governance. Accessed at 25.03.2016, from www.financialstabilityboard.org/publications/r_130212.pdf.

Hoag, D. L. (2010). *Applied risk management in agriculture*. Boca Raton, Florida: Editura CRC Press.

OECD. (2004). *Principles of corporate governance*. Accessed at 05. 12. 2015. http://www.oecd. org/document/49/0,3343,en_2649_34813_31530865_1_1_1_1,00.html.

Shleifer, A., & Vishny, R. W. (1996). A survey of corporate governance, National Bureau of Economic Research, Cambrige MA 02138, April 1996, Accessed at 27.08.2015. http://www. nber.org/papers/w5554.pdf.

Stiglitz, J. E. (2010). *În cădere liberă. America, piaţa liberă şi prăbuşirea economiei mondiale.*, Editura Publică, Bucharest.

Tricker, B. (2011). The cultural dependence of corporate governance. Accessed at 29.08.2015. http://corporategovernanceoup.wordpress.com/2011/11/07/the-cultural-dependence-of-corporate-governance.

Tripa, S. (2006). Guvernanţa corporativă în contextul globalizării. Accessed at 15.05.2016. http:// steconomice.uoradea.ro/anale/volume/2006/economie-si-administrarea-afacerilor/72.pdf.

Chapter 21
Importance and Perspectives of Protected Areas in Romania

Daniela Antonescu

Abstract Currently, the human impact exerted on the taxonomic diversity of vegetation and wildlife is very high. Human activities erode biological resources and reduce biodiversity. Biodiversity loss is the effect of agricultural and forestry intensive activities, industrialization, advanced fragmentation of natural habitats by infrastructure and urbanization, water, air pollution and tourism development. After accession to the European Union (EU), one of Romania's priorities was to increase protection of its natural areas. In these circumstances, the Romanian Academy initiated a project entitled "Natural resources—strategic reserves, what we use and what we let to the future generations," which aimed to realize the primary aspects regarding conservation of biodiversity and protection of natural areas in Romania. This chapter aims to present the main findings of this research project.

Keywords Protected area · Sustainable development · Biodiversity
Natural habitat · Regional development · Ecosystem

21.1 Introduction

Biodiversity is a system of life support, the basis for economic and social activities and development, and ensures the survival of all living things. Eco-natural systems are those that determine the specific conditions which require exchanges of energy, materials, and information, contributing to adaptability, resilience, and productivity. The relations established between different ecosystems are very complex, with it being difficult to estimate the importance of each individual, as well as the potential consequences of losing an individual or groups.

D. Antonescu (✉)
Institute of National Economy-Romanian Academy, Calea 13 Septembrie,
050711 Bucharest, Romania
e-mail: daniela.antonescu25@gmail.com

© Springer International Publishing AG, part of Springer Nature 2019   241
V. Vasile (ed.), *Caring and Sharing: The Cultural Heritage Environment
as an Agent for Change*, Springer Proceedings in Business and Economics,
https://doi.org/10.1007/978-3-319-89468-3_21

Organizing and conducting different economic activities generates environmental pressures related to land use, changing landscapes and ecosystems, destruction of natural spaces, irrational use of land, overconcentration of activities in very sensitive areas with high environmental value, etc. Population growth, agricultural development, and the economy have determined an increase in anthropogenic activities.

In the last three decades the diversification of human activity, acceleration of globalization, and chronic pollution have been the dominant traits of environmental deterioration. The damage to natural capital is a real process which is extremely complex and lengthy, evolving in strict dependence on pace, forms, and forces of socioeconomic development systems.

To protect biodiversity and to ensuring public access to outstanding natural areas for recreation and tourism, Protected Areas (PAs) have been proposed. Whatever the definitions in each country and in international organizations, it is certain that they provide environmental, scientific, educational, recreational, economic, and cultural benefit, while the coverage of PAs is an indicator of the degree to which biodiversity components are protected.

Given that we are actually witnessing the visible degradation of biodiversity, with its irreversible effects and major imbalances on the environment, it is very important to establish an inventory of all natural and biodiverse resources in Romania.

21.2 The national natural context

Located in Central Europe, at an equal distance between the North Pole and the Equator, and between the Atlantic Ocean and the Ural Mountains, the Danube River and the Black Sea, Romania has a balanced climate and landscape regime: 28% mountains; 42% hills and plateaus; and 30% plains—having high biological diversity. Romania's geographical location and radial natural distribution determines the existence of a wide range of meso–micro climates and soil conditions.

Romania owns 54% of the Carpathians and almost 97.8% of the national rivers flowing into the Danube. The Black Sea region includes coastal platform and territorial waters as well as an exclusive economic zone under the Strategy of Marine Networks (Directive 2008/56/EC).

To maintain and preserve species and habitats, in the European Union (EU) there are seven statutes of preservation, covered by Directive 2009/147/EC (Birds Directive) and Council Directive 92/43/EEC on the conservation of natural habitats and of wild fauna and flora (Habitats Directive). These directives are implemented in Romania through the following:

- Monitoring the conservation status of species and habitats (Art. 17 Habitats Directive).
- National System of bird monitoring (Art. 12 Birds Directive).

The concept of "natural habitat" is defined by Habitats Directive no. 92.43/EEC on the conservation of natural habitats and wildlife: "terrestrial or aquatic areas, which are distinguished by comprehensive geographic features, no biotic and biotic, natural and semi-natural, similar with the concept of ecosystem".

At the national level, PAs represent 24.84% of the country (PAs of national interest representing 7% and Natura 2000 representing 17.84%). Meanwhile, natural ecosystems represent 47% of the country; agricultural ecosystems 45%, and construction/infrastructure 8%.

The great diversity of Romanian ecosystems is determined, mainly, due to their very high numbers:

- 357 habitat types, most of them being equivalent to the major classification systems used at the European level.
- 199 habitats—equivalent in Natura 2000.
- 213 habitats—Emerald equivalent.
- 170 habitats—Corine Program.
- 357 habitats—Palearctic Program.
- 263 habitats—European Nature Information System (EUNIS).

After Romanian's entry to the EU, on a national level there was an increase in protected natural areas (both in terms of number and size). Thus, the national protected area network gradually expanded as a consequence of a series of Government Decisions (GDs), during the period 2004–2010 (GD no. 2151/2004, no. 1581/2005, no. 1143/2007, no. 1066/2010, and no. 1217/2010). Currently, in Romania, there are 998 PAs, namely: 79 scientific reserves; 13 national parks; 230 nature monuments; 661 nature reserves; 15 natural parks; three biosphere reserves—Delta (1991), Retezat (1979), and Pietrosul Rodnei (1979); 19 Ramsar Sites; and one World Heritage Site—the Danube Delta.

21.3 Evolution of Protected Areas in Romania

Due to growing interest in PAs in Romania, their number has increased in recent years, from 1384 (2008) to 1503 (2013)—an increase of 8.6%. Wetlands of international importance grew by 280%, followed by PAs of Community Importance with a growth rate up by 40.3% in 2013 compared to 2008. However, there are two categories of PAs that did not follow the general trend, recording a numerical reduction: scientific reservations and natural monuments (Fig. 21.1).

The authorities responsible for protecting natural areas in Romania are those who develop strategies, programs, and legislation (Table 21.1).

Management of protected natural areas is carried out according to Emergency Ordinance (OUG) no. 57/2007 on the regime of protected natural areas, conservation of natural habitats, wild flora and fauna, approved by Law 49/2011, with Government Decision (HG) 1000/2012 regarding the reorganization and

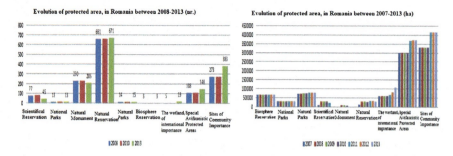

Fig. 21.1 Evolution of PAs in Romania. *Source* Author's contribution

Table 21.1 Central institutions involved in managing PAs in Romania

Ministry of environment, water and forests	Developing national strategies on environmental protection (Romania's national strategy on climate change, 2050) life + programme
Environment fund administration	The main institution that provides financial support to environmental protection programmes. It is coordinated by the Ministry of Environment
Ministry of European funds	Develops and manages the operational programme large infrastructure during the period 2010–2020
Ministry of regional development and public administration (territorial development) National agency for cadastre and land	Spatial Development Strategy of Romania Coordinate the integrated strategy for sustainable development of the Danube Delta Implements the National and Regional Spatial Programme (RSP) Provides documentation endorsement landscaping, according to the competencies established by law
Ministry of agriculture	National program for rural development, 2014–2020

Source Author's contribution

functioning of the National Agency for Environmental Protection and subordinate public institutions.

At the end of 2013 there were 10 approved management plans:

- Natural Park Grădiştea Muncelului.
- Cioclovina National Park.
- Macin Mountains National Park.
- Iron Gates Natural Park.
- Calimani National Park.
- Bucegi Natural Park.

- Small Marsh Braila Natural Park.
- Blindly Rezervation Apahida.
- Beresti Rezervation.
- Plopeni Site, Natura 2000.

21.4 SWOT Analysis of Romania's Biodiversity

A comprehensive strengths, weaknesses, opportunities, threats (SWOT) analysis for PAs was undertaken as part of an evaluation process. It identified the following opportunities and threats.

Strengths

- Romania has a high biodiversity (about 3700 plant species and almost 33,800 animal species), including species of Community interest and/or species on different lists under World Heritage protection.
- The existence of adequate legislation and institutions empowered to act in this area.
- Romania has continuously participated in international environmental policy making, signing, and ratifying international conventions regarding the protection of World Heritage (cultural and natural).
- The existence of major natural areas 31 (3 biosphere reserves, 13 national parks, 15 nature parks) and 671 nature reserves.
- Significant growth identified in nationally protected natural areas mainly through setting up networks covering about 23% of the country.
- The existence of an integrated geographical information system (GIS) database at the national level (a cadastre of PAs, national park zoning, creating a database in accordance with Natura 2000) which is available free of charge on the Ministry of Environment website.
- The existence of the Natural Monuments Commission of the Romanian Academy, founded in 1950, and its involvement in the decision-making process on PAs.
- A large number of non-governmental organizations (NGOs) in environmental protection associations.
- The existence of national programs directly aimed at protected areas.
- The existence of protected areas (monasteries, archaeological sites, churches, etc.) under statute of Biodiversity Area.

Weaknesses

- Lack of management plans and effective protection for most natural reservations and Natura 2000 sites.
- Increasing anthropogenic pressure on protected natural areas (deforestation, tourism, mining, overgrazing, etc.).

- Large areas of Natura 2000 sites include land use which is contrary to the objectives of nature protection.
- Lack of rules for the application of laws aimed at PAs and their management.
- Lack of funds for implementing the objectives of management protected natural areas.
- Lack of staff to implement protection and management objectives.
- Localities in the vicinity of PAs are generally underdeveloped and have limited potential for growth/development; they have limited access to infrastructure, and the population is in a continuous process of migration.
- Irrational use of natural resources (e.g., forestry).
- Excessive use of coastal areas, without considering the ecological balance; gradual erosion and steep coastal zones, reducing areas of beach.
- The management of PAs does not result in a correlation between economic and social development objectives and conservation, given that communities are fragile PAs (mountain areas, border isolated).

Opportunities

- The existence of important European sources of funding should permit elaboration of management plans and enhancement of the public awareness of the importance of PAs.
- Implementation of projects through the effective management of protected natural areas (ex. National Protected Area Management System (SINCRON http://www.teamnet.ro/solutions/magnitudeprojects/sincron-national-protected-areamanagement-system/)).
- Increased involvement of NGOs, educational institutions, and research institutions on issues related to PAs and their management.
- Provision of grants to reduce human pressure on natural PAs.

Threats

- Habitat loss and fragmentation of habitat due to urbanization, infrastructure development, and exploitation of natural resources, especially forest resources.
- Uncontrolled and illegal logging in protected natural areas.
- The draining of wetlands for cultivation or other uses for obtaining economic profits.
- The abandonment of traditional uses of land, especially for pastures and meadows, incineration of forests, and overgrazing.
- The overexploitation of ecosystems and species through various economic activities.
- Penetration and expansion of invasive species.
- Environmental pollution and uncontrolled waste effecting biodiversity (acid rain, eutrophication, etc.).
- Wind farms, especially those build across bird migration routes.
- Global environmental change, climate change, and extreme weather events (droughts, floods, heat waves or cold spells, wind intensification, etc.).

SWOT analysis is the main instrument for evaluating threats to PAs in Romania. Local and regional authorities play an important role in the process of protecting biodiversity by providing advice on how to:

- Strengthen adaptive management and monitoring of the whole process.
- Enhance organizational and developmental learning.
- Enable informed decision making and enhance the long-term sustainability of the achievements of different programs.

21.5 The Vision of Protected Area Development

By comparing the internal and external factors of SWOT analysis acceptable visions and perspectives were formulated and outlined here. The general vision regarding PAs, up to 2035, is that Romanian biodiversity, including the ecosystem services it provides (natural capital), will be protected, valued, and restored. It will take account of the intrinsic value of biodiversity and the vital contribution of the services provided by nature to human wellbeing and economic prosperity. The vision proposed is consistent with EU and national objectives and strategies: EU Strategy for biodiversity and Strategy Europe, 2020; National Strategy of territorial development of Romania, 2035 (Horizon 2050); Sustainable Millennium Development Goals; Romania's National Strategy 2013–2020–2030; The National Sustainable Development Strategy for the agri-food sector and rural areas in the period 2014–2020–2030; Prioritised Action Frameworks—Habitats Directive, Natura 2000.

In the author's opinion, the main actions which will support this vision are:

- Generating an inventory of all species in order to determine measures for maintaining/improving their conservation status.
- Elaboration of research studies to assess and monitor the conservation status of species and habitats.
- Economic and social analysis of the impact of human activity on Natura 2000 sites and species of community interest or internationally interest.
- Prioritization of action depending on the seriousness of environmental situations.
- Implementation and follow up of management plans.
- Identifying invasive species and prioritizing ways to counter them—control/ eradication.
- Maintaining ecological corridors, for migratory species and maintaining and/or improving the network of connectivity between PAs, including Natura 2000 sites.
- Ecological reconstruction of degraded ecosystems in PAs, including Natura 2000 sites.

21.6   Scenarios for 2035 horizon

Regardless of the time period to which they relate, territorial planning scenarios should consider nature and the environment, among other factors. From this perspective, we propose a further four spatial planning scenarios, which can be applied to individual regions, and can provide an overview of the evolution and status of biodiversity and PAs in Romania.

Scenario 1: Knowledge-regions according to Europe 2020. In this scenario, regions turn to modern technology, exchange of information, and modern systems of communication in order to identify new solutions to environmental issues. It relies on good information being made available to citizens and, at the same time, their effective participation in the management of the ecosystem in which they live. In this scenario, research and new technologies are the main driving forces that enable sustainable use of natural capital throughout the region. An increase in the dissemination of information will allow residents better awareness of the natural living environment, this is turn will lead to society as a whole becoming more involved in the management of the areas in which they live. The three sectors that contribute significantly to the environmental concerns—urbanization, tourism, and agriculture—will benefit from a number of inventions and innovations that will help protect the environment and maintain or restore biodiversity.

Scenario 2: Regions based on endogenous potential (New Economic Geography). This scenario relies on local resources and traditions, in pursuit of a regional flexible economy, one which is able to adapt to the outdoor environment. This scenario is specific to regions that promote long-term programs, capitalizing on regional strengths, including the natural environment. The scenario opposes the market liberalization trend (trend promoted by the EU), and the recovery, at any price, of endogenous potential by large international companies. The effects of climate change and unsustainable agricultural policies, which seek to maximize economic benefits, affecting biodiversity in protected areas. Consequently, part of the local population will migrate from the affected area due to worsening environmental conditions, while the differences between rich and poor will increase. Inhabitants of these regions want to live in a sustainable environment in terms of environmental quality and social framework.

Scenario 3: So-called red-zone regions (with important environmental problems), showing clear signs of environmental damage as a result of uncontrolled human action: continuously increasing temperatures, reduction of precipitation, flooding, etc. In this scenario, the region is influenced by the environmental crisis and the economic and social one. Biodiversity is increasingly threatened, water use is strictly controlled, agriculture returns to dry crop varieties, tourism activity decreases, urbanization increases, etc. As a result, it is necessary to invest funds increasingly into research for clean technologies (green technologies). Researchers and NGOs will become key members of the local community. This will result in a new paradigm of sustainability.

Scenario 4: Adaptive-regions. This covers the main features of each of the scenarios described above. The main principle of this scenario is that global knowledge will support the development and application of new technologies in the context of an economic–social–ecological system. Under this scenario, the region will develop sectors of agriculture/forestry, and eco-basic tourism and urbanization will take account of the landscape and land-use conditions in protected areas. In this regard, these regions will attract inhabitants, companies, NGOs, public institutions, etc., thereby maintaining territorially a high level of social cohesion.

Because human activities (economic, social, cultural, etc.) cannot be separated from nature, it is necessary to promote a model of thought on the development of PAs based on the principle of a conservation framework for development. Besides this, in areas with many natural landscapes, future practices have to enforce both economic and social services, in parallel with protection of ecosystems. The stimulation of economic activities must respect the environment unconditionally whilst promoting human welfare.

21.7   Conclusion

In Romania and the EU, biodiversity is negatively influenced by the inaction and depletion of financial and internal resources. Threats to biodiversity are both quantitative and, especially, qualitative, highlighting the need for better knowledge of the current situation. Moreover, there are many strategic documents and action plans, remaining in statements that have reported negative effects of human activities on nature: wild species threatened with extinction (fourth EU), many ecosystems degraded habitats modified as a result of increasing urbanization, overexploitation of natural resources, introduction and spread of invasive species, climate change, extreme, landslides, floods, etc.

Under actual, global and dramatic environmental changes, conservation of PAs is a strategic priority at both the national and international level. In this respect, Romania should promote and implement urgently a strategy for the conservation of natural areas based on policies and integrated development measures regarding to a sustainable approach.

PAs represent 24.84% of Romania's total land surface. These PAs are under the coordination of both national and county authorities. Research has shown that local factors play a very important role in implementing strategies for protecting biodiversity. Taking into account the low levels of financial resources available it is important that funds are managed wisely, establishing clear priorities in both the short term and long term. In addition, it is important to ensure stability, over time, of these priorities and not to allow conjectural modifications for the sake of short-term interests.

References

Antonescu, D. (2013). The regional development policy of Romania in the post-accession period, Postdoctoral Research, http://www.ince.ro.

Bălteanu, D., Dumitraşcu, M., Ciupitu, D., & Geacu, S. (2006). Protected natural areas, în vol. Romania. Space. Society. Environment, The Publishing House of the Romanian Academy, Bucureşti.

Borza, A. (1924). Protecţiunea naturii în România, Buletinul de informaţii al Grădinii Botanice şi al Muzeului Botanic de la Universitatea de Cluj, IV, 1, Cluj.

Borza, A. (1930). *Problema protecţiunei naturii în România, Întâiul Congres Naţional al Naturaliştilor din România.* Societăţii de Ştiinţe, Cluj: Edit.

Buza, M., Geacu, S., & Dumitraşcu, M. (2005). Die Nationalparks in Rumänien im Kontext der EU-Erweiterung. Ein Überblick, Europa Regional, 13, 3, Leipzig.

Hotărâre nr. (2151/2004). privind instituirea regimului de arie naturală protejată pentru noi zone.

Hotărârea Guvernului nr. (1066/2010). privind instituirea regimului de arie naturală protejată asupra unor zone din Rezervaţia Biosferei Delta Dunării şi încadrarea acestora în categoria rezervaţiilor ştiinţifice.

Hotărârea Guvernului nr. (1143/2007). privind instituirea de noi arii naturale protejate.

Hotărârea Guvernului nr. (1581/2005). privind instituirea regimului de arie naturală protejată pentru noi zone.

Legea nr. 5 din 6 martie. (2000). privind aprobarea planului de amenajare a teritoriului naţional, secţiunea III—zone protejate, Bucureşti.

Legea nr. 137 a protecţiei mediului, Bucureşti.

Lepşi, I. (1937). Ocrotirea monumentelor naturii din Basarabia, Buletinul Muzeului Regional al Basarabiei, 8, Chişinău.

Ordinul Ministrului Mediului şi Pădurilor nr. (2387/2011). pentru modificarea Ordinului ministrului mediului şi dezvoltării durabile. nr. (1964/2007) privind instituirea regimului de arie naturală protejată a siturilor de importanţă comunitară, ca parte integrantă a reţelei ecologice europene Natura 2000 în România.

Pop, E., & Sălăgeanu, N. (1965). *Monumente ale naturii din România.* Meridiane, Bucureşti: Edit.

Popescu, GH., Pătrăşcoiu, N., Georgescu, V. (2004). Ariile protejate din fondul forestier în România, în vol. *Pădurea şi omul", Edit. Nord-Carta, Suceava.*

Popova-cucu, A., & Muică, C. (1983). Ocrotirea naturii, în vol. *Geografia României", I, Edit. Academiei R.S. Română, Bucureşti.*

Racoviţă, E. (1937). Les Monuments Naturels. Définition, Classification, Normes pour l'application des lois et règlements. Ce qu'il faudrait faire et ce qu'il faudrait ne point faire. Essais d'exposé sommaire, Société de Biogéographie, 5, Paris.

Strategia Naţională pentru Conservarea Biodiversităţii. (2013–2020). Ministerul Mediului şi Schimbărilor Climatice.

Strategia Naţională privind Schimbările Climatice. (2013–2020). Ministerul Mediului şi Schimbărilor Climatice.

Toniuc, N., Oltean, M., Romanca, G., Zamfir, M. (1992). List of protected areas in Romania, Ocrotirea Naturii şi a Mediului Înconjurător, 36, 1, Bucureşti.

Chapter 22
Training for Heritage Promotion in Rural Areas

Marius-Răzvan Surugiu, Valentina Vasile, Raluca Mazilescu, Ioana-Alexandra Login and Camelia Surugiu

Abstract Revitalizing rural areas can be done on the basis of innovative ideas provided by well-trained staff with high skill levels. Education and training should be a priority due to the continuing high rate of growth in the demand for new skills in the labor market. Currently, employers are seeking, in the labor market, people with social skills, computer skills, foreign language speakers, and people who demonstrate initiative, coming up with new ideas which may be productive for businesses. People have become more sensitive about the environment, they are more educated and seek quality in both services and products. This cannot be provided without the assistance of stakeholders (local communities, authorities, entrepreneurs, employees, trainers, etc.) who also need to be trained in accordance with their duties and roles.

Keywords Training · Heritage · Rural areas

22.1 Introduction

Human resources are of particular importance to the economy, especially given the challenges arising nationally and internationally. Human resources represent the driver of development in rural economies. This underlines the fact that there is a connection between the level of training of human resources and the development level attainable. This makes it necessary to bring into question the methods used for counseling and raising awareness of the effects of human resources on economic, social, and cultural aspects influencing life in rural areas.

It is well known that agriculture, animal husbandry, and other traditional activities from rural areas have, over a period of time, shown a decrease in

M.-R. Surugiu (✉) · V. Vasile · R. Mazilescu · I.-A. Login · C. Surugiu
Institute of National Economy-Romanian Academy, Bucharest, Romania
e-mail: mariussurugiu@yahoo.com

C. Surugiu
Faculty of Administration and Business, University of Bucharest, Bucharest, Romania

© Springer International Publishing AG, part of Springer Nature 2019   251
V. Vasile (ed.), *Caring and Sharing: The Cultural Heritage Environment
as an Agent for Change*, Springer Proceedings in Business and Economics,
https://doi.org/10.1007/978-3-319-89468-3_22

importance to the local economy. Thus, identifying new alternative sources of revenue is of great importance. Valuing cultural heritage and tourism may represent effective solutions for improving rural areas. Romania has a great tourism potential and heritage assets with unmatched value.

22.2 Training to Manage and Promote Cultural Heritage

Revitalizing rural areas can be done on the basis of innovative ideas provided by well-trained human resources with high skill levels. The role of training in developing human resources is evident in all countries throughout the world. Education and training should take priority due to the continuing high rate of growth in the demand for highly skilled labor.

The process of training human resources is a complex one, with many issues to be considered by human resource specialists and also by stakeholders. The problems that may occur are varied. The sustainable development of the heritage and tourism sectors requires the involvement of all stakeholders (local communities, employees, professionals, entrepreneurs, and trainers) with each stakeholder receiving some type of training, adapted to the needs and to the specificity of the activities. For the development of the heritage and tourism sectors in rural areas, it is important to attract entrepreneurs, residents of these areas, local authorities, etc., all of whom need to understand the importance of these activities for both themselves and the community.

The heritage and tourism sectors will not be able to provide quality products and services without a well-trained workforce. For all stakeholders feedback is important, because stakeholders will, sooner or later, be influenced by the activities of others. Therefore, it is necessary that each one understands the others' needs, benefits, and risks, to be able to make wise decisions in order to support such activities. This underlines the need for the development of networking between interested actors from all sectors.

In order to reform the Romanian heritage and tourism sectors, and to have internationally competitive sectors, better working conditions and improved quality of training are needed, so that the products and services coming from those sectors of the Romanian economy can better develop. Rural businesses must have the maturity to invest in human resource development in order to encourage staff to acquire new skills and abilities. In turn, government bodies and educational institutions should promote training and stress its importance in relation to skills, knowledge, and the needs of individuals.

Heritage assets represent a region's main attractions, also representing one of Romania's main tourism products. It is important to develop the sustainability of such assets in order to provide economic opportunities to communities.

Considering the benefits for rural areas, it is important to protect heritage assets by promoting sustainability in both the heritage and tourism sectors. Thus, public decision makers may adopt measures focused on protection of heritage assets and tourism products and services, ensuring that those sectors meet their potential, representing after all, important drivers for the development of rural areas. Preserving heritage assets may represent a very complex activity, due to the fact that various stakeholders need to collaborate for preservation to happen. Thus, it is important to develop networking between key actors, with the purpose of developing sustainable policies and strategies. Also, it is important to identify project ideas which may bring innovative results regarding various approaches to promote sustainable products and services in both the heritage and tourism sectors. In addition, it is important that all key stakeholders (tourism organizations, heritage organizations, etc.) are continuously trained and involved in preservation projects.

Nowadays, the number of tourists and their requirements have increased. This requires a rise in the level of training given to employees from heritage and tourism sectors. There is also a need for training in the use of new technologies. The use of information and communication technology (ICT) registered a growth, also in various rural areas. The need for sustainable development, for national and international networking, requires a high level of training. The need for a highly qualified workforce is not only a requirement but also an economic priority, with training representing the activity through which economic progress can be sustained. Training also provides satisfaction to individuals and supports the revival of rural areas.

In rural areas, educational assistance is extremely important, since rural areas tend to have small budgets and poorly trained staff that rely on volunteer leadership. Training and professional development programs can provide valuable assistance in strategic planning, identifying available resources for development, and managing new or expanding tourism businesses (South Rural Development Center 2000).

Moreover, the idea that an important part of the workforce might transfer from agriculture to other sectors, such as heritage and tourism, requires some investment in human resource training. Many of the problems faced by farmers which may be involved in heritage or tourism businesses may be overcomed by investing in knowledge and training for skills used in managing these kinds of businesses.

Any economic activity developed requires a training period. However, some farmers consider they can provide services to different categories of visitors with little or no training. Many business owners and employees in rural tourism are not well prepared, or have a low level of training, considering that the holiday experience they offer to consumers of tourism products and services is sufficient (OECD 1994). A business in the heritage or tourism sectors may be complex, with many problems which need to be solved—success may be obtained only with proper training and additional qualifications.

The training of human resources represents a key factor to the quality of heritage and tourism products and services. It is therefore necessary that a minimum training be given to rural heritage and tourism services and products providers, together with technical assistance regarding various aspects related to rural area development.

The development of some learning centers can be extremely useful to the rural community, especially in periods of economic and social change. These centers may offer programs for the development of knowledge and skills, and also programs to support rural businesses.

Competence and skills may be obtained through seminars, personal counseling, sharing success stories and lessons learned, local papers, roundtables, forums, and so on, thus helping communities and raising awareness about present situations as well as initiating an assessment of owned and desired knowledge levels.

Advising and assisting future entrepreneurs in rural tourism can be achieved by organizing training courses presenting the difficulties they will have to meet when starting up, and running, their businesses. The modern vision in running new businesses must prepare entrepreneurs in the use of scientific methodology of risk assessment (Zirra 2005). Making and implementing specialized training programs for key stakeholders (entrepreneurs, employees, the local community, etc.) will bring economic and social benefits locally, having effects on the development of products, services, and rural areas.

Training of stakeholders can generate economic development in rural areas by creating a support for new businesses and by supporting local initiatives aimed at developing traditional crafts and specific art, and reducing regional imbalances, etc. Knowledge in terms of management will contribute to better organization of work, which in turn will lead to increased profitability and business efficiency.

Human resource training has positive effects on society and culture through mobilizing and encouraging local people, creating a professional attitude, increasing the commitment of human resources, increasing job satisfaction, increasing cooperation between different stakeholders, developing a culture and positive attitudes, and so on. Better trained stakeholders, possessing different skills in certain fields, will be able to identify with the mission and objectives of rural area policies. Individuals will be more motivated toward their work and will be able to perform their actions at a higher qualitative standard. Stakeholders within local communities with a higher education will understand the benefits that this activity can bring and will be more interested in supporting training. Also, they will be interested in enhancing cooperation with other local stakeholders, at both regional and national levels.

Training programs are of great use as they provide an additional opportunity for pre-qualified young people to build a career. Strategies and measures taken to improve skills show a trend for solutions, based on partnership and dialogue between the institutions organizing training courses and other stakeholders such as the public authorities. However, this needs to be developed further, beyond training, to look in a broader sense at the learning process by combining aspects of learning with practical experience. The direct correlation between learning, employment, and the labor environment leads to consider economic and social dimensions when there is a desire for the improvement of knowledge and skills. This can be done by adopting a common philosophy regarding the learning process, the so-called "areas of learning" approach, involving all stakeholders from a particular sector and training field in the learning and innovation processes through practical and active cooperation, leading to improved competitiveness. In addition, supporting and developing entrepreneurship, having an awareness of the importance of encouraging tourism activities in rural areas, fostering public–private and private–private partnerships, and encouraging local leadership are all solutions which can revitalize human resources in rural areas. It is important that these should not be viewed in isolation, but combined and tailored to each region. Moreover, they support the professional development of human resources in rural tourism and create preconditions for progress in rural tourism activities (Surugiu 2008).

Youths represent an important segment of human resources. Youth involvement in heritage protection can be of great importance. Young people are the future of any region or country, and they tend to be the ones who have the most innovative ideas, and can bring new visions and strategies to various fields of an activity.

Youth participation in cultural programs and their participation in programs of heritage protection are important aspects, mainly because these are long-term processes, therefore making necessary to ensure that skills and knowledge are transferred successfully between participating generations. For younger generations, gaining awareness of the importance of heritage and tourism products and services is a learning process.

Young people represent a powerful driver for promoting development in many areas. This is underlined by the fact that young people strongly believe that they have the potential to make significant changes to both the economy and society in general.

Besides this, young people are very influenced by ICT, respond faster to the changes in technology and are easily adapting to developments in this area. Regarding the involvement of youths in the heritage and tourism sectors, "the most dynamic market segment of potential consumers of innovative cultural heritage products are youth, either foreign tourists or locals, more familiar with ICT devices and information viral dissemination" (Vasile et al. 2015).

Training programs, for young people in particular, should include different approaches to heritage and cultural tourism, for example, aspects related to financing programs in these sectors, aspects of marketing the products and services offered by these sectors, developing strategies, models of community involvement, and so on.

Young people, and other stakeholders interested in training, may benefit from the expertise of specialists from sectors of heritage and tourism through organised workshops, visits to cultural sites, lectures in classrooms, and study travels, all focusing primarily on providing essential theoretical knowledge, but some providing the chance to see the reality of life on the ground and offering the opportunity to develop networking. Thus, such training enables young people to develop the skills necessary in various sectors.

22.3 Promoting Cultural Heritage and Tourism

There are various aspects related to culture, mainly underlined by economic, social, and political realities, which are strongly connected with local governance competencies. Heritage and tourism services and products are significantly more environmentally friendly than other products and services from other sectors and have an important role to play in the local and national economy.

Promotion of the rich diversity of heritage assets and tourism services and products from Romania can be encouraged through training sessions, local study visits to rural areas, and through developing highly qualitative materials with rich and important information for stakeholders.

Direction for the development of activities related to cultural heritage valorisation may refer to the following:

- Identifying and correctly evaluating potential.
- Obtaining knowledge and assessment by specialists of the important issues related to heritage valorisation.
- Obtaining knowledge of the economic, social, and cultural potential of heritage by entrepreneurs.
- Promoting innovative products and services to beneficiaries to stimulate knowledge and mobility (in situ participation).

In order to achieve this, the manner of educating stakeholders regarding heritage management in general, especially in rural areas, must be changed, i.e.:

- Information should be presented in schools, to communities, and incorporated in activities which refer to knowledge.
- Understanding of heritage value and the need for its protection/preservation is required.
- Entrepreneurial potential and opportunities offered by entrepreneurship and good management should be highlighted.
- Knowledge and skills for beneficiaries of products and services—hard and soft skills—should be taught.

Training from this perspective takes the following forms:

- Education on the current value of heritage.
- Expertise on the reinterpretation of the potential benefits of local cultural development.
- Specific entrepreneurial education.
- Knowledge of efficient and protective (preserving) management.
- Social and cognitive skills necessary to develop another cultural consumption behavior (participatory, in situ presence, interpretation).
- ICT knowledge, required for any current cultural consumption action.

It is important to train people to use ICT, computers, and dedicated software, thus permitting better promotion of heritage assets on social media. Such training should also be given to managers of heritage assets. Another important aspect is to learn about creating events in terms of historical topics, dedicated to segments of tourists or visitors. For this to happen it is necessary and important to develop partnerships to attract substantial funding.

Promotion and preservation of cultural heritage are linked to efficient digitization, to developing virtual information databases on heritage assets. At a local level (in rural areas) is important to implement custom heritage asset cataloging and other documentation solutions. Another measure connected to advances in ICT is related to developing onsite digital exhibitions, supported by interactive applications for smartphones, tablets, infokiosks, and so on.

22.4   Connections Between Economic Activities from Rural Areas and the Promotion of Heritage

A rural area is an area with low population density, where agriculture is the most important activity, and where technology is not at its highest level of development. However, rural areas generally have the lowest levels of pollution and have a lot of possibilities regarding starting a business. Rural areas may offer some unique business environments that may not often be available in urban areas. That is why many business ideas may be used and applied in rural areas, but it is of course essential to check their viability.

Starting a business in a rural area may have its challenges, but also advantages. One may be the fact that the human resources may be more cooperative in small rural areas, since people know each other, having a positive impact on the process of running a business. Another advantage might be the small amount of capital required to start a rural business. Challenges in this respect may be related to the fact that, before deciding to start a business in a rural area, is important to have a picture of the types of activities that might be developed in such areas, therefore, creating a good business idea requires significant thought and effort.

In rural areas, businesses may be started in various sectors. A good example is one of creating a connection between an agricultural business and offering some products or services for tourists interested in understanding the main characteristics of local heritage. This represents a method for generating income from tourist activities developed in a rural area, perhaps associated with local festivals, fairs, and so on. The same type of business, producing fruits and vegetables, may provide tourists/visitors with activities from which they may learn historical facts and information about that particular rural area.

In a business related to agriculture, some high-return products may be offered to nearby restaurants, food stores, etc. Also, locally made products, related to farming activities, such as milk lotions, herbal soaps, and so on, may represent attractive products to visitors, going on to determine a strong presence in the market.

22.5   Conclusions

The rural labor force needs to be trained for rural tourism particularly in the areas of acquisition of local, national, or European sources of finance for rural tourism businesses, marketing of rural tourism and heritage assets from rural areas, management of accommodation in rural areas, development of business plans, operating leisure activities in rural areas, etc. The development of activities in the sectors of rural tourism and heritage can only occur if there is cooperation and partnership with other local communities or other stakeholders (trainers, professionals) who are willing to assist.

Increasing individuals' levels of knowledge through training generates benefits and added value not only on a personal level, but also on a group level (tourists, community, etc.). Only people who have a rich knowledge in this field can identify viable solutions to the various situations that may arise during the development of activities. Therefore, training at specialized institutions should not be replaced.

This underlines the fact that at the local community level it is necessary to conduct specialized human resource–training programs, developing organizational strategy, development and promotion of cultural assets and tourism in rural areas with the participation of all stakeholders involved. In conclusion, human resources are the key element to ensuring the quality and content of the products and services from the heritage and tourism sectors. This requires a skilled workforce able to meet the changing needs of the tourism market while maintaining business competitiveness.

Currently, employers are seeking employees with social skills and computer skills, who are able to speak foreign languages, able to come up with new ideas, and be productive in terms of business. However, the heritage and tourism sectors remain unattractive to a large part of the workforce in the economy due to their low wages, difficult working conditions, low career prospects, etc. Therefore, many problems are encountered with recruiting and retaining staff.

It is important in terms of the human resource–training process to start with staff dealing directly with customers and work through to top management. Workforce training is the answer to many of the problems that occur during the development of an economic activity. Any measure adopted by the authorities, businesses, training institutions, etc., aiming to stimulate and supporting heritage and tourism in rural areas must encourage and promote giving and receiving feedback between different levels in the workforce, something which if neglected, will create a negative effect in terms of the sustainable development of rural areas.

In today's society, which is in a constant state of change, tourists and visitors seek new destinations, heritage assets, tourism services, and products. The activities of heritage and tourism in rural areas represent an alternative for many tourists eager to learn more about a country's nature, culture, traditions, village life, authenticity, etc. People have become more sensitive to the environment, they are more educated, and seek quality of services and products. This cannot be provided without the assistance of stakeholders (the local community, authorities, entrepreneurs, employees, trainers, etc.), all of whom need to be trained in accordance with their duties and roles.

References

OECD. (1994). Tourism strategies and rural development, Paris.

South Rural Development Center. (2000). The rural south: Preparing for the challenges of 21st Century, No. 10, June 2000, http://srdc.msstate.edu/publications/smith.pdf.

Surugiu, C. (2008). *Dezvoltarea turismului rural din perspectiva formării și perfecționării profesionale a resurselor umane*. București: Editura Universitara.

Vasile, V., Surugiu, M. R., Login, I. A., & Stroe, A. (2015). Innovative valuing of the cultural heritage assets. Economic implication on local employability, small entrepreneurship development and social inclusion, *Procedia—Social and Behavioral Sciences, 188*.

Zirra, D. (2005). *Ocuparea forței de muncă și șomajul în neoliberalismul economic*. București: Editura Universitară.

Chapter 23
Employment Profile in Tourism Sector in Romania—Skills Demand and Quality of Jobs' Perspectives in the Context of Local Heritage Valuing Using Business Innovation and ITC Support

Valentina Vasile and Ana-Maria Ciuhu

Abstract Using official statistics at national level, the paper aims to contribute to tourism studies in Romania from the perspective of employment in tourism industry. Romania's specific characteristics will be identified in terms of quality and structure of employment. National level is considered for analysing the social productivity of labour in terms of GDP and employment for the tourism sector. The quality of employment is reviewed also in terms of permanency of job and average seniority of work with the same employer. The employment is analysed from the perspective of full-time and part-time activity, age groups and educational attainment level.

Keywords Tourism sector · Tourism industry · Employment · Quality of employment · Social productivity of labour

23.1 Introduction

Tourism is a major economic activity in the European Union with wide-ranging impact on economic growth, employment and social development. Moreover, it represents an industry that prove resilient to the economic crisis and provide jobs for women and young people (Eurostat, 2015). The prospects at 2020 and 2030 horizons (World Tourism Organization, 2016: 5) show that the seven emerging economy destinations in the EU-28 (Bulgaria, Croatia, Hungary, Latvia, Lithuania,

V. Vasile (✉) · A.-M. Ciuhu
Institute of National Economy-Romanian Academy, Calea 13 Septembrie,
050711 Bucharest, Romania
e-mail: valentinavasile2009@gmail.com

© Springer International Publishing AG, part of Springer Nature 2019
V. Vasile (ed.), *Caring and Sharing: The Cultural Heritage Environment
as an Agent for Change*, Springer Proceedings in Business and Economics,
https://doi.org/10.1007/978-3-319-89468-3_23

Poland and Romania) are expected to grow faster, at 3.7% a year on average, than the 21 advanced economy destinations (1.9% a year).

Romania is a country with enormous tourism potential. Actually, the travel and tourism direct contribution to employment was just 2.5% in 2008 and 2.6% in 2015 (World Travel and Tourism Council).

A particularity of Romania's tourism market is that it prioritised support for tourism in rural areas, with a particular focus on training people that had previously been reliant on subsistence agriculture (European Commission 2016: 8). The regional dimension of the tourism was debated in the literature (Zaman et. al, 2012), in terms of typology of regional development, in the form of touristic regionalization or zoning of the country.

Using official statistics at national level from Eurostat and National Institute of Statistics, the study aims to contribute to tourism studies in Romania from the perspective of employment in the industry. Romania's specific characteristics will be identified in terms of quality and structure of employment.

We are considering for the analysis the period 2008–2015, for ensuring the comparability of the data, as in 2008 NACE rev.2 was introduced.

For the data sets used in the analysis, the tourism sector comprises the following sub-sectors: air transport, accommodation and food service activities, accommodation and travel agency, tour operator reservation service and related activities.

23.2 Changing Professional Profile of Employment in Tourism Sector

23.2.1 General Considerations

The main characteristics of changing professional profile of employment in tourism sector will be analysed in this section.

The tourism industry offers a considerably wide range of employment opportunities, starting with professional, skilled positions and finishing with unskilled or semi-skilled work, either paid full-time, part-time, casual or temporary employment.

In the tourism sector, the employment structure is changing by activities. Besides the specific sub-sectors (air transport, accommodation and food service activities, accommodation and travel agency, tour operator reservation service and related activities), more and more complementary activities in tangent sectors are developing, such as vendors of souvenirs and gifts, manufacturers and producers of handicraft, employees of cultural organizations and promoters for local tourism.

Another important aspect is the developing of tourist facilities in peripheral areas. Therefore, the reconsideration and promoting the value of cultural, economic and social heritage assets, which are less known or were not included before in package tours, will lead to local investments.

23.2.2 Employment Profile in Tourism Sector

Tourist industry involves, besides the presence of natural and anthropic potential, the quality of human resources, a factor which ensures actually functionality of components of the offer.

The employment profile in tourism sector will be analysed in the following, considering the professional status, age groups, education level and residential areas.

During the analysed period, the structure of the employment in tourism sector has suffered important changes, in terms of professional status. In the tourism labour market, new specializations appear, which leads to positive trends in terms of entrepreneurship.

In the context of the Labour Force Survey, an employed person is a person aged 15 and over who during the reference week performed work—even if just for one hour a week—for pay, profit or family gain. Alternatively, the person was not at work, but had a job or business from which he or she was temporarily absent due to illness, holiday, industrial dispute or education and training.

An employee is a person who has a contract to carry out work for an employer and receives compensation in the form of wages, salaries, fees, gratuities, piecework pay or remuneration in kind.

A self-employed person is the sole or joint owner of the unincorporated enterprise (one that has not been incorporated, i.e. formed into a legal corporation) in which he/she works, unless they are also in paid employment which is their main activity (in that case, they are considered to be employees).

Figure 23.1 shows clearly the evolution of these three professional groups. Most of the workers in the industry are employed persons or employees. Yet, the trend of self-employed persons is a positive one. In 2011, 6.8 thousands workers in the industry were self-employed persons, and in 2015, the number raised at 8.9 thousands. This positive trend owes to the fact that, in the tourism labour market, new specializations appear, i.e. entrepreneur, manager, promoter/travel agent.

Fig. 23.1 Employment structure in tourism sector by professional status in Romania, 2008–2015 (thousands). *Source* Eurostat database (2016), online data code tour_lfs1r2

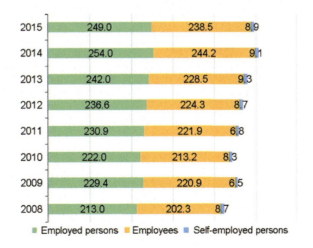

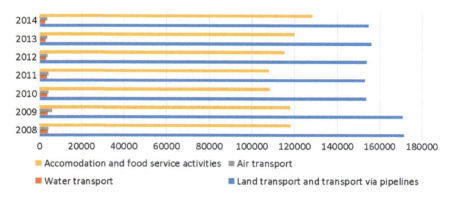

Fig. 23.2 Average number of employees in tourism sector in Romania, 2008–2014. *Source* National Institute of Statistics (2016), Tempo database, online data code FOM104G

The average number of employees in specific sub-sectors (accommodation and food services and selected transport services) is highlighted in Fig. 23.2. The average number of employees in accommodation and food services has risen from 118.3 thousands in 2008 to 128.2 thousands in 2014. In the tangent sectors specific to transport, this number has decreased.

The average monthly labour cost per employee, which includes all the expenditures supported by the unit for the labour force, is another indicator important for analysing the changing professional profile of employment. The literature indicates that the labour cost does not clearly indicate whether an employer employs a few people at high rates of pay or a large number of people at low rates of pay (Boella and Goss-Turner, 2005: 233). In tourism sector, the average monthly number cost per employee has a positive evolution during 2008–2014. As Fig. 23.3 shows, the

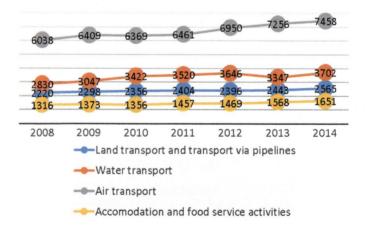

Fig. 23.3 Average monthly labour cost per employee in tourism sector in Romania, 2008–2014 (RON). *Source* National Institute of Statistics (2016), Tempo database, online data code FOM111C

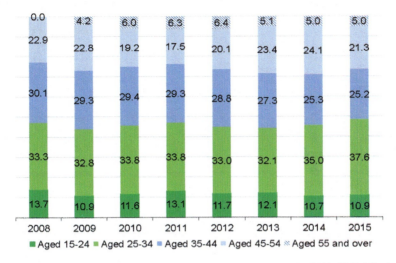

Fig. 23.4 Employed persons by age group in tourism sector in Romania, 2008–2015 (%). *Source* Eurostat database (2016), online data code tour_lfs2r2

highest monthly number cost is registered for the air transport sub-sector: 6038 RON in 2008, 6461 RON in 2011 and 7458 RON in 2014. Accommodation and food service activities sub-sector has the lowest average monthly, 1316 RON in 2008, 1457 RON in 2011 and 1651 RON in 2014.

Regarding the employment structure by age groups, data is available for two selected tourism sub-sectors: accommodation and food service activities and accommodation. Figure 23.4 shows the evolution in the employment structure, considering the age groups 15–24, 25–34, 35–44, 45–54 and 55 years and over.

The tourism sector is attractive for young people. The age groups 15–24 and 25–34 totalled 47% of the employed persons in 2008 and 48.5% in 2014. The age group 35–44 has declined in the structure, from 30.1% in 2008 to 29.3% in 2011 and 25.2% in 2015.

In Fig. 23.5, the employment structure by education level is illustrated.

The education levels were defined as follows, according to ISCED 2011:

- Low: less than primary, primary and lower secondary education (levels 0–2)
- Medium: upper secondary and post-secondary non-tertiary education (levels 3 and 4)
- High: tertiary education (levels 5–8).

The share of low education level employed person is decreasing, from 13.3% in 2008 to 11.9% in 2015. Nevertheless, most of the employed persons are the ones with medium education level, as many of the specific positions in the industry have this requirement. Surprisingly, the share of the people with high education level is growing, from 5.3% in 2008 to 10.9% in 2011 and 14.2% in 2015.

Employment structure has important changes also in the residential areas. The tourism has moved from large cities and urban areas to small villages in rural areas,

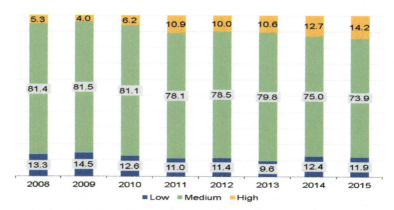

Fig. 23.5 Employed persons by education level in tourism sector in Romania, 2008–2015 (%). *Source* Eurostat database (2016), online data code tour_lfs3r2

through specialization with integration of residents. Therefore, some new activities have risen among these areas: agro-tourism, ecotourism, small business development by harnessing local traditions as handicrafts, area-specific events, etc.

In 2008, 19.4% of the total persons working in tourism industry were in rural areas. In 2015, the share increased by 3.5 p.p. In rural areas, new tourist facilities are developing; local investments are stimulated by reconsidering and promoting the value of cultural, economic and heritage assets less known or even not included in cultural tours or tourist. Therefore, the rural areas are characterized by an increase in the self-employed persons (9.9% in 2012 and 22.9% in 2015) (Table 23.1). Contributing family workers (OECD definition, 2001) are registered mostly in the urban areas.

23.3 The Quality of Employment in Tourism Sector

The quality of employment in tourism sector in Romania will be analysed in terms of the following aspects: permanency of job, social labour productivity, average seniority with the same employer and full-time/part-time activity.

The permanency of job refers at the number of permanent versus temporary jobs. Regarding its evolution as it is illustrated in Table 23.2, the results show that in Romania the number of permanent jobs grew: a 2.47 p.p. annual increase was registered. For the same period, the number of temporary jobs in tourism sector has decreased with 0.04 p.p. annually.

Secondly, another important aspect that characterizes the tourism labour market of Romania is the social productivity of labour (Fig. 23.6). It was computed as the ratio between GDP (million RON) and civil employed population (persons), for the sector accommodation and food service activities.

Table 23.1 Employment structure in tourism sector by professional status and residential areas in Romania, 2008–2015 (%)

	2008	2009	2010	2011	2012	2013	2014	2015
Urban								
Total	80.6	77.1	79.0	78.8	77.7	76.5	76.9	77.1
Self-employed	61.3	83.0	62.8	63.5	90.1	90.3	95.5	73.7
Employer	92.8	98.5	84.8	79.9	89.7	70.6	64.5	89.2
Employee	80.4	76.3	79.0	78.8	77.0	76.6	77.0	76.6
Contributing family worker	0.0	0.0	100.0	100.0	100.0	32.7	66.1	0.0
Rural								
Total	19.4	22.9	21.0	21.2	22.3	23.5	23.1	22.9
Self-employed	38.7	17.0	37.2	36.5	9.9	9.7	4.5	26.3
Employer	7.2	1.5	15.2	20.1	10.3	29.4	35.5	10.8
Employee	19.6	23.7	21.0	21.2	23.0	23.4	23.0	23.4
Contributing family worker	100.0	0.0	0.0	0.0	0.0	67.3	33.9	0.0

Source Authors' calculation, based on National Institute of Statistics (2016), online data code AMG110T

Table 23.2 Permanency of job in tourism sector in Romania, 2008–2015 (thousand persons)

	2008	2009	2010	2011	2012	2013	2014	2015
Permanent job	192.1	211.8	205.3	212.7	204.1	218.6	228.9	231.0
Temporary job	6.9	6.6	7.1	6.5	7.0	6.8	6.8	6.8
Total	202.3	220.9	213.2	221.9	213.9	228.5	235.7	238.5

Source Eurostat database (2016), online data code tour_lfs4r2

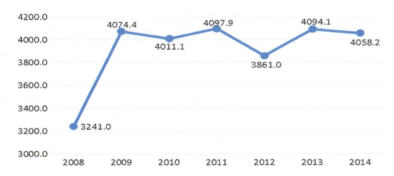

Fig. 23.6 Social productivity of labour in tourism sector in Romania, 2008–2014 (Million RON/ person). *Source* authors' calculation, based on National Institute of Statistics (2016), online data code CON11M and FOM103D

Given relatively modest performance of the tourism sector in Romania, performed mainly in the traditional way, it was facing low economic efficiency, i.e. low social productivity of labour. In 2008, the social productivity was 3241 million RON/person, but in 2009 and 2014, it was registered at approximately 4000 million RON/person.

Another important standpoint that characterizes the tourism sector of Romania is the average seniority with the same employer, which shows employees' tendency to keep their job with a certain employer and maybe advance in their careers, or move from one job to another depending on certain circumstances.

Based on the data provided in Table 23.3, results show that in Romania, during the 2008–2015 period, an average number of 50.6 thousand employees (22.8% of the total) had been working for less than two years with the same employer, while an average of 168.1 thousand employees (77.2%) had been working for three years or more with the same employer.

Data show that in Romania the number of employees who had been working for less than two years with the same employer has decreased by 2.55 p.p. annually, while the number of employees who had been working for two or more years with the same employer has increased by 6.09 p.p. annually between 2008 and 2015.

Finally, a statistical indicator for the quality of employment is the measure of full-time/part-time activity.

According to Labour Force Survey, the share of people working full time in the industry did not changed significantly among the analysed period. Yet, in 2012, 6.1% of the people working in the industry had part-time jobs, comparing with 0.8% in 2008 and 1.2% in 2014 (Table 23.4).

Table 23.3 Average seniority of work with the same employer in tourism sector in Romania, 2008–2015 (thousand persons)

Duration	2008	2009	2010	2011	2012	2013	2014	2015
Less than 2 years	60.1	55.9	44.7	48.0	49.0	44.2	49.4	53.4
3 years or over	134.6	161.2	166.7	171.7	164.0	179.7	184.2	182.3
Total	202.3	220.9	213.2	221.9	213.9	228.5	235.7	238.5

Source Eurostat database (2016), online data code tour_lfs5r2

Table 23.4 Employed persons by full-time/part-time activity in tourism sector in Romania, 2008–2015 (thousand persons)

	2008	2009	2010	2011	2012	2013	2014	2015
Total (thousands)	424.0	459.0	443.9	461.5	469.6	479.8	507.2	496.4
of which, in %								
Full time	99.2	99.5	99.0	98.5	93.9	98.2	98.8	98.7
Part time	0.8	0.5	1.0	1.5	6.1	1.8	1.2	1.3

Source Eurostat database (2016), online data code tourlfs1r2

Other qualitative changes were noticed in terms of jobs quality. The low-skilled jobs based on job simple specialization have been replaced with integrated training requirements: specific knowledge of foreign languages, know-how, ICT skills and ability to manage communication networks and to develop specialized and tailor-made services, based on consumers' profile. Also, the job requirements imply new skills, such as knowledge about the history of the places, local legends and the ability to reinterpret cultural heritage through the development of intangible assets and promote their values.

23.4   Conclusions

Tourism sector has a plenty of challenges, regarding the specific employment. New complementary services are going to appear.

Also, the touristic sector is expected to improve in rural areas. More clearly, a new business model is developing in rural areas: on the one hand, we have the stays in countryside for life experiences related to local tradition; on the other hand, there are the cultural routes, thematic sequences of activities, which are integrated in standard touristic packages.

Between the tourism industry, the environment and the local community there is a strong relationship because the presence of tourists in an area increases local economy and revenues and creation of new jobs. A recommendation which would support this relationship would be the public local partnership and community planning action plan.

References

Boella, M. J., & Goss-Turner, S. (2005). *Human resource management in the hospitality industry: An introductory guide* (8th ed.). Oxford: Elsevier Butterworth-Heinemann.

European Commission. (2016). *Mapping and performance check of the supply side of tourism education and training.* Written by the Centre for Strategy and Evaluation Services. Available http://ec.europa.eu/growth/tools-databases/newsroom/cf/itemdetail.cfm?item_id=8762&lang=en&title=EU-tourism-skills%3A-%27Mapping-and-performance-check-of-the-supply-side-of-tourism-education-and-training%2720 May 2016.

Eurostat. (2015). *Tourism industries—employment.* Available http://ec.europa.eu/eurostat/statistics-explained/index.php/Tourism_industries_-_employment 18 May 2016.

Eurostat. (2016). *Tourism database.* Available http://ec.europa.eu/eurostat/web/tourism/data/database 18 May 2016.

National Institute of Statistics. (2016). *Tempo online database.* https://statistici.insse.ro/shop/ 18 May 2016.

OECD. (2001). *Glossary of statistical terms.* Available https://stats.oecd.org/glossary/detail.asp?ID=443 20 May 2016.

World Tourism Organization. (2016). *International tourism trends in EU-28 member states—current situation and forecast for 2020–2025–2030.* Prepared for the European Commission, Directorate General for Enterprise and Industry. Available http://ec.europa.eu/growth/tools-databases/newsroom/cf/itemdetail.cfm?item_id=8828&lang=en&title=International-tourism-trends-in-EU-28-member-states—Current-situation-and-forecast-for-2020-2025-2030 28 May 2016.

Zaman, G., Vasile, V., Goschin, Z., Rosca, E. (2012, June). Typology and planning of the tourism regional development in Romania. *The USV Annals of Economics and Public Administration,* *12*(1(15)), 7–17 (Stefan cel Mare University of Suceava, Romania, Faculty of Economics and Public Administration).

Chapter 24
Cultural Heritage Tourism Export and Local Development. Performance Indicators and Policy Challenges for Romania

Valentina Vasile and Elena Bănică

Abstract Tourism activity is an important driver of the global economy, ensuring monetary circulation, through tourism receipts, to other economic circuits. By developing tourism activities, countries can increase their national production, with a positive effect on their Gross Domestic Product (GDP). Tourism services and cultural products should be promoted together in development efforts, as generators for regional progress in areas with partially valued heritage potential. A strategic and integrated approach of sustainable cultural heritage tourism development must include all types of externalities, both positive and negative, and should be included in local policies for development as a priority, offering economically driven opportunities. Intensive development of tourism, which contributes to an increased added value, must be implemented in services through technology. Cultural heritage, promoted through tourism, creates jobs, drives innovation, supports public services development and local entrepreneurship (including transport and communication infrastructures), generates prosperity, and encourages participation of citizens. This chapter presents proposals and recommendations for national policies and strategies for ensuring that inbound tourism, based on current national and cultural heritage, constitutes a supplementary factor to economic growth in the region.

Keywords Tourism · Export · Sustainable development · Economic growth Strategies

V. Vasile · E. Bănică (✉)
Institute of National Economy-Romanian Academy, Bucharest, Romania
e-mail: elenabanica77@gmail.com

24.1 Export of Tourism Services as Facilitators of Cultural Consumption

The export of goods and services from a country implies both (a) support for the production and technological potential development and (b) dissemination of national specific products/services.

Export of tourism services promotes the specific national cultural uniqueness of a place to be used for artistic events, while also sharing knowledge about, and promoting, common European values. National history blends with regional history while culture finds its roots and basis on common confluences and/or values, on common and specific customs, as well as behavior (Licciardi and Amirtahmasebi 2012).

Tourism, in all its forms (traditional–classical or modern, based on the digital economy) represents the transmission and diffusion of cultural heritage to a large number of indigenous and foreign consumers. The export of tourism services in areas with heritage potential acts as a barometer of interest for cultural consumption, regardless of whether such consumption is business or leisure related. Knowing about places and local habits is to understand the present through cultural heritage, the (re)discovery of common and/or perennial cultural values.

Knowing and understanding "diversity" may support and strengthen the foundations for a "demand for historical memory." In addition, learning from the past is a way to better communicate and develop common business, strengthening multilateral and communitarian collaboration for innovation in tourism and cultural consumption of onsite visits. More than ever, the personal experience as beneficiar, the active involvement in cultural tourism consumption and social media development, increases the importance of sharing experience as business driver for tourism; it provides a smoother path from information and individual demand to cultural tourism consumption. The demand is more targeted as destinations (validated by social networking) and increases the quality standards for supplied services. For less known/valued heritage assets, the move from local and personal experiences to global sharing strengthens the local community roadmap for development, beyond the service sector, providing incentives for job creation, urban upgrading, physical improvement of the local environment, general infrastructure, education, and manufacturing industries including information and communications technology (ICT) industries, etc. It also facilitates social inclusion, poverty reduction or increased community wealth, and social network development, i.e., small business development and social distributive networks, etc.

Onsite visits increase people's knowledge about places and events while enriching their experiences and emotions, facilitating widespread curiosity about other places, which in turn drives a higher demand to visit and personally experience other societies. Tourism and cultural sectors revitalize local communities and facilitate integration in (inter)national chains of values, stimulating interest in creative and attractive venues for both tourists and residents alike. A demand-driven, flexible approach to heritage product development gives a boost to small enterprises and the development of social economies as well as increasing demand for the export of tourism services.

24.2 Service Exports as Drivers for Sustainable Development at the Local Level

Tourism activity is an important driver of the global economy, ensuring monetary circulation, through tourism receipts, to other economic circuits. By developing tourism activities, countries can increase their national production, with a positive effect on their Gross Domestic Product (GDP). This domain is also an important contributor, ahead of other industries, to the achievement of added value, because it requires a high consumption of manpower, intelligence, and creativity. Another positive effect of transport and tourism sector (T&T) for cultural heritage consumption consist of driving, stimulating, and developing the up and down stream industries, being a way of diversifying the structure of an economy, both on local, regional, and national levels. Part of the income from the export of tourism services can be used as a source of investment for the development of the cultural heritage sector and heritage assets (onsite and for promotion via the media), requiring the creation of new jobs and innovative complementary activities.

Valuing local potential means activating resources and increasing interest in integrated businesses. Local materials and human resources represent the starting point in redesigning a local business model of products and services, with heritage being a strong stimulus for specialization, preservation of cultural identity, and the development of innovative activities. The economic concept of cultural heritage capital is based on a new model of local development in areas with such assets, contributing to development of the cultural heritage sector (Peacock 1995; Hutter and Rizzo 1997; Schuster et al. 1997; Throsby 1997; Rizzo and Towse 2002; Mason 2005; Peacock and Rizzo 2008; Benhamou 2010; Vasile and Login 2013). The economic concept of cultural capital took shape decades ago (Throsby 1999, 2001; Shockley 2004; Cheng 2006; Wang 2007; Bucci and Segre 2011) and its potential for cultural–creative industries boosted the importance of such a sector to economic development. Cultural heritage assets, in both tangible and intangible forms, exist as a capital stock held by a country, a region, a city, an individual economic agent, or an individual person. The proper valuation of these assets implies knowledge based approach and creative forms for market oriented products/ services.

The cultural heritage sector interacts readily with the core of the cultural creative industries and is part and/or a complement to the wider creative sector. "Cultural production is young, inclusive and entrepreneurial" (EY 2015). Europe, as the second largest cultural creative industries market, accounts for one third of the total revenue and one quarter of employment in the sector. Cultural creative industries, economically measured by copyright based industries sector (industries that make use of copyright and related rights protection) contributes to economic outputs with 2–11% of GDP and employment, differentiated by countries. The world average values in 2015 were of 5.48% of GDP and 5.34% of employment (WIPO 2015). Romania's performance is slightly above average in terms of contribution to GDP (5.55%) and lower than average for employment (4.19% in 2010) (Zaman et al. 2010a, b, c, d, e, f).

For less developed countries in integrated economic spaces (like the EU), it is easier to create specific business opportunities based on activation/valuation of local strong points for development, i.e., heritage promotion, tourism services, and associated/complementary local activities. Stakeholders map development, as complementary services provided to cultural consumers, could attract also other forms of tourism, with possibilities for developing associated activities—business events, social network activation, educational activities etc.

In economic and social terms, tourism is the third largest socioeconomic activity in the EU after retail and construction (EC 2010). Tourism contributes 5% to the EU's GDP and total workforce. However, this activity is not evenly distributed throughout Europe, its capacity and intensity registering a strong variation from one region to another. According to a study of the Political Department of the European Parliament, tourism plays a small role in most EU member states that joined after 2004 (European Parliament 2015).

In recent years, and especially after the financial crisis, there has been increased interest in tourism's role in economic development. The debate on the need to promote the national tourism sector, to ensure long-term economic growth, is a relatively new issue. In literature there are many studies on the contribution of exports of goods to economic and social development. Tourism, belonging to the services sector, acquires growing attention, although it is not an accepted product in the classic sense. In this regard, international tourism might be considered an export since it is a source of income and consumption. Tourism activity produces multiple effects in many other economic sectors, like reducing deficit of trade balance or increasing tax revenues. As pointed out by Sinclair (1998), it is important for emerging countries to consider and analyze patterns that led to the success of tourism, such as in Spain, for example; at the same time, these patterns should not be copied and applied as such, but adapted to the specificities of each country, in terms of geographical, social, and cultural tradition. However, tourism literature gives only modest attention to the relationship between tourism development and economic growth.

In the literature, there are two main ideas that are based on the assumption that the export of tourism services generates economic growth. On the one hand, assuming tourism development is based on the idea that economic growth can be generated by stimulating countries' international tourism, as the export alternative, Cortés-Jiménez and Pulin (2009) provides an overview of tourism in Spain and Italy, considering the above mentioned hypothesis. On the other hand, Nowak et al. (2007) considers that economic development can be achieved by increasing the volume of imports. This hypothesis was tested and sustained in the case of Spain, confirming that the economic and industrial development in Spain was driven by imports of capital goods financed mainly by receipts from tourism (Bote Gómez and Sinclair 1996). The potential link between exports and economic development has been presented and studied many times. It was thus demonstrated theoretically that exports contribute positively to production growth by reducing exchange-type constraints (McKinnon 1964) or by increasing efficiency through enhanced competition (Krueger 1980). The specific contribution of the export of tourism services on economic growth is mentioned in just a few studies. In 2004, for example, Durbarry conducted an analysis of Mauritius' exports, by assessing its various types, including the role of international tourism on economic growth (Durbarry 2004).

Investing in tourism as an alternative to boosting and increasing the external demand for cultural heritage consumption is associated with investing in heritage for livability, job creation, and local development, branding it both nationally and internationally [with robust inclusion within the green growth agenda (World Bank 2012)].

International tourism is an invisible export that contributes positively to the destination country. Thus, international tourism makes a significant contribution to the growth and diversification of international trade. Furthermore, tourism helps to equilibrate the balance of payments of host countries, especially where tourism is the main economic activity or source of income.

From a sociocultural point of view, tourism contributes to the material and spiritual needs of people, positively influencing the size and structure of individual consumption, as well as restoring physical and intellectual capabilities through leisure, medical spa treatments, etc. Another positive effect is the contribution to enriching people's education—improving knowledge for both tourists and local populations through direct or indirect contact with new cultures and civilizations. As a distinct economic sector and an integral part of the economy, tourism has efficient management of resources and achieving positive economic results as its priorities, while at the same time meeting the needs of tourists by improving visiting conditions.

In places where local or regional development strategies have proven the existence of a real development potential, investments can be attracted to optimize local development.

Romania has many UNESCO World Heritage sites including a nature reserve (Delta Dunarii) and six cultural reserves: the churches in Moldova, the Dacian fortresses in the Orastie Mountains, the historic center of Sighisoara, the Horezu Monastery, the fortified churches in Transylvania, and the wooden churches from Maramures. Romania has therefore significant potential for tourism development from multiple points of view: cultural, historical, natural, health-based, etc.

The National Master Plan for Tourism Development 2007–2026 in Romania is the main strategic document for tourism. It sets targets for the development of different tourist activities in many areas of Romania.

Investments in tourism mainly fall into two categories: the so-called "small investments," which are completed within one year and therefore take effect from the following year, and "large investments" which represent the achievement of integrated tourism objectives, based on diversified tangibles (complex tourism)— investments in the latter case exceed a one-year period and start to produce effects only after they are fully complete.

It should be noted that one of the specificities of Romanian tourism is the presence of small and medium businesses and for this reason investments are only relatively modest. Important investments can only be made by medium and large companies especially from the point of view of technological developments in the sector.

Investments in tourism are addressed exclusively to completing-type services and not for innovation in tourism, which could gain higher added value and higher social productivity. For example, construction of new hostels represents an extensive development based, in technological terms, on already known technologies and to a lesser extent on high-tech applications. Intensive development of tourism, on the other hand, which could contribute to an increased added value, should be made in services based on new high-tech products, such as associative wellness treatment facilities for people with mobility problems, beauty/spa services including foe elderly, medical gymnastic for targeted groups, etc.

At the same time, capital investments cannot be considered as being supported by revenues from the tourism sector, as corporate profit is allocated for investment or dividends, as decided by the shareholders or associates. In addition, there are no mandatory accounting standards according to which amounts set as depreciation (cost to company) can be allocated as development resources for technological renewal and development of production capacities. Sources of funding for the tourism sector are generally modest and rely mainly on the ability of private investors and, more recently, the possibilities of absorption of structural funds dedicated solely to global development or tourism.

In the framework of the Regional Operational Program 2014–2020, the development of cultural heritage and tourism, as a driver for local economic development, is considered to be a funding priority. It is foreseen that 45 additional cultural sites will be renovated under this priority.

The current fiscal regime on reinvested profit, the relatively low net profit rate and difficult access to other financing sources (Structural Funds, local funds, etc.), create fewer opportunities to invest consistent amounts for technological transfer and for structural changes toward a new business model. Moreover, the actual structure of the tourism business model in Romania does not intensively help the development of the sector.

Among EU countries, Romania registers the lowest current T&T infrastructure quality and capacity, being at the bottom of the ranking of EU countries (68 out of 136 countries), with a very low increasing score of WEF (World Economic Forum) composite infrastructure, from 3.6 in 2013 to 3.8 in 2017 (out of 7) (WEF 2017; WTTC 2017). Romania has a good position in terms of its safety and security environment (ranked 39), health and hygiene (ranked 31), and environment sustainability (ranked 43), along with an acceptable level of ICT readiness (ranked 60). However, it does not perform as well in terms of business environment (ranked 76) and human resources (ranked 81).

From a tourism performance point of view, international openness (ranked 45) is acceptable, but tourist service infrastructure (ranked 62, within which the quality of tourism infrastructure was ranked 129), quality of roads (ranked 126), and price competitiveness (ranked 85) were unsatisfactory compared with its good position in terms of cultural resources and business travel (ranked 45) and country brand strategy rating (ranked 35). The tourism sector is not a high priority in terms of policy support (ranked 108 for prioritizing this sector) and transport infrastructure is equally underdeveloped, being a severe limit to the potential development of tourism. The lowest ranked positions (ranked 130 or lower, out of 138) were registered for the most important components for supporting cultural heritage sector development: government prioritization of the T&T industry (ranked 131) and effectiveness of marketing and branding to attract tourists (ranked 131). We also should add that there are further limitations to investment in the sector, some economic constrains, such as effect of taxation on incentives to invest (ranked 125) and to work (ranked 117), the extent of staff training (ranked 101), the ease of finding skilled employees (ranked 130), and T&T government expenditure as a percentage of government budget (ranked 107).

In terms of declared and available cultural heritage, Romania holds a better position than the average WEF composite infrastructure index for the number of World Heritage Cultural sites held (ranked 36) and for intangible cultural heritage (ranked 24). A week point for Romania, representing the modern style of heritage consumption, is the very low digital demand for cultural and entertainment tourism (ranked 80). A similar imbalance is registered for natural heritage, with the digital demand for natural tourism being ranked 77 and for total protected areas 38 (23.8% of total territory represent protected areas). Having good potential but being improperly valued and supported with weak policies in terms of cultural heritage sector development, tourism export demand will remain at low levels and tourism competitiveness will continue to decrease [in the last 2 years (2014–2016) Romania dropped 2 places on the Travel and Tourism Competitiveness Index (TTCI)].

24.3 Performance Indicator Analysis—Main Results

Cultural heritage assets, from an economic valuing point of view, could be considered as:

1. Facilitating market benefit increases—i.e., tourism revenues and spillovers to the hospitality and service sector, start-ups based on innovative entrepreneurship, innovation through digitalization of the specific goods/services, etc.
2. Supporting non-market externalities—i.e., attracting investment in terms of qualified personnel involvement in intangible innovation; increasing the

self-esteem of inhabitants and (inter)national visibility of peripheral cultural areas; motivating local regeneration and restructuring plans, including livability standards, etc.

The socioeconomic value of cultural heritage has been redefined. Even though there are no short-term generators of tangible/measurable benefits, at large, cultural heritage assets represent for society an economic and social "perennial potential for growth," difficult to integrate in conventional monetary metrics but something which ought to be integrated as a driver/multiplier factor in local development strategies.

Cultural heritage through tourism activities and especially visitor exports, creates jobs, drives innovation, supports public service development and local entrepreneurship (including transport and communication infrastructure), and generates prosperity and citizen participation. According to the WTTC (World Travel and Tourism Council) Report for 2017, the T&T sector promotes cultural values, diversity, and heritage activating resource efficiency for inclusive and sustainable economic growth, promoting social inclusiveness, augmenting and refining employment and (in work) poverty reduction, supporting mutual understanding, peace, and security. All in all, the T&T sector contributes on average 10% of global GDP and one tenth of jobs in the global economy, with an expectation that it will show continued growth in both areas. Romania's performance in terms of these metrics is much less than half, with its convergence process being very slow, despite its high dynamic in the sector, due to its very low actual performance (Table 24.1).

Romania's ranking of relative positon for T&T contribution to GDP in 2016 was 163 out of 185 countries with a direct contribution of 1.3% and total contribution of 5.2%. It is estimated to improve to 152 in 2027 with its direct contribution and total contribution to GDP also estimated to increase to 1.6% and 5.8%, respectively.

As for its contribution to employment—2.4% for direct and 6.2% for total in 2016, if jobs indirectly supported by the industry are included, slowly increasing to 2.6 and 6.9% in 2027 (WTTC Country Report for Romania 2017). This performance is far lower than other EU countries even though Romania's potential is higher than other member states.

Visitor exports generated 2.8% of total exports in 2016 and are expected to increase only to 2.9% in 2027, despite an average annual increase rate estimated at 3.5%. If we consider the levels reached in the year 2007 for this indicator and the effect of the financial crisis, we notice that the recovery period is still ongoing. The effect of the crisis on employment was higher (2.2% in 2013), and time lagged, compared with the effect on GDP (1.2% in 2010, as bottom level for direct contribution). In a similar manner to the EU and the rest of the world, the indirect and induced contributions of the T&T sector are higher than the direct contribution, with estimates suggesting an increase over the next decade.

Visitor exports are a key component of direct contribution. After 2008 Romania lost its attractiveness to foreign tourists, registered as a share of its total exports— from over 4.5% at its highest performance in early 2008 to less than 3% after 2010 without likelihood of making a recovery in the following decade. The last increase

Table 24.1 Contribution of the T&T sector to economic growth and employment in Romania in 2016 and 2027 (forecast), in a comparative context (% to contribution)

	Reference year	Romania		EU 28		World	
		Direct	Total	Direct	Total	Direct	Total
1. Contribution to GDP of which:	2016	1.3	5.2	3.7	10.2	3.1	10.2
Direct			25.6		36.3		30.3
Induced			18.8		19.5		18.0
Indirect			55.6		44.2		51.7
(a) Supply chain			19.9		34.8		36.6
(b) Investments			32.2		4.2		8.4
(c) Government collective			3.6		5.2		6.7
	2027 (forecast)	1.6	5.8	4.1	11.2	3.5	11.4
2. Contribution to employment	2016	2.4	6.2	5.0	11.6	3.6	9.6
	2027 (forecast)	2.6	6.9	5.8	13.1	4.0	11.1
3. T&T capital investments	2016		8.1		4.9		4.4
	2027 (forecast)		8.4		5.4		5.0
4. Visitor exports	2016		2.8		5.9		6.6
	2027 (forecast)		2.9		6.6		7.2
5. Foreign visitors spending or international tourism receipts, as a percentage of T&T GDP	2016		38.6		30.8		28.2

Source World Travel and Tourism Council Report 2017. https://www.wttc.org/-/media/files/reports/economic-impact-research/regions-2017/europeanunionlcu2017.pdf; https://www.wttc.org/-/media/files/reports/economic-impact-research/countries-2017/romania2017.pdf

of T&T's share of total national investment from around 7.5% in 2013 to 8.1% in 2014–2016, did not produce significant improving in specific offer quality and the estimated increase share up to only 8.4% is not suitable to better performances. Domestic travel spending share of T&T in GDP in 2016 was 1.6 times higher than visitor exports (i.e. foreign visitor spending orinternational tourism receipts). More than a half of the T&T industry contribution to GDP and employment is generated by indirect activities (i.e., supply chain contributes and investments, the collaborative government representing the smallest one). Visitor numbers are estimated to increase from 4.75 million international tourists in 2016 to 9.435 million by 2027.

Cultural tourism is the form which attracts the largest numbers of foreign visitors, but we also note the importance given in recent years to rural tourism as a source of sustainable niche tourism, which is less expensive for investors. Specialists have linked rural tourism to sustainable business by demonstrating that tourism creates jobs and thus is a source of rural development.

The conventional economic evaluation of cultural heritage usually finds its origin in the quantitative analysis of associated tourism services—number of visitors, average length of visit, travel cost, etc. Also, some qualitative estimates based on surveys complete the picture of multidimensional aspects of tourism and cultural consumption. Usual research methods used to assess this willingness to pay are, among others, based on survey techniques and interviews. An important aspect related to the financing issue is represented by β and σ convergences and their typology (slow, fluctuating etc.).

In Romania there are considerable regional disparities between the number of nights spent by domestic tourists and inbound tourists. Similar to Poland and Germany, around four out of five nights spent in tourist accommodation were accounted for by domestic tourists, mainly outside the capital city (Eurostat data). Most inbound tourists are attracted to regions in and around the capital cities of Romania (with a similar situation being registered in Denmark, France, Hungary, the Netherlands, Slovakia, Slovenia, and the United Kingdom). The most popular regions are the South-East (RO22) and Bucharest–Ilfov County (RO32). The lowest occupancy rate is in the Center region (RO12)—the 5th among the bottom 10 EU tourist regions in terms of bedroom occupancy rates in hotels and similar establishments, with less than 30% occupancy in 2014 [lower rates were registered by Bulgaria (BG 31, BG 32) and Greece (EL 64, EL 53)] (Statistical Classification of Territorial Units - NUTS-2 classification).

Romania's tourism exports, according to Eurostat data, increased over a 25-year period by only 13.5%, from 4.238 million nights spent by non-residents (hotels, holiday and other short-stay accommodation, camping grounds, recreational vehicle parks, and trailer parks) in 1990 to 4.812 million in 2016. This trend showed an oscillating evolution with its lowest value in 1999—only 1.98 million registered nights (Eurostat 2016).

The share of Romania's travel exports in total exports of services has decreased in the last few years—its trade balance being negative. In Bulgaria or Hungary, the share of tourism exports in terms of total exports of services is much higher—in all other cases in southeast Europe the trade balance is positive (Table 24.2).

Romania's exports consist of 75% goods and 25% services. While its external trade in goods balance is negative year by year, as far as services are concerned the balance is positive, which has a positive influence on economic growth. Nevertheless, taking into consideration the low level of services in total exports, this sector does not generate progressive forces for other economic branches and the global economy (Fig. 24.1).

Tourism export intensity, measured as the number of nights spent by non-residents per 1000 inhabitants, increased in the period 1990–2015 with 22.4%, decreasing Romania's population being higher than the tourism export dynamics. After 1990 tourism export intensity decreased in the first decade to half, reaching its lowest value of only 96 nights spent by non-residents per 1000 inhabitants in the year 2000. Recovery from this drop took until 2014 (Table 24.3).

Table 24.2 Travel exports as share of total exports of services (given as percentages), and travel balance in Romania and other EU countries from southeast Europe (million euro), in 2015 and 2016

Country/time	2015				2016			
	Export		Import	Balance	Export		Import	Balance
	Exports[a]	Euro (millions)	Euro (millions)	Euro (millions)	Exports[a]	Euro (millions)	Euro (millions)	Euro (millions)
Bulgaria	40.1	2,838.3	1,006.4	1,831.9	43.8	3,284.8	1,226.6	2,058.2
Hungary	24.1	4,814.9	1,650.1	3,164.8	24.1	5,109.7	1,954.1	3,155.6
Poland	23.2	9,429.5	7,149.2	2,280.3	22.4	9,908.1	7,204.1	2,704.0
Romania	9.3	1,542.0	1,854.5	–312.5	8.7	1,562.5	1,940.4	–377.9
Slovenia	37.5	2,257.3	822.2	1,435.1	36.0	2,346.3	848.5	1,497.8
EU 28	18.1	335,029.6	302,526	32,503.6	18.4	340,402.3	314,733.3	25,669

[a]Share of travel exports to total exports of services
Source Authors' calculation based on Eurostat data, Database "International trade in services (since 2010) (BPM6 - Balance of Payments Manual 6)" [Dataset: bop_its6_det], last update 21.11.17

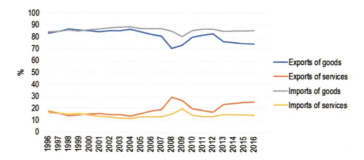

Fig. 24.1 Share of goods/services as part of the total foreign trade of Romania (% in total export, % in total import, respectively), 1996–2016 (*Source* Eurostat database, author's calculations, Database: "GDP, and main components (output, expenditure, and income)" [Dataset: nama_10_gdp], last update 23.11.2017)

For the transition period, the convergence was registered only with 4 countries albeit with very high values of ratio of export intensity (Austria, Denmark, Cyprus, and Luxembourg).

After 2007, the impact of the financial crisis was significantly higher for Romania, export intensity sharply decreased, and the convergence process with almost all EU countries ceased. Also, divergence continued in a more accentuated manner with Lithuania, Latvia, Estonia, Spain, Croatia, and Bulgaria. Compared with 2007, the year of Romania's accession to the EU, the convergence process was modest up to 2015, despite recent years of higher economic growth, mainly because of the effects of the crisis. As averaged against EU 28 levels, Romania registered a divergent evolution, the tourism export intensity gap increased from 12.13 in 2007 to 15.45 in 2010 and partially recovered to 12.67 in 2015. A similar oscillating evolution was registered with 18 EU countries. A divergent trend, partially reduced in recent years, was registered with 8 EU countries. Compared to Germany, Portugal or Greece, export intensity had a different evolution, the disparities increased and remained higher than 2007 values.

Romania is not the first choice as a tourism destination. The total number of nights spent in Romania by non-residents increased 1.8 times in 2016 as against 2009, however, Romania remains a modest tourism destination in this part of the Europe (Fig. 24.2).

Tourists visiting Romania are mainly from EU countries, with the highest numbers coming from Germany, Italy, France, and Hungary, in 2017. This is the result of the single market, of the freedom of movement for both capital and people. However, it is also linked to investment possibilities in Romania across all economic sectors, including tourism (Table 24. 4).

In this context the main concern of policy makers is to support consistent improvement of the quality and attractiveness of Romania as a tourist destination, to develop new products and services based on valuing national cultural heritage and identifying common European values in culture and heritage assets as the main source of connectivity among EU member states, and to develop a network of

Table 24.3 Romania's tourism export intensity disparities as against EU member states (2015–2007; 2015–2000; 2015–1990)

Country/ Date	Gap ratio evolution			Gap (divergence)	Gap (convergence)	Year of maximum value
	2015[a]– 2007	2015[a]– 2000	2015[a]– 1990			
EU 28	0.54			3.32	–2.78	2010
Poland	–0.11	–0.27		0.32	–0.43	2010
Slovakia	–2.10	–3.56	1.60	0.40	–2.50	2008
Germany	0.35	–1.07	1.63	1.68	–1.33	2010
Finland	–1.59	–3.73	1.37	1.33	–2.91	2009
Lithuania	1.73	2.70		2.81	–1.07	2013
Hungary	–0.22	–5.60		1.33	–1.55	2009
Sweden	–1.17	–3.98	2.00	2.46	–3.63	2009
Latvia	1.35	3.39		2.52	–1.17	2014
Belgium	–1.78	–8.38	0.36	2.33	–4.12	2009
Bulgaria	–1.14	1.67	0.29	2.37	–3.51	2011
France	–1.50	–10.03		4.19	–5.69	2010
Denmark	–1.50	–10.81	–1.17	2.29	–3.79	2010
Netherlands	–0.44	–7.26	3.78	2.27	–2.71	2010
Czech Republic	–2.20	–6.01	6.16	1.61	–3.81	2009
Estonia	–0.27	12.79		6.47	–6.73	2011
Ireland		–44.50				
Slovenia	0.02	–3.12	0.68	4.38	–4.36	2009
Italy	–2.51	–11.64	5.93	4.78	–7.29	2009
Portugal	0.44	–9.71	6.10	2.71	–2.27	2009
Luxembourg	–8.38	–36.29	–14.08	4.50	–12.88	2009
Spain	–4.64	–35.16	15.16	5.72	–10.35	2011
Greece	6.23	–12.94		15.21	–8.97	2009
Austria	–10.20	–42.44	–8.90	17.74	–27.94	2009
Cyprus	–35.88	– 188.37	–31.45	16.07	–51.95	2009
Croatia	23.63	7.40		35.88	–12.25	2012
Malta	–25.62	88.64		20.66	–46.28	2010
United Kingdom	1.80	–2.94	0.82	2.20	–0.40	2010

[a]2015 or last available data, i.e., 2014 for EU 28 and 2012 for United Kingdom
Source Authors' calculations based on Eurostat data, Database: "NACE_R2, nights spent at tourist accommodation establishments" [Dataset: tour_occ_ninat], last update 07.11.17, (NACE_R2 = Statistical classification of economic activities in the European Community, Revision 2)

cooperation based on thematic cultural routes. Because domestic investment is much lower than is needed for consistent improvement, both in the cultural heritage and tourism sectors, sources of European finance could be a good opportunity for

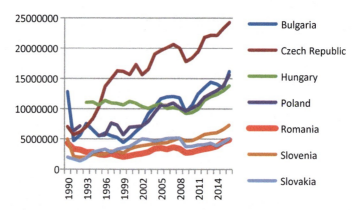

Fig. 24.2 Total nights spent by non-residents in Romania and other EU countries, 1990–2015 (number of nights) (*Source* Eurostat data, Database: "NACE_R2, nights spent at tourist accommodation establishments" [Dataset: tour_occ_ninat], last update 07.11.17)

Table 24.4 Non-resident tourists to Romania in 2017, by country of origin

Origin of non-resident tourists to Romania	Number of tourists	Percentage of total
	1,863,929	100.0
Germany	221,697	11.9
Israel	193,706	10.4
Italy	162,152	8.7
France	111,987	6.0
Hungary	107,465	5.8
United States	106,991	5.7
United Kingdom	106,405	5.7

Note Reference period January–August 2017
Source National Institute of Statistics (NIS), Romania, Press release October 2017. http://www.insse.ro/cms/ro/content/turism-26

smart investments in valuing heritage assets and for tourism infrastructure modernization, to create connectivity between different European destinations, to create innovative products, to design and share good practice (Babic et al. 2014; Vasile 2015), and to develop a multiparty road map for local development (Grobbe and Hendriks 2014).

24.4 Some Conclusions and Policy Recommendations

Heritage is a public good but the responsibility for its valuing in the cultural benefit belongs to both public and private sector. The business sector designed for valuate the uniqueness is widening and more integrated to digital economy, both for innovative preservation, ingénue presentation for public consumption (innovative cultural products), promoting green development of specific economic and social environment (preserving natural habitat) and for attracting onsite visitors.

Tourism services and cultural products should be considered co-determinants for local development in areas with partially valued heritage. A strategic and integrated approach of sustainable cultural heritage tourism development must include all types of externalities (positive and negative) and should be included in the local roadmap for development as a priority and an economically driven opportunity.

The balance between indigenous and foreign consumers is part of the cultural education of the population and an open gate for embracing diversity and creatively integrating multiculturalism.

Present research showed that sustainable and inclusive growth through the export of cultural heritage products could be an engine for local development re-designs in lower income areas. In general, these regions have unvalued, under-valued, or just partially valued heritage assets, but investment efforts need to address both public and private business. Investments in tourism are the backbone for cultural heritage openness to national and international networks for specific business sector development through exports providing authentic and unique cultural tourism products.

The conservation and proper valorization of local heritage enhances local identity and historical and cultural backgrounds. Promoting a variety of policies to use all local resources—innovative, cultural, heritage products involves both talent, business hub development, and young creative consumers interested in onsite active participation/involvement in cultural consumption.

Insufficient domestic investment in the cultural heritage sector and smart investments remain the main challenges for Romania. Demand for cultural tourism export is increasing; as well, the quality of complementary consumption services provided by local stakeholders. The business development/diversification and modernization is the central challenge for local communities. Upgrading the UNESCO World Heritage List with both tangible and intangible cultural heritage assets and a proper preservation (in time and space) of the local authenticity, could support the efforts for local business development, as the most straightforward way to align private incentives with optimal innovation.

For Romania, the most beneficial way to approach increasing cultural heritage exports is:

- To develop local creative hubs for valuing heritage potential and providing cultural outputs for export.
- To support private–public partnership, in the development of local stakeholders map for cultural tourism; sharing the costs and benefits from heritage interpretation and valuation, respectively, as market and non-market value, as active and passive use etc.
- To stimulate intergenerational technological transfer for traditional cultural products for preserving authenticity and taking care of heritage in the interests of future generations.

- To enhance local cultural centers for joint activities for consumers/tourists, learning through knowledge and by doing specific artisan activities—handicrafts, participation in traditional events, etc.
- To stimulate agrotourism and integrate it within the digital economy, to develop and integrate niche tourism based on preservation of the environment.
- To value, from economic and cultural point of view, of the multiplier effects of the heritage capital stock, both in tangible and intangible forms.
- To understand and measure the externalities of cultural goods/services components (the aesthetic, symbolic, spiritual, social, historic, scientific, and/or authenticity values).
- To educate youths in heritage economics, cultural investments, and innovative sustainable cultural tourism.
- To support heritage policy—preservation/conservation, adaptive reuse, economic and social (re)interpretation of common values.
- To promote efficiency in the production of both economic and sociocultural benefits through heritage valuing, fiscal incentives, etc.
- To support σ and β convergence of regions through share of T&T sector in GDP, based on common values and increased qualitative offer, strengthening the local leadership in tourism management and boosting smart investments.

Appendix

Nights spent by non-residents per 1000 inhabitants in Romania and ratio of tourism export intensity with other EU member states.

Country/date	1990	2000	2007	2008	2009	2010	2011	2012	2013	2014	2015
Romania—tourism export intensity	183	96	166	156	124	129	143	164	173	189	224
Romania = 1.00											
EU 28			12.13	12.73	15.13	15.45	14.84	13.69	13.62	12.67	0.00
Poland	2.01	1.88	1.72	1.71	2.03	2.05	1.92	1.88	1.87	1.81	1.61
Slovakia	2.70	7.17	5.70	6.10	5.52	5.36	5.17	4.56	4.58	3.77	3.60
Germany	3.12	5.39	3.98	4.38	5.32	5.66	5.39	5.09	5.03	4.91	4.33
Finland		8.21	6.07	6.65	7.40	7.25	7.15	6.56	6.26	5.55	4.49
Lithuania		1.89	2.86	3.10	3.36	3.66	4.30	5.45	5.66	5.46	4.59
Hungary	4.22	11.46	6.08	6.38	7.41	7.25	6.93	7.00	7.00	6.63	5.86
Sweden		10.20	7.39	7.62	9.85	9.29	8.41	7.28	6.94	6.74	6.22
Latvia		3.06	5.10	5.97	6.06	6.60	7.59	7.25	7.55	7.62	6.45
Belgium	7.10	15.84	9.24	9.83	11.58	11.57	10.61	9.04	8.57	8.08	7.46
Bulgaria	7.97	6.59	9.40	9.89	10.02	10.82	11.77	11.21	11.43	10.30	8.26
France		18.78	10.26	10.71	12.36	14.44	13.23	11.69	11.68	10.54	8.75
Denmark	9.96	19.61	10.30	10.43	12.13	12.59	11.91	10.51	10.25	9.99	8.79
The Netherlands	6.05	17.09	10.27	9.87	12.23	12.54	11.62	10.16	10.97	10.84	9.83
Czech Republic	3.68	15.85	12.05	12.33	13.66	13.56	12.93	12.67	12.20	11.15	9.84
Estonia			13.06	14.01	16.48	18.54	19.52	17.61	17.15	15.79	12.79
Ireland		57.45						15.77	13.72	12.98	12.96
Slovenia	13.42	17.22	14.08	16.21	18.46	17.74	17.38	16.94	16.56	15.45	14.10
Italy	8.19	25.75	16.62	17.39	21.40	21.24	20.32	18.56	17.93	16.29	14.11
Portugal	10.60	26.42	16.26	16.97	18.98	18.51	18.39	16.81	17.72	18.12	16.70
Luxembourg	35.10	57.31	29.40	29.79	33.90	26.53	28.06	26.73	24.95	24.81	21.02
Spain	10.69	61.01	30.48	31.66	35.26	35.98	36.20	31.74	31.29	29.59	25.84

(continued)

(continued)

Country/date	1990	2000	2007	2008	2009	2010	2011	2012	2013	2014	2015
Romania—tourism export intensity	183	96	166	156	124	129	143	164	173	189	224
Greece		45.05	25.88	27.41	41.08	40.61	40.43	33.51	36.12	36.31	32.11
Austria	50.62	84.16	51.91	57.56	69.66	67.22	61.16	56.03	53.75	48.99	41.72
Cyprus	97.46	254.38	101.90	107.22	117.97	117.87	108.98	95.53	87.99	79.61	66.01
Croatia		61.86	45.63	48.96	60.61	58.24	55.98	81.50	80.70	76.24	69.26
Malta			114.26	118.38	127.62	134.92	123.55	109.65	112.34	105.04	
United Kingdom	9.36	13.12	8.38	8.42	10.46	10.58	9.82	10.18			

Source Authors' calculation based on Eurostat data, Database: NACE_R2, nights spent at tourist accommodation establishments [Dataset: tour_occ_ninat], last update 07.11.17

References

Babic, D., Papathanasiou-Zuhrt, D., & Vasile, V. (2014). Heritage as development mediator: Interpretation and management. In *SEE TCP project Sagittarius interpretive guide book, Faculty of Humanities and Social Sciences* (71 p). Croatia: University of Zagreb (ISBN 978–953-175-512-2).

Benhamou, F. (2010). Heritage. In R. Towse (Ed.), *Handbook of cultural economics* (2nd ed., pp. 229–235). Cheltenham: Edward Elgar.

Bote Gómez, V., & Sinclair, M. T. (1996). Tourism, the Spanish economy and the balance of payments. In Tourism in Spain (pp. 89–117). Oxon.

Bucci, A., & Segre, G. (2011). Culture and human capital in a two-sector endogenous growth mode. *Research in Economics, 65*(4), 279–293.

Cheng, S. W. (2006). Cultural goods production, cultural capital formation and the provision of cultural services. *Journal of Cultural Economics, 30*(4), 263–286.

Cortés-Jiménez, I., & Pulina, M. (2009). Inbound tourism and long-run economic growth of Spain and Italy. https://www.researchgate.net/publication/249024205_Inbound_Tourism_and_Long-run_Economic_Growth.

Durbarry, R. (2004). Tourism and economic growth: The case of mauritius. *Tourism Economics, 10,* 389–401.

European Commission (EC). (2010). *Europe, the world's no. 1 tourist destination—a new political framework for tourism in Europe (COM(2010) 352 final).* Brussels.

European Parliament (EP). (2015). *From responsible best practices to sustainable tourism development.* Study, 2015, European Parliament, Directorate General for Internal Policies, Policy Department Sructural and Cohesion Policies, Transport and Tourism, Research for Tran Committee.

Eurostat. (2016). *Eurostat regional yearbook* (2016 ed.). http://ec.europa.eu/eurostat/documents/3217494/7604195/KS-HA-16-001-EN-N.pdf/76c007e9-6c1d-435a-97f8-e5ea700aa149.

Ey. (2015, December). *Cultural times: The first global map of cultural and creative industries.* http://www.worldcreative.org/wp-content/uploads/2015/12/EYCulturalTimes2015_Download.pdf.

Grobbe, F., & Hendriks, J. J. M. (2014). *Valentina Vasile, Cornelia Dumitru, Alexandru Stratan, Dumitru Stratan, contributors-CommunityPlanning-a multi-party roadmap* (74 p). Netherland: AO Organization Development (2014), english version as printed version (ISBN: 978-90-822432-0-8). www.ao-organisatieontwikkeling.nl.

Hutter, M., & Rizzo, I. (Eds.). (1997). *Economic perspectives on cultural heritage.* London: Macmillan.

Krueger, A. (1980). Trade policy as an input to development. *American Economic Review, 70,* 188–292.

Licciardi, G., & Amirtahmasebi, R. (Eds.). (2012). *The economics of Uniqueness.* World Bank.

Mason, R. (2005). *Economics and historic preservation: A guide and review of the literature.* Washington, DC: Brookings Institution.

McKinnon, R. (1964). Foreign exchange constraint in economic development and efficient aid allocation. *Economic Journal, 74,* 388–409.

Nowak, J. J., Sahli, M., & Cortés-Jiménez, I. (2007). Tourism, capital good imports and economic growth: Theory and evidence for Spain. *Tourism Economics, 13,* 515–536.

Peacock, A. (1995). A future for the past: The political economy of heritage. *Proceedings of the British Academy, 87,* 189–243.

Peacock, A., & Rizzo, I. (2008). *The heritage game: Economics, policy and practice.* Oxford: Oxford University Press.

Rizzo, I., & Towse, R. (Eds.). (2002). *The economics of heritage: A study of the political economy of culture in Sicily.* Cheltenham: Edward Elgar.

Schuster, J. M., de Monchaux, J., & Riley, C. A., II (Eds.). (1997). *Preserving the built heritage: Tools for implementation.* Hanover, NH: University Press of New England.

Shockley, G. E. (2004). Government investment in cultural capital: A Methodology for comparing direct government support for the arts in the US and the UK. *Public Finance and Management, 4*(1), 75–102.

Sinclair, M. T. (1998). Tourismand economic development: A survey. *The Journal of Development Studies, 34,* 1–51.

Throsby, D. (1997). Seven questions in the economics of cultural heritage. In M. Hutter & I. Rizzo (Eds.), *Economic perspectives on cultural heritage* (pp. 12–30). London: Macmillan.

Throsby, D. (1999). Cultural capital. *Journal of Cultural Economics, 23*(1), 3–12.

Throsby, D. (2001). *Economics and culture.* Cambridge: Cambridge University Press.

Vasile, V., & Login, I-A. (2013). *Innovative interpretation of cultural heritage and local sustainable entrepreneurship development. Case study on Romania—In(di)visible bucharest, in European research development in Horizon 2020.* In H. Elena H & Bostan I (Eds.) (pp. 573–593), hardback (ISBN: 978-1-910129-00-5); paperback (ISBN: 978-1-910129-01-2). London, United Kingdom, United Sates of America: Printed in Lumen Media Publishing, Romania: Lumen Publishing House. https://www.bookdepository.com/European-Research-Development-Horizon-2020/9781910129012.

Vasile, V. (Ed.). (2015). *Procedia—social and behavioral sciences* (Vol 188, pp. 1–334) (14 May 2015). Heritage as an alternative driver for sustainable development and economic recovery in South East Europe-Project. SEE/B/0016/4.3/X SAGITTARIUS. http://www.sciencedirect.com/science/journal/18770428/188/supp/C.

Wang, X. (2007). An analysis of optimal allocation and accumulation of cultural capital. In *Departmental bulletin paper 2007-08-03* (pp. 197–213). Kyoto: Graduate School of Policy and Management, Doshisha University.

WIPO. (2015). *Guide on surveying the economic contribution of copyright industries.* revised edition. http://www.wipo.int/edocs/pubdocs/en/copyright/893/wipo_pub_893.pdf.

World Bank. (2012). *Inclusive green growth: The pathway to sustainable development.* http://siteresources.worldbank.org/EXTSDNET/Resources/Inclusive_Green_Growth_May_2012.pdf.

WTTC. (2017). *Travel and tourism.* Economic impact 2017, World Travel and Tourism Council. https://www.wttc.org/-/media/files/reports/economic-impact-research/regions-2017/world2017.pdf.

Zaman, G. H., Vasile, V., Parvu, R., Darasteanu, C. (2010a). *The economic contribution of copyright-based Industries in Romania.* http://www.wipo.int/export/sites/www/copyright/en/performance/pdf/econ_contribution_cr_ro.pdf, http://www.wipo.int/copyright/en/performance/.

Zaman, G. H., Vasile, V., Parvu, R., Darasteanu, C. (2010b). *Eurostatstatistical database.* http://ec.europa.eu/eurostat/data/database.

Zaman, G. H., Vasile, V., Parvu, R., Darasteanu, C. (2010c). *EUROPA-official website of the European union-member countries-Romania.* http://europa.eu/about-eu/countries/member-countries/romania/index_en.htm.

Zaman, G. H., Vasile, V., Parvu, R., Darasteanu, C. (2010d). *European commission-DG ECFIN (economic and financial affairs)-country page for Romania,* May 2016. http://ec.europa.eu/economy_finance/eu/countries/romania_en.htm.

Zaman, G. H., Vasile, V., Parvu, R., Darasteanu, C. (2010e). *World travel andtourism council.* http://www.wttc.org/research/economic-research/economic-impact-analysis/country-reports/.

Zaman, G. H., Vasile, V., Parvu, R., Darasteanu, C. (2010f). *National Institute of Statistics.* Romania. http://www.insse.ro/cms/.

Chapter 25
Weather Risk Management's Instruments Used in Tourism Industry

Mirela Panait, Irina Radulescu and Marian Catalin Voica

Abstract The weather is an important factor that affects the businesses, because the climate change determined the intensification of natural phenomenon, sudden temperature changes or large amounts of rainfall or snowfall. The traditional instruments offered by insurance industry are not suitable for these new challenges determined by climate change. A new market was born, and new tools for weather risk management appeared. The weather derivatives are traded on OTC market and on stock exchange. The article is focused on the use of the weather derivatives by the companies from tourism industry. Taking in account the success of weather derivatives traded on Chicago Mercantile Exchange Group, the authors of this paper analysed the possibilities of tourism industry's companies from other parts of the world to cover risks arising from weather.

Keywords Weather derivatives · Insurance industry · Hedging strategies
Climate change · Stock exchange

25.1 Introduction

Tourism is an important economic field in most countries. In many developing countries, tourism is a force of development, taking in account its contributions to the growth of the national economy: the generation of income, employment and foreign exchange earnings. With increasing level of development of these countries, they turn from net receivers of foreign tourists in provider countries of tourists for foreigner countries. The importance of this field is greater if we take in account not only direct economic impact, but also indirect and induced impacts (Table 25.1).

Despite major differences that exist between countries in terms of tourism's contribution to the economic development of a country (Surugiu and Surugiu 2013), at international level, tourism plays an important role taking in account the

M. Panait (✉) · I. Radulescu · M. C. Voica
Petroleum-Gas University of Ploiesti, Avenue Bucharest 39, Ploieşti, Romania
e-mail: mirematei@yahoo.com

© Springer International Publishing AG, part of Springer Nature 2019
V. Vasile (ed.), *Caring and Sharing: The Cultural Heritage Environment as an Agent for Change*, Springer Proceedings in Business and Economics, https://doi.org/10.1007/978-3-319-89468-3_25

Table 25.1 Importance of local product buying

Type of contribution	Effects		
Direct impact	Commodities – Accommodation – Transportation – Entertainment – Attraction	Industries – Accommodation services – Food and beverage services – Retail trade – Transportation services – Cultural, sports and recreation services	Sources of spending – Residents domestic T & T spending – Businesses domestic travel spending – Visitor exports; – Individual government T & T spending
Indirect impact		T & T investment spending Government collective spending Impact of purchases from suppliers	
Induced impact		Food and beverage Recreation Clothing Housing Household goods	

Source World travel and tourism council, travel and tourism economic impact 2016, p. 2

data reported by World Travel and Tourism Council and presented in Table 25.2. For example, in 2015 the direct contribution of this sector (travel and tourism) to GDP was USD 2,229.8bn (3.0% of GDP) and it generates directly 107,833,000 jobs in 2015 (3.6% of total employment).

Table 25.2 Economic contributions of tourism: estimates and forecasts

	2015 USD bn[a]	2015% of total	2016 growth[b]	2026 growth[c]
Direct contribution to GDP	22,229.8	3.0	3.3	4.2
Total contribution to GDP	7107.3	9.8	3.5	4.0
Direct contribution to employment[d]	107,833	3.6	1.9	2.1
Total contribution to employment[d]	283,578	9.5	2.2	2.5
Visitor exports	1308.9	6.1	3.0	4.3
Domestic spending	3419.9	4.7	3.3	4.0
Leisure spending	3621.9	2.3	3.0	4.2
Business spending	1106.9	0.7	3.9	3.7
Capital investment	774.6	4.3	4.7	4.5

[a]2015 constant prices and exchange rates
[b]2016 real growth adjusted for inflation (%)
[c]2016–2026 annualized real growth adjusted for inflation (%)
4000 jobs (*Source* World Travel and Tourism Council, Travel and Tourism Economic Impact 2016, p 7)

In the last two decades, at international level, tourism activity experienced major changes under the impact of globalization, financial crisis (Podasca 2010; Haralambie 2013), food crisis (Stancu 2015), terrorism or climate change (Nedelcu 2015; Ielenicz and Nedelcu 2015). In spite of the negative influences exercised by economic crisis, climate change or terrorist attacks, the tourism flows are expected to raise taking in account factors like population growth, shorter working weeks, rising incomes. In addition, the forecasts regarding the evolution of the tourism activity are influenced by "the complex character of this branch as a consumer of production from other branches and the production supplier to the other branches" (Zaman et al. 2010).

25.2 Weather Derivatives as Financial Instruments Used in Tourism Activity

Before 1997, there were a small number of financial instruments that offered insurance against the risks of climate change: the insurance policies used to cover damage of this kind. It can be said that in the market there is a zone not covered on protecting companies against the risks arising from exposure to weather changes. Even in modern society, highly engineered, weather and climate changes still affect the lives and human choices and have a significant impact on revenue and earnings of companies from sectors like agriculture, tourism, constructions (Matei et al. 2008; Keen et al. 2003).

Weather affects, to a greater extent, the volume of consumption than the price of certain assets. For example, warmer winters may mean higher stocks of oil or natural gas for utilities' companies and energy's corporations. Also, cool summers may result in empty hotel rooms or fewer passengers for airlines. Although the price of a good, an airplane sit or hotel room, may change depending on high or low demand, price adjustments do not necessarily cover low incomes (Scott 2003).

The first transaction on weather derivatives market took place in September 1997 and was conducted by ENRON and KOCH on OTC market, since we observe a rapid development of this market in quantitative and qualitative dimensions. Thus, products for specific risk management were launched: options, cap, floor, collar and swap that are available for OTC market. These products use various temperature indexes. For these financial products, the amounts that buyers pay their vendors are calculated by multiplying the difference between the contract value index and value index recorded weather during the contract period, with a certain amount expressed in dollars. So, the payout of a weather derivative is based on a weather index and not on a demonstrated loss like in the case of conventional weather insurance products (Cao et al. 2003; Cao and Wei 2004; Zeng 2000).

Other differences between traditional insurance products and weather derivatives are:

- The insurance products cover events with high risk and low probability; the weather derivatives are used to cover events with lower risk and higher probability like small changes in temperature that may affect the sales of energy companies;

- Weather derivatives are transparent because the payments are made based on the evolution of an index and all data are public; in the cases of insurance contracts, the compensation is paid by the insurance company after damage assessment.

The weather derivatives' market is dominated by OTC sector that is "fuelled" by many institutions from Europe and USA like investment funds, insurance companies and some of the larger energy companies that offer weather derivatives used for hedging or speculative strategies.

Weather derivatives are new financial instruments traded on OTC and stock exchange. In 1999, Chicago Mercantile Exchange launched weather derivatives for some American, European and Asian towns, and the underlying assets used for these derivatives contracts being temperature, rainfall or snowfall indexes. There are many differences to commodities or financial derivatives taking in account the following considerations:

- Weather is by its nature a location-specific asset and non-standardized commodity;
- For standardization of the weather, indexes are used: temperature index, rainfall index or snowfall index;
- Underlying asset of traditional derivatives is traded in a spot market; the launch and traded of futures and options for commodities, securities or currencies are normal stages that follows trading on spot mark of those assets;
- The standard derivatives are used for price hedging strategies and not quantity hedging strategies, and weather derivatives are useful for quantity hedging; (Campbell and Diebold 2011).

25.2.1 Weather Derivatives—Study Case for Romanian Market

Weather derivatives may take different forms, but the most known form is the temperature derivatives. Temperature derivative contracts use temperature index. The most used are heating degree days (HDD), cooling degree days (CDD) and cumulative average temperature (CAT). Usually, the period of the contracts are months or seasons.

The main components of a contract on temperature are:

1. Type of contract (futures or options);
2. Period of contract (month or season);
3. Contract unit;
4. Official station from which weather data are obtained;
5. Definition of the index (W) on which the contract is based;
6. Minimum price fluctuation;
7. Settlement method: financially settled.

In Romania, the main touristic destinations are mountain resorts concentrated in Prahova and Brasov counties (Adrian 2015), seaside resorts from the Black Sea and balneal resorts (Ungureanu 2014). Taking in account the climate change that affected Romanian territory, the authors highlight the importance for companies from travel and tourism fields to have the possibility to hedge the weather risk like temperature or rainfall/snowfall risk for some Romanian traditional destinations.

Forward, we propose the development of weather options contracts based on temperature for the main winter and summer season resorts at the Sibex Exchange, which is the main exchange from Romania where futures and options are traded.

For the winter season we think that the contracts will be used in resorts that have at least 8 km of ski slopes and four cable installations, so we propose the initiation of contracts for: Sinaia, Predeal, Poiana Brasov, Straja, Parang and Semenic. For these locations, the temperature data will be recorded by the next stations of The National Meteorological Administration: Sinaia 1500, Predeal, Poiana Brasov, Petrosani, Parang and Semenic.

The support for the contracts will be the HDD index or the CAT index available for the ski season months: December, January, February, March and April. The length of the contract may take two forms, a month or a season.

Further, we propose the use of the Chicago Mercantile Exchange contract unit as 20 USD times the HDD/CAT index and the minimum price fluctuation of 1 index point, equivalent with 20 USD.

For the summer season we think that the contracts will be used by the seaside resorts like: Mamaia, Neptun-Olimp, Eforie Nord, Eforie Sud, Costinesti, Mangalia and Jupiter. For these locations, the temperature data will be recorded by the next stations of The National Meteorological Administration: Constanta and Mangalia.

The support for the contracts will be the CDD index or the CAT index available for the summer season months: May, June, July, August and September. The length of the contract may take two forms, a month or a season.

Further, we propose the use of the Chicago Mercantile Exchange contract unit as 20 USD times the CDD/CAT index and the minimum price fluctuation of 1 index point, equivalent with 20 USD.

25.2.2   Methodology Used to Determine the Index Value for Temperature Variation Contracts

All three versions of temperature variation contracts have at their core the daily average temperature computed as

$$T_i = \frac{T_{i_{min}} + T_{i_{max}}}{2}$$

where

T$_i$ average recorded temperature on the day i;

T$_{(i\_min)}$ minimum recorded temperature on the day i;

T$_{(i\_max)}$ maximum recorded temperature on the day i.

After determining the daily average temperature, we can compute each of the three indexes.

Cumulative average temperature index represents the sum of the daily average temperature in a period (month, season or year) determined as:

$$CAT = \sum_{i=1}^{n} T_i$$

where

CAT cumulative average temperature for a period of n days;

T$_i$ average recorded temperature on the day i.

Cooling degree days' index is based on the assumption that the normal temperature for human activities is 65 °F (18 °C). Temperatures that are above this value will incur costs to cool down to the normal temperature and higher temperatures require higher costs. As a result, CDD calculates the number of degrees that are above the normal temperature using the next formula:

$$CDD_i = \max(T_i - T, 0)$$

where

CDD$_i$ cooling degree day;

T$_i$ average recorded temperature on the day i;

T temperature of 18 °C (65 °F).

After determining the CDD for each day, we determine the CDD index with the next formula:

$$CDD = \sum_{i=1}^{n} CDD_i$$

where

CDD cooling degree day index;

CDD$_i$ cooling degree day.

Heating degree days' index is also based on the assumption that the normal temperature for human activities is 65 °F (18 °C). Temperatures that are below this value will incur costs to heat up to the normal temperature and lower temperatures require higher costs. As a result, HDD calculates the number of degrees that are below the normal temperature using the next formula:

$$HDD_i = \max(0, T - T_i)$$

where

HDD$_i$ heating degree day;
T$_i$ average recorded temperature on the day i;
T temperature of 18 °C (65 °F).

After determining the HDD for each day we determine the HDD index with the next formula:

$$HDD = \sum_{i=1}^{n} HDD_i$$

where

HDD heating degree day index;
HDD$_i$ heating degree day.

25.2.3 Application for Romanian Market

In this paper, the authors made a proposal regarding the trade of temperature derivative contracts for Sinaia resort—the most popular Romanian mountain resort. In our case study, we use the data from Sinaia meteorological station for three months, December, January and February, which are the main months of the skiing season. We chose Sinaia because it is one of the most known destinations for winter sports and it is also known as the Pearl of the Carpathians. Sinaia has almost 22 km of ski slopes.

In Table 25.3, we compute the average temperature for each day using (1) and the value of CAT using (2). The value of CAT for the season is obtained by summing the values of CAT for each month, and we compute a seasonal value of CAT of 63.9 °C. If we acknowledge that the temperature of 0 °C would be a feasible average value for the accumulation and maintaining of snow on ski slopes and that the multiannual average temperature is around 0.7 °C, we can say that the value of CAT we obtain is almost equal to the multiannual value.

In Table 25.4, we compute the daily HDD using (5) and then we use (6) to compute the HDD index for the entire period. The value of HDD index is 1574.13 °C. This value is very close to the multiannual value of HDD index. This means that this value of the HDD index may be used as a starting point for the creation of financial instruments.

These instruments may take a lot of forms and can be used in many different ways. In our case, we are interested to have a season with a sufficient amount of

Table 25.3 Daily temperatures for skiing season

Day	December			January			February		
	Max	Min	Avg.	Max	Min	Avg.	Max	Min	Avg.
1	1.67	0	1.11	0.56	−4.44	−2.22	5	−6.11	−0.56
2	8.89	0	4.44	−2.22	−5	−3.33	11.67	−3.33	4.44
3	8.89	0	4.44	−4.44	−7.22	−5.56	10	0	5
4	11.67	5	8.33	−7.22	−11.11	−8.89	5	2.78	3.89
5	16.67	2.78	10	−9.44	−14.44	−12.22	5	1.67	3.33
6	11.67	0	5.56	−4.44	−12.22	−8.33	5	2.78	3.89
7	12.78	5	8.89	−3.33	−8.33	−5.56	3.89	2.78	3.33
8	5.56	1.67	3.33	−1.11	−7.22	−4.44	2.78	0	1.11
9	5	−1.11	2.22	−4.44	−7.22	−5.56	3.89	0	2.22
10	6.67	−4.44	1.11	−6.11	−9.44	−7.78	1.67	−2.22	0
11	5	−4.44	0	−7.22	−9.44	−8.33	0.56	−4.44	−1.11
12	7.78	0	3.89	−7.22	−11.11	−8.89	2.78	−6.11	−1.67
13	3.89	0	2.22	−5	−11.11	−8.89	1.67	−7.22	−2.78
14	0.56	0	0	−2.22	−6.11	−4.44	5.56	−7.22	−1.11
15	1.67	0	1.11	−2.22	−5	−3.33	5.56	−4.44	0.56
16	3.89	0	2.22	0.56	−3.33	−1.11	0	−8.33	−4.44
17	7.78	2.78	5.56	1.67	−6.11	−2.22	−2.22	−12.22	−7.22
18	10	6.67	8.33	1.67	−1.11	0	0.56	−12.22	−5.56
19	11.67	5.56	8.89	1.67	−1.11	0	8.89	−6.11	1.11
20	6.67	3.89	5.56	0.56	−3.33	−1.11	11.67	−3.33	4.44
21	5.56	2.78	4.44	5	−2.22	1.11	12.78	−2.22	5.56
22	7.78	−3.33	2.22	8.89	−2.22	3.33	15.56	−1.11	7.22
23	8.89	−1.11	3.89	5	0	2.22	16.67	2.78	10
24	5	−4.44	1.11	3.89	−2.22	1.11	15	−1.11	6.67
25	0.56	−5	−2.22	3.89	−4.44	0	18.89	1.67	10
26	1.67	−7.22	−2.78	2.78	−3.33	0	15.56	2.78	8.89
27	−2.22	−7.22	−4.44	6.67	−2.22	2.22	20.56	0	10
28	−3.33	−7.22	−5.56	5	−2.22	1.11	20	5	12.22
29	−3.33	−11.11	−7.22	5	−4.44	0	13.89	1.67	7.78
30	−1.11	−7.22	−4.44	5.56	−5	0	–	–	–
31	3.89	−8.33	−2.22	2.78	−7.22	−2.22	–	–	–
CAT			70			−93.3			87.2

Source Author's calculation

snow on the slopes. If the temperature is too high through the season the snow on the slopes will melt and with no snow tourists will stop coming to Sinaia. This happened in the season 2015–2016 and generated a lot of losses to the tourism companies from the area.

Table 25.4 Number of daily HDD

Day	December	January	February
1	16.89	20.22	18.56
2	13.56	21.33	13.56
3	13.56	23.56	13
4	9.67	26.89	14.11
5	8	30.22	14.67
6	12.44	26.33	14.11
7	9.11	23.56	14.67
8	14.67	22.44	16.89
9	15.78	23.56	15.78
10	16.89	25.78	18
11	18	26.33	19.11
12	14.11	26.89	19.67
13	15.78	26.89	20.78
14	18	22.44	19.11
15	16.89	21.33	17.44
16	15.78	19.11	22.44
17	12.44	20.22	25.22
18	9.67	18	23.56
19	9.11	18	16.89
20	12.44	19.11	13.56
21	13.56	16.89	12.44
22	15.78	14.67	10.78
23	14.11	15.78	8
24	16.89	16.89	11.33
25	20.22	18	8
26	20.78	18	9.11
27	22.44	15.78	8
28	23.56	16.89	5.78
29	25.22	18	10.22
30	22.44	18	–
31	20.22	20.22	–
Total	488.01	651.33	434.79

Source Author's calculation

25.3 Conclusion

Weather derivatives have a lot of possibilities to develop. The main constraints that they encounter are represented by the lack of providers for more areas of the world, the lack of education among potential users, and the effects of their use. As a result, these are the main areas where a lot of improvements need to be made. They are one of the best alternatives to insurance with a quicker resolution. While on insurance contract you have to wait until the provider evaluates and compute the value of the damage and if it is covered by the insurance policy, the weather derivative contracts provide a fast resolution by executing the contract and no other complicated procedures. The weather variables may be the base of numerous types of contracts, providing coverage of an enormous range of situations that cannot be hedged by traditional methods.

The authors analysed the possibility of launching weather derivatives by one of the Romanian stock exchanges—Bucharest Stock Exchange (BSE) or Sibiu Stock Exchange (SIBEX). The authors consider that SIBEX is the most indicated "host" exchange for these products taking in account the offer of this institution for derivatives having as underlying shares, indexes, commodities and currencies (currently, no longer futures contracts are traded on BSE). In the case of mountain resorts, in winter season, the companies operating in the area depend largely on maintaining a low temperature to be profitable. To protect against warm winters, these companies can sell (take short position) HDD index futures at a certain level. A warm winter will lead to low index HDD, and those companies are hoping to buy temperature derivative contracts at a lower price, profit result using it to cover losses.

References

Adrian, U. (2015). The importance of Romanian mountain tourism for the national economy. *Ekonomika poljoprivrede, 62*(3), 849–868.

Campbell, S. D., & Diebold, F. X. (2011). Weather forecasting for weather derivatives. Journal of the American Statistical Association.

Cao, M., Li, A., & Wei, J. Z. (2003). Weather derivatives: A new class of financial instruments. Available at SSRN 1016123.

Cao, M., & Wei, J. (2004). Weather derivatives valuation and market price of weather risk. *Journal of Futures Markets, 24*(11), 1065–1089.

Haralambie, A. G. (2013). The impact of globalization in the context of the current crisis. Ovidius Univ Ann Ser Econ Sci, *13*(1).

Ielenicz, M., & Nedelcu, A. (2015). An appropriate and complete tourism lexicon. *International Journal of Sustainable Economies Management (IJSEM), 4*(3), 16–27.

Keen, M. M., Freeman, M. P. K., & Mani, M. M. (2003). Dealing with increased risk of natural disasters: Challenges and options (No. 3–197). International Monetary Fund.

Matei, M. (coord.), Stancu, A., Enescu, G., Geambaşu, C. (2008). *Burse de mărfuri şi valori.* Petroleum-Gas University of Ploiesti Publishing House.

Nedelcu, A. (2015). *Geografia turismului.* Bucharest: Universitară Publishing House.

Podasca, R. (2010). Advantages and disadvantages of globalization. *Ovidius University Annals, Economic Sciences Series, 10*(1), 768–771.

Scott, D. (2003, April). Climate change and tourism in the mountain regions of North America. In *1st International Conference on Climate Change and Tourism* (pp. 9–11).

Stancu, A. (2015). The relationship among population number, food domestic consumption and food consumer expenditure for most populous countries. *Procedia Economics and Finance, 22,* 333–342.

Surugiu, C., & Surugiu, M. R. (2013). Is the tourism sector supportive of economic growth? Empirical evidence on Romanian tourism. *Tourism Economics, 19*(1), 115–132.

Ungureanu, A., & TEŠIĆ, A. (2014). Romanian balneary tourism prospects in the context of services globalization. In *Sustainable agriculture and rural development in terms of the republic of Serbia strategic goals realization within the Danube region* (p. 88). Rural development and (un) limited resources.

World Travel and Tourism Council, Travel and Tourism Economic Impact. (2016). http://www.cmegroup.com/trading/weather/.

Zaman, G., Vasile, V., Surugiu, M., & Surugiu, C. (2010). Tourism and economic development in Romania: Input-output analysis perspective. *Romanian Journal of Economics, 31*(2).

Zeng, L. (2000). Weather derivatives and weather insurance: Concept, application and analysis. *Bulletin of the American Metrological Society, 81,* 2075–2982.

Chapter 26
Social Innovation—a Key Driver for Cultural Sustainability

Irina Anghel

Abstract Sometimes regarded as not only one of the dimensions of sustainability but even the central pillar of sustainable development, cultural sustainability is itself an agent, lever and catalyst for non-destructive socio-economic and demographic transformation. Defined as the ability to preserve the cultural identity and to ensure consistency and congruency between the future developments and the cultural value of a community, achieving cultural sustainability seems a continuously increasing challenge in the current global socio-demographic landscape. In the context of highly unpredictable and uncontrollable challenges stemming from the local as well as global environment, this paper looks into the potential of social innovation, through its intrinsic features, to serve the strategic objectives of preserving cultural values and heritage, at local level. Also, it may prove a valuable lever to reconcile social, economic and cultural interests and challenges critical to local sustainable development. Beside some theoretical considerations, the authors will draw on available good practice examples from the Romanian as well as international experience.

Keywords Cultural sustainability · Social innovation · Cultural heritage
Social economy · Sustainable development

26.1 Introduction

Along the last decade, on the scientific research and public policy agendas, cultural sustainability has grown into a major pillar of sustainable development, increasingly closely intertwined with the other three traditional versants of sustainability: economic, environmental and social (UNESCO 2012; Dessein et al. 2015; Daniel et al. 2012; Duxbury and Gillette 2007 etc.). On the one hand, a well-thought

I. Anghel (✉)
Institute of National Economy-Romanian Academy, Calea 13 Septembrie,
050711 Bucharest, Romania
e-mail: irina_c_anghel@yahoo.com

© Springer International Publishing AG, part of Springer Nature 2019   303
V. Vasile (ed.), *Caring and Sharing: The Cultural Heritage Environment
as an Agent for Change*, Springer Proceedings in Business and Economics,
https://doi.org/10.1007/978-3-319-89468-3_26

valorisation and promotion of cultural heritage may boost up the income and economic activity at local and national levels (Hernandez-Ros 2014; European Commission 2014, 2015). Tourism development, job creation, higher public budget inflows and poverty reduction are direct or indirect consequences of well preserved and capitalised upon cultural assets. At the same time, high income availability is directly associated with higher propensity to engagement in cultural activities. According to a recent EU report (European Commission 2013a), people in Northern European countries allocate the highest interest, time and resources for a wide range of cultural activities. To the other end of the spectrum, the Southern and Eastern European countries display the least engagement in cultural activities and the highest sensitivity of their cultural engagement to the economic welfare. In the Central and Eastern European countries, the economic crisis that settled in 2007 brought forth a steep decline in the involvement of their citizens in cultural activities.

On the other hand, strengthening the cultural identity through the stimulation of culture creation and consumption activities represents a valuable lever for enhancing social cohesion, inclusion, participation and resilience. Actually, between culture and society there has always been an interactive and reciprocal determinative relationship: culture, an expression of the society's evolvement, has, at its turn, moulded society.

Moreover, between cultural- and environmental-related projects and investments there is high potential for direct mutual reinforcement. Heritage preservation and promotion initiatives may draw the necessary interest and resources for the protection and the sustainable development of landscape and natural environment.

Beside considering culture as a lately added self-standing dimension of sustainable development alongside the economic, social and environmental pillars, some scientists and policy makers associate culture with broader roles, from that of mediator of the other three traditional pillars and of guidance among the economic, social and ecological considerations and imperatives, to even the foundation of the sustainable development structure, integrating, coordinating and guiding every aspect—by itself or in network with the whole system—of sustainable strategy and action (EU Council 2014).

Understanding culture as an overarching paradigm of the sustainable development thinking renders a different political attitude that should integrate the cultural policy with the social, economic and environmental strategies and policies which should imperatively be at least culturally informed. Education, RDI, social development, urban and regional planning, tourism, and environmental policies ought to integrate culture to the core (Dessein et al. 2015).

At EU level, many official documents, papers and initiatives, as well as the Horizon 2020 strategy (European Commission 2014), acknowledge the potential of the cultural heritage and activities as strategic drivers for economic growth, competitiveness, social cohesion and welfare, and environmental sustainability. Through its Research Framework Programmes, EU has supported research and innovation on, and excellence in, cultural heritage since the 1980s. Cultural heritage and assets are now perceived and presented as productive factors (Dessein et al.

2015 European Commission 2015), a perspective that replaces the traditional perception of culture-related activities as mainly morally justified cost-bearers. A recent report of the Expert Group on Cultural Heritage (European Commission 2015) explains and endorses the particular function of the innovative use of cultural heritage as investment opportunity leading to social cohesion, on the one hand, to environmental sustainability as well as to economic development, job creation and expansion of new markets.

To this end, however, the human society, at all aggregation levels, needs to find new, innovative more effective ways to preserve, create and valorise cultural assets. This paper explores the role that innovation—and, particularly, social innovation—may play for achieving the goal of cultural sustainability.

26.2 Cultural Sustainability Through Social Innovation

Cultural sustainability may be defined as the ability to preserve the cultural identity and to ensure that the ongoing transformation and development within a certain society are consistent and congruent with the cultural value of that particular community. This provides the necessary basement for a durable development and enforces resilience. It promotes community well-being, and it definitely requires community participation.

Cultural identity preservation and a societal development consistent with the cultural values of a particular community encompass, in the authors' opinion, three main areas:

A. Heritage conservation and preservation. It is the most direct lever for preserving the historical identity and values of a certain community, for passing it on to the future generations. It is a publicly assumed responsibility towards the past and the generations to come. At the same time, it is increasingly considered a source of inspiration for the cultural and creative industries, and thus, a potential driver for economic growth and well-being.

B. Creation/redesigning of cultural assets. Increasingly encouraged within the currently flourishing creative industries, the creation of cultural assets ensures the continuity of culture, the consistency of the new sociocultural developments with the historically determined cultural identity while allowing for cultural diversity and human development. Within the perimeter of the creative and cultural industries, under the protection of various legislations such as the IPR, the creation of cultural products translates creativity and talent into economic value. Therefore, the creation of cultural values and products encourages cultural engagement of the current generations, allows for continuity, and strengthens community identity, individuals belonging, inclusion and participation. At the same time, active creative sectors are generators of jobs and economic well-being.

C. Promotion, popularisation and valorisation of cultural assets through consumption of cultural products. This dimension is what actually turns potential into economic welfare gain for the individual and for the whole community. Moreover, this is what attracts further public and, more important, private investment and what stimulates the individuals' engagement and support. The effectiveness of the economic valorisation of cultural assets and potential depends largely on the quality and relevance of the other two main facets of cultural sustainability strategy.

The role of research and innovation for achieving cultural sustainability has been largely acknowledged and promoted. Innovation is instrumental in each of the main directions of action for cultural sustainability. The preservation, restoration of the cultural heritage, and the production of valuable, relevant cultural assets through the creative and cultural industries, as well as the valorisation of cultural heritage and cultural products, require a strategic approach to research and innovation which would apply the cutting-edge results of the latest research in ICT. At the EU policy level, the EU Research and Innovation Agenda for cultural heritage proposes three main interrelated and comprehensive strategic objectives that systematically emphasise the innovative approach, paradigm, mindset and framework: innovative finance, investment, governance, management to translate cultural heritage into an effective economic production factor; innovative use of cultural heritage as a means to increase social integration, cohesion and inclusiveness; and innovative use of cultural heritage that would support the environmental sustainable development.

It is, thus, apparent that technology—supported by research and innovation—stays at the core of each pillar of cultural sustainability. Optimal heritage preservation relies on innovative methods and solutions involving technology. The creative and cultural industries draw heavily on IT, while successful promoting and popularising of any cultural site is dependent on involving IT.

Innovation is essential, on the one hand, for enhancing the creative processes that aim either at generating cultural assets or at a higher and more sustainable valorisation of the already existent cultural assets. On the other hand, especially when targeting the younger public, it is important to understand, and capitalise upon, the potential of ICT to increasing the interest for cultural products and participation in cultural events. The ICT component in the creation and distribution within creative industries is unquestionably important. We would mention the EC-level initiative—Europeana—that involves a European Digital Library.

Under the Horizon 2020 platform, an explicit target is leveraging cutting-edge ICT technologies, through tight cooperation between ICT innovative technologies providers and creative industries, for the development of innovative tools, products, services and applications—such as 3D reality, advanced virtual user interfaces—in the creative industries (Hernandez-Ros 2014). Research for the benefit of cultural heritage preservation is supported through the FP7, the main areas in focus being the conservation and ICT technologies; heritage conservation and disaster resilience and climate change; underwater cultural heritage as well as art, culture and humanities (with special interest for transnational dialogue and understanding,

European common identity etc.). A special but an innovative approach does certainly not involve only technological innovation. Generally speaking, to the end of shaping behaviours and attitudes at societal level, social innovation is as important as the technological innovation (Bankinter Foundation of Innovation 2009) For successful projects of cultural assets preservation, creation and promotion, social innovation is critical, as well, as it furnishes the cultural sustainable objective with the proper and viable motives, access to untapped human and financial resources and with no trade-offs between social, economic and environmental development goals. It may, actually, provide a mediating platform between the social, economic and environmental interests at local level, while ensuring cultural sustainability. These functions and role are fostered by the intrinsic defining features of social innovation (Nicholls and Murdoch 2012; Caulier-Grice et al. 2012; European Commission (EC) 2013b; Mulgan et al. 2007; Moulaert et al. 2013):

a. Social innovation prospers there where the three traditional sectors—public, private or non-profit—have not proved satisfactory in quality or coverage.
b. It is inspired by predominantly social motives, and the main beneficiary is not an individual, but the society as a whole.
c. It does not only produce a social impact, it also creates and employs new social instruments in the form of new interactions, of new relationships. Social innovation brings forth changes in the interactions network, it redesigns social interactions, and it transforms institutions and develops the system of values within a determined society.
d. Social innovation engages multiple stakeholders in society, reconciling interests and attitudes, and transforming the main receiver in co-contributor.
e. Social innovation opens access to needed resources which would be hardly available within the public, private or non-profit sectors.

A complex approach, generally accepted in the EC documents, defines social innovation as new solutions (products, technologies, services, patterns, markets, processes) that provide better answers to a specific social need than the already existent solutions, and that lead to the improvement or creation of capacities and relationships, as well as to the optimisation of the utilisation of the society's assets and resources (Caulier-Grice et al. 2012). Social innovation serves thus to meeting the social needs while improving the society's capacity to act and react. It empowers and strengthens resilience, and it increases the social capital and improves the management and functionality of the society's institutions (Hamalainen and Heiskala 2007; Moulaert et al. 2005; Nicholls and Murdock 2012).

Considering each aspect described above, cultural sustainability (involving cultural assets conservation, creation and promotion) seems definitely one such fertile ground for social innovation (Nicholls and Murdoch 2012). Achieving cultural sustainability requires new relationships and linkages between social actors, a re-positioning of interests and responsibility, the assumed engagement of all stakeholders and the active involvement of the beneficiary community. Transforming the passive local beneficiary community into an active actor at all stages is maybe one of the most critical elements for a successful, culturally driven project.

One example of best practice that displays the interlacing between social and technological innovation along a complex project integrating heritage conservation, cultural assets creation and promotion/valorisation is …. Lagopesole (Aici as avea nevoie de cateva elemente de identificare plus o legatura catre un document, ceva. Acestea sunt doar amintirile mele de la conferinta de la tg. mures). Cutting-edge technology attracts young and adult tourists, through a virtual interactive map, robotic guide, while historical movies and other art products which actively involved the local community (many locals are movie actors) enrich the virtual and real cultural experience of the visitors. New relationship patterns have been created within an intersectoral framework, such as pro-sumption and co-production.

Capitalising upon each and every potential historical asset, a rather obscure historical site has attracted necessary funding for restauration and conservation, has become a prosperous touristic attraction and has brought forth higher community and cultural identity, higher social cohesion and integration, as well as higher general social and individual welfare.

26.3 Opportunities for Social Innovation Towards Cultural Sustainability in Romania

Social innovation and technological readiness are a prerequisite for any effective initiative related to, or aiming at, cultural sustainability in the Romanian economic and social landscape.

A general outlook on the engagement of the Romanian individual towards cultural activities, events and opportunities presents an alarming picture. According to recent statistics, it is apparent that, regardless of the economic ups and downs, the Romanian people are less inclined towards engaging in consumption or production of cultural assets or activities. While in Sweden, Netherlands or Denmark the percentage of those who read a book along the 2012 year was between 80 and 90%, the figures for Romania are down to 50% (by 18 p.p lower than the EU average rate, as well). An overall index of cultural practice places Romania among the countries with the lowest engagement in cultural activities. A very interesting and relevant aspect revealed by the EC barometer (European Commission 2013a) is that the Romanian respondents justified reluctance, non-involvement or low interest in each type of cultural activity mainly by the "lack of time" (Table 26.1). An alarming issue is that another frequent explanation—almost as common as the "lack of time"—was the "limited choice or poor quality of that particular activity in the place the respondent lives". While this is among the least mentioned barriers at EU level (about 10% of respondents), in Romania, the percentage of respondents considering it as the main reason for not getting involved in most of the cultural activities is double or even triple. The third most common justification is the

Table 26.1 Main barriers to participation in cultural activities in Romania, 2012

	Lack of time (%)	Lack of interest (%)	Limited choice or poor quality (%)	Too expensive (%)	Lack of information (%)	Other (%)	Do not know (%)
Seen a ballet, a dance performance or an opera	25	24	30	14	3	3	3
Visited a public library	36	26	23	4	2	6	3
Been to the theatre	30	19	29	15	3	3	1
Visited a museum or a gallery	32	22	26	12	2	4	2
Cultural programme on TV or radio	46	16	20	4	4	6	4
Been to a concert	28	18	30	15	3	4	2
Visited a historical monument or site	35	26	18	10	4	4	3
Been to the cinema	31	29	19	13	2	4	2
Read a book	49	22	14	3	2	6	4

Source European Commission 2013a, Cultural Access and Participation Report, Eurobarometer 399, processed by authors

"lack of interest". Surprisingly, high costs were mentioned by only 15% of respondents at the most.

Despite the non-apparent linkage between affordability and participation to cultural activities, the level of welfare is a precondition to the disposition to manifest interest for cultural events or consumption. "Lack of time" may, actually, be the result of a low prioritisation of cultural involvement among interests, directly linked to the unavailability of the psychological time, for a mind absorbed with the imperative of covering the basic living needs.

That low prioritisation may also be a direct cause of the poor quality of the local cultural products and services or of the limited choice—an explanation which has been far more often given than on average, at EU level (10% at most, for going to theatre or concert).

It is apparent, thus, that, in Romania, achieving cultural sustainability through increasing participation in cultural activities and cultural products consumption relies mainly on raising real interest for cultural events. That would follow the improvement of the quality and diversity of the cultural products' offer, as well as the improvement of the individual's perception. To this end, an innovative approach and openness towards learning from national and international good practice examples are essential. This surely involves social as well as technological innovation or, at least, technological readiness. That last issue is related to meeting a critical level of the national absorptive capacity that may allow for effective intake of the available technology already successfully employed in other culture-oriented initiatives.

A relevant example of good practice, in Romania, related to social innovation as a lever and driver of cultural sustainability lays in the concept-initiative "the durable village" launched by the "Mihai Eminescu Trust" Foundation. The target village is the Transilvanian village where the massive emigration of the population of German origin left behind a cultural and social void and discontinuity, together with economic downfall. In order not to waste the valuable and precious local cultural heritage, an intervention was critical.

Through its goal, through the means and impact, this programme is, in itself, a social innovation. The ultimate objective that defines the very mission of the programme is improving the quality of life in the target village. The beneficiary is the local community. The programme addresses its main needs and vulnerabilities and relies on local resources, while targeting the preservation and valorisation of the local cultural heritage.

The means employed also label the initiative as social innovation, due to the new pattern of relationships that arise along the programme implementation. The local community—the beneficiary—is directly and actively involved in designing solutions, in prioritising actions, in ensuring implementation. The key instrument is the responsible valorisation of the local cultural and natural heritage with the involvement of local available human resources, knowledge, tools and techniques.

The "integrative" character renders the projects a wide temporal and structural impact, at all levels of local sustainable development: social, cultural, economic as well as environmental. It empowers local community through investing in its people, through providing educational and entrepreneurial opportunities while capitalising on available resources and potential. The Foundation programme has been operationalised through about 1100 specific projects in 49 villages of four countries (Brasov, Mures, Covasna and Sibiu). Three key objectives are pursued: the restauration and conservation of the cultural heritage—historical buildings, traditional agricultural techniques, landscape as well as traditional crafts; the development of the local entrepreneurial spirit through professional training and qualification, through supporting small rural businesses, job creation and career development opportunities; stimulation of sustainable cultural tourism. Consequently, nearly 240 of local people have been trained in traditional building techniques and agro-tourism and 40 villagers attended English classes. About 200 seasonal and permanent jobs were created, and 50 small rural businesses—in agro-tourism and traditional crafts—were supported and mentored. More than 2500 children in seven nearby public schools have been involved in ecological and educational activities.

Apart of the three above-mentioned objectives, the "durable village" projects meet the basic local needs. School buildings have been restored, school busses have been provided, and professional waste collection services were partly funded.

The local community is involved and co-interested in the creation and preservation of cultural assets. Given intensive and well-designed popularisation and advertisement strategies, the consumption of local products and services has considerably increased. For example, in the Viscri village—one of the most popular and successful project of the MET Foundation—the number of tourists visiting and accommodating in the village exceeds 30–40 per day during summer. This project of social innovation has proven successful even in attracting investors, such as the World Bank, the German Foundation for the World Heritage. On the social side, local ethnic communities at risk of social exclusion and poverty have also been involved and integrated in the programme's projects, receiving support for acquiring education and training, for running their own businesses, for training others.

Concluding, once half-deserted and forgotten villages have now become lively, flourishing and cohesive communities who fathomed they have something special to provide the world with, a heritage that defines the place they live in, precious values and cultural assets that deserve being safeguarded and cherished. While preserving and developing cultural values, this social innovation allowed for better living standards, access to education, opportunities for entrepreneurship, for employment and even career development.

26.4 Conclusions

In a knowledge-based economy and a highly technologised society, in order that cultural heritage and culture-oriented activities may achieve their full potential as economic production factors, as strategic assets for higher social integration, cohesion and participation, as well as levers for ensuring the protection and sustainable development of the natural environment, it takes innovative mindset, innovative approaches, innovative cooperation towards innovative solutions. Cultural sustainability cannot be achieved without innovation (European Commission 2015). Technological research and innovation are essential for finding and applying the best alternatives for cultural assets preservation as well as for their promotion and optimal sustainable economic valorisation/capitalisation.

Securing the necessary investment for funding restoration and preservation of cultural heritage, stimulating the potential cultural assets creation as well as the promotion and economic valorisation of the cultural assets cannot be achieved but within an innovative framework and approach. While one may notice some positive examples throughout the country, a general change in attitude and pace should guide the public strategies and actions at all levels. A cultural sustainability focused political mindset requests an intersectoral approach, as policies for education, research, social welfare, urbanism, tourism are to various degrees interrelated with cultural aspects.

This paper endorsed the role that social innovation may play, if properly stimulated and fostered, for achieving cultural sustainability. For further research, we consider collecting national and international examples of best practices where social innovation together with technological innovation has been successfully employed for cultural sustainability.

References

Bankinter Foundation for Innovation. (2009). *Social innovation*. Reinventing Sustainable Development. http://www.fundacionbankinter.org/system/documents/6998/original/XII_FTF_Social_Innovation.pdf.

Caulier-Grice, J., Davies, A., Patrick, R., Norman, W. (2012). *Defining social innovation. A deliverable of the project: The theoretical, empirical and policy foundations for building social innovation in Europe (TEPSIE), Euroepan Commission—FP 7—Brussels*. European Commission, DG Research.

Council of the European Union. (2014). *Conclusions on cultural heritage as a strategic resource for a sustainable Europe*, 20 May 2014. http://www.consilium.europa.eu/uedocs/cms_data/docs/pressdata/en/educ/142705.pdf.

Daniel, T. C., Muhar, A., Arnberger, A., et al. (2012). Contributions of cultural services to the ecosystem services agenda. *Proceedings of the National Academy of Sciences of the United States of America, 109,* 8812–8819. https://doi.org/10.1073/pnas.1114773109.

Dessein, J., Soini, K., Fairclough, G., Horlings, L. (eds.). (2015). *Culture in, for and as sustainable development*. University of Jyvaskyla, Finland: Conclusions from the COAST Action IS1007 Investigating Cultural Sustainability.

Duxbury, N., Gillette, E. (2007). *Culture as a key dimension of sustainability: Exploring concepts, themes and models*. Workgin paper no. 1, centre of expertise on culture and communities.

European Commission. (2013a). *Cultural access and participation report, Eurobarometer 399*. http://ec.europa.eu/public_opinion/archives/ebs/ebs_399_en.pdf.

European Commission (EC). (2013b). Guide to Social Innovation. *DG Regional and Urban Policy*.

European Commission. (2014). *Towards an integrated approach to cultural heritage for Europe, communication from the commission to the European parliament, the council, the European economic and social committee and the committee of regions, COM (2014) 477*. http://ec.europa.eu/culture/library/publications/2014-heritage-communication_en.pdf.

European Commission. (2015). *Getting cultural heritage to work for Europe*. Report of the Horizon 2020 expert group on cultural heritage. DGRI KI-01-15-128-EN-N. http://bookshop.europa.eu/en/getting-cultural-heritage-to-work-for-europe-pbKI0115128/.

Hämäläinen, T. J., & Heiskala, R. (Eds.). (2007). *Social innovations, institutional change and economic performance: Making Sense of structural adjustment processes in industrial sectors*. Regions and Societies: Edward Elgar Publishing, Cheltenham, UK.

Hernandez-Ros, J. (2014). *Research and innovation actions for creative and cultural industries*. The EU Framework Programme for Research and Innovation Horizon 2020 Creativity DG CNECT, European Commision. http://nem-initiative.org/wp-content/uploads/2014/04/2_17GA_G2_Creativity_NEM_1-avril-2014.pdf.

Moulaert, F., Maccallum, D., Mehmood, A., & Hamdouch, A. (2013). *The international handbook on social innovation: Collective action, social learning and transdisciplinary research*. Chetlenham: Edward Elgar.

Moulaert, F., Martinelli, F., Swyngedouw, E., & Gonzalez, S. (2005). Towards alternative models of local innovation. *Urban Studies, 42*(11), 1969–1990.

Mulgan, G., Tucher, S., Rushanara, A., Sanders, B. (2007). *Social innovation: What it is, why it matters and how it can be accelerated social innovation oxford.pdf.*

Nicholls, A., Murdock, A. (2012) *Social innovation: Blurring boudaries to reconfigure markets.* Macmillan: Palgrave.

UNESCO. (2012). Culture, a driver and an enabler of sustainable development. *Thematic Think Piece.* https://en.unesco.org/post2015/sites/post2015/files/Think%20Piece%20Culture.pdf.

www.mihaieminescutrust.ro.

Chapter 27
From Smart Cities to Smart Buildings— Tools for Promoting Cultural Heritage

Andreea-Clara Munteanu

Abstract Changing Europe to be smart, sustainable and inclusive, able to generate and manage high employment levels, productivity, and cohesion is a still goal which is hard to attain which launches several challenges in the field of growth. With a background of deep structural changes, and also some extremely favorable developments, the tourism industry has turned into a sector playing a decisive role in attaining Europe 2020 goals. Cultural heritage is a fundamental resource of sustainable development, but also a basic factor for differentiating the touristic products. In this respect, we can notice that cultural heritage has as a background the need of integrating the touristic resource (natural and cultural) within the local community, but also the need to avoid that this process would lead to alteration, deterioration or even loss of the cultural heritage. The attractiveness of a tourist destination depends on the degree to which it succeeds in satisfying demand. In this context, the role of cultural heritage is defining, due to its uniqueness, and to the multitude of individualized possibilities in some of its complex packages, based on natural resources, cultural–historical heritage, personalized services, etc. Cultural heritage, especially for low-income communities, represents an important asset and a significant source of finance for local budgets. Promoting smart buildings on the internet and creating digital access solution for them, may lead to a new understanding in the public administration of smart cities. Our chapter aims to point out the opportunities emerging for small communities in the cultural heritage management area.

Keywords Cultural heritage · Smart city · Smart building · Tourism development

A.-C. Munteanu (✉)
Institute of National Economy-Romanian Academy, Bucharest, Romania
e-mail: acmunteanu@gmail.com

27.1 Rationalities

Changing Europe to be smart, sustainable, and inclusive, as well as being able to generate and manage high levels of employment, productivity, and cohesion is still a hard goal to achieve, launching several challenges in the field of growth. With a background of deep structural change, but also favorable development, the tourism industry has turned into a sector playing a decisive role in attaining the three goals of the Europe 2020 strategy:

- Smart growth resulting from stimulating knowledge, innovation, education, and the digital society.
- Sustainable growth, promoting production that makes more efficient use of resources, while encouraging competitiveness.
- Inclusive growth, based on raising the employment rate, improving qualifications, and fighting poverty.

Thus, on a global level tourism contributes to the direct or indirect support of over 226 million jobs, while registering growth of approximately 4% against the year 2014 in terms of its contribution to world GDP, and a 5% growth in terms of numbers of airline passengers (1.14 billion). According to the opinion of experts, the tourism sector may play a crucial role in increasing territorial cohesion, especially in less developed countries and regions or those on the periphery, as well as achieving required competitiveness, and supporting adjustments to demographics, the environment, and economic challenges.

From the viewpoint of contribution to GDP, on the European Union (EU) level, tourism ranks third with over 5% growth, thereby ensuring about 5.2% of labor force employment. The outcomes of recent research (RCI 2012) show that the number of international passenger arrivals to Europe increased constantly over recent years, with estimates for 2020 indicating the achievement of a 45% of total international arrivals worldwide under the conditions of maintaining an increase rate of 6.5%.

One of the most marked phenomena faced by the EU is demographic ageing, forecasts of experts in the field indicate that for the year 2020 some 20% of the population will be considered elderly, aged 65 years and over. In this context, it becomes imperative that the tourism sector adjusts to the needs of this demographic.

On the other hand, some studies about the preferences of customers (Nikitina and Akimova 2013) indicate both a refinement in tastes, and also an increased demand for what is considered to be "authentic." The attractiveness of a tourist destination depends on the degree to which it succeeds in satisfying the demand placed upon it. In this framework, the role of cultural heritage is defining due to its uniqueness of character, as well as the many possibilities available to tourists to individualize their complex holiday packages, based on visiting natural resources, appreciating cultural–historical heritage, requiring personalized services, etc.

At the same time, acknowledging cultural heritage as a fundamental resource of sustainable development, and also as a basic factor in the differentiation of tourist products, means there is a need to integrate tourism resources (natural and cultural) into local communities, without allowing this process to lead to alteration, deterioration, or even loss of cultural heritage.

27.2 Smart Cities—Insights

As urban spaces developed and become ever more complex, the requirements formulated by the public administration sector become increasingly more difficult to meet regarding both the qualitative aspects, and the acceptable time-intervals for citizens. The high demand, diversity, and dynamics of emerging needs have imposed the creation of modern solutions for public management. The multiple solutions and facilities provided by increasing technical progress in the field of ICT (information and communication technologies), by using wide-scale information dissemination, and also an increased degree of technological readiness, including less well–prepared communities, have all contributed to the emergence of the smart city concept. The smart city represents a stage in urban development in which the quality of life and public services is ensured by means of a management system that provides integrated IT (information technology) solutions (public transport, community services, waste management, drinkable water supply, spaces for cultural events, etc.).

The smart city has organic-type communication with its citizens and provides them with the opportunity of being involved in real-time decision-making processes and to be engaged more actively and diversely in various aspects of community life. On the other hand, the management of smart cities allows its managers to deal more swiftly with various issues, preventing the emergence of instances calling for intervention, and ensuring better community safety (currently, the most frequently used applications of the smart city are related to interventions in emergency situations and traffic management). At the same time, the facilities provided by the smart city allow the gathering of information regarding the needs of its citizens and the identification of personalized solutions, or those which can be personalized (e-government and e-citizenship). The main fields of interest to citizens in relation to smart cities refer to access to quality education, to ensuring modern and quality utility infrastructures, easy access to information of public interest, easy access to medical services including online monitoring, adequate road and public transport infrastructures, and safety.

The Europe 2020 strategy includes smart cities among its assumed programmatic objectives and The European Innovation Partnership on Smart Cities and Communities adopted, in 2015, the document "Smart cities as driver of a new European industrial policy." In this document is substantiated the integration of six enabling pillars:

- Technologies and tools for energy efficiency and integration of renewable sources.
- Dissemination of technology platforms and connectivity to set up new digital service systems.

- New digital services to improve the quality of life and work of the public and business.
- Upgrading infrastructure and urban redesign.
- Education and training of individuals, businesses, and the public sector in digital skills.
- An economically and financially viable model for investment.

However, the operation of a smart city within these designed parameters pre-supposes the existence and availability of some resources, including financial, human, and infrastructure. In the case of communities that rely for their existence on intensive economic activity, the functionality of the smart city is ensured by the availability of resources and by a high level of absorption of new technologies by people and local economic agents.

Less developed communities, from an economic viewpoint, are faced with a multitude of issues triggered either by a lack of basic infrastructure, or by their lack of technological readiness. Moreover, cities with marked migration in terms of the age of their employed population, may also have an elderly population which may display opposition, or even hostility, to changes generated by the creation of a smart city.

The change into a smart city, especially in the case of less developed regions is a huge challenge for local authorities because:

- it involves money;
- asks for qualified human resources; and
- asks for digital access.

In turn, managing a smart city provides local authorities with:

- good value for money;
- a new, efficient way of decision making; and
- new development directions for the city.

27.3   Smart Buildings: The Use of the Internet in Cultural Heritage Promotion

In parallel with the development of the smart city concept, the idea of the smart building was born. Smart buildings are an integrated assembly of technology, energy systems, and facilities for housing or working that allow residents the optimum use of sustainably managed space. Smart buildings use technological processes, integrating computerized telecommunication, safety, lighting, catering, or entertainment systems.

The advantages of using smart buildings within public administration resides mainly in its efficient responsiveness to the needs of citizens as well as in its capacity for savings regarding available resources by means of intelligent facilities (movement sensors, hourly regulation of ambient temperature, etc.). Practically, smart buildings represent a vital component of smart cities.

Network integration of smart buildings represents a new development stage in the smart living concept and provides among other things the possibility of interoperability, remote control, and real-time data exchange.

The development of tourist activities is a source of increased income for public local administrations, however, in areas with conditions of low levels of development, barriers emerge related to the absence of access, accommodation, or entertainment infrastructures, meaning that the attractiveness of the location to tourists is diminished. A solution for overcoming these barriers is represented by virtual tourism. By making use of smart solutions through new technologies, the tourist attractions, such as museums, memorial houses, archaeological sites, etc., can become accessible and visible. Among the smart tools used currently for promoting virtual tourism, we should mention: virtual (static or dynamic) tours, interactive mapping, 3D modeling, social media, etc.

In Europe, virtual tours are common practice for museums, memorial houses, exhibitions, tourist areas, etc., with online visitors being able to see with their own eyes the main areas, or most important elements, exhibited at these sites.

In Romania, we notice some progress in the area of "smart development," but we have to add that this still mainly happens in the richest areas (Bucharest, Constanta, etc.) or the most popular or well-known sites like the Memorial of the Victims of Communism and the Resistance in Sighetul Marmatiei or the Histria Museum.

For instance, between 2011 and 2013, the Histria citadel (Constanţa county) was included in a project aimed at the promotion of cultural–historical heritage and biodiversity conservation in Constanţa, Istria, in the area of Cheile Dobrogei (Fig. 27.1).

One of the main activities of this project was a 3D reconstruction and animation of the city of Istria (Fig. 27.2).

Fig. 27.1 Project map "Following the Argonauts: promoting the tourist route Constanta, Istria, Cheile Dobrogei" (*Source* http://histria-cheiledobrogei.ro/Harti-4/)

Fig. 27.2 Histria archeological site and 3D reconstruction (*Source* http://www.i-tour.ro/cetatea-histria-reconstituita-3d/)

27.4 Small Cities—Challenges

Darabani (Botoşani county) is a northern city of Romania (Fig. 27.3) and dates from the 16th century. Currently the city has budget difficulties due to the large number of unemployed people, but, despite this, in the local development strategy for 2014–2020 there is a project aimed to promote Darabani as a tourist destination by valorizing local cultural heritage. In this respect, the Leon Danaila Museum will be restored and digitized, with all its features becoming available online.

Using multimedia technology to put together art, archaeology, and architecture could bring tremendous success, even to small cities, transforming them as tourist destinations and also triggering economic development.

Fig. 27.3 Darabani city, Botoşani county

References

Nikitina, O., & Akimova, O. (2013). Cultural historical heritage as a factor of regional economic development. In *Proceedings of the International Conference on sustainable cultural heritage management, Roma*, pp. 499–511.

RCI. (2012). Case study: Tourism development in the Western Balkans. Regional Competitiveness Initiative.

Part II
Best Practices

Chapter 28
The Importance of Using New Technology in Museums

Mutlu Erbay

Abstract Global society has experienced a radical transformation due to massive social, demographic, technological, and economic shifts in recent years. Today, there are questions about how technology will affect society in the future. New technological equipment and tools have started to be used in museums. Contemporary museums cannot be imagined without such technical achievements, hence the use of these technological innovations in museums is very significant to reflect the features and characteristics of this era. The main reason for the use of the most advanced technology in museums originates from collaboration between universities, museums, and the private sector. The use of information and communication technology at the beginning of the 21st century is important for museums. This chapter examines areas where technology is used in museums and considers exhibitions organized recently utilizing technology in Turkish museums.

Keywords Technological developments · Technology use in museums
Turkish museums · QR codes · Datamatrix codes · Global positioning system

28.1 Introduction

Global society has experienced a radical transformation due to massive social, demographic, technological, and economic shifts in recent years. Today, there are questions about how technology will affect society in the future. New technological equipment and tools have started to be used in museums. Contemporary museum cannot be imagined without their utilizing technology. Hence, the use of technological innovations in museums is very significant, reflect their contemporary nature. The main reason for use the most advanced technology in museums originates with collaboration between universities, museums, and the private sector. The use of information and communication technology at the beginning of the

M. Erbay (✉)
Fine Arts Department, Boğaziçi University, Bebek, Istanbul, Turkey
e-mail: erbaym@boun.edu.tr

© Springer International Publishing AG, part of Springer Nature 2019
V. Vasile (ed.), *Caring and Sharing: The Cultural Heritage Environment
as an Agent for Change*, Springer Proceedings in Business and Economics,
https://doi.org/10.1007/978-3-319-89468-3_28

21st century is important for museums. This chapter examines areas where technology is used in museums and the exhibitions organized recently using technology in Turkish museums.

Advanced technologies were firstly used militarily (such as bomb disposal robots or mine clearance robots), in places where people might be in dangerous situations, such as in nuclear plants, in the health sector, in micro-surgical eye and innominate bone operations, and in the entertainment sector (with the help of robots or simulators). Since then, such technologies have started to be used in museums or cultural heritage areas. The importance of using new technology in future museums was revived by researchers studying at the Science Museum in London in the 1980s. The London War Museum's simulator and Natural History Museum's use of robot technology represent pioneering approaches in this specific area.

28.2 Literature Review

An agreement was signed between National Geographic and the Egyptian government in 2002, to explore the special room of Pharaoh in the Great Pyramid of Giza, Egypt, which was reached for the first time at the end of a 10-year study using robotic cameras.

The use of technology in archeological expeditions is quite new. Archeologists have benefited from satellites (such as Spot, Radarsat, Ikonos, and Aster) viewing the Earth from space and collecting data from the Earth's surface to determine areas of archeological sites. Devereux et al. (2005) state that today, the quantity and quality of information about the surface of the Earth obtained remotely is increasing rapidly. Nowadays, remote-sensing technology pushes the boundaries on all fronts. This satellite archeology, or satellite remote sensing, represents great potential for Egyptian archeology. The buildings of the city of Ur were discovered as a result of examination of images taken by the Aster satellite. Loeb (2012) indicated that satellite images are significant in the search for ancient settlements like the discovery of the city of Ur. Loeb (2012) also stated that if he had completed this survey on the ground, the search would have taken his entire life, asserting that computer science techniques, can immediately generate enormous maps providing new archeological opportunities.

The application of technology is reflected in the museum's exhibition areas: a technology center of the Orsay Museum (the most famous of its times); the exhibition of the new museology with the architectural plans of the Gugenheim Museum in New York; Bilboa Gugenheim Museum; architectural example of the new museum/culture, such as Pompedu, the spirit of time and building technology. In Turkey, Haydarpaşa Station is similar to the Orsay Museum in France. Nowadays, the Haydarpaşa train station is planned to be turned into a hotel or mall.

This chapter aims to assert the importance of advanced technology use in museums, art galleries, and archaeological sites. This study is the result of descriptive survey model research that contains samples regarding visual cultural practices with recent advanced technology in both Turkish museums and museums around the world.

28.3 Methodology and Results

Reasons for using technology in museums are not only to improve the visual, preservation or transportation aspects of museum pieces, but also to provide superior projection and presentation of exposed pieces. Nowadays, the biggest portions of contemporary museum budgets are used for the presentation, protection, and transfer of knowledge.

Technology is used for various purposes in Turkey, classified into five categories:

1. To inform visitors and for promotion.
2. To collect information about visitors.
3. To ensure security.
4. To determine restoration and original pieces, i.e., the origin of a piece of art.
5. To provide and implement demonstrations.

Contemporary museology mainly concentrates on presentation of information. In this respect, technology may be used for simulations, headphones, data matrices, surround sound, screens displaying images and movies, and at kiosks using touch-screen systems. CD-ROMs represent an important method for promoting museums. They provide easy transfer of information. They achieve this with use of the Internet and digital software and hardware tools such as iPads and iTunes. Today, the use of technology in museums is something natural, as more and more museums are promoted with the help of the Internet.

28.3.1 Using Technology to Promote Museums to Visitors

Today, technology is frequently used for information provision and promotional purposes. Museums are places where examples of buildings, as well as cultural artifacts and evidence of civilizations, can be displayed systematically and sequentially to the public. The main purpose of museums is to provide public information about works of art. Also, museums are careful in choosing the staff responsible for these works, as there are some individuals who refuse to perceive the idea of seeing museums as a treasure chamber of superior quality. Technology enables locating information on a virtual platform in a faster manner, enables storage of information, and enables people to reach specific information.

Computers provide information to visitors regarding the number of works in the museum, the kind of works, exhibitions, opening days and hours, and museum itineraries. This information is quite important to visitors, people working in museums, and people researching museums.

Today, people can visit the most famous museums and art galleries on their computers, mobile phonesF, or iPads remotely from their homes or offices. They can also obtain detailed information about works of art. A museum's information can be transferred to users thanks to an uncountable number of websites, i.e., YouTube, Twitter, or Facebook. Sometimes, documentaries, conferences, and exhibits from museums can also be transmitted to visitors electronically via YouTube. In the following text we consider three ways technology is used, by museums, to transfer information to visitors.

QR Codes and Datamatrix Codes

QR codes have been used in some museums in Istanbul since 2012. People can obtain information about a museum, gallery, work of art, and exhibit areas through the Datamatrix program which can be downloaded to their mobile phones. The first instances of this use of technology were in the Topkapı Palace, the Hagia Sophia Museum, the Istanbul Archaeology Museum, and the Kariye Museum in 2012. A GSM company has created an application for mobile phones which can be downloaded, at a cost, by the public. With the revolving funds of the Ministry of Culture administration, visitors from 78 different countries have accessed museum information using QR codes. Approximately 22,000 people have used this application since October 2015.

Simulations and Rejuvenations

Simulations and rejuvenations are the most widespread exhibition devices in Turkish museums. An example of rejuvenation can be found in the computer environment created at an exhibit about Constantinople in 2012. Constantinople's castles, which were demolished in the past, were revived in a computer environment at the Istanbul Archaeology Museum.

In an exhibition at the Archaeology Museum in July 2013, original objects from Yenikapı wrecks, as well as information on boat making, cargo, and why and how certain ships sunk, was narrated with the support of visual effects. Also displayed at this exhibition was a computer-generated skull of a woman, a fired stove, and images of Jannissary camps from different eras.

Some simulations are 3D or 5D. Istanbul's observation terrace simulation in the Saphire shopping mall is quite effective for children. This sort of arrangement could be used in museums.

Besides Datamatrix, simulations, and rejuvenations, museums can use digital labels (with QR codes), audiovisual systems, ear flaps, photos, movies, videos, CD-DVDs, and the internet (Twitter, Facebook, YouTube) to inform visitors about galleries and exhibits. By a combination of these methods, museum visitors can get the most information in the least time. These sorts of visual exhibiting techniques will begin to rapidly replace conventional models in museums.

28.3.2   The Use of Technology to Collect Information About Visitors

The underlying concept of utilizing technology for presentation techniques in world museums is gathering pace. Computer forms source information about the age and sex of visitors, the dates and times they visit websites, how often individuals visit museums or use search engines to look for virtual museums, most frequently used words linked to museum searches, and major problems faced by museum visitors. It is possible to gather information, using surveys, about the demographical properties of museum visitors, their reasons for visiting museums, their profiles, frequency of visitation, length of visit, transportation to museums, etc. This data can then be examined and used in future decision making.

Numbers of tickets sold, touch-screen computers, thumbwheel switches placed at museum exits, computer surveys, sensor devices in front of showcases, book sales, restaurant revenues, and camera and video-recording systems all provide museums with information about visitors. The information obtained by visitors, about the number of visitors, profiles (women, men, children) of visitors, the proportion of the museum's blank and repletion, the day in which the museum is frequently used, the visitor's attitudes and behaviors in the museum, being determined relevancy to works, the museum's tour route, the intensity of visitors for halls, the day demand of the visitors, the average visiting time in the museum, the frequency of visit is embroidered in the level of director.

Information obtained by museum visitors can then be evaluated in the future. Gathering visitors information is also important for improving or refreshing services used in museums.

All this information is effective for determining a museum's future policies, strategies, and investment. For example, if children represent the biggest population visiting a museum, then the museum can take this into account in terms of its future growth strategy. If handicapped people frequently visit a particular museum, then its exhibit planning may be changed accordingly. Hence, promotions and investments in the museum sector are based on targeted populations. In this respect, it is necessary for museums to collect data on its visitors. The rich information gained about visitors is used to determine their future requirements and to consider the distribution of costs in the future. This is particularly noticeable in American museums where the culture of advertising and promotion has been developed in this manner. More than this, to receive income and donation is possible for museums through a sponsor aid.

28.3.3   Technology Used to Ensure Security in Museums

Nowadays, modern museums have financial power and use their revenues to meet their own specific needs. Most of these financial resources are used to protect the works of art in museums by means advanced technology.

Museums need to ensure the safety of exhibitions to protect works of art. The protection of exhibits uses many electronic tools such as special temperature probes, specific sensors for dampness, ventilation, and powder and smart illumination systems. However, a well-equipped security system is also required to prevent theft. Materials emitting radio frequencies and microchips are indispensable security instruments used when displaying and storing works in museums, taking inventories, and traveling to international exhibitions and fairs.

Vehicle-tracking Systems—Global Positioning System

Vehicle-tracking systems are used to monitor transportation routes of vehicles carrying historical artifacts and works of art during their transfer from one place to another. Transportation trucks with global positioning systems (GPS) were first used to ensure the security of the Prince Tut's Treasures traveling exhibit which was opened in America in 2000. This international exhibition was transferred between Egypt and the United States and was opened in Seattle and Melbourne, Florida. The route of traveling exhibition was followed by this way. This was done for the first time, the USA used transportation trucks with GPS to follow the exhibition of an important civilization. This kind of system informs museum directors and teams about the current locations of works of art.

Magnetic Reader Cards

Magnetic reader cards are used for local and foreign visitors in municipality museums, the most famous being the Miniatürk. A visitor can obtain any information in his/her language with the help of a reader card when standing in front of any exhibit.

The Barcode

The barcode system is used to find and define works of art exhibited in museums. This tool makes it easier to track the work in storage, at foreign exhibitions, at demonstrations, and while being restored.

Chips

The Ministry of Culture requires chips to be located on the back of valuable works and paintings in museums, especially on paintings or invaluable historical archaeological objects. In this manner, it becomes possible to find them if stolen.

With the use of security cameras and recent developments in technology, the issues of controlling an exhibition's environment, i.e., ventilation, temperature, dampness, as well as other tools for protection, have become common. Besides the physical protection of works of art, camera systems in exhibition areas, voiced security systems, safe door panels, window sensors, and heat sensors are also used in museums. Smart, sensor-based light fixtures have become common with the development of technology. Lamps are now more durable, with increased lifetimes, and can even be used in flooring. Protection of an exhibit against damage caused by damp, heat, and light can be managed using a glass case containing many of these kinds of advanced technologies. Such cases are effective systems at securing works of art from fires, floods, earthquakes, robberies, etc.

28.3.4   Restoration/Conservation and Determination of Originals (Recovery Protection)

Museums sometimes use technology to renovate works of art. Technology is used to identify which works are made using which materials. According to the information collected, works can either be protected or renovated. The best examples being the cleaning of corrosion on bronze works, and the calculation of the conservation and restoration needed for materials such as skin, which spoils rapidly, bone, wood, and stone removed from subway excavations in Istanbul.

A private museum called the J. Paul Getty Museum in the Unites States visualizes earthquakes in a virtual environment simulator in order to protect its sculpture collections. Results from the simulations permit the management team to determine a plan for the protection of exhibits during an earthquake. People who share an interest in these virtual demonstrations can watch them on YouTube. For example, the process of conservation which cleans deterioration and rust on a candlestick surrounded by figures of Eros is shown step by step. Visitors are able to watch and learn about the advanced technologies used at the J. Paul Getty Museum as well as the methods of conservation they employ, on YouTube.

Some computer programs which include various software color programs can show approximately what kind of result would be achieved after restoration. In addition, whether a picture or an object is an original can be determined by the use of technology. Technology can be very beneficial particularly when determining the origin of cultural entities and their dimensions, as well as for use in completing missing segments of works of art, or repairing and restoring them.

28.3.5   Technology Use for Demonstrations

Museums often run demonstrations and advertisements at fairs, funfairs, and exhibition stands. Museums systematically organize objects and open new exhibitions and collections to express stories in the most interesting way. World and national museums play a significant role in the world of education.

The modern staff of museums that look at museums like some trendy halls and refuse the traditional image of the museum are trying to respond to the needs of visitors in the shortest possible time. In recent years, new demonstration techniques have emerged, according to which commercial sector competition has a bad influence on the public of traditional museums and galleries. However, new demonstration techniques are used in private and municipal museums in Turkey, where advanced technology is being developed.

Using robots in demonstrations was a technique used in museums in the United States in 1997. Rhino and Minerva were two prototypes prepared to be guide robots in a museum. Mobile robots created by University of Washington are important to reflect the cooperation between museum and university. Robots are particularly good at getting children's attention. Science and technology museums and museums related to planetariums, space, mineralogy, geology, and botany are able to use high levels of technology. Museums increase their interest to the public through demonstrations combining entertainment and education, with many effective examples being found in the United States and the continent of Europe.

28.3.6   Museums and Exhibitions Using Technology

İş Bank Museum

The museum that describes the developmental history of Turkey, İş Bank, is an institution that brings innovation with the use of touch-screen system, kiosks, and riggings with computers. Sound effects (sounds of cases and chains) and image effects (illuminated numbers used in the entrance of the showroom) are used. Workers' images are visually reflected on the wall in the first floor which is quite effective to visitors.

Eskişehir Eti Archaeology Museum

The Eskişehir Archaeology Museum selected a new exhibition technique using a sponsor, linked to the Ministry of Culture and Tourism. It enables visitors to enter a tumulus in a sepulcher and to travel within a virtual environment. There are specially designed salons to project visitors into a virtual three-dimensional world. There are computer games for children, brochures and a virtual book. It is allowed to insert a basket into a device that projects images on the floor. By this way, visitors can imagine the subject.

Kırşehir Kaman/Kalehöyük Archaeology Museum

The Çağırkan Kalehöyük was excavated by Japanese archeologists. There is a cinevision demonstration in the museum. The art works discovered in the tumulus and during the archeological investigations are exhibited in the museum. Japanese

Prince Mikasa gave this museum to the city of Kırşehir as a gift. There is a Japanese garden inside the museum which is shaped in the form of a tumulus.

Rezzan Has Museum

This museum organized an exhibition called "Kayıp Dillerin Fısıldadıkları (Whispers of Extinct Languages)," to shed light to the evolution of writing from its birth, as pictograms, to present day. They used various photography and illumination techniques. An investigation has been conducted on these objects to establish the old languages used, but also to decipher the old Greek writing style.

İstanbul Archaeology Museum

An exhibition called "Boyalı Tanrılar (Painted Gods)" was organized at the Istanbul Archaeology Museum in 2011. Reliefs and sculptures made of plaster were colored in the exhibition. In this way, the works in their real stage were displayed to visitors. A similar version of this exhibition was opened in the Athens Museum.

Vedat Nedim Tör Museum

The Yapı Kredi Exhibition was placed in the area of Tatarli Museum, Frig Cemetery and Inner Ornaments. This exhibition was organized with support and advice from specialized chemical engineers and information on the colors and materials used was collected.

Van Gogh Alive Exhibition

Original works were not used in the exhibition entitled "Çerçeve Yok İçindesin (Van Gogh Alive)" in 2012. Van Gogh's original works were shown in detail on large screens. Visitors felt as if they were inside the works, almost living them. This was the first digital art exhibition that did not belong to a dead artist. For this reason, hundreds of visitors came to Istanbul and visited the third Antrepo to see these non-original works for the first time. The exhibition was exhibited in Bursa and Antalya as well.

Body World

Around 150,000 people visited an exhibition called "Yaşam Döngüsü Vücut Dünyası (Body World)" in 2010. This anatomy exhibition was made with the cooperation of private firms.

Dinosaur Exhibition

This exhibition was organized with the cooperation of the Natural History Museum in London. Over 70 million artifacts were exhibited, incorporating information about animals, planets, minerals, and fossils. Three dimensional and mobile systems were used in this exhibition. The exhibition was also taken to Istanbul and the Antalya shopping mall. The animatronic dinosaurs used in the exhibition were created by Kokoro, in Japan.

Aviation and Space Exhibition

A NASA exhibition was opened in Marmara Expo shopping center between 21 September 2012 and 17 February 2013. The exhibition plotted the last 50 years of aerospace history. The exhibition was organized by an American company, Sierra Nevada Corporation, and was visited by 100,000 people. This exhibition was undertaken for commercial purposes.

A Shark's World Exhibition

"Prey or hunter?" was exhibited in the Trump shopping center in the first quarter of 2013. In this exhibition, children and teenagers had the chance to learn about a shark's life. This exhibition was undertaken for commercial purposes.

28.4 Conclusion

Nowadays, the Museum's subscriptions, museum-schools collaboration, and the collaboration between the museum and the private sector have contributed to improving the museum's finances, using new technologies and technologies in museums.

There are many advantages to using computers in museums. Quick access to information, processing information, and storing data, all require an advanced network system. On the other hand, there are also some disadvantages. Technology use is sometimes not suitable for traditional museums. Ventilation devices occupy a large place and create annoying sounds. These pieces of equipment are expensive both for museum and visitors. In addition to these, giving a selection chance to visitors is necessary for democracy and museum ethics. Also, the occupational future of human tour guides is at risk.

In modern museums, it's important to reach visitors in a faster way. To do so, Twitter, Facebook and others are used by the public relations and resource development departments. The museums are trying to become a center of art that reaches visitors faster. The most important aim of museums is to be known and accessible to visitors. Thus, in the new conception of museology, museums need to be renewed, comfortable, retful and relaxing. They can do this by reorganizing tourist routes, renewing information panels, standardizing labels, translating English correctly, arranging ambient temperatures by season, and opening new cinemas, shops, restaurants and cafes near museums or even in their premises.

Today, museums should be included on the agenda. The museums should be living centers. They can do this by organizing exhibitions and activities. They have to make international collaborations and provide income. Museums must be accessible to visitors. These should be located in city centers or transport routes. In addition, their web pages should be easily accessible. Museums should be sustainable. In this age, museums do not belong to any time and place, they are unlimited and have no public target.

To conclude, nowadays, technology can be used to supply information, introduce new works of art, determine the preferences of visitors, ensure the safety of works of art, assist with restoration, and check the originality and diversity of exhibits. Technologies used in exhibitions will carry museology into the future ensuring the wellbeing of mankind's heritage.

References

Devereux, B. J., Amable, G. S., Crow, P., & Cliff, A. D. (2005). The potential of airborne lidar for detection of archaeological features under woodland canopies (Vol. 79, Issue 305). Cambridge: Cambridge University Press.

Loeb, J. L. (2012). *Using Satellite Images to Search for Ancient Settlements, 2012*. USA: Harvard University.

Paul Getty Museum. (2012a). Protecting art in an Earthguike/The PaulGetty Museum/Seismic Isolator Technology. YouTube video, 2012.

Paul Getty Museum. (2012b). Conserving Bronze: The Lamp with Eroses Bronz. YouTube video, 2012.

Chapter 29
The Trail of the Romanian Ancient History at the Black Sea Coast

Steliana Cojocariu and Iulia Dăngulea

Abstract Paper presents the Trail of the Romania Ancient History at the Black Sea Coast from Constanta County, created and implemented within ALECTOR Project —Collaborative networks of Multilevel Actors to advance quality standards for heritage tourism at Cross Border Level. The trail includes ten assets from Constanta County as follows: the Museum of National History and Archaeology from Constanta, the Roman Edifice with Mosaic from Constanta, the Archaeological Park from Constanta, Tropeum Traiani Monument from Adamclisi, Tropeum Traiani Fortress from Adamclisi, Tropeum Traiani Museum from Adamclisi, Histria Fortress, Capidava Fortress, Callatis Fortress and Callatis Archaeology Museum. The project from Romania focuses on Constanta County heritage assets and their values in an effort to create and promote The Trail of the Romania Ancient History at the Black Sea Coast. The trail is designed for the visitors who want to learn about 2000 years of history in 2 days.

Keywords Heritage · Cultural route · Alector project · Touristic products
Constanța

29.1 Introduction

The Project "Collaborative Networks of Multilevel Actors to advance quality standards for heritage tourism at Cross Border Level" with ACRONYM "ALECTOR" belongs to the ENPI CBC Black Sea JOP Programme.

Project ALECTOR appears from the need to produce high-added value tourism products and establish novel tourism policies to sustain later on locally produced

S. Cojocariu (✉) · I. Dăngulea
The Ministry of Tourism, Bucharest, Romania
e-mail: steliana_cojocariu@yahoo.com

I. Dăngulea
e-mail: iulia.dangulea@gmail.com

© Springer International Publishing AG, part of Springer Nature 2019
V. Vasile (ed.), *Caring and Sharing: The Cultural Heritage Environment as an Agent for Change*, Springer Proceedings in Business and Economics, https://doi.org/10.1007/978-3-319-89468-3_29

heritage tourism. It is strictly interwoven with the need to let collaborative networks and strategic partnerships emerge at cross-border level.

Project ALECTOR (alector.org) involves actors from various administrative and social levels, so as to strengthen their capacity to effectively manage heritage for tourism. These collaborative networks will deliver three main outcomes: (a) (re) activation of human capital by intense know-how transfer of innovative practices directly deriving from research conducted, (b) local authority empowerment by diffusing policies regarding heritage management and tourism planning and (c) the development of local and regional strategic partnerships.

ALECTOR proposes a cognitive and educational framework for using of a place's assets, which would guide final beneficiaries (regions, communities, SMEs) to identify, signify, valorise and manage their natural and cultural resources, in order to use heritage potential as a vehicle for tourism strictly connected with a unified signage and interpretation system.

Most up to date innovative know-how will result in visitor-centric communication policies, and policies about the management of leisure time, an issue directly related to the competitiveness of places' and regions' in the sector of tourism. These policies will enable final beneficiaries to develop tailor-made heritage strategies and defend their cultural assets against a globalising world. By delivering a series of pilot projects to serve regions and localities as best practices, ALECTOR helps diffuse project results at a cross-border-wide level giving birth to further economic and social development.

The local pilot project objective was: to explore place image and cultural reputation in each Pilot Project Areas among potential domestic and foreign visitors; to evaluate the status quo of cultural products and services in each Pilot Project Area; to provide suggestions for playing institutions based on strategic development approach—new/innovative cultural heritage products and services.

29.2 The Trail of the Romania Ancient History at the Black Sea Coast

Following the e-survey, NAT 1 selected ten heritage locations from Constanta County: the Museum of National History and Archaeology Constanța (MINAC), the Roman Edifice with Mosaic from Constanta, the Archaeological Park from Constanta, the Callatis Archaeology Museum from Mangalia, Callatis Fortress from Mangalia, Tropaeum Traiani Monument from Adamclisi, Tropaeum Traiani Fortress from Adamclisi, Tropaeum Traiani Museum from Adamclisi, Histria Fortress from Istria and Capidava Fortress from Capidava.

The sample for the e-survey consisted of the travellers residing in the country and the questionnaire applied followed the model provided within ALECTOR project, being focused on Constanta heritage locations. Totally there were received and analysed 30 questionnaires.

The e-survey results showed that people are aware of the cultural and historic sites selected for the pilot project. The source of information about the ten selected locations for the majority of respondents is school, internet, media and travel agency. 100% of respondents would like to know more about the selected locations and 75% of the total would choose private tours with guide, applications for smartphones and printed guides for the proposed route. The majority of the respondents think ALECTOR project is important for the development of cultural tourism and thus business development in tourism.

The purpose of the project is to explore the Constanta archaeological sites in order to promote them within the Trail of the Romanian Ancient History at the Black Sea Coast. Constanta County heritage assets are numerous and diverse, attesting the succession of many civilisations on this territory during the centuries, starting with the Greek colonisation in the 7th century BC, when large urban centres were developed known as polis (Histria, Callatis, Tomis), and continuing with the rise and fall of several empires from Roman and Byzantine to the Ottoman one.

The Trail of the Romania Ancient History at the Black Sea Coast includes ten objectives like fortresses, museums, ruins and monuments with significant historical value and connected to the cultural and historic development of Constanta County, defined by a fascinating mixture of civilisations where European features happily coexist with Oriental ones.

The motto of the route "2000 years of history in 2 days" suggests the historical experience related to the Romanian people legacy in general and Constanta people legacy in particular obtained by the visitors after visiting the objective. The trail is created to start on the first day with Constanta (old Tomis), Istria (old Histria) and Capidava and to continue on the second day with Adamclisi (old Tropaeum Traiani) and Mangalia (old Callatis).

The Museum of National History and Archaeology Constanta is over one century old. It has been founded following an initiative by Remus Oprean, the first Prefect of Constanta County in 1879. After 1877, works undertaken to expend the city of Constanta have led to the discovery of important vestiges belonging to the ancient city of Tomis (ceramics, statues, inscriptions, coins, etc.). At present, the museum is situated in the old town (Ovidiu Square) and hosts a collection of more than 430,000 items presenting the profile of Dobrogea settlements over the centuries, from prehistory to 1940. The museum owns unique items like the "Tanagra" type statuette collection, the statuette group Fortune with Pontos, the statue of the Serpent Glykon, Hamangia culture pottery which is the oldest culture in Romania and the national collection of Roman glass (Alexandrescu-Vianu 2009).

The Roman Edifice with Mosaic, situated in the old town of Constanta in the vicinity of the Museum for National History and Archaeology, is one of the most important ancient commercial complexes from Romania. The pavement with mosaic, covering an area of more than 2000 mp—one of the largest on the whole territory of the former Roman Empire—is made of small pebbles (tesserae) of different colours: white, black, yellow, cream-coloured, dark green, brick red and purple red, combining in a unique and refined manner geometrical and vegetal ornamental motifs. The squares are subdivided in different geometrical shapes to which there are inscribed images of Greek vessels made of small pebbles (tesserae) of different colours: white, black, yellow, cream, green and red. Only one zoomorphic motif can be noticed in the rich and varied design of the mosaic pavement: a white dove which can hardly be seen through the leaves of the ivy emerging from a stylised kantharos. It can be linked to the Christian practices of the time when the edifice was functioning.

The Archaeological Park spreads on a generous surface, in the old part of Constanta and it has been arranged with double purpose: on one side it draws attention on the archaeological value of the place, and on the other side it has an educative role. It is vibrant, ancient and cultured, an area rich in vegetation and where the spirit of the old Tomis is still alive. It represents a gate to the history of Constanta, where traces of Tomis architecture can be found, both from the Hellenistic and Roman epochs like limestone bases, columns, capitals, ceramic vessels, cornices, friezes or wall fragments, making the alleys seem like exhibition halls from a history museum. The large map displayed on a building wall nearby the park gives a whole image of the numerous ancient sites to be visited in Dobrogea.

Tropeum Traiani Monument, located at 60 km from Constanta in Adamclisi village, is a key monument of Roman imperial art, and one of the most important ancient monuments of Romania. It was built between 106 and 109 for celebrating Trajan Emperor, for the victory of the Roman army over the alliance made of Dacians, Burs and Sarmatians in 102. On the monument, there was discovered an inscription that indicates the fact that it was dedicated to Mars the Avenger by Nerva Traian August, emperor and Caesar. It was realised after a project of the famous architect Apollodorus of Damascus, bearing 54 relief carvings, called metopae, showing scenes of the fight between the Romans and Dacians' allies, as well as 27 battlements. The trophy itself was placed at the upper part of the monument.

The monument is part of an isosceles triangle of three items: the monument and the funerary tumulus mark the base, while the upper point is the altar. The altar was raised to honour the soldiers fallen during the battles fought by the Romans led by Emperor Trajan (98–117 AD) against an alliance formed by the Dacian king Decebal. The tumulus grave was placed behind the monument and was also built in 102, short time after the altar. The tumulus contained the grave of a Roman officer who died during the battle in Adamclisi.

Tropaeum Traiani Fortress is located at north-west of Adamclisi village, at 2 km from the Tropaeum Traiani monument. It was one of the most important religious centres in the Black Sea area during the Roman Empire and also after during the Byzantin Empire. It also represents one of the most interesting chapters of the birth of Romanian people on these lands. Spread over more than 16 ha the fortress has one of the richest and longest histories from Dobrogea area. A Getic fortress at origin, very well protected by walls and an ingenious defence systems, it was always a threat that had to be conquered. It had four large basilicas, four gates and like any Roman town two main street that crossed at half way: Via Principal's and Cardo. Near the main gate there still are two ditches made to fit the carriages of the local people. If the watchers would have fallen asleep, the noise made by the wheels that could not fit the ditches would have waken them up and the intruders would have been revealed.

The fortress was built along with the monument on the founding place of a Geto-Dacian establishment. Since its foundation, veterans and settlers who were involved in agriculture were brought along with the Geto-Dacians. After AD 170 the city receives the rank of "municipality" and the people called themselves "Traianenses", according to the inscriptions. Until Justinian and during his reign (527–563), the city became an important civil and religious centre.

Tropaeum Traiani Museum, is designed like a lapidarium and is housed in the modern museum building (inaugurated in 1977), situated in Adamclisi village. It is the depositary of the original blocks of stone and stone statues of the Roman monument. The main attractions of the museum are the original sculpted blocks of stone, called metopae, which are exhibited in plain view and invite to closer examination and understanding of the fierce battle they depict. Out of the 54 original stones, 48 are exhibited at the museum in Adamclisi and are in incredible good condition for their age, one is in Istanbul and five were lost or destroyed during time (Ghidul Muzeelor website).

As the monument was initially created as a symbol of the military supremacy of Rome, the blocks of stone depict a triumphant Emperor Trajan saluting his troops, inspecting the battlefield or dominating the new territory he conquered, his right hand raised in salutation. The victorious Roman soldiers are always shown dominating their opponents, slaying, fighting and overwhelming them with their superior weapons and military equipment. Still, the Dacians and their allies were considered fierce fighters against the Romans.

The original statues on the top of the monument are also exhibited at the museum, the armoured soldier trunk and the prisoners at his feet, together with the blocks containing the inscription that shows that the monument was dedicated to Mars, the god of war.

Histria Fortress or Istros, the first Greek colony on the western shore of the Euxine, near the mouth of the Danube (known as Ister in ancient Greek) (Lordkipanidze 2001). Nowadays the Istria-Sinoe area of 400 ha on which the site is situated is included in the Danube Delta Biosphere Reserve declared UNESCO patrimony.

Histria was continuously inhabited for 1300 years from the Greek to the Byzantine period, being destroyed by the attacks of the Avars and the Slavs.

Archaeological works begun in 1914 have revealed vestiges from all periods of habitation. Thus, the Temple of Zeus and the Temple of Aphrodite indicate the rich religious life in the Greek period; the baths and the paved streets are a vivid testimony to the prosperity in the Roman period; basilicas public squares and living quarters demonstrate its importance in the Roman–Byzantine age. In Histria, there were issued the first coins on the present territory of Romania around 480/475 BC. They were silver coins which bore the symbol of the town represented by an eagle and a dolphin.

29.2.1 Capidava Fortress

Capidava Fortress (the Getae toponym meaning the city of turning) is located on a rocky promontory of the right branch of the Danube, halfway between Cernavodă (the ancient Axiopolis) and Hârșova (ancient Carsium). The military camp was built under Trajan the Emperor, together with the Roman border defence fortifications at the Danube, with the help of squads Legion XI Claudia and Legio V Macedonica. Various military units were quartered in Capidava camp, until the beginning of the 7th century AD, given its strategic position at the Danube.

Capidava Fortress is an open-air history lesson, a lively archaeological worksite, an unforgettable experience. Here there were discovered 100 tombs of 1.000 years old. Given the proportions, it is considered the second medieval necropolis of Romania.

The fortress was very well integrated within the surrounding environment, as the walls were linked to the impressive Danube cliffs, recognised nowadays as a landscape and nature reserve.

Callatis Fortress is a Dorian creation of Greek colonists from Heraclea Pontica, since the end of the 6th century BC. The mythical founder of the fortress was considered to be Heracles. Because of the invasions in the second half of the 5th century AD, the flourishing Callatis started to decay. The old ruins of Callatis can be visited near the beach where there can still be seen the remains of the fortress walls. Archaeologists are convinced that most of the ruins are sunk on the bottom of the Black Sea (Allard 2013).

A very important discovery made here in 1959, is the Papyrus Tombstone, dated from the 4th century BC. Its interior is built of large blocks of limestone, carved on the interior and covered above with stone slabs, three being dug to a depth of 1.50 m above the ancient ground level. Around it stood a stone ring, with a diameter of 14 m, in the south-western side with a small shrine for officiating the ceremonies. In the earth, covering the tomb there were found 4 Greek vases and on the top stone, fragments of a coronet comprising bronze leaves and grains, trapped on a bone frame, all gilded, imitating the ancient crown of laurel. Inside the tomb, along with the skeleton of the dead, there were found remains of a coronet similar to that on the cover, fabrics and clothing and the debris of a papyrus written in Greek in a state of preservation quite precarious, being the only document of its kind discovered in Romania. Above the tomb, it was built a mound of earth, a toumba, according to the Greek custom of the time, which protected the entire complex.

Another important discovery refers to the fact that under Emperor Gordian (238–244), at Callatis functioned, the first association of hunters attested in Romania, as it results from an inscription on a marble slab with the names of 43 members, written in Latin and Greek.

Also, the oldest Greek gymnasium sports profile from Romania worked at Callatis in the 1st century AD and the town is the first health resort in our country, mesothermal sulphurous baths being known since Burebista, the Dacian king.

29.2.2 Callatis Archaeology Museum

The Archaeology Museum is situated in Mangalia, numerous artefacts from the ancient Callatis being exhibited in the museum building which was inaugurated in 1978. The archaeological items exhibited date from Neolithic, Greek, Hellenistic Roman and Roman–Byzantine periods. The most important item of the museum is papyrus dated in the 4th century BC, discovered in 1959 in a tomb included now in the permanent exhibition of the museum. It is the only ancient papyrus discovered in Romania, being written in old Greek language, with brown ink.

In the museum, there are exhibited archaeological items of significant value such as: columns, gorgerins, friezes, cornices, inscriptions, statues, Tanagra statuettes, jewels, coins, ceramics, agriculture tools. The museum exhibition includes also three tombs conserved in situ, of which also the tomb with papyrus.

29.3 Conclusion

The urbanisation in Romania has a long history. Since antiquity there were known the cities Histria, Tomis and Callatis, which were founded by the Greek colonists on the Black Sea coast. The remains of antiquity are numerous and of great significance for the Romanian history, culture and civilisation. The temples and public edifices are testimonies of the impact of the Greek colonisation in the area but also of the economic and politic relations with the local population.

The conquest of Dacia by the Roman Empire was followed by a period of urban development of continental Dobrogea and of strengthening the Danube Limes (Custurea et al. 2007). New fortresses were built, there were systemised and refurbished entire quarters from the old Greek colonies at the Black Sea coast, there were built imposing edifices like the monument in Adamclisi, the whole area being in a period of economic, cultural and religious life blooming. The local Getae elements were gradually integrated in the Greek–Roman multicultural mix, even the rural areas being strictly organised and included in the new Roman administrative system.

Beginning with 1900, on the Black Sea Coast urbanisation knows a significant development which led to the construction of impressive buildings as well as to buildings especially dedicated to museums. Thus appeared the monumental building in New Romanian style which will shelter later the Museum of National History and Archaeology of Constanța, the little and coquet building of the Callatis Archaeology Museum, the museum building near the famous Histria Fortress and the lapidarium-like building which shelters the original metopae of the Tropaeum Traiani Monument.

The project from Romania focuses on Constanta County heritage assets and their values in an effort to create and promote The Trail of the Romania Ancient History at the Black Sea Coast. The trail is designed for the visitors who want to learn about 2000 years of history in 2 days.

To ensure success the local project team shall look for ways to involve heritage authorities, government officials, heritage and tourism-related businesses, special interest groups and citizens into the process of planning for and developing the Local Interpretive Project.

The Trail of the Romania Ancient History at the Black Sea Coast will be addressed to travellers from Romania, Black Sea Basin and to international travellers who want to discover the captivating ancient history of Romania.

References

alector.org

Alexandrescu-Vianu, M. (2009). *The treasury of sculptures from Tomis. The cult inventory of a temple* (pp. 27–46). Bucharest: Dacia NS, N.T.Tome LIII.

Allard, C. (2013). *Între marea Neagră și Dunăre, Dobrogea 1855*, ed. Non Lieu, Paris. ISBN: 978-2-35270-135-4.

Custurea, G., Dima, M., Talmatchi G., & Velter, A. (2007). *Coin hoards of Dobrudja* (1st ed.). Ex PONTO.

ghidulmuzeelor.cimec.ro

Lordkipanidze, O. (2001). The golden fleece: Myth, euhemeristic explanation and archaeology. *Oxford Journal of Archaeology, 20*(1), 1–38.

Chapter 30
Financial Instruments for Tourism and Agrotourism in Romania

Otilia Manta

Abstract In the European Union (EU), the tourism sector in 2012–2013 represented over 5% of GDP, providing over 7 million jobs. Rural tourism is universally accepted as a type of travel practiced in rural areas. Buildings in these areas are small, usually present architectural interest, and are decorated in a style reminiscent of traditional homes. Rural tourism may feature traditional local gastronomy and most often is conducted within a family system. "Rural tourism is a concept that includes tourist activity organized and led by the local population, based on a close connection with the environment, natural and human". Tourism in rural areas has been maintained in its authentic form practiced, but was shaped, appreciated and requested the evolvement of civilization amid the higher phenomena of industrialization and urbanization. Rural tourism in its pure form should be located in rural areas, be functional from a rural point of view, be small in scale, both in terms of construction and settlements, and represent the traditional environment, economy, history, and location.

Keywords Rural · Tourism · Microfinance · Agrotourism

30.1 Introduction

One particular form of rural tourism, called agrotourism is limited to peasant housing, harnesses the natural environment, and provides accommodation and agrotourism services. It forms a subset of rural tourism. Rural tourism is linked to the structure of tourist accommodation, tourism activities, and the local economy. Both agrotourism and rural tourism are two concepts that identify up to a certain level in rural areas, each of these concepts having specific elements such as inputs, outputs, conversion, and the external environment. A specific element of rural

O. Manta (✉)
Department of Financial Microeconomics, Romanian Academy-CCFM,
Bucharest, Romania
e-mail: otilia.manta@ince.ro

© Springer International Publishing AG, part of Springer Nature 2019   345
V. Vasile (ed.), *Caring and Sharing: The Cultural Heritage Environment
as an Agent for Change*, Springer Proceedings in Business and Economics,
https://doi.org/10.1007/978-3-319-89468-3_30

tourism is the type of accommodation it incorporates: motels, hotels, tourist hostels, and school camps. The most popular forms of rural tourism are:

1. Family-run rural tourism, in which the household hosts make available their own kitchen to tourists, encouraging them to prepare their own meals and by using traditional local products, thus directly contributing to the sustainability of local suppliers' activity.
2. Rural tourism practiced by households running hostels for groups of 10–20 people, offering accommodation and breakfast.
3. Rural tourism practiced directly in rural households, which takes place at country level, occasionally, uncontrolled, with solitary isolation or in small groups in households for a short period of time and without special requests for comfortable accommodation, meal preparation or other services.

30.1.1   Tourism Statistics in Romania (2013–2014)

- The number of tourists in Romania experienced a major decline in 1990–2002, from 12.3 million in 1990 to less than 5 million in 2002.
- Since 2003, amid stabilization of Romania's economic situation, there has been an upward trend in the number of tourists, increasing from 5.06 million in 2003 to 5.08 million in 2004, 6.2 million in 2006, reaching a peak of 7.12 million in 2008.
- The global economic crisis had a strong impact on the tourism industry. The number of tourists dropped to about 6 million in 2009 and 2010. Since 2011, tourist numbers have improved.
- In 2012, accommodation in Romania processed almost 7.7 million tourists, of which about 1.7 million were foreigners. However, balance of payments and external debt provided by the National Bank of Romania shows that Romania recorded a deficit in the years 2011 (−296 million Euros) and 2012—389 million Euros)—showing a rising trend.
- According to the World Tourism Organization (2013), the direct contribution of tourism to gross domestic product (GDP) was only 1.5% in Romania, compared to 5.2% worldwide. The share of tourism to GDP is significantly lower than other countries in the region: being 11.9% in Croatia, 4.2% in Hungary, and 3.8% in Bulgaria.
- Direct contribution of tourism to employment represents only 2.3% in Romania (193,000 jobs), compared to an average 5.4% globally. Contributions within the region include 13.1% in Croatia, 5.8% in Hungary, and 3.8% in Bulgaria.

These statistics are more worrying considering that some of the states that have recorded higher contributions of tourism to GDP and employment do not have the same level of tourism potential as Romania. An example of one such country is

Hungary, where the impact of tourism on the economy is higher than Romania's, although the country does not have mountainous or coastal regions.

30.1.2 Recoverable Natural Resources in Terms of Tourism

Romania has significant natural tourism potential, with a varied landscape that allows the practice of many forms of tourism. It is important to mention the high degree of uniqueness of these resources which offers Romania a competitive advantage relative to other European tourist destinations. The Danube Delta, with its resorts and spas, is considered as having strategic importance for the development of tourism. Thus, the Danube Delta, a United Nations Educational, Scientific and Cultural Organization (UNESCO) biosphere reservation, is a unique area in Europe in terms of biodiversity having the potential to become an attractive destination for tourists, with good opportunities for the development of ecotourism. With over one third of the spring's and spas in Europe, Romania has a significant advantage compared to other countries in the region. Considering the sociodemographic trends in Europe—an aging population, a greater concern for healthcare, expansion of alternative forms of treatment—the potential for development of health tourism is indeed significant. The value of tourism linked to the cultural heritage available to Romania is at least as large as the value offered by Romania's natural heritage. Just as in the case of natural resources, cultural resources may confer a competitive advantage to Romanian tourism because of the number of sites with high degrees of uniqueness.

Romania has six cultural sites included in UNESCO:

1. The Dacian fortresses of the Orastie Mountains.
2. The saxon settlements with fortified churches in Transylvania.
3. The wooden churches of Maramures.
4. The churches with exterior frescoes in Bucovina.
5. The Horezu monastery.
6. The historic center of Sighisoara.

Although some of these sites receive international recognition (such as Sighisoara and the Saxon settlements with fortified churches), other parts remain less known to the general public (such as the Dacian fortresses), given precarious access and limited promotion. To this cultural heritage are added many elements of intangible heritage—traditions and customs, legends, music and dances—which can become tourist attractions independently with effective promotion.

30.2 Materials and Methods

Using classical scientific research tools, based on analysis and synthesis, induction and deduction, we used observation and examination tools, research methods based on the basic principles of scientific research, and we created procedures based on factual analysis as a result of a practical experience and extensive documentation of national and international literature. Personal contributions are highlighted in the paper together with the importance of the theoretical and applied values resulting from the conclusions and proposals that we have formulated and promoted. Research results are presented using tables, figures and graphs. The theoretical information needed for research was taken from literature and specialized papers (books, studies, papers, articles, etc.) in the field of microfinance both from the country and abroad. Statistical information and specific data on microfinance opportunities were taken from the reports and statistics of institutions involved in microfinance both in the country and abroad, as well as from public bodies and private specialists.

Current theoretical approaches to microfinance are:

- Regarding the methodology of research on microfinance, the complexity and diversity of the issues addressed require the use of methods, techniques, tools, and procedures of scientific investigation and interpretation, in which particular importance is given to: As regards the methodology of microfinance research, the complexity and diversity of issues addressed requires the use of methods, techniques, tools and procedures for scientific investigation and interpretation, in which particular attention is paid to microfinance criteria, access to and study of micro-credit typology aspects, such as and tackling the issue of knowing and investigating rural microfinance for scientific substantiation.
- The rational method, used as an instrument of knowledge, reflection, analysis, organization, and ongoing scientific research.
- The integration method of forms, methods, and logic operations carried out through the use of analysis and synthesis, abstraction and concretization, comparison, generalization, and systematization.
- The statistical method through the use of descriptive statistics and statistical analysis.
- The method of observation, conducted systematically and analytically.
- Discussions with experts from within national and international institutions, as well as with the beneficiaries of microfinance products and services.
- Data analysis and interpretation, using graphs, charts, and figures to highlight various developments in microfinance.

30.2.1 Rural Microfinance Opportunities Are a Research Topic of Great Interest Worldwide in the Present Economic Environment Generated by the Global Economic Crisis

Building microfinance theories aims to establish correlations between the values of funded entities (firms, etc.), the financial structure and the cost of capital purchases. Although some specialists argue that the theories developed on the optimal microfinance structure have a positive effect on the market value of the funded entity, there are theories that assert that the developed financial structure has a neutral effect on it. In this respect, the relevance of theories on the evolution and structure of the optimal legal entity for microfinance (e.g., a farm) is highlighted in this chapter. However, the theories presented regarding the optimal structure of microfinance entrepreneurs in rural areas offer some important lessons. First of all, these theories justify the opportunity to identify the factors that influence the structure of the capital and, therefore, the financing structure is not optimized. The objectives of the capital structure can be a series of loan rates that change over time while the generation conditions change. Secondly, entrepreneurs should aim at a specific capital structure that is compatible with the overall strategy of the funded entity (e.g., the farm) on revenue growth, market position, etc. Decisions on microfinance should be developed on the basis of this structure. Thirdly, establishing an optimal microfinance structure is a complex process involving a combination of quantitative analysis with value assessments characteristic of each enterprise management area.

30.3 Results and Discussions

30.3.1 Agrotourism and Local Ecotourism

Romania's countryside is extremely diverse, with differences existing between the regions and traditional villages. At present, rural Romania is well preserved, maintained with all its traditional elements and historical architecture, including agricultural activity specific to peasant households, which makes agritourism and rural tourism a favorable climate for sustainable development. Among the limiting factors to rural tourism are issues with rural infrastructure, with local housing often considered unacceptable to tourists and a generally low demand for peasant household accommodation, the education and practical training of local people (minimum knowledge of tourism is required as well as being able to speak a foreign language), the security of tourists, etc. Economic indicators reflect the reality of rural tourism in terms of its contribution to the economy; approximately 0.1% of Romania's income is from rural tourism, compared to an average 4.4% in EU countries. Tourism requires substantial investment and resources (educational, financial, infrastructure, etc.). Agrotourism through its specific elements contributes in an integrated way to the development of the peasant household, the goods and services are directly produced within the household, which, in economic and financial terms, makes the activities carried out generating income sources that support the families in rural areas, this activity having a direct impact on the development of technical and financial capacity of the peasant households at the local level. Calculations carried out by experts in tourism show that the price of breakfast in all agrohostels is less than 40% of the price of breakfast in the hotels with standard classification. The reason for such a difference in price is expected because different standards and services are offered. In addition, other economic aspects make agrotourism products cheaper than standard competitive tourism products. Policies for agrotourism should stimulate these advantages, reducing the tax burdens, to permit lower prices and therefore maintain clients. Supporting and expanding rural tourism has an important educational component that relates primarily to knowledge of cultural traditions and historical values of rural landscapes. The educational component is addressed, predominantly, to the children from urban areas who, in terms of their knowledge of agriculture and nature, suffer largely because they have not experienced such rural conditions, spending most of their lives in built-up urban spaces. Participation for two weeks a semester in farm activities, including hiking, bathing in fresh water, horse riding, etc., contributes to a broader knowledge for those children brought up in urban environments. In fact, in many EU countries, the national curricula of urban schools provide holiday periods and/or practical working opportunities on farms and rural guesthouses. Most noticeably, this happens in Austria, Switzerland, and Sweden, where there are consequently great educational outcomes.

30.3.2   Types of European Union Financial Support

EU programs have financial instruments which support members to different degrees with financial intervention subsidies (direct payments) or financial agency/ financial intermediary assistance. One part of EU policy opens up competition for grants and loan support via local commercial banks. EU programs offer research and education through co-financing policies. Beneficiaries of EU funds aim indicators in their projects and documentation of financing based on EU programs it funds. The basic rule the EU adopts for funding of grants is to only fund activities not already finalized, with double funding prohibited.

30.3.2.1   European Regional Development Fund

The European Regional Development Fund (ERDF) is one of the structural funds and investments offered by the EU. Its main objective is the development of economic and social cohesion with a direct impact on the imbalances between member states. Direct financial support under this fund is used to increase the competitiveness of entrepreneurs in tourism while sustaining quality tourism at the state, regional, and local level, especially in rural areas. The ERDF has 11 themed horizontal objectives in line with Europe 2020 policy priorities. These objectives include: the integrated development of tourism infrastructure, industry research and innovation, a digitization sector through innovative technologies of information and communication, increasing the competitiveness of small and medium-sized enterprises (SMEs), labor mobility and increasing workforce, competency-based education programs of correct competition and protection of the real economy, environmental protection, etc. The types of eligible activities in tourism are:

1. Research, development and technological innovation related to tourism, including innovations and services specific to rural tourism clusters (service incubators, laboratories, demonstration projects, etc.).
2. Developing ICT products related to tourism (applications, data mining).
3. Development of innovative services for rural tourism, especially in areas affected by industrial restructuring, namely underprivileged and underdeveloped areas. This development is directly dependent on best practice existing in the rural area European.
4. Development of new types of tourism like cultural tourism, ecotourism, gastronomic tourism, and sports tourism, etc., all encouraging local resource mobilization thereby increasing sustainability and regional specializations.
5. Clustering activities between the different industries of tourism and recreation, allowing product diversification and the expansion of regional tourism seasons (e.g., nautical tourism, that is, boating and cruising).
6. Improving, through innovation, energy efficiency and promoting the use of alternative energy resources to SMEs.
7. Protecting, promoting, and developing local brands and services for tourism and agrotourism.
8. Improving tourism infrastructure on a regional and local level.
9. Introducing measures to promote entrepreneurship, employment, and business creation, as well as internationalization of SMEs and clusters of tourism.
10. Providing training and upgrading of skills.

30.3.2.2 European Agricultural Fund for Regional Development

The European Agricultural Fund for Regional Development (EAFRD) has as its main objective the promotion and economic development of rural areas through financial instruments. The main types of tourism-related actions eligible for funding under EAFRD are:

1. Training and skills (training, workshops, coaching, etc.).
2. Integrated consultancy services to support farmers, SMEs, travel, and tourism, as well as integrated packages incorporating agriculture and tourism.

3. Develop support through financial support services in rural areas in terms of business services, catering services, transport services, etc.
4. Expand integrated development plans and local development strategies in rural areas.
5. Develop tourism infrastructure at regional and local scales.
6. The elaboration of feasibility studies on the restoration of buildings of cultural value, the protection of local patrimony in villages and the protection of natural heritage. This would involve multi-entity cooperation and the creation of operational groups, including research / innovation clusters between research institutes, farmers, universities and consultancy firms specialized in the development of integrated strategic projects on rural tourism and agritourism.

30.3.2.3 European Fund for Fisheries and Maritime Affairs

The European Fund for Fisheries and Maritime Affairs (EMFF) replaces the former European Fisheries Fund (EFF). Its priority is to increase the number of new jobs and develop cohesion projects in fishing and aquaculture. The types of actions related to tourism which are eligible for funding under the EMFF are:

1. Feasibility and technical studies.
2. Priority projects, including pilot projects, operation groups, and cooperation projects.
3. Conferences, seminars, workshops, public information, exchange of best practices, awareness campaigns, and activities associated with communication and dissemination, such as advertising campaigns, events, development and maintenance of websites, platforms for stakeholders, etc.
4. Training—lifelong learning enabling participation in tourism or complementary activities to tourism.

Along with funding these types of programs, as part of the 2014–2020 programing period the European Commission decided upon new financial instruments for tourism, among which is included the Competitiveness Operational Program which supports smart growth, promotes investment in research and promotes investments in research and innovation, technology and development, innovation and applied research, increasing quality and access to information and communication technologies within tourist units.

30.3.2.4 European Social Fund

The European Social Fund (ESF) aims in particular to improve employment, mobility, and professional qualifications in the EU in in terms of the tourism sector, with infrastructure and human factors being considered the most valuable investments. Furthermore, international cooperation between tourist facilities play a major role in projects financed by the ESF, with support for the transfer of best practices in the EU and the development of policies on the orientation of tourism units towards very specific market segments.

30.3.2.5 Competitiveness of Enterprises and Small and Medium-Sized Enterprises

Competitiveness of Enterprises and Small and Medium-sized Enterprises (COSME) is a program that supports the competitiveness of SMEs in the EU. Among its objectives are the financial support of the tourism sector, namely: the development and/or promotion of thematic tourism products which are sustainable, and direct cooperation between tourism and traditional creative industries, as well as the transfer of best practices from European countries; public–private partnerships that develop transnational tourism products aimed specifically at seniors and youths to promote an increase in tourism in the low season.

30.3.2.6 Creative Europe

Creative Europe aims to help creative and cultural organizations to operate transnationally. Reuniting three pre-existing programs (Culture, MEDIA, and MEDIA Mundus), Creative Europe consists of 3 parts: media, culture, and a complementary support component, dedicated to guaranteed bank loans for cultural and creative sectors and cooperation with cultural policy (available from 2016). This program is a complementary thematic program specifically geared to supporting the development of niche tourism / rural tourism through supporting actions such as: cooperation projects between tourist units from several countries, networks of European cultural capitals in the European cooperation sector. Along with these EU funding programs, sources of funding for tourism units at local level have to be identified, and as an example we mention microfinance.

30.3.2.7 Microfinance—A Tool for Tourism and Agrotourism in Rural Romania

Specialized microfinance development in rural areas is the pillar of support available to small businesses, improving their sustainability and rural existence. A major percentage of rural households state they need the new programs for microfinance in rural area. Currently in Romania there are more than 2.5 million small farms (semi-subsistence farms), which need diversification of complementary services such as agritourism or rural tourism. Moreover, due to the lack of financial resources due to the financial crisis, financial and banking institutions and non-bank financial institutions have developed new innovative financial products and services, such as microfinance, aimed at financially supporting rural activities. The progress of financial inclusion is the result of the digitization trend in the financial sector, having a major impact on financial institutions. Creating new distribution models (networks of external agents, banks with branch networks), the emergence of new technological innovations regarding customer access to financial services (such as mobile banking) are just some examples of the current microfinance challenges in the current context of financially developed innovations (the new concept fintech). The phenomenon of "microfinance" has created new opportunities for customers: easy management of household savings, revenue collection, and payment of bills and taxes. Its use in Romania still needs to become more concrete and consistent, and customers need educating in terms of these new digital tools. It is undeniable that a revolution is taking place! In the context of the financial crisis, microfinance continues to grow, offering new digital opportunities—access for new customers or help and services provided to beneficiaries. Furthermore, all funding programs both in Europe and the United States, in the current context of the crisis, are geared very much toward the safety of small businesses in rural areas (farms, support services, and agro tourism or rural tourism), promoting innovative financial technologies as well as suing in identifying solutions for promoting microfinance grant programs and financial support for rural areas. The issue of a microfinance company can not be scientifically investigated without an appropriate approach to the "cost of capital" indicator as the main variable of microfinance, i.e., the ratio between those who make available capital (financiers) and those who need them (entrepreneurs and households peasant). There is nowhere free microfinance resources, which is why special attention should be paid to the microfinance product, especially in terms of its cost, relative to the financial capacity of rural demand. The microfinance system, at national or international level, offers rural companies a limited range of solutions, which is why my approach is directly related to the development of innovative microfinance models based on international best practice models, but adapted to realities from the Romanian rural environment.

These are two aspects of fundamental microfinance policy. In terms of decisions about microfinancing, rural entrepreneurs must be given rigorous criteria allowing them to choose and combine resources. Undoubtedly, the cost of microfinance is the main criterion in choosing microfinance resources. Without knowing the cost of microfinance capital, it cannot be said that we can maximize the market value of services and products in rural areas. Moreover, a correct estimate of the cost of capital (the cost of the financing source) is important in the process of investment decisions taken by the contractor in rural areas (e.g., agro-enterprises and micro-farms). Many of us have gone through the situation of being unable to access loans which are necessary to meet unexpected expenses in terms of trying to develop a small business. The difficulty accessing microfinance pushes people into poverty, increasing ever more the number people seeking social assistance. What can be done to change the situation and how can we prevent increasing poverty? The answer lies in providing a current microfinance policy directed especially at those who are financially excluded. However, access to credit which is too expensive can also contribute to debt and have serious macroeconomic consequences, such as those of the crisis in 2007. Therefore, poverty and social exclusion can be fueled by the inability to access credit or access inappropriate forms of finance. Such difficulties are undermining economic growth and social cohesion. Instead, poverty and financial difficulties are supporting social exclusion. Low-income households are most likely to be unable to access appropriate financial services. Along with poverty, age, area of residence (rural or urban), and gender are direct causes of financial exclusion. Starting from the real needs of those who are involved in daily activities in rural areas, any proposed lending program must take account of the type of financing structure corroborated with the common agricultural policy, namely the National Rural Development Plan in each state. On the other hand, the existing models in the world must give their input so that the concept of microfinance model structure is covered by regulated institutions. In general, banks offer less financial projects to rural areas—due to the associated risks of such areas. The question is why? Why there are no institutions involved in this type of risk taking? Why are financing products not tailored to the realities of rural areas? Maybe it is time to create additional institutions which can adapt to such risk factors and be closer aligned to the needs for microfinance in rural areas. Starting in 2013, by Regulation (EC) No 1305/2013 of the European Parliament and of the Council on support for rural development by the European Agricultural Fund for Rural Development (EAFRD) and repealing Regulation (EC) No. 1698/2005 (www.reterurale.it), the financial support framework for the rural environment has been created, more precisely the types of investments to be financed through this program. Moreover, in order to help farmers, for the first time in the history of European funds for agriculture and rural development, a special funding measure was created to set up a mutual fund to take financial risks from agriculture and rural areas (estimated funding for a such fund is about EUR 350 million). Moreover, for a long time there has been a discussion about the creation of special funds to support farmers and non-agricultural activities in rural areas, funds that, I strongly believe, must be adapted to our real rural needs, also by existing microfinance models of good practice worldwide and by designing new innovative models that have elements that match our microfinance needs in rural areas. Based on these considerations, we propose in our research a financing package with programs that provide loans (microcredits), subsidies and loan guarantees by type of destination in rural areas, namely:

- Programs for public utility services (medical clinics, schools, fire centers, community centers, equipment and vehicles for first aid and many other initiatives coming from the local community);
- Programs for financing infrastructure networks (roads, village water supply, communications, etc.) linking rural residents to the global economy and, not least, national, regional and local;
- Financing programs that support business creation and development at local level and have a direct impact on the creation of new jobs in rural areas.
- In Romania, through the Ministry of Agriculture and Rural Development, there is the "National Rural Development Plan" financing program that includes more

Fig. 30.1 The Farm Bill as model for rural microenterprise. *Source* http://www.usda.gov/wps/portal/usda/usdahome?navid=farmbill

rural investment funding measures and has a bottom up approach (from local needs), which makes the sustainability element of rural development policies available at local, regional and national level. Moreover, these financial support measures also create the support framework for attracting new co-financing solutions, which leads us to affirm that there is a need for microfinance models to ensure the sustainable development of rural areas.

- The model from which I start in my scientific approach has two inputs: Model Farm Bill and the strategic project POSDRU/135/5.2/S/ID135486—"Microcredit, the fundamental component of rural entrepreneurship", personally coordinated and implemented with a team of experts between April 2014 and November 2015. As a result we can mention: professional training and professional orientation in the field of rural microfinance of more than 2000 participants, the creation of a network of 25 microfinance micro-enterprises and a network of 156 specialized brokers rural microfinance.

If we consider the Farm Bill as a model for rural microenterprise (farms, agritourism pensions, etc.) the model of microfinance must be directly related to it, and microfinance products must be adapted to its type of intervention: commercial microcredit, social microcredit, microcredit for business investments in farms (Fig. 30.1).

30.4 Conclusions

The Consultative Group to Assist the Poor (CGAP) estimates that the world has over 500 million family farms, farms that provide food to more than 2.5 billion people, people who live daily with less than US\$ 2. I consider it is our duty, as economists, to identify the most efficient models of microfinance to support those people who are in absolute or relative poverty. The challenges and constraints of those working in the field of microfinance for rural areas are numerous and the risks and limitations must be guaranteed by optimal solutions, especially if we consider this vulnerable segment in terms of banknotes. Nevertheless, the non-performing loan (NPL) indicator is much lower compared to other financing segments, which is also possible as a result of innovative solutions in the area of financial and social inclusion of rural areas (paper Otilia Manta, www.ibima.org).

Specialized microfinance development in rural areas represents a pillar of support for small businesses by improving their sustainability. The progress of financial inclusion is the result of trends in digitization of the financial sector, having a major impact on financial institutions. Creating new business models in microfinance through innovative distribution channels (external agent networks, branch network banks) as well as emerging new customer access and back office management opportunities are just some of the current challenges to which the microfinance sector knows in the process of innovation and adaptation to the needs of the rural environment (especially in the field of tourism and agrotourism).

The phenomenon of "microfinance" has created new opportunities for customers, allowing them easy management of household savings, revenue collection, and payment of bills and taxes. Its use in Romania still needs to become more concrete and consistent, and customers need educating in terms of these new digital tools. It is undeniable that a revolution is taking place! In the context of the financial crisis, microfinance continues to grow, offering new digital opportunities, be it access to new customers or help and services provided to beneficiaries.

A typical feature of the rural economy is the presence at local level of SMEs, many of which are microenterprises (over 98%) with a high percentage of self-employed persons. Microfinance innovations for rural areas (especially for small farmers with limited financial resources) have great potential, with a direct impact on sustainable local development and having a direct impact on global food safety and security. Microfinance in rural areas has been reduced, especially as regards the possibility of integrating services into agricultural microfinance, but we are currently witnessing major progress in developing this new business model of rural microfinance for agriculture, rural tourism, agritourism and other environmental services rural.

The International Food Policy Research Institute (IFPRI), part of the World Bank's Vision 2020 was to conceptualize and assemble the concept of rural microfinance and agriculture to bridge the knowledge gap by promoting innovation in the provision of financial services to rural households and create new innovative directions and manage the risks facing the poor in rural areas. The importance of the realities of life, facing small-scale farmers, including low education levels (according to statistics provided by the National Institute of Statistics) and the lack of access to modern financial instruments, leads us to say that the subsistence farms currently (in Romania currently have about 2.5 million semi-subsistence farms according to the data provided by the National Institute of Statistics). These conditions mean that people involved in developing new models for microfinance institutions must create new and innovative means to achieve the funding needs of small and medium-sized farms. Existing digitization technologies offer us new concepts in microfinance with direct impacts on final costs. Microfinance models and programs have a direct impact on the development of activities and services in peasant farms, especially as a result of addressing the risk coverage policy for small and medium-sized farmers through financial support such as guarantee funds. The combination of financial services and non-financial services (such as technical support, marketing and financial consulting) offers integration of production and services across the value chain. Moreover, through a micro-macro-policy approach, as well as through the creation of innovative microfinance and funding programs, we can join together to develop a favorable environment for both sustainable local development and, above all, the right framework for the implementation of both European and international funding programs, reimbursable and / or non-reimbursable, to finance rural activities.

Currently, UN member countries have signed and assumed sustainable development objectives (Sustainable Development Objectives), targets that each Member State will respect for the next 14 years in the global sustainable development context. Given that the world's number one problem is currently the worst rising poverty, unlike the targets set out in Agenda 2015 (where the major goal was the millennium development), the richest must be directly involved voluntarily or indirectly through fiscal policies, to support the poor in need (disadvantaged). Moreover, Agenda 2030 mentions the major involvement of states through policies and programs, the state being the element of balance between the present generation and the next generations.

References

Borzaga Euricse, C. (2013). *Unlocking the potential of social economy and social enterprises.*
Cibian, O. (1930). *Agriculture interests in the light of rural credit—Excerpt from the study published in "National Economy".*
Emilian, D. M. (2008). *Structural funds.* Eurolobby House: Bucharest.
Faim, S. (2014). Une microfinance plus en plus Verte: Effet de mode tendance Lourde, https://www.sosfaim.be/publication/zoom-microfinance/.
Future, New York: United Nations World Commission on Environment and Development, www.environnement.ens.fr.
Gusti, D. (1938). *Status today Romanian village.* National Culture Printing House: Bucharest.
Herman, E., & Stefanescu, D. (2009a). *Impact of lending in agriculture lending process.* PIM Printing House: Iaşi.
Herman, E., & Stefanescu, D. (2009b). *An analysis of domestic credit granted for types of institutional sectors.* PIM Printing House: Iaşi.
Loredana, C. (2013). *Agricultural capital—Opportunities and constraints for Romanian rural communities.* Agriculture Capital Printing House: Bucharest.
Madgearu, V. N. (1914). *Structure and trends popular banks in Romania.* Romanian printing: Bucharest.
Noya, A. (2013). *Social Innovation and social economy in the 3RD National Conference of social economy,* Bucharest, http://www.ies.org.ro/library/files/prezentare_antonella_noya_cnes_2013.pdf.

Otiman, P. I. (2011). *Alternativele economiei rurale a Romaniei: Dezvoltarea agriculturii sau insecuritate alimentara si desertificare rurala severa*", Editura Academiei Romane, Bucuresti, 2011 ISBN 978-973-2720-660.

Pelinescu, E. (2009). *Impact of lending policies on the Romanian economy*. PIM Printing House: Iaşi.

Robert, B. (2015). *Schemes in developed countries*. Geneva: International Labor Organization, website, http://conspecte.com/Geoeconomia/agricultura-si-strategiile-deindustrializare-in-tarile-indezvoltare.html.

Sen, A. (1999). *Development as freedom*. Oxford: Oxford University Press, www.se2009.eu.

Slăvescu, V. (1924). *Appropriation of land in Romania*. locul aparitiei, Ed "Romanian Book".

Stern, N. (2006). *Stern review: The economics of climate change*. Cambridge: Cambridge University.

Vulturescu, G. (1889). *About Land credit companies and their establishment in Romania*. Bucharest Printing House: Bucharest.

WCED. (1987). *Report of the World Commission on Environment and Development*, www.sarpn. org.za, Organization website, http://conspecte.com/Geoeconomia/agricultura-si-strategiile-deindustrializare-in-tarile-indezvoltare.html.

Chapter 31
The Hagia Sophia Soup-Kitchen Furnishing Exhibition Project

Nuri Özer Erbay

Abstract A furnishing project has been started to exhibit the carpets carrying some of the most distinguished characteristics of Turkish Islamic Civilization between thirteenth and nineteenth century. Museum allocation design was performed, and restorations were planned to carry out the functionality of the building in an effective way. Fifty-two ancient carpets and 50 ancient rugs were controlled for this purpose. During preparation process of the project, studies were initiated to determine the current situation. Some particular issues such as horizontal layout of the building, areal division, venues, and sizes of the carpets were examined.

Keywords Museum projects · Carpet Museum · Restoration project

31.1 Introduction

A furnishing project has been started to exhibit the carpets carrying the most distinguished characteristics of Turkish Islamic Civilization between thirteenth and nineteenth century (Erbay 2007a). Museum allocation design was performed, and restorations were planned to carry out the functionality of the building in an effective way. Fifty-two ancient carpets and 50 ancient rugs were controlled for this purpose (Erbay 2007b). During the preparation process of the project, studies were initiated to determine the current situation (Akgündüz et al. 2012). Some particular issues such as horizontal layout of the building, areal division, venues, and sizes of the carpets were examined. Number and quality of the pieces to be exhibited were transferred to the digital media. The number of showcases to be placed in exhibition area and number of carpets to be exhibited were projected with three-dimensional exercises during pre-study process. Projects prepared in three different styles have been presented to Regional Directorate of Foundations. Exhibition is supported by interactive technology and has been placed in three halls.

N. Ö. Erbay (✉)
Museology Department, Istanbul University, Istanbul, Turkey
e-mail: erbay.nuriozer@gmail.com

© Springer International Publishing AG, part of Springer Nature 2019   361
V. Vasile (ed.), *Caring and Sharing: The Cultural Heritage Environment
as an Agent for Change*, Springer Proceedings in Business and Economics,
https://doi.org/10.1007/978-3-319-89468-3_31

A well-defined business plan with time details was prepared and distributed among different working groups. Joint studies were initiated with museum officers, foundation officers, museum experts, consultants, and architectures. Discussions were carried out with consultation boards and control teams for all stages of the project. Work flows, programming, design, and application studies were examined during the process of planning (Erbay 2006). The areas of current buildings are planned for restoration purposes; museum and exhibition areas have been constructed as three separate galleries. Exhibition halls have been planned as entrance halls through atrium and gallery 1, 2, and 3. Carpets are divided into three main groups as Seljukian, Early Period Ottoman, and Classical Period Ottoman, which should be exhibited in these three exhibition halls.

31.2 The Project

Emergency exits have been specified for visitors and employees. These buildings were transformed into museums (Erbay 2009); hence, they require new designing process. Box office and security areas are located next to the entrance door. Static and dynamic projection techniques are used in the halls and exhibition designs. Showcase exhibition was suggested by considering humidity and moisture problems in the building and within the area. The works of art from thirteenth, fourteenth, and fifteenth centuries required first-degree protection and were suitable to be exhibited in special showcases. Twelve wall showcases were virtually designed by Prof. Dr. Fethiye Erbay, an instructor at Boğaziçi University, and the Museum Consultant of Regional Directorate of Foundations and attained as the museum planner of this building. Showcase samples were approved convenient with the world standards which are commonly implied at museums in England, Germany, and Japan. A special vacuum wall cabinet and floor showcases with airflow cut were used for the carpets within the scope rare works of art as in Victoria and Albert Museum, London and British Museum. The project proposal was discussed with the museum officers and museum administrators from England (Fig. 31.1).

(a)   **(b)**

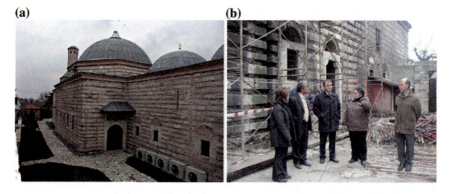

Fig. 31.1 a Front Side of the Building. **b** The Construction Process (Ozer Erbay visual collection)

Upstairs was designed to show the historical transformation. Soup-kitchen building had been modified through restoration studies. This area was designed as venue mainly for research and information purposes. Folding platforms, electronic devices, kiosks, flat screens, written data for public information, labels, and all other presentation materials were designed in the exhibition halls. This place was converted into a museum with its whole environment. The fountain, cistern, administration building, and single-story wooden building were re-functionalized with atrium arrangements (Fig. 31.2).

Administration building has been renewed as a two-story building and a management office. A single-story wooden building has been suggested for social issues; however, it has been argued that the project should include areas for museum services as WC for visitor service area, cafe, and warehouse which were not included in Hagia Sophia Lead Depository and Soup-Kitchen Restoration Project. It was stated that there was a need for a research center, library, and warehouse area. A portable souvenir shop was planned at the back door of the soup-kitchen. Emergency exits, toilet directions for the visitors, and needs of disabled visitors were identified. On the other hand, there was a requirement for a detailed professional study related to air-conditioning, lighting, security, exhibition conditions, and administrative offices of the building to be converted into a museum. A modern ventilation system was required to be able to keep humidity values in the warehouses within a range to fit the healthiness of the work and blow at a sufficient level and maintain consistency. Detailed technical projects should be prepared with their physical designs, heat, light, sound, and arrangements for

Fig. 31.2 Soup-kitchen building (Ozer Erbay visual collection)

Fig. 31.3 Soup-kitchen building (Ozer Erbay visual collection)

air-conditioning installations. A security planning was defined to ensure the safety of the works considering visitors in the building and air circulation. Experts reported that the climate conditions in the warehouses of the museum where a large portion of artworks could be periodically checked. Therefore, humidity and temperature fluctuations between mid-season and night and day could be avoided and main factors causing deterioration, such as harmful gases, could be regularly controlled.

Hagia Sophia soup-kitchen building was revitalized with these restoration and museum projects. Hagia Sophia soup-kitchen building was opened to public through the international carpet exhibition curated by Prof. Dr. Fethiye Erbay (Fig. 31.3).

31.3   Conclusion

The "Museum Exhibition Organizing Implementation" took place in 2010. As Hagia Sophia Soup-Kitchen Encyclopedia states, this building was transformed into a Carpet Museum in 2013. Forty-six carpets and prayer rugs are exhibited in three galleries with their chronological order. Carpets and prayer rugs from Principalities Period, Ottoman Period, and Usak region (Eyice 1982, 1984) finally met with the audience. Damages should be avoided in order to maintain durability of the unique carpet collection placed in Hagia Sophia soup-kitchen building. Environmental temperature, relative humidity, light, and air pollution should be always kept under control, and preventive protection endeavors need to be conducted. Security of visitors and employees should be sustained with physical and technological security systems as well. Unique protection techniques in the context of contemporary museology should maintain sustainability of the museums. To utilize Hagia Sophia's soup-kitchen as a museum is a significant project to be transferred to the future generations.

References

Akgündüz, A., Öztürk, S., & Baş, Y. (2012) *Hagia Sophia one chapel at three periods*. Istanbul: Ottoman Research Foundation Publications.

Erbay, F. (2007a). *Project of converting Hagia Sophia soup-kitchen building into a museum*. Istanbul: Republic of Turkey Regional Directorate of Foundations Presentation.

Erbay, F. (2007b). Ancient foundation carpets and rugs met with the experts. *Bahariye Art Journal*, 7–16.

Erbay, N. Ö. (2006). Hagia Sophia Soup-Kitchen Building Technical Report (prepared for construction and Monuments Branch Directorate), 2006.

Erbay, F. (2009). *Endeavor of Institutionalizing the Museum Administration (1984–2009), Project of converting Hagia Sophia soup-kitchen building into a museum*. Architecture Foundation Institute.

Eyice, S. (1982). Sultan I. Mahmud Fountain in Istanbul: A Piece of Work Perishing. JTS (1982, 1984), pp 119, rs. 16–19.

Eyice, S. (1984). Hagia Sophia. İslamic Encyclopedia, FC. IV, p.

"Hagia Sophia Soup-Kitchen" Religious Affairs Administration İslamic Encyclopedia, Turkish Religious Affairs Foundation. (2014). http://www.diyanetislamansiklopedisi.com/ayasofya/. Accessed November 30, 2014.

Chapter 32
Cultural Tourism and the Stimulators RDI and ICT for Its Development

Maria Valkova Shishmanova

Abstract Anthropogenic and intangible cultural heritage are the basis for socioeconomic development of certain areas. Cultural tourism is one of the sub-sectors of the economy that is developing dynamically, especially if RDI and ICT (Web site and database) are used. For detection, conservation, preservation, protection, stimulation, socialization, maintenance, management and promotion of cultural values also need to use RDI and ICT. In today's world of global challenges and drastic upheavals, sustainability of cultural heritage and cultural tourism is very vulnerable. Development activity and innovation, communication and information technologies are unbelievable need for stability. New significant developments and innovations that can change the tourism industry are associated with the introduction of ICT. General utilization of ICT, Internet, and mobile smart devices (for information, booking, and payment function) in tourism will create a direct approach for the tourists to communicate with tour operators and other service providers. The use of broadband Internet access to ICT increases the value and quality of travel services and products without raising the price, while supporting cluster associations in the sector. Development and enrichment of promotional services and products must be based on ICT and its dissemination. Use of RDI and ICT to promote business and services in the field of tangible and intangible cultural heritage would be a decisive step toward better practices. Here are presented the logical model and the technology of the process leading to elaboration of a marketing municipality profile of developing cultural tourism. The steps that are necessary for its construction and the profile itself must be unified and standardized for all municipalities to obtain a synergistic and multiplier effect.

Keywords Cultural tourism · Logical model · Innovation · RDI
ICT · Mobile devices

M. V. Shishmanova (✉)
Faculty of Mathematics and Natural Sciences, South-West
University "Neofit Rilski", Blagoevgrad, Bulgaria
e-mail: valkova_chich@abv.bg

© Springer International Publishing AG, part of Springer Nature 2019   367
V. Vasile (ed.), *Caring and Sharing: The Cultural Heritage Environment
as an Agent for Change*, Springer Proceedings in Business and Economics,
https://doi.org/10.1007/978-3-319-89468-3_32

32.1   Introduction

Globally, tourism is the most rapidly growing economic activity and the largest source of revenue. Tourism is the leading sector in the policy of the European Union and the Republic of Bulgaria with the aim its competitiveness to be world class by creating conditions for the preservation and maintenance of natural and cultural heritage, balance of economic activity and environmentally friendly lifestyle, innovations in technological aspect, sharing of best practices. At the local-level tourism, it is necessary to continue to lead the economy where there is the right level of resource, attracting a significant part of the revenue of the municipality and representing the main occupation of part of the local population. For areas—locations known and established tourist destinations—their development should continue in line with modern requirements of tourists and challenges facing the European Union in economic terms.

32.2   Cultural Tourism as Sub-sector of the Economy with Greater Significance—Year-Round Workload

Cultural tourism is an important and expanding sector, which attracts visitors with higher cultural and cognitive needs, and whose financial situation ranks them in the middle or wealthy classes of society. Any territory—municipalities own cultural values—should take repositioning of their cultural services and develop innovations aimed at increasing value through culture. These municipalities should diversify the types of tourism they supply and to increase the number of overnight stays by offering more affordable and attractive travel packages and promotional initiatives through a variety of cultural activities and events that are held throughout the year.

Individual activities exhibiting the cultural values (archaeological excavations, restoration, reconstruction of infrastructure, protection, advertising, promotions, etc.) are included in an integrated development plan needed to become a worthy heritage into a valuable resource capable of activating mechanisms for regional and local development and thus generate:

- Increase investment in the region;
- Creating jobs and increasing employment;
- Increasing the income generated on the basis of increasing the number of tourists;
- Increase the social welfare of the population that has no monetary terms (cultural development of civil society, restoration and preservation of monuments, and values inherited from the past).

Development of cultural tourism also generates on the territory attracting: visitors; financial resources; highly qualified professionals; tourism companies, and creating business opportunities for companies from other sectors of the economy (Bozhikov and Yankov 2003).

Culture could be represented by concentric circles.

In the center is the circle—the cultural heart representing the main elements of traditional culture. This is the activity of people producing culture. Cultural tourism with its elements fits here. One element is the tourism of the artistic values of the past—cultural goods and products and the tourism art—modern architecture, literature, virtual arts, and so on. The next round brings the essence of the secondary elements of cultural tourism—a style of life (faith, traditions, rituals, folklore, and cuisine) and creativity (including all types of design and art, fashion, filmmaking and media projects, entertainment, amateur arts).

In some countries, these circles converge and are mutually reinforcing, thus producing a common cultural offering (http://www.montana-vidin-dolj.com/home/)

Some subtypes of cultural tourism can capture trends and moods of consumers in the most significant market share segments, taking into account their needs, motivating demand and behavior. These are: tourism of cultural and historic heritage, creative and art tourism, rural tourism, tourism of urban sightseeing, contemporary and local cultural tourism (Strategic Plan for the development of cultural tourism in Bulgaria 2009).

Normally, overall strategy cannot cover in detail and consider all issues in different directions. This requires the development of specific strategies for the improved management of museums, cultural exchange and tourist activities, and new technologies. Based on overall strategy, these specialized strategies will develop priorities outlined in detailed programs for the respective directions (Strategy for sustainable development of tourism in Bulgaria 2014–2020).

32.3 Innovations in Tourism—Crucial for the Sustainable Development Strategy

The growth and affirmation of tourism will be helped by schedules of such employment with which to enhance the quality and working conditions, measures to support entrepreneurs (networks, marketing, promotions) that implement permanent innovation.

Given the growing importance of Internet booking for travel and tourism, of small and medium enterprises in the tourism sector, should be offered training or simplified access to appropriate service providers in order to develop a successful presence on the Internet and to earn new and new customers.

Innovation is at the root of the current economic policy in the EU (the Lisbon Strategy and the "Europe 2020"), as well as at regional level, with increasing public investment in research, education, training, and support of the "most innovative sectors" (transport, energy, and environmental industries). This also applies for services requiring a certain level of knowledge, skills, or qualifications, which should be characteristic of most tourist activities (accommodation, catering, real estate).

Changes and innovations in tourism can occur with the use of information and communication technologies (ICTs). This is particularly important for small businesses in the tourism industry where required widespread use of ICT and the Internet will allow users to communicate directly with service providers. The sector as a whole can lead to cost savings (for transactions), which subsequently leads to progress in the reduction of intermediaries such as travel agents or even tour operators. Major innovations in the area of mass travel such as the emergence of low-cost airlines have largely influenced the growth and future improvement of the tourism industry.

In large tourist companies, implementing innovative measures is routine and a standard component of corporate governance. To ensure that not be caught off guard by unexpected innovations, companies today include innovation as part of their everyday planning. For them, innovation is simply just an additional production factor.

The problem is small businesses in the tourism industry specialized for a particular destination to take the opportunity to fully benefit from innovation. The main limitation is the lack of staff and resources. SMEs in tourism are primarily to meet the everyday needs of regular customers, and they cannot devote resources to research and development.

The tourism industry has always strived to introduce new technologies (such as worldwide systems for distribution). Progress in communications, Internet-based networks and databases, and widely spread practice of online marketing reveal endless new opportunities for the tourist branches. They have a significant impact on traditional business models in tourism. The use of broadband Internet access with information and communication technologies (ICTs) adds value to tourism services and products and supports the development of tourism networks and clusters in the sector. The problem is the lack of broadband technology and the lack of specialized knowledge and skills of staff to fully benefit from ICT. To overcome these gaps should provide their special training (https://www.oecd.org/.../Competitiveness_Policy_Outlook_brochure.pdf).

The consumers of tourist services use widely Internet communication technologies while arranging their tourist trips. The EU's current two-thirds of tourists organize their trip via Internet, and more than 50% buy their trip online. Flexible and affordable products for direct connection to tourist services are required. Tourists and the Internet service providers use the high potential of the Internet technologies in the online business (https://www.oecd.org/.../Competitiveness_Policy_Outlook_brochure.pdf) (Gauci 2010).

Regulations should allow innovative companies to achieve certain economies and strive to innovate through associations and other forms of networking. Through cooperation, usage of networks, new technologies, advertising, marketing, and sharing of quality trained staff of human capital.

Cooperation in tourism is negligible, especially for small businesses. In this regard, the industry and the government should support innovative tourism policies that promote cooperation, coherence, and synergies in the activity.

32.4 Creation and Development of Networks for the Organization of Innovations in Tourism Companies and Destinations

Certain sub-branches of the tourism industry, such as hotel companies, airlines, rent-a-car agencies, participate generally at the international market.

However, nationally and globally most tourist services are offered by companies classified as small and medium enterprises. While the first group occupies more and more market share, broaden the product, successfully diversify their palette of offered services and activities, and innovate to achieve competitive global products, in the second group can get that firms compete for the same market, which will lead to convergence products and pricing issues.

This is important for small- and medium-sized tourism enterprises to work together to be constructive competition. To survive among large companies, small businesses in tourism should participate in the competition not only constructively, but to work in networks by implementing best-speed all the latest achievements in the field of innovation.

Small entrepreneurs in tourism are more vulnerable to competition from their bigger partners than to the benefits of the common work. In the field of tourism, geographical networks/clusters and networks/clusters based on the different activities and different types of tourism are created. Clusters in tourism have the opportunity to create capacity for the operators by carrying out various innovations (https://www.oecd.org/.../Competitiveness_Policy_Outlook_brochure.pdf).

RDI and ICT are promoters in the development and prosperity of cultural tourism. They can be used as measures to control access to cultural values through innovative technologies, approaches, activities, and protection measures (Alexandrova 2011: 76–83).

32.5 Logical Model and Process Technology to Create a Tourist Profile of a Tourist Core (Municipality)

32.5.1 Cultural Tourism Marketing Profile of Municipalities

The main goal is positioning a municipality or area as a year-round tourist destination with focus on cultural tourism. This was announced by the Ministry of Tourism. A list of specific cultural and historical routes is presented that will be finally discussed with the Ministry of Culture and presented to the industry in order to develop detailed tourist products so as to attract more tourists. To achieve the objectives assigned, it will work with both traditional and non-traditional advertising, including so-called celeb tours with celebrities who will be invited to visit specific sites of cultural and historical routes.

The analysis of marketing profiles with their positive and weaknesses is the basis for the creation of updated profiles not only for potential investors, designers of territorial and other projects, but also for users of administrative and other services in the municipality, its citizens, and potential guests of the municipality.

These marketing strategies and marketing profiles of the municipalities are "frozen" picture in a given stage of the municipality status quo—the moment in which they are drawn. They represent the economic and social situation, but without the territorial factor that is essential for sustainable development of the municipality. The area is one on which processes develop and are facilitated.

The methodology applied in Bulgaria is entirely consistent with this of the reports "Digital control worldwide." The index aims to provide an objective assessment of the state of the tested Web sites. For this purpose, index covers five categories that need to measure fundamental elements of electronic control. Of course, it is important to stress that this methodology was developed based on existing theories and key research on philosophy and the core of e-governance. The authors of the Index E-Government have included the following five categories: security and privacy; applicability; contents; available services; citizen participation and social commitment.

32.5.2 Nature of the Marketing Profile

Drawing up a marketing profile and successful start-up will improve the image of the municipal center and municipality through exposure of its main resources. In profile, it is intended to complete, integrate, and create added value for many initiatives started and planned on the territory of the settlements in the municipality in recent years.

Marketing profile should create a basis for sustainable economic, social, territorial, and environmental development of the municipality. Marketing profile of cultural tourism in the municipality must be part of the sector "tourism" and presented creative industries of each municipality in order the Web site to be functional, innovative, and perfect for serving advertising and to underpin attracting tourists, investors, and other users.

32.5.3 Objectives of the Marketing Profile

Strategic objectives of the marketing profile are:

- Create adequate image outside the municipality, and promote investment and use of services. The aim is to highlight the history, cultural heritage, economic, social and territorial resources, strategic initiatives that are already implemented and those in progress as well as the planned investment opportunities for new business initiatives to achieve on the territory;

- Support small business development by creating a favorable environment for development of entrepreneurship, providing consulting services and planning, marketing, information, and funding;
- Support the strengthening and development of existing businesses in the region by identifying new opportunities and better use of local resources and completion of infrastructure;
- Provide information about training and business services necessary for the development of the local economy;
- Identification and promotion of those industrial sectors for which the municipality provides advantages for the localization, implementation of program contracts for attracting foreign investments;
- Provide complete information for users of tourism infrastructure, natural resources, construction of technical and social infrastructure;
- Identify and support a range of projects, including in particular the participation of the private sector (Shishmanova and Signagina 2015).

32.5.4 Approaches to Achieve the Objectives in the Formation of the Marketing Profile

- Promoting the economic benefits of the region in order to attract new businesses and industries;
- Promotion of territorial, natural, cultural, and historical resources for tourism development;
- Presentation of the progress in construction of technical and social infrastructure complementary the image of the municipality.

32.5.5 Terms of Solving the Above Objectives

The necessary condition for solving the above objectives will be determined by the creation of reliable and complete information materials for the municipality. It should summarize the existing heterogeneous information about it, deliberately structured so that extolled virtues and its favorable possibilities in view triggers interest by potential business partners, investors, designers, and users of services in the municipality. In this direction should focus the group's efforts in developing the marketing profile of a municipality.

32.5.6 Problems of Created Marketing Profiles and Functioning Sites

It is necessary to describe the existing problems. Attracting foreign investment to solve the problems of the municipality is a major milestone in the guiding of any good municipal management.

At the same time in comparison with the tools that are used in the country so far, it needs to highlight the following key issues as:

- Poor architectural structure of the site to reach clearly and easily the required information by the user—investor, designer, citizen of the municipality, visitor —who are users of certain services offered in the municipality, as well as tourists;
- Lack of specific information that is of interest to potential investors—planning security, land and terrain, built-free warehouses, construction of technical infrastructure reaching them, etc.;
- Information available is inadequate and unstructured; it is of interest more for tourist visitors, than for businessmen and investors who are actually targeted marketing of the municipality;
- Insufficiently complete and total information for tourist construction: direct access to information of the tourist site, opportunity to reach by transport or walking to it, correct presentation of information about the natural, cultural, and historical heritage, etc.;
- Lack of technical capacity for timely updating of the fast-changing economic information;
- Unattractive photographs included in the profile that do not contribute to better illustration of existing competitive natural and anthropogenic objects;
- Costly form of presentation of the municipality in traditional printed brochure.

32.5.7 Opportunities of the Marketing Profile

Marketing profile should create the opportunity for:

- Delivering quick and easy access to important data to potential investors; brief and specific information;
- Possibility to obtain additional detailed information through links to other addresses;
- Profile opportunity to benefit from an unlimited number of users because the information is in electronic form;
- Direct access at any time to any user, anywhere in the world is;
- Quickly reflect any change;
- Quickly supplement with new information;

- Providing rapid content update, owing to changes in the local economy;
- Access to information also in foreign languages—English, German, French, and languages of neighboring countries if the municipality is border;
- Smaller cost to update the site compared with preparation of brochures; opportunity to prepare specific target printed materials.

32.5.8 Example Content of the Municipality Profile

The content of the profile must be selected in terms of the interest of foreign investors, planners, users of the municipality services, foreigners, and locals. Extensive information is given to the economic characteristics and qualifications of the labor forces, taxes and fees, legal requirements for environmental protection, and others. Technical infrastructure—transport, telecommunications, energy, water, and gas supply—is limited, including only the minimum for the potential user. Existing services means for inclusion and/or use of the specified service and useful contacts are also included. It provided the characteristics of territorial resources and their security plans and schemes. Distinctive and specific information about the municipality and information about quality of life is flanking and selected mainly in terms of opportunities for good leisure in short stay or to provide a fulfilling life of the family in residence of foreign nationals. For comprehensive information about culture, art, history (areas considered most widely so far in existing brochures) must be provided through links (by subsequent links) (http://www.flgr.bg/en).

32.5.9 Technology Process for the Preparation of a Marketing Profile

Creating a unified and standardized basic "template" for a marketing profile based on ICT will unfold over time and will be supplemented. Its algorithm aims to create such a profile that will be run on a pilot municipality, taking approve through opinion of all users—investors, designers, citizens of the municipality, visitors and users of services in general, and the administrative staff. This move will be made at the national level.

The technology of the process leading to a marketing profile consists of five stages. Working group on economy of the municipality defines as primary task to create favorable conditions to attract and absorb foreign investments.

The first and most essential phase is to develop a concept for marketing profile. This phase changes the view on the vision of the municipality and presentation of information in terms of the interest of potential investors and other users; for example, in this case a tourist or tourist company arised from familiarization with various practices that could serve as a model for the preparation of the electronic document.

The second phase includes preparing the structure of the marketing profile, i.e., selection and arrangement of the types of information to be included as content. It is a look at all the information available to the municipality, hitherto existing presentations and brochures, etc. It includes determining what information is of interest to foreign customers, what is missing and must be supplemented or revised. A draft of initial structure of the material is elaborated. A working group of experts from the municipality is created on which to offer this initial version for comments and additions. The working group should include experts from all major areas reflected in the marketing profile and an IT specialist of the municipality. It should conduct several discussions and adoption of the final version of the structure (http://www.flgr.bg/en).

In the third phase, the whole structure of the marketing profile is completed with information, as it is previously collected, processed, and sorted by relevant specialists.

The next fourth phase provides editing of all the information in order to be unified in one style for a document. In this case, concise and succinct style of presentation is very important. As marketing profile is aimed at people who do not have much time and are looking for specific information, having to be told as much as possible with the least possible resources.

The fifth and last stage is uploading via marketing profile of the Web site and the design of the electronic document by IT specialists of the municipality. The further development of electronic marketing profile is associated with additional appropriate graphic design and connection with the rest of the information existing on the Web site of the municipality, as well as with continuous and periodic updating of the information.

From the examination and analysis of various papers cited in the study and the literature, I can summarize the following:

Similarities:

- Cultural tourism is part of the creative industry;
- Cultural tourism could revive settlements;
- The cultural corridors and cultural routes improve the competitiveness of cultural tourism in a certain area, region, or country;
- The innovative cultural tourism creates a network of cultural—tourist products established along these corridors;
- Cultural tourism can lead to sustainable growth;
- Differences and new suggestions in the current study;
- The entry of the cultural areal of a given areal a party in the general treasury of the world represents a unit of the total network of cultural values and streams;
- This node of the general network leads to social and economic revitalization;
- In the development of tourist cluster segments the niches in the market must be clearly defined through multiple marketing research upon which can be promoted cultural and creative services satisfying the consumers;

- In the marketing researches for the compilation of the cluster, the entire leg of the journey having regard to the cluster itself must be present;
- Creative industry must accurately be incorporated into a single mechanism to cultural tourism in order to form and act creatively in a tourist cluster.

32.6 Conclusion

Anthropogenic and intangible cultural heritage are the basis for socioeconomic development of certain areas. Cultural tourism is one of the sub-sectors of the economy that is developing dynamically, especially if it used RDI and ICT (Web site and database). For detection, conservation, preservation, protection, stimulation, socialization, maintenance, management and promotion of cultural values also need to use RDI and ICT. In today's world of global challenges and drastic upheavals, sustainability of cultural heritage and cultural tourism is very vulnerable. Development activity and innovation, communication and information technologies are unbelievable need for stability. With ICT are conducted all the innovations and changes in the tourism economy. Widely distributed are the ICTs, Internet, and mobile smart devices (for information, booking, and payment function) for ordering and delivery of tourism services. Many innovative products of cultural tourism are already introduced in numerous European destinations. The use of broadband Internet access to ICT increases the value and quality of travel services and products without raising the price, while supporting cluster associations in the sector. Development and enrichment of promotional services and products must be based on ICT and its dissemination. Use of RDI and ICT to promote business and services in the field of tangible and intangible cultural heritage would be a decisive step toward better practices. Here are presented the logical model and the technology of the process leading to elaboration of a municipality marketing profile of developing cultural tourism. The steps that are necessary for its construction and the profile itself must be unified and standardized for all municipalities to obtain a synergistic and multiplier effect.

References

Alexandrova, E. (2011). Cultural tourism in high urban centres. *Journal of Science and Research, The Bulgarian Chamber of Education, Science and Culture, 1,* 76–83.

Bozhikov, V., & Yankov, N. (2003). *Strategy for conservation and sustainable development of cultural—historical heritage in Bulgaria, Guidelines, Fields, Sofia.*

Cultural Tourism. http://www.montana-vidin-dolj.com/home/.

Gauci, C. (2010). Innovation in Island Tourism European Economic and Social Committee, ESO/ 62 Brussels, pp. 1–13.

Marketing profile of the municipality of Blagoevgrad, Foundation for Local Government Reform. http://www.flgr.bg/en.

Research, Development and Innovation (RDI). 13. Digital society. 14. Cultural and creative sectors. 15. Transport. 16. Environmental policy. 17. Access to finance. https://www.oecd.org/ .../Competitiveness_Policy_Outlook_brochure.pdf.

Shishmanova, M., & Signagina, N. (2015). Creative industries. Cultural tourism in the marketing profile of municipalities. SWU University "Neofit Rilski", pp. 188–194.

Strategic Plan for the Development of Cultural Tourism in Bulgaria 2009.

Strategy for Sustainable Development of Tourism in Bulgaria 2014–2020.

Chapter 33
Cultural Heritage of Beysehir from Eleventh Century Until Today

Halil Akmeşe, Ahmet Büyükşalvarcı, Zübeyde Över and Sercan Aras

Abstract The phenomenon of cultural heritage is a treasure that narrates the common history to the people of a nation, strengthens the feelings of solidarity and unity among them, and is shared by everybody. In this context, the works of art created in Beysehir by Turkish presence which has continued from eleventh century until today still exist uniquely also across the world. The objective of this study is to demonstrate the cultural heritage works of Beysehir and to attract attention of authorities on this matter.

Keywords Beysehir · Culture · Cultural heritage

33.1 Introduction

The whole values of a community and all kinds of works which are produced by people, having a physical presence, received as a heritage from the past and wished to pass down to the future for some justifications, are named as cultural heritage. Meanwhile, the phenomenon of Tangible Cultural Heritage contains buildings, historical sites, monuments, and all sorts of things produced by human hands, and they are important works conserved and maintained on behalf of future generations.

Although little objects can be easily maintained and protected in museums, it is essential for immovable things to be preserved onsite. But nowadays these prob-

H. Akmeşe (✉) · A. Büyükşalvarcı · Z. Över · S. Aras
Necmettin Erbakan University, Nişantaşı Mah., Dr. Mehmet Hulusi Baybal Cd. No: 12, 42060 Selçuklu/Konya, Turkey
e-mail: halilakmese@gmail.com

A. Büyükşalvarcı
e-mail: abuyuksalvarci@konya.edu.tr

Z. Över
e-mail: berra_1305@hotmail.com

S. Aras
e-mail: arassercan1@gmail.com

lems are largely solved. Of course, the activities carried out in this sense vary from country to country in connection with the importance attached to this matter and how much they want to adopt their cultural heritage assets.

The researches made about Beysehir and Beysehir Lake Basin show us that the region was started to be used for settlement after Neolithic Age. These researches tell us that there are many settlements belonging to Chalcolithic Age, Bronze Age, and Iron Age, and Beysehir region has been used uninterruptedly for a period more than thousands of years. In light of this information, the works generated by Turks in Beysehir since the last quarter of eleventh century have reached from past to present.

From this point of view, these works reached today are required to be preserved and to be exhibited both on national and international platforms. Thus, the cultural heritage will have the importance deserved and the future generation will also be allowed to benefit from this.

33.2   Geographical Location of Beysehir

Beysehir District, which is under Konya Metropolitan Municipality, is located in a pit among West Taurus Mountains. A large part of this pit is covered by Beysehir Lake. Beysehir Plain extends to the southeast of the hollow lake. Taurus Mountains descend toward the plain with high, steep escarpments from the west and southwest (Alperen 2001: 4).

Surface area of Beysehir District is 2652 km^2. ¼ of this figure comprises Beysehir Lake, and 2/4 comprises mountainous areas. With these figures, it is the seventh largest district of Konya in respect of land width. Its land comprises 1 of 293 of Turkey, and its lake area comprises one of 1172 (http://beysehirkultur.org/ Access: 23/04/2016). Summers are hot and dry, and winters are quite cold and snowy in the district which has a transition characteristic between Mediterranean climate and continental climate (Günaydın 1999: 48).

The increase in height from the surroundings of Beysehir Lake toward the environment causes some changes on temperature and precipitation. Because of this, the decrease in temperatures and abundance of continental nature reduce the productivity of agricultural products and decrease the diversity (Kaya and Şimşek 2014). The surroundings of Beysehir Lake have gained national park status since February 20, 1993, and its national park area is 88,750 ha. The population of Beysehir is 71.730 as of 2015. This number is composed of 35.311 men and 36.059 women (www.nufusu.com).

33.3 History of Beysehir

The region containing Beysehir and the lake had been called Pisidia during the ancient times. The city known as Karallia in Pisidia took the name of Skerlos during the times of Byzantines (Alperen 2001: 3).

The city referred to as Karallia took the name of Viransehir in time. It had been re-established by Turkmens mostly comprising Ucoklar during the period of Sultan Alaaddin Keykubat in the first half of thirteenth century (Erdoğru 1995: 84).

Seyfeddin Suleyman among the Esrefogulları princes which is one of the Anatolian principalities had encircled this city with walls, and the city began to be called Suleyman Sehir after this period. This city was called the city of the prince after some while because of being the center of the principality, and its name was registered as Beysehir in time (Alperen 2001: 3).

Beysehir, which has been settled after Neolithic Age, shows us that there are many settlement areas belonging to Chalcolithic Age, Bronze Age, and Iron Age and Beysehir has a history of thousands of years. In consequence of our subject, we are going to mention the history after Turkish domination. Accordingly, it is known that Beysehir and surroundings had stayed under the domination of Byzantine Empire for many years, and Turks appeared in Beysehir region toward the end of eleventh century (Musmal 2005).

It is stated that Greeks living around the lake when Beysehir was an end region had established commercial relations with Turks and as a result of these relationships they have adopted Turkish customs and traditions in time. Seljuk Sultan I. Izzeddin Mesut wanted to conquer Antalya region when Greeks had friendly relations with Turks, and for this reason Seljuk forces were making attacks constantly to Antalya region (Turan 1993: 177). When Emperor Ioannes Komnenos was advancing toward Antalya at the expedition launched for Seljuks in order to secure Istanbul–Antalya road and to stop the attacks done in 1142, saw that the Christian people living on the islands of Beysehir Lake were subject to Seljuks, and attacked the castles located on the islands with rafts and skiffs, conquered these islands, and exiled the Christians under the administration of Seljuks to Konya (Musmal 2005: 4).

The region was on Istanbul–Antalya road and had a quite strategic importance during this period. Afterward, it also did not lose its importance after fell under Turkish domination, and even Seljuk Sultan Alaaddin Keykubat had a palace constructed in his name on the shore of Beysehir Lake (Arik 2000: 43).

33.4 Cultural Heritage

33.4.1 The Concept of Culture

The first scientific culture concept in the family of anthropology sciences was explained by an English Anthropologist Tylor (1871) as a whole containing the habits and skills learnt like arts, knowledge, tradition by human beings which are a member of a community or a culture (Güvenç 1993: 102). This concept, later, began to be used in Spanish, English, and Slavic languages. European ethnologists preferred to use the term of Culture for the groups that they came across after the second half of ninetieth century and described them as little, primitive. The word of culture means civilization in the field of science; education in the field of humanities; fine arts in the field of aesthetics; production, agriculture, and cultivation in the field of biology (Güvenç 1993: 98).

33.4.2 Cultural Heritage

It may also be called that this is the concrete example for looking at this concept, culture from a view of philosophy. It would not be a wrong expression to say culture has meaning intertwined with heritage. Even though discussions are made on whether culture is a heritage and whether heritage is a culture at various times, the heritage should not be ignored as an inseparable part of culture. Therefore, the cultural heritage may be mentioned as the essence of concretized, objectified, or conceptualized structures of the culture. Cultural heritage is a concept without boundaries and times. Therefore, it has become a deep area of interest for historians, sociologists, and philosophers. The difficulty in identification of what are heritages and what are not heritages underlies this versatile interest. The widespread of cultural heritage concept may be put forward as the reason of this (Üçcan 2002: 4). Cultural assets can be defined, in the widest sense, as movable and immovable works in the nature of documents providing information of past cultures, existing above ground, underground, or underwater (Asatekin 2004: 22).

33.4.3 Intangible Cultural Heritage

UNESCO has adopted the Convention for the Protection of Intangible Cultural Heritage at 32nd General Conference dated October 17, 2003. The second article of the Convention defines Intangible Cultural Heritage as follows: "Intangible Cultural Heritage" means practices, representations, descriptions, knowledge, skills defined by communities, groups and individuals in certain cases as a part of their cultural heritage and tools, instruments related thereto and cultural spaces. This intangible heritage passed down from generation to generation is recreated continuously depending on the interactions of communities and groups with their environments, nature, and histories, and it gives them a sense of identity and continuity; thus, it contributes to the respect for human creativity and cultural diversity. In the context of this Convention, only the Intangible Cultural Heritages, which are in accordance with sustainable development principles and mutual respect necessities of communities, groups, and individuals and conform to the fundamentals of international human rights documents, will be taken into consideration. The second clause of same article of the convention defines as follows the areas where Intangible Cultural Heritage appears:

- Oral traditions and narrations together with the language serving as conveyor for passing down Intangible Cultural Heritage;
- Performing arts;
- Societal practices, rituals, and feasts;
- Applications related to the nature and universe;
- Handicrafts tradition.

33.4.4 Tangible Cultural Assets

It is possible to classify Tangible Cultural Heritage as follows:

- Movable Cultural Heritage (paintings, sculptures, manuscripts, archeological artifacts, and so on);
- Immovable Cultural Heritage (monuments, archeological sites, historical city textures, and so on);
- Underwater Cultural Heritage (sunken wrecks, underwater ruins, and cities);
- Natural Heritage (natural sites having cultural aspects, like cultural landscapes, physical, biological, and geologic formations) (Ünsal and Pulhan 2012: 34).

33.5 Cultural Heritage of Beyshir Reached Today from the Turkish History

As mentioned above, Seyfettin Suleyman Bey, who was one of the margraves of Seljuk Sultan III. Gıyaseddin Keyhusrev, established Esrefogulları Principality by designating Beyshir as the administrative center. Historians were of the same mind that Beyshir had experienced its Gold Age during the period of Esrefogulları Principality (1277–1326) (Konyali 1991: 12). The throne was taken by Mubarizeddin Mehmet son of Suleyman Bey who constructed Esrefoglu Mosque bearing his name in 1297 and a castle in 1288 in Beyshir. Esrefogulları

Principality has been abolished upon the conquest of the city by Ilhanlılar's Anatolian General Governor Demirtaş in 1326 during the period of II. Suleyman Bey (Erdoğru 2006: 39). After abolishment of the principality, the city that was conquered by Eratnalılar after Ilhanlılar, came under the domination of Hamitogulları after a while. Later, I. Murat among Ottoman Sultans has bought the provinces of Akşehir, Beyşehir, Karaağaç, and Isparta from Hamitoglu Huseyinbey. Now Beysehir was under the domination of Ottoman state. However, this domination would cause Ottoman to confront with Karamanogulları constantly. This is because Beysehir was very close to Konya and Karaman cities which were the administrative centers of Karamanogulları power (Erdoğru 2006: 41–44). At the last time, Fatih Sultan Mehmet has conquered entire Karaman lands excluding İçel with second Karaman expedition in 1466 (Erdoğru 2006: 44).

33.5.1 Esrefoglu Mosque

Esrefogulları has almost become immortalized by granting a marvelous Islamic social complex in terms of Art History behind them in spite of their short life-lasting half century (Erdemir 1999a: 7). Esrefoglu Mosque has a worldwide reputation in this social complex which is the continuation of Seljuk architecture. It is the original and largest one of the mosques with flat roofs and wooden poles across Anatolia (Efe 2014: 23). Esrefoglu Mosque, which is standing in all its glory today and still continuing to serve, is located in İçerişehir Neighborhood in Beysehir city center (Konyali 1991: 217). It is understood from the inscriptions placed on the main door and subsequent arched interior passageway that the mosque has been constructed by Esrefoglu Seyfeddin Suleyman Bey between the years of 1296 and 1299 (Erdemir 1999b: 19). It is known that Esrefoglu Suleyman Bey Mosque constituting the most important structure of Esrefoglu Social Complex had a very important function with regard to the establishment and development of Beysehir.

33.5.2 Ismail Aka Madrasah

The madrasah is located directly opposite the west side of Esrefoglu Mosque. It is probable that the first status of the building also known as Taş Medrese was built by Suleyman Halil Bey. Afterward, it has been rebuilt by Grand Emir Ismail Aga. This is because there is a statement on the marble inscription of the madrasah: "This honorable madrasah has been built on behalf of Grand Emir. It was renovated in 771 hegira by the Father of Graces, honor of the religion and world, glorious Emir Ismail Aga son of Halil. May Allah reward his labor" (Konyali 1991: 255).

33.5.3 Castle Gate and Ramparts

It was constructed by Eşrefoğlu Seyfeddin Süleyman Bey who was a Beysehir Prince during the times of Seljuk Sultan II. Mesud, and the city inside was named as Suleyman Sehir. The ramparts of the castle, of which only the northern gate has survived until today, have been completely demolished and its foundations substantially remained under the ground. It is a castle ending at the northern gate by breaking northward after passing through the east about thirty meters from fish house, along the shore of the lake, behind the timber office located opposite the çömçem fountain (Suslu 1934: 40). The width of the castle gate that is the most obvious side of the remains of the castle is 2.80 m. Its arch has been made of white and black 11 stones. There are ruins of the bastions protecting the gate and protruding on both sides of the gate. The height above the ground of the gate is 7 m (Konyali 1991: 200).

33.5.4 Kubat Abad Palace

Kubat Abad social complex has reached today as a site ruins spreading around the bronze age mound called soil road and rocky hill protruding toward the lake, in the plain located along the foots of Anamas Mountains that is a branch of Taurus Mountains, in the southwest shore of Beysehir Lake. Building remains of all sizes can be watched in this region where Kubad Abad Palace is located at about 3 km to the town of Beysehir, which is known as Hoyran and called Golkaya in today's name. Three of them are the largest and high-quality ones. There is large palace in the northernmost, small palace at its south and the section called shipyard or boathouse located at water level in the southernmost (Arik 2000: 49). This is a palace constructed between the dates of 1235 and 1236 during the expedition to Antalya–Alanya organized by Seljuk Sultan Alaaddin Keykubat (Serin 2008: 5).

33.5.5 Malanda Mansion

The ruins known as Malanda Mansion are also known as the mansion of Saddeddin Kopek as mentioned by Ibn-I Bibi. This mansion, located on one of the mountain foot's waists, among streams, springs, in a pine forest, is 6 km away from Kubad Abad Palace and has a position easily overlooking the palace (Arik 2000: 272).

33.5.6 Maiden's Castle

Maiden's Castle, the second bird paradise after Manyas bird paradise in Turkey, was the shipyard and harem of Kubad Abad that was the summer Capital of Anatolian Seljuks. There were ruins of mortared walls, rampart, and palace remains from this castle. This historical island of 5 decares harbors more than 210 bird species (Arik 2000).

33.5.7 Vaulted Bazaar

It was constructed at the end of thirteenth century, and a person named Çavuşbaşı had it repaired at the dates of 1566–67 according to the inscription (Konyali 1991: 281–282). There is the castle gate at a distance of about 100 m in the north and Esrefoglu Turkish Bath in the west of the vaulted bazaar that seems to have great importance for the city. It was made ready for use after restoration during the years of 1975–1976 while it was in a wrecked condition. It is a subject of discussion whether this building, which sets a typical example for Ottoman Vaulted Bazaar with its current condition, has same plan with Bezziye Khan (Akyurt 1940: 120). It is also not known when the Vaulted Bazaar, that seems not used so much during nineteenth century, has been abandoned. After abandonment of the Vaulted Bazaar, center of the city should have shifted toward the other side, namely the square area (Ergenç 1996: 411).

33.5.8 Stone Bridge

This bridge has been constructed at the intersection of the lake and the Beysehir Creek, the tributary of Beysehir Lake. Even this location is named as bridgehead (köprübaşı) in documents, and there is even a madrasah known by that name in Beysehir during our examination period. Beysehir Bridge had been in need of repairs from time to time because of maintaining its importance during every period, and for this reason, it has been repaired or renovated many times. Sarre, who saw the bridge in 1895, has described as "a beautiful bridge built out of cut-stones and having seven arches", but now it has been destroyed insomuch that nobody can pass over it. The bridge was in ruined condition even in the years of 1868. Konya Governor, who came to Beysehir at this date, requested the bridge to be repaired, and it was ordered in the request sent to the center on this subject that the bridge would be repaired with the help of local people, but it was also stated that the people were not wealthy enough for helping. Although it is now known whether the bridge was repaired at this time, or whether another bridge was built in place of it, Beysehir People would attain a big and monumental bridge in 1912–1913. This bridge also functions as a

Regulator being a part of Konya Plain Irrigation. This bridge (Regulator), located in Beysehir, has also been built by Anatolia–Baghdad Railway Company during the period of Konya Governor Ferit Pasha because the task of irrigating the Konya Plain was assigned to this company (Muşmal 2005: 215).

33.6 Conclusion

It should be known that objects are always important for people. Because they give direction to the activities of humankind and concretize their thoughts and so people can create permanent works with concretized ideas. Still it can be said that not only the works, but also the masters who created those works have also gained great importance, and they drew interest from people.

Objects have presented information and idea of their period by reason of being able to exist for long term, provided the opportunity to evaluate the past lives of societies, and thus, they have caused important decisions to be taken for preservation of their presences. In light of these objects coming from the history, the formation of activities that give direction to the future of people has become possible.

However, these objects may be damaged by natural impacts like bad light, rain snow, and applications done knowingly or unknowingly by human beings. For these reasons, the protection of these works is of great importance when cultural heritage works are also considered to provide income to countries nowadays on account of their significant tourism potential in particular. Upon passing down the works that can be conserved to future generations, survival of the values, consequently the identities of the societies, which become increasingly important across the world, is ensured.

Beysehir, which has been a Turkish city since the last quarter of eleventh century, is fairly rich in respect of cultural heritage today. At the same time, many steps have been taken for preservation of cultural heritages in Beysehir having the status of national park. Konya Metropolitan Municipality is paying strict attention to achieve this and has undertaken the restoration works of historical buildings by performing necessary studies.

Apart from this, some activities are carried out to cause the Esrefoglu Mosque and Social Complex to enter the Permanent List of World Heritage of UNESCO.

When considered in this context, there is a splendid civilization, mathematics, information, and aesthetic lying in the background of Esrefoglu Mosque. This distinguished work is making contributions to the development of many science branches such as fine arts, mathematics, painting as well as science of history with correct applications. However, when we consider Esrefoglu Mosque and Social Complex in terms of faith tourism, it is seen that due importance is not given. Moreover, it can also be said that Beysehir cannot get necessary concern within scope of Silk Road. Considering the lack of required touristic promotion activities, Beysehir can be taken to the place it deserves in respect of tourism and particularly cultural tourism by bringing cultural heritages to the forefront. As it might be observed from the compilation of local researches such as Sumela Monestry and similar architectural and cultural heritages spread over Turkey, it might be concluded that Beysehir does not receive satisfactory attention with its cultural and architectural accumulation. Regarding the main limitation of this research, it might be said that there is not statistical or numerical facts and figures related to the exposition of cultural heritage of Beysehir.

References

Akyurt, Y. (1940). *Inscriptions, Beysehir inscriptions and Esrefoglu Mosque and Tomb*. TTAED, IV, Istanbul.
Alperen, B. B. (2001). *Beysehir and history*. Beyşehir: Büyük Sistem Dershanesi Printing House.
Arik, R. (2000). *Kubad Abad*. Ankara: Turkiye Is Bank Publications.
Asatekin, G. (2004). *Kültür ve Doğa Varlıklarımız, Neyi, Niçin, Nasıl Korumalıyız?*. Ankara, T.C.: Kültür ve Turizm Bakanlığı DÖSİM Basımevi.
Beysehir Culture and Promotion Website, Geographical Location of Beysehir. http://beysehirkultur.org/viewpage.php?page_id=1. Access March 23, 2016.
Edremir, Y. (1999a). *Beysehir Esrefoglu Suleyman Bey Mosque and social complex*. Beysehir: Beysehir Foundation Publications.
Erdemir, Y. (1999b). *Beyşehir Eşrefoğlu Süleyman Bey Camii ve Külliyesi*. Konya: B. Vakfı Yayınları.
Erdoğru, M. A. (1995). *BeysehirMaddesi*. Istanbul: Religious Foundation of Turkey, Islam Encyclopedia, TDV Publications.
Erdoğru, M. A. (2006). *BeysehirSanjak under the administration of Ottomans (1522–1584)*. Istanbul: Kültür Sanat Yayınları.
Gunaydin, H. (1999). *Human geography of Beysehir district*. Master's Thesis. Ankara. Gazi University Institute of Social Sciences.
Güvenç, B. (1993). *Türk Kimliği - Kültür Tarihinin Kaynakları*. Ankara: Kültür Bakanlığı Yayınları.
Kaya, B., & Şimşek, M. (2014). A research on the relationship between temperature, precipitation and Vegegation in Beysehir Region (Konya), Turkish Studies. In *International Periodical For The Languages, Literature and History of Turkish or Turkic Volume 9/8*.
Konyali, İ. H. (1991). Beysehir history with monuments and inscriptions (Haz. Savran A.). Erzurum: Ataturk University Publications.
Muşmal, H. (2005). *Social and economic structure of Beysehir and surroundings during first half of nineteenth century (1790–1864)*. Doctoral Dissertation. Konya: Selcuk University; Institute of Social Sciences.
Population by Years. http://www.nufusu.com/ilce/beysehir_konya-nufusu. Accessed March 23, 2016.
Serin, D. (2008). *Vegetal ornamentation on cruciform tiles of Kubad Abad Palace*. Unpublished Master's Thesis. Çanakkale: Onsekiz Mart University Institute of Social Sciences, Department of Art History.
Suslu, M. Y. (1934). *History of Esrefogulları*. Istanbul: Babalık Printing House.
Turan, O. (1993). *Turkey during the period of Seljuks*. Istanbul: Bogazici Publications.
Tylor, E. B. (1871). *Primitive cultures: researches into the development of mythology, phylosophy, religion, art and custom*. London: John Murray.
Ünsal, D., Pulhan, G. (2012). Türkiye'de Kültürel Mirasın Anlamı ve Yönetimi. In A. Aksoy, D. Ünsal (Eds.), *Kültürel Mirasın Yönetimi*. Eskişehir: Anadolu Üniversitesi Yayınları.

Chapter 34
Sustainable Tourism as a Factor in the Successful Development of the Regional Economy

Timur Absalyamov, Svetlana Absalyamova, Albina Absalyamova and Rustem Sakhapov

Abstract Nowadays, tourism has an enormous impact on the economy of many regions. However, not all regions are able to provide long-term sustainable tourism development in their territory. One of the most important causes of problems in the development of regional tourism is the imperfection of the regional system of tourism management. The article presents the study of sustainable tourism and investigates the conditions of the approach of modern tourism to this model. We analysed the impact of sustainable tourism on social processes. The article explores both positive effect of tourism on the economy of the region and negative consequences, primarily the problems of sociocultural character. The paper offers a number of measures to improve the management of tourism at the regional level. Their implementation will contribute to the self-development of tourism; it will increase the interest of local authorities and communities in the improvement of the quality of tourism resources, development of social infrastructure, transport, communications, telecommunication systems, culture, folk art and crafts.

Keywords Sustainable tourism · Regional economy · Self-development of tourism

T. Absalyamov (✉) · S. Absalyamova · A. Absalyamova
Kazan (Volga Region) Federal University, Institute of Management,
Economics and Finance, Kazan, Russia
e-mail: abstimur@yandex.ru

S. Absalyamova
e-mail: s.absalyamova@yandex.ru

A. Absalyamova
e-mail: albina@absalyamova.ru

R. Sakhapov
Department of Road Construction and Machinery,
Kazan State University of Architecture and Engineering, Kazan, Russia
e-mail: rusakhapov@gmail.com

© Springer International Publishing AG, part of Springer Nature 2019
V. Vasile (ed.), *Caring and Sharing: The Cultural Heritage Environment
as an Agent for Change*, Springer Proceedings in Business and Economics,
https://doi.org/10.1007/978-3-319-89468-3_34

389

34.1 Introduction

The problem of the development of sustainable tourism as a region's development driver is relevant to many countries and attracts the attention of scientists. Scientists search for an effective development model of sustainable tourism and the study of its impact on the sustainable development of the region (Eurostat 2016). Different countries develop the concepts of sustainable development of tourism at national level (WTTC 2016; UNESCO 2016; UNWTO 2016). The study of these concepts allows us to explore the best practices in this area and use them in our research.

Today, Republic of Tatarstan set the task of formation of the modern competitive tourism industry as one of the leading sectors of territorial specialization that will provide maximum opportunities to meet the expectations of Russian and foreign citizens in the tourism and recreational services (Absalyamov 2015). Tourism should contribute significantly to the socio-economic development of the Republic of Tatarstan in such ways as the increase of a profitable part of the regional and local budgets, investments, number of jobs and raising incomes.

34.2 Literature Review

The problem of the development of tourism and its impact on sustainable development of the territory is the subject of numerous studies of scientists from different countries. Andersson (2007) investigated tourists' attitude to ecological problems. Ballantyne et al. (2011) showed the level of tourist impressions and attraction of wildlife for tourists. The behaviour of tourists was explored in the work of Chiu et al. (2014). Choi and Sirakaya (2006) paid attention to community tourism. Most of them reflect the national characteristics of sustainable tourism, which are useful for the study of best practices in this area. Biggs et al. (2012) demonstrated the experience of Australia; Blancas et al. (2011) studied Andalusian case in Spain. Galley and Clifton (2004) went through the specialities of Indonesia. Thus, the novelty of our work is to study the Tatarstan model of sustainable tourism and its impact on the economic development of the region. This problem is very relevant nowadays because of the upcoming great events in the region (FIFA Confederations Cup 2017, FIFA World Cup 2018, Tatarstan's 100th anniversary).

34.3 Methods

We have developed a management model of development of sustainable tourism in the region, presented in the form of successive events (Fig. 34.1) that allow achievement of the goals, objectives and expected results.

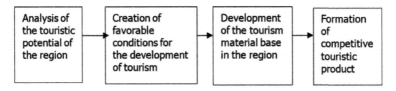

Fig. 34.1 Implementation plan of the management model of sustainable tourism development in the region

34.4 Research and Results

34.4.1 Analysis of the Tourist Potential of the Region

Analysis of the tourist potential of the region allowed us to identify strengths and weaknesses of the region.

Strengths:

1. The favourable geographical position and good transport accessibility. The Volga River is one of the well-known Russian brands.
2. The high cultural and historical potential (Kazan Kremlin is a UNESCO World Heritage Site, 13 historic towns and numerous sites of cultural and historical heritage, the diversity of cultures and traditions, etc.).
3. The presence of religious buildings of various denominations (Our Lady of Kazan, Qol Sharif Mosque and others.).
4. The presence of the tourist infrastructure and dynamic emerging sports facilities and leisure and entertainment centres.
5. Seasons' variety.
6. Local cuisine.
7. Carrying out a huge number of events designed to attract a variety of visitors (conferences, congresses, sports competitions at various levels, festivals, etc.).
8. Attractive conditions of the tourist market.

Weaknesses:

1. Lack of information about Tatarstan as a tourist destination.
2. Insufficient promotion in world and region tourist markets.
3. Lack of diversity of a particular tourist product.
4. Insufficient number of tourist accommodation facilities for mass tourist traffic.
5. Lack of organized tourism transport (air, rail lines, specialized bus and motor-ship voyages, etc.).
6. The lack of competitiveness of the Republic's tourist product (the ratio of price —quality is not compliant with world standards).
7. The predominance of excursion activity with its characteristic "peak" loads and short stays tourists.
8. The uneven distribution of tourist flow by seasons.

34.4.2 The Creation of a Conducive Environment for Tourism Development in the Republic of Tatarstan

The creation of a conducive environment for tourism development in the Republic of Tatarstan assumes implementation of the following activities:

1. Creation and improvement of the Republican normative legal base of tourism and regulation of tourist activity.
2. Providing a favourable investment climate in the Republic to attract investment for the construction and reconstruction of objects of the tourism industry.
3. The introduction of a system of activities aimed at the development of small businesses and tourism as its priority.
4. Perfection of tax regulation in the direction of creating a favourable tax climate.
5. Providing the necessary amount of state capital investments in reconstruction, construction and maintenance of major infrastructure related to tourism.
6. Development and implementation of a system of measures of state support of the enterprises of the tourist complex, working on the reception of tourists.

34.4.3 The Development of the Material Base of the Republic's Tourism

The activities for the development of the material base of tourism in the region are presented in the framework of formation of system of Republic tourist and recreational zones, identified as priorities on the basis of cluster approach. These include:

1. The development of tourism cluster "Sviyazhsk" with the formation of a tourist "core" (Sviyazhsk Island) in accordance with the guidelines of the concept of socio-economic, environmental and architectural and artistic revival of Sviyazhsk as a small, historical town, including the creation of local mooring sites for boats and service zones of tourists reception on routes of road and water transport.
2. The development of touristic recreational area "Bolgar" with the formation of tourist cluster "Bolgar State Historical and Architectural Museum-Reserve" that provides the creation of service zones of tourists reception on the routes of cruise and passenger water transport, the creation of guest houses and hotels and organization of a special place for festival and entertainment events, mass, national and ethnic festivals.
3. The development of touristic recreational area "Kazan" with the formation of the tourist "core" in Kazan with the use and further development of accommodation and restaurant facilities.

Implementation of the model involves risks that may impede the achievement of the planned results.

These risks include:

1. Macroeconomic risks associated with the possibility of deterioration of the internal and external environment, a slowdown of economic growth, investment activity level, inflation and the crisis of the banking system.
2. The financial risks associated with the emergence of budget deficits and the lack of budget funding.
3. Technogenic and environmental risks. Change of climate conditions. Global climate change may significantly affect the dynamics of tourist flows.
4. Geopolitical risks. The development of the tourism industry, both domestic and outbound, is greatly influenced by the political situation in the country and in the adjacent countries. The military and terrorist actions may lead to a decrease in tourist flow and reduce the investment attractiveness of the region.
5. International risks. The successful functioning of the tourism industry is directly dependent on the conditions of Russia's international relations with other countries. In addition, the situation on international markets, exchange rates, the degree of integration of the states is important in the tourism industry.

The evaluation of the effectiveness of tourism positioning model in the Republic of Tatarstan was conducted on the following assumptions:

1. The need to determine the effectiveness of the entire tourism industry, not every single specified direction.
2. Expectations of the planned growth of living standards of the Republic of Tatarstan population in the coming years.
3. Expectations of growth in business activity.

In Fig. 34.2, you can see the distribution of money flows, according to the model.

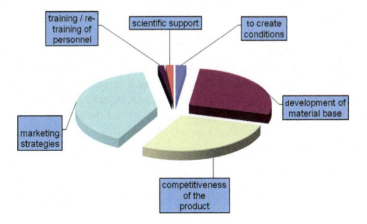

Fig. 34.2 Money flow distribution

Total amount of the investment in the development of the material base for servicing tourists includes the following types of costs:

• Development of tourist complexes, the creation and improvement of park areas, the establishment of information centres.
• The creation of new facilities of hotel complexes, recreational clubs and hotels, guest houses, camping sites, etc.
• Improvement of tourist zones.

Tourist service system is divided into two groups (Sakhapov and Absalyamova 2014):

• Direct service
• Indirect service.

The first group includes service accommodation facilities and catering, where there is a direct contact with the tourists.

The second group includes a range of businesses that serve the entire tourism structure.

The main social effect of the implementation of the programme of activities is the increase of welfare of the Republic of Tatarstan population.

It will appear from the two kinds of budgetary effects: increase in tax revenues and investment income.

The growth of tax revenues can be achieved by increasing the tourist flow.

34.5 Conclusion

On the basis of created model of management of positioning and sustainable development of tourism in the region, there were identified the main socio-economic benefits: welfare of the Republic of Tatarstan population, growth of business activity in the tourism sector, increase the total number of jobs, an increase in the financial revenues of the region, stimulating the development of related industries, the elimination of existing differences in the level of infrastructural development in the region.

The implementation of this model will allow consolidation of the positive trends in the sustainability of tourism in Tatarstan, which would entail the creation and renewal of existing tourist infrastructure and, consequently, the creation of the modern competitive tourism industry on the territory of the Republic of Tatarstan.

References

Absalyamov, T. (2015). The influence of cultural and sport mega-events on sustainable development of the cit. *Procedia—Social and Behavioral Sciences, 188*, 197–201. https://doi.org/10.1016/j.sbspro.2015.03.372.

Andersson, J. E. C. (2007). The recreational cost of coral bleaching—A stated and revealed preference study of international tourists. *Ecological Economics, 62*(3–4), 704–715. https://doi.org/10.1016/j.ecolecon.2006.09.001.

Ballantyne, R., Packer, J., & Sutherland, L. A. (2011). Visitors' memories of wildlife tourism: Implications for the design of powerful interpretive experiences. *Tourism Management, 32*(4), 770–779. https://doi.org/10.1016/j.tourman.2010.06.012.

Biggs, D., Ban, N. C., & Hall, C. M. (2012). Lifestyle values, resilience, and nature-based tourism's contribution to conservation on Australia's great barrier reef. *Environmental Conservation, 39*(4), 370–379. https://doi.org/10.1017/s0376892912000239.

Blancas, F. J., Lozano-Oyola, M., González, M., Guerrero, F. M., & Caballero, R. (2011). How to use sustainability indicators for tourism planning: The case of rural tourism in Andalusia (Spain). *Science of the Total Environment, 412–413*, 28–45. https://doi.org/10.1016/j.scitotenv.2011.09.066.

Chiu, Y. T. H., Lee, W.-I., & Chen, T.-H. (2014). Environmentally responsible behavior in ecotourism: Antecedents and implications. *Tourism Management, 40*, 321–329. https://doi.org/10.1016/j.tourman.2013.06.013.

Choi, H. C., & Sirakaya, E. (2006). Sustainability indicators for managing community tourism. *Tourism Management, 27*(6), 1274–1289. https://doi.org/10.1016/j.tourman.2005.05.01.

Eurostat official website. www.epp.eurostat.ec.europa.eu/portal/page/portal/eurostat/home/. Access February 2, 2016.

Galley, G., & Clifton, J. (2004). The motivational and demographic characteristics of research ecotourists: Operation Wallacea volunteers in South-east Sulawesi, Indonesia. *Journal of Ecotourism, 3*(1), 69–82.

Sakhapov, R. L., & Absalyamova, S. G. (2014). The usage of telecommunicational technologies in the integration of universities and business. In *Proceedings of 2014 11th International Conference on Remote Engineering and Virtual Instrumentation, REV 2014* (Article number 6784248, pp. 21–23). https://doi.org/10.1109/rev.2014.6784248.

UNWTO official website. www.unwto.org. Access February 2, 2016.

UNESCO official website. www.unesco.org. Access February 2, 2016.

WTTC official website. www.wttc.org. Access February 2, 2016.

Chapter 35
Efficiency of Cultural Routes: Between Wish and Reality

Andreea Andrei, Aurel Mototolea and Cătălin Nopcea

Abstract The fruitful conjugation of two factors (Romania's EU accession on 1 January 2007 and the fact that there is a large number of cultural and tourist landmarks in Dobrudja) led to the implementation of various national or cross-border cultural and tourist programmes. Museum of National History and Archeology, Constanta, depositary of a valuable cultural heritage, was partner in numerous such projects, among which a significant part was dedicated to promoting various national or cross-border cultural routes. Despite the generous and comprehensive concept, many of these cultural routes have fallen into oblivion, soon after the project was finished. We may mention here routes that included religious landmarks, art monuments or historic and archaeological monuments, many of them being unique in the country or in SE Europe (Roman Edifice with Mosaic in Constanta, the Monastic Cave Complex from Basarabi-Murfatlar, Triumphal Monument at Adamclisi). Most of the projects implemented in Dobrudja, either with European or with national funding, were based almost exclusively on promoting the cultural and natural heritage and not on finding solutions to the fundamental problems of this region. Present paper aims to identify the causes of this situation and possible solutions to revitalize these cultural routes in order to achieve the initial goals: promoting the historic and archaeological heritage and increasing the benefits for local communities. For an efficient tourism, it is not enough to create mere touristic routes, to highlight points of interest on a map, as long as the reality on the ground does not meet the expectations of the ones interested. Discovery of monuments and points of interest have a positive effect only as long as a contribution it is made to their preservation and protection. In this case, it does not suffice only to promote, but also to preserve the cultural heritage for sustainable exploitation from a cultural, touristic and economic point of view. As curators, we

A. Andrei (✉) · A. Mototolea · C. Nopcea
Museum of National History and Archaeology, Constanta, Romania
e-mail: andreiandreea03@yahoo.com

A. Mototolea
e-mail: aurelmototolea@yahoo.com

C. Nopcea
e-mail: nopceacatalin@gmail.com

© Springer International Publishing AG, part of Springer Nature 2019   397
V. Vasile (ed.), *Caring and Sharing: The Cultural Heritage Environment as an Agent for Change*, Springer Proceedings in Business and Economics, https://doi.org/10.1007/978-3-319-89468-3_35

have approached this case study by observing the contribution of historic and archaeological landmarks on the efficiency of this type of projects. In order to do so, we have collected data about the 16 cultural projects, in which our institution was involved, either as applicant, partner or just subject of the project.

Keywords Cultural routes · Dobrudja · Archaeology · Historical monuments Cultural tourism

35.1 Introduction

As it joined the European Union on 1 January 2007, Romania set on a rapid process of integration, modernization and economic growth, the access to various European funding programmes contributing greatly to this goal. One of the directions considered neatly winning in this process was the tourism, with an important component—the cultural tourism, as it is unambiguously stated in all official strategies (as it is stated in National Strategy for Regional Development 2014–2020. Development Priority 6: the sustainable tourism development requires fostering a competitive and sustainable tourism development regionally and locally through a sustainable promotion of the cultural patrimony with touristic potential and setting up/modernization of the touristic infrastructure). Cultural tourism plays an important role in the knowledge, preservation and promotion of cultural and touristic heritage of each country. While tourism was considered a primarily economic activity, heritage (either local, national or universal) represents a richness that cannot be considered a classic consumer product. In this respect, it is necessary to establish joint strategies for the cultural tourism development, which should be considered not only in terms of economic contribution, but also as a means of preserving both values and cultural heritage, by a better promotion of the history, local and national values among tourists and by supporting the intercultural exchanges that contribute to the communities' economic, social and cultural development.

35.2 Literature Review

The idea of the present paper came from studying some articles that analyse the phenomenon of cultural tourism in countries such as Spain and Italy, countries with a thriving tourist industry, which have accumulated a vast experience over the years. Referring to Spain, we may mention the comparative analysis of Urtizberea et al. (2016) regarding the provinces Andalusia and Basque country, or the one of Fernández Vázquez et al. (2016) for Galicia (Camino de Santiago). Regarding the experience of the Italians, of a great help were the papers included in the volume Il turismo culturale: Nuovi orientamenti di sviluppo economico-sociale (2010), presenting situations and various cases from different regions of Italy, as well as the unpublished Ph.D. thesis Analisi economica del turismo culturale in Italia (2013), especially for the methodology used. For the local area, a useful paper was Profilul consumatorului de turism rural (2013). We mention that our study is in its early stages, and further on, we intend to analyse other similar projects in Dobrudja region, projects that involved also other institutions, cultural or administrative; finally, this effort will result in comparative analysis with situations encountered in tourist areas by excellency.

35.3 Methodology of the Research

The present paper aims to highlight the importance of continuing the activities developed within the cultural and tourist projects, like cultural routes, even after the projects are successfully finished. As curators, we have approached this case study by observing the contribution of historic and archaeological landmarks on the efficiency of this type of projects. In order to do so, we have collected data about the 16 cultural projects, in which our institution was involved, either as applicant, partner or just subject of the project. These projects were developed beginning with 2007 and until present or, as in the case of LIMES project (see the list below, position 14), its implementation will be finished in 2018. The data analysed by us are the ones referring to the expenses on promotion and materials used, number of people involved in implementation and the receptivity (or not) of the local communities. In order to comply with publishing requirements, we have presented only the general conclusions, without cluttering the text with statistics.

35.4 Presentation and Analysis of Cultural Routes

On a regional level, Dobrudja (south-eastern region set between the Danube and Black Sea), suitable for housing since ancient times, has a high touristic potential, marked by two basic components: natural (landscapes, favourable climatic conditions, therapeutic value) and anthropogenic (historical and archaeological artefacts, monuments and works of secular and religious art, museums and museum collections, ethnography and folklore elements, recent accomplishments). Therefore, on the Dobrudjan territory a large number of touristic–cultural sights can be found, some of Southeastern European (the Monastic Cave Complex from Basarabi-Murfatlar; the Triumphal Monument from Adamclisi) or even European (the Glykon Snake) importance. The various programmes and projects drawn up in the post-EU accession aimed to highlight the economic and exploit of these objectives, one of the ways chosen being the cultural routes' establishment.

A significant part of the historical–archaeological sites from the southern part of the region (Constanta County) is in the patrimony and management of the Museum of National History and Archeology (acronym MNHAC), and here, we mean both exhibited heritage pieces, located in its Constanta headquarters and in four museums in the county, as well as the archaeological sites managed by the museum (the ancient cities of Histria, Adamclisi and Capidava; the Monastic Cave Complex in Basarabi-Murfatlar). This situation led to the institution's engaging into numerous local and international projects regarding cultural routes, initiated by private legal entities or by national or local authorities. Two complementary factors are worked in the favour of this achievement: the existence of the rich patrimony mentioned above and that the major museum sights (ancient fortresses and archaeological sites) are generally located in rural areas, around some small human communities. It all started from the premise, perfectly feasible in theory, that a cultural route means an increased tourists inflow, which is—in turn—followed by an economic revival of these rural villages, an income sources' diversification of the respective communities (where revenues come mainly from agriculture) and, last but not least, the creation of new jobs. The approach is consistent with the tourism's general trends, knowing that the activity is an important cog in the global economy gearbox, both in terms of international trade and as an employment's basic condition, being an increasingly complex phenomenon and bringing together people and resources, products and services, companies and their economic activity (Morère Molinero and Perelló Oliver 2013: 8). In addition, in an accelerated way, tourism is an activity that identifies, differentiates and exploits the advantages of a geographic region; therefore, the public administration shows an increasing interest in the creative powers of cultural tourism as a source of economic value (Fernández Vázquez et al. 2016: 241).

Starting with 2007 until this year, the Museum of National History and Archeology participated in a total of 16 projects proposing cultural routes and implementing the cultural tourism in Dobrudja and, in particular, in Constanta, projects that we present in the list below.

Projects with international funding:

- **Venus at the Lower Danube (Financed by: PHARE—CBC Romania—Bulgaria 2005**; Target: itinerary exhibition, scientific symposium, publishing of the volume "Venus at the Lower Danube"; Implementation period: 2007–2008)
- Development centre for elaboration of effective models for cultural tourism in the regions of Kavarna and Constanta (Financed by: Joint Small Projects Fund, PHARE—CBC Bulgaria—Romania; Target: cultural routes, 2 days long; Implementation period: 2008)
- Religious monuments of Dobrudja: identification and certification (Financed by: PHARE—CBC Bulgaria—Romania; Target: promoting the religious monuments at the Lower Danube, publishing a catalogue for presentation; Implementation period: 2008)
- Archaeological sites in Constanta County (Financed by: Ecos-Ouverture Programme; Target: Romanity route, trilingual brochures (RO-EN-FR) which present the touristic landmarks Histria, Tropaeum Traiani, Tomis, Roman Edifice with Mosaic, Callatis, Capidava; Implementation period: 2009–2010)

- Rehabilitation of the Triumphal Monument Tropaeum Traiani (Financed by: Regio—Regional Operational Programme 2007–2013; Target: architectural rehabilitation of the Triumphal Monument Tropaeum Traiani, arranging access road, parking lot and others; Implementation period: 2010–2013; http://www.mdrap.ro/userfiles/publicatii_regio14_2012.pdf)
- TRANS-TOUR-NET: Creation and Marketing of Pilot Cross Border Tourist Products in Dobrudzha (Financed by: Romania—Bulgaria CBC Programme 2007–2013; Target: are promoted MNHAC, Callatis Museum, Romanian Navy Museum, city of Histria, archaeological site of Adamclisi; Implementation period: 2011)
- Constanta County: A timeless discovery (Financed by: Regio—Regional Operational Programme 2007–2013; Target: 1 day long touristic routes (Murfatlar—Adamclisi—Ion Corvin—Oltina; Medgidia—Capidava—Topalu—Hârșova; Constanța—Ovidiu—Gura Dobrogei—Casian—Istria) and 2 days long (Mamaia—Eforie Nord—Eforie Sud—Techirghiol—Costinesti—Olimp—Neptun—Jupiter—Cap Aurora—Venus—Saturn—Mangalia—Hagieni—Vama Veche—2 Mai); Implementation period: 2011)
- Constanța, the first step in your long journey—promoting the touristic area of Constanța–Mamaia (Financed by: Regio—Regional Operational Programme 2007–2013; Target: promoting and developing tourism in the area of Constanta–Mamaia; Implementation period: 2011–2013; http://www.constanta-turistica.ro/)
- On the footsteps of the Argonauts: promoting the touristic route Constanța, Istria, Cheile Dobrogei (Financed by: Regio—Regional Operational Programme 2007–2013; Target: to promote the biodiversity and the cultural and historical heritage of the Istria–Cheile Dobrogei area, within the thematic route "On the footsteps of the Argonauts"; Implementation period: 2011–2013; http://www.histria-cheiledobrogei.ro/)
- Itineraries and novel events in Dobrudja (Financed by: Regio—Regional Operational Programme; Target: (a) enogastronomia—six itineraries in Constanta County which include vineyards, wine cellars and cultural, historical or natural landmarks; (b) natural and therapeutic factors characteristic to Constanta County—balneary tourism (Eforie, Techirghiol, Mangalia); (c) ethnic diversity characteristic to Constanta County, customs and traditions—cultural tourism (presentation of ethnic communities and of their specific cultural events—Turkish, Tatar, Lipovans, Russians, Bulgarian, Romani, Greek, Italian); Implementation period: 2012)
- LIMEN: Cultural Ports from Aegean to the Black Sea (Financed by: Joint Operational Programme "Black Sea Basin 2007–2013"; Target: to include Constanta in international cultural maritime routes and to establish cultural routes in the city for the passengers of the cruise ships coming to Constanta; Implementation period: 2013–2016; http://www.limenproject.net/)
- OLKAS: From the Aegean to the Black Sea—Medieval Ports in the Maritime Routes of the East (Financed by: Joint Operational Programme "Black Sea Basin 2007–2013"; Target: promotion of the Medieval city-ports of the Black Sea and Aegean Sea; Implementation period: 2012–2014; http://www.olkas.net/home/)

- RER: Route of Roman emperors and the Danubian wine route (Financed by: Government of Federal Republic of Germany; Target: to increase competitiveness between the two transnational touristic products; countries involved: Croatia, Bulgaria, Serbia and Romania; Implementation period: 2014–2015)
- LIMES: Development and promotion of an integrated tourist product and of cultural heritage: The route "Roman Frontier in the cross-border is between Romania and Bulgaria" (Financed by: Interreg VA Romania–Bulgaria 2014–2020; Target: creation of a touristic product, the route "Roman Frontier in the cross-border area between Romania and Bulgaria"; Implementation period: 2016–2018)

Projects with national funding:

- Archaeological sites in Constanta County (Financed by: Constanţa City Council; Target: trilingual brochures (RO-EN-FR) which present the touristic landmarks Histria, Adamclisi, Tomis, Callatis, Capidava; Implementation period: 2009–2010)
- Religious monuments and places of worship in Constanta County (Financed by: Constanta City Council; Target: promotion of religious monuments in Constanta County; Implementation period: 2009–2010)

As shown above, the mentioned projects are primarily focused on activities aimed to promote cultural routes, trails and activities proposals, as the common ground is the existence in the localities these routes involve of historical and archaeological or religious attractions, intended to be the main sightseeing points, other activities or sights being presented in a subsidiary. We believe that these aspects are the general line noticeable for both small communities and in the urban poles. In terms of typology, these cultural routes are a touristic product addressing mainly to "institutionalized" tourists and/or "mass individuals", less to the "non-institutionalized" and occasional "dawdlers" (Pop 2013).

35.4.1 Results, Comments and Suggestions

In our view, the aim of these projects was not fully achieved because, most of the times, even if the projects' implementation has been completed successfully, there is a lack in diversity (a wider cultural and touristic offer) and continuity (after the projects' conclusion). In order to give a boost to this kind of tourist activity, we believe we need a paradigm shift.

First, a relevant diagnostic of the cultural tourism sector reality is needed. Starting from this activity's focus—the tourist—we recently observed that, in the tourism industry, the tourists target alternative forms to mass tourism, based on the return to nature and authentic cultural values. The ascending evolution of eco-tourism and cultural tourism is influenced by the growing demand of the urban society (which focuses the financial resources) to be more active. The increased mobility of those tourists preferring to travel from one place to another, searching and discovering new attractions, contributes to the need of creating competitive touristic products on the local and national market.

The patrimony's role needs repositioning. Three types of patrimony can be detected as subject to touristic "exploitation": tangible (immovable heritage, in the general acceptance), intangible (spiritual events, artistic) and vivant (street show). Regarding our target region, most of the projects have mainly considered the tangible heritage, the cultural routes in general including visits to historical and archaeological or religious attractions. There are prerequisites for capitalizing the intangible heritage, as in recent years great strides in this direction were made, but the process must be boosted. Regarding the vivant heritage, as much as it is present in the urban areas, this one is not nearly as highlighted. Unlike other cities, the Constanta region attributes are not easily identifiable (Constanta—the peninsular area (maximum concentration of patrimonial offer) is being renovated and is touristic feasible only during the summer; Mangalia—touristic city by definition—preserves few of the initial characteristics; the two Eforie—summer villages; Techirghiol—health tourism can be a solution, but without a well-structured cultural tourism offer, success will be greatly diminished; Medgidia—once an important commercial pole currently provides little in terms of tourism); neighbourhoods are not cultural sights themselves (i.e. unguided trails through old neighbourhoods, urban areas well defined—banking area, commercial area, administrative area, etc.), and their inhabitants have no awareness of belonging to a particularly well-defined community (street, neighbourhood, town).

The efficiency of these popularization projects and the desired cultural tourism boost is contingent on creating and maintaining the technical structures of the beneficiary administrative units able to manage the post-completion process. For an efficient tourism, is not enough to create simple touristic routes, to underline the sights on a map, as long as the reality in the field does not live up to the expectations of those informed about these routes (either through own documentation on the Internet, on the concerned institutions' websites, through the tourist offer presented by travel agents, or by participating in various tourism fairs, advertising, media).

An important factor in this process is to create or maintain one's own identity, given that the rapid globalization advance means that every country, every city and every region must compete with others for its ration of consumers, tourists, investors, students, cultural and sports events (Anholt 2007: 1), which can unequivocally identify and place it on the world map. Although the battle seems to be given mainly for the economic resources, it does not mean the neglect of the local specificity that defining something the identity (Urtizberea et al. 2016: 52). We believe that we can identify an explanation for this kind of project failure: the lack of an established brand for each community; it—the community—broken from the cultural route chain, must be perceived as an independent entity, through what it represents itself, not through its belonging to something, not to be conferred on attributes not its own. Therefore, we consider advisable to maintain an identity where appropriate, and, when needed, a new analysis and a new approach to the objectives' specific features as to create one's own identity/local brand, with a high force of attraction for potential visitors.

As Constanta is the largest city in the region and, due to its economic potential and location, it is included in most touristic–cultural routes, we will present its patrimonial–historic situation in detail. Among Constanta's attractions (the biggest port on the Black Sea, the second largest city in the country, has no tourist information point!) present in almost all routes and widely promoted, many of them are not visited or are in an advanced state of decay. For example, the Museum of Sculpture "Ion Jalea" is open only 3–4 months a year, and together with the Port Museum—"the Queen's Nest", they remain quasi-unknown, not just to tourists, but also to the locals. The Municipal Casino, an emblematic building of the city, is in an advanced state of decay and can be visited only on rare occasions and only wearing protective equipment. The "Great Synagogue" of the city is a particularly important monument for the local history and is also in a deplorable state, being even in danger of completely disappearing in the near future unless measures of restoration and preservation are taken. This religious monument completes the picture of Dobrogea's ethnic and religious diversity—model of interethnic coexistence—along with other places of worship belonging to all ethnic groups and confessions established at some point in Constanta and Dobrudja (the Greek "Metamorphosis—Transfiguration" Church, the Armenian "St. Mary" Church, the Bulgarian "St. Nicholas" Church, "St. Peter and Paul" Orthodox Cathedral, the Roman Catholic "St. Anthony of Padua" Basilica, the "Carol I" Mosque, the Hunchiar Mosque), all concentrated in a relatively small area in the old city centre. Hotel "Intim", built in the early twentieth century, on the former Hôteld'Angleterre, where our national poet Mihai Eminescu lived for 10 days in 1882, is currently non-functional, though it is located in an area with many touristic and economic advantages.

Other archaeological remains scattered in the old city and the ruins of ancient Tomis included in the cultural routes are actually overshadowed by the new constructions which, although should protect and capitalize on them by the law, they hide them from the visitors' gaze (applicable to the basilica under Hotel Ibis, the North Gate of Tomis city, the Painted Hypogeum Tomb of Tomis, etc.). Although they are mentioned in the tourist maps, they cannot actually be visited and remain closed to the public for conservation reasons.

The "Roman thermae", along with the "Roman Mosaic Edifice", enjoys a good position at the exit from the Constanta Port Passenger Terminals and would therefore constitute an important tourist attraction. However, in this case as well, the inclusion of the above-mentioned attractions in the projects promoting tourism and cultural routes did not mean an increase in the tourists' number. The main reason is that the minimum conditions for visitation are not insured—sanitation area, ancient vestiges' restoration and preservation in order to stop their increasing degradation, correctly signalling the attractions with international languages explanations and finally permanent security service to protect the monuments and tourists. Unless urgent measures to rehabilitate these vestiges of great value (the largest ancient mosaic in Romania and given its initial size of approximately 2000 mp supposedly the largest in the SE Europe), the immediate risk is to remove it from the tourist circuit, which means, in addition to a great cultural loss, a great economic damage.

Therefore, the historical heritage, considered to be a cultural capital, generates an economic income stream that offsets and exceeds the material efforts made in its conservation and recovery efforts. (Hierro and Fernández 2010: 77–88) Therefore, we emphasize once more the urgent need to restore and preserve the existing cultural heritage, without which the cultural tourism, which has grown worldwide in recent decades, would no longer exist.

Regarding our museum, emblematic for the city and looked at on the whole problem, it is a necessary concern for bringing it into this century, increasing its diversity and attractiveness, making it more dynamic, more interactive (Nogues Pedregal 2003), using cutting-edge technologies designed to arouse the interest of young people and to get them closer to the exhibition spaces considered, often rightly, as being outdated. Property management involves not only conservation and research, but also has an educational function (formal and non-formal), with an important role in the regional development and tourism.

An important aspect is the rural–urban ratio and the disparities between the two categories in establishing of some touristic–cultural routes.

The urban environment is clearly favoured in this tandem, at least at this time, although the ongoing and rapid cityscapes' transformation (systematization, beautification, change of destination) makes—at least in some cases—the touristic presentation of the town to require frequent updates. Another significant aspect is the "change" of the tourist itself, the expectations and requirements; often its expectations are linked to the touristic product's personalization, which is relatively difficult in urban environments. However, there are shy beginnings, the concept of "volunteer guide", being currently applied only in Constanta.

In rural areas, the solution must be sought elsewhere. Here, the tourists appreciate more the local specifics and are interested in landscapes, wineries, local cuisine, folk performances. We consider suggestive example of Adamclisi town. In this area, there are three important historic-archaeological attractions: the Roman–Byzantine fortress, the Tropaeum Traiani shrine and monument, an important Danube Romanity vestige. This Triumphal Monument was restored in 2010–2013 period (see list above, position 5). The fact is that these rehabilitation measures did not have the desired effect, the increase in the visitors' number being insignificant following the monument's rehabilitation. Certainly, however, it will prove to be a good investment in a far or close future, but only unclear currently.

Perhaps one solution would be (both in urban and rural areas) looking for a mix between history and entertainment, culture and consumerism, tourism and inherent urban–rural processes, as it is highly plausible that the tourists can be attracted to theme parks, with multimedia shows and events, located both in urban and rural areas. Certainly we can say, however, that the travel consumer's habits are in constant change, therefore travel must always fold on its requirements.

35.5 Conclusions

Discovering monuments and interesting sights has a positive effect only as far as they contribute to their preservation and protection. In this situation, it is not enough only to promote, but also to preserve the heritage for a sustainable exploitation in cultural, touristic, economic terms.

A well thought out strategy, in the long term, for the tourism sector development requires close collaboration between operators (especially tourism, but not only) and patrimony managers to develop the attractions' management plans. They should involve all stakeholders, including the local community, but especially the local authorities and to contribute to developing the necessary infrastructure to attract a growing number of tourists. We mention among them: improving the access roads, car parks, toilets, tourist services, accommodation diversification, recreational and leisure facilities, proper functioning of the administrative, scientific and commercial services and, only then, the product's presentation and sale. Therefore, a collaboration between the cultural environment and tourism sector is imperative in order to bring forward ideas and proposals directed towards the diversification and improvement of the ties between the two sectors, aimed at creating a high-quality cultural offer, well structured for both tourists and local population.

The cultural heritage of Dobrogea and, in particular, of Constanta (the area we refer to herein) is particularly rich. However, funds raised mostly focus only on projects promoting tourism and not on the substance matters that we still have this area. Promoting the cultural tourism implies a valuable patrimony, or at least some outstanding sights, but well restored, conserved and enhanced in terms of tourism. Some other fundamental problems on the cultural routes infrastructure should be noted in this context—roads unsuitable for the organized tourism's development, unmarked cultural attractions, without a historical description, lack of parking lots, tourist information centers and other facilities absolutely necessary. In this way, many historic and archaeological attractions are not presented to the public and cannot be included in the visited circuits. Thus, we have untapped rich cultural resources; therefore, touristic and cultural potential in the area is not fully exploited in cultural, educational and economic terms.

Acknowledgements Information presented in this article was taken, if it was necessary, also with the approval of the management of the Museum in Constanta, from projects involving our institution, even though the authors of the present paper were not personally involved in all of these projects. This is why we present our gratitude to our colleagues involved in the implementation of these projects and who gave us useful information, as well as to the management of the Museum in Constanta.

References

Anholt, S. (2007). *Competitive identity. The new brand management for nations, cities and regions*. London: Palgrave Macmillan.

Fernández Vázquez, J., López Rodríguez, C., & Arévalo Iglesias, L. (2016). Turismo cultural y nuevastecnologías de la información: el caso del camino de Santiago y el fomento de la marcapaís. *Questión, 1*(49), 241–251.

Hierro, J. A., & Fernández, J. M. (2010). Un análisis económico de la conservación del patrimonio historic en España. *Patrimonio cultural de España, N., 3*(2010), 77–88.

Morère Molinero, N., & Perelló Oliver, S. (2013). *Turismo cultural*, Madrid.

Nogues Pedregal, A. M. (Ed.). (2003). *Cultura y turismo, Sevilla*.

Pop, I. (2013). *Profilul consumatorului de turism rural*. Ph.D. thesis, mss, Cluj-Napoca.

Urtizberea, I. A., Hernández León, E., & Tomàs, A. A. (2016). Local heritage in a global world: Heritagization of culture in Andalusian and Basque local contexts. *MemóriaemRede', Pelotas, 8*(14), 41–57.

II turismoculturale: nuoviorientamenti di sviluppoeconomico-sociale (BIT—BorsaInternazionale del Turismo, 18–21 February 2010, Milano) [Online] Available: http://www.beniculturali.it/mibac/multimedia/MiBAC/documents/1266332066827_OpuscDef_bassa.pdf [16 May 2016].

Chapter 36
Cultural Symbols in the Context of Communication—Identity Label and Link of Social Cohesion

Varvara Buzilă and Svetlana Lazăr

Abstract The authors highlight the value of the communication by means of symbols in the context of tourism, a kind of communication that helps individuals learn, in a rather short time, the culture and the cultural heritage of a people or of a community. The verbal symbols, object and gesture-like, spatial ones, etc., become in the touristic language visual attractions, edible, dancing, musical ones, etc., aiming to describe the constant historic effort, a defining one for a society and a culture, in order that it may preserve its tangible and intangible cultural heritage by means of the historical memory. The authors argue that the basic symbols of a culture represent a generous potential, always attractive for tourism development. It is because they represent very efficient tools for accomplishing the objectives assumed by tourism. The paper analyses and presents several main symbols of the communities from the Republic of Moldova, with significant parallels in the culture of other states from a large geographical area. They underline the necessity to offer local communities and touristic agents the possibility to develop local specific artistic activities that maintain the viability of the cultural heritage in all its acknowledged manifestations, by offering it an international cultural reception. The innovation of the project consists in identifying and promoting at a cross-boundary-level common heritage value. These values fit best of all the touristic practice of learning the unique originality, considered in the whole world, of three axiological symbols of the Moldovan society: ritual bread, wine and the tree of life. Thanks to the implementation of a pilot project was created the touristic route "HUNTING FOR SPIRITUAL TREASURES" which offers the possibility to know lively, through participation, the significances of these symbols that refer to the triumph of life and human creativity in an ecological natural environment. The project matches the European aims of asserting and promoting the cultural identities and of acknowledging the values of the tangible and intangible cultural heritage, as a guarantee of social cohesion. It views the development and diversification of the national and cross-border touristic product, the socio-economic development of

V. Buzilă (✉) · S. Lazar
National Museum of Ethnography and Natural History, ANTREC-Moldova,
82 Mihail Kogălniceanu Street, Chisinau MD 2009, Republic of Moldova
e-mail: buzila.varvara@gmail.com

© Springer International Publishing AG, part of Springer Nature 2019
V. Vasile (ed.), *Caring and Sharing: The Cultural Heritage Environment as an Agent for Change*, Springer Proceedings in Business and Economics, https://doi.org/10.1007/978-3-319-89468-3_36

communities, by means of the respect of the general human values. The paper is based on the results of theoretic and practical investigations of the common aspects in the development of culture and civilization for the durable touristic assessment of the anthropologic cultural heritage, of the tangible and intangible cultural goods, being the main identity basis for the socio-economic development and for the cohesion of the community.

Keywords Cultural symbol · Tree of life · Wine · Ritual bread Hospitality · Cognitive tourism · Social cohesion

36.1 Introduction

The man of the postmodern society lives in a universe of signs, as rich as the one where the archaic and traditional societies once lived. Like its predecessors, this man cannot imagine his/her own existence without the communication by means of signs. The formation, survival and progress of societies depend as well, why not acknowledge this evident fact, on their ability to develop their semiotic set of cultural tools: languages, codes, channels, signs, symbols, etc. Human communities build their social, cultural and ethnic identity by means of updating permanently, reconsidering and reviving this set of tools that leads, firstly, the social, the historic and ethnic memory. These identities relate between themselves on several levels within the most developed and organized structures of the "Semiosphera", i.e. the language and the life of signs (Лотман 2004). The ethnologist Jean Cuisenier considers that the ethnicity of a people is that something due to which a people bear its identity as people. And this identity "consists neither in language, nor in territory, religion, in that or other peculiarity, but in the project and the activities that make sense of the usage of language, of ruling a territory, of practising customs and religious rituals" (1999). This project unites and harmonizes the social, economic and cultural efforts of all the structures of the society. According to the same author, the identity discourse of Europe is shaped by the cultural communication at local, regional and world level of over 200 peoples or ethnos living on the continent. After the lapse of two millennia and a half, by "ethnic groups" we understand "communities that bear a certain cultural heritage, passing it from one generation to another, in order to display themselves in contemporary life, in order to give value to their identity and make it known, sometimes even through bombs and weapons" (Cuisenier 1999). As for us, like many other people, we consider that it is much more useful to make known your identity by means of knowledge and promotion of identity, so that these would be respected.

Knowing about your own culture and of other people—an always up-to-date touristic objective—becomes more efficient by using signs and symbols. In this context, tourism may be understood as a pleasant communication, well structured, of a group of people, over a certain time span. In the meantime, it is a convention among the participants in the tourist activities, a fact that supposes the usage of a symbolic set of tools, specific for the cultures that interact. From a symbolic perspective, man acquires the statute of tourist for a limited time span, always a short one, while his expectations are maximal as value. Persons, who offer services in the field of tourism, practise this quality much more time, in order to offer services according to the requirements of tourists. In order to increase the efficiency of communication during the time allotted to touristic activities and to fulfil the expectancies of guests, hosts frequently appeal to symbols, assuring themselves that all the participants in the event know and accept the conventions of the symbolic thought. We can demand ourselves how much would increase the pleasure of a communication specially focused upon discovering symbols in a culture with a considerable age and symbolic structures relatively well preserved, which maintain their viability by means of traditional institutions, of cultural, educational and economic ones.

The study of the symbolic tools, of the strategies of integration, and of the local and regional symbolical behaviours enforces, on one hand, the identity spirit and, on the other hand, it offers new perspectives to the social practices of cooperation between different nations.

A tourism based on knowledge, on enjoying and consuming symbols, these being essential for a society, offers a large number of axiological, multicultural and economic opportunities. Considering the region of south-eastern Europe, to which belongs the Republic of Moldova, Stahl wrote about a unitary whole, a result of the historical evolution, comprising a great variety of features: "... mentalities and practices reminding of Prehistory or heathen Antiquity coexist with Christian and scientific ones; modern industries have established in places where people still travel by carts driven by oxen, or ride donkeys; strong traditional regions are situated in the neighborhood of regions where the past seems to have disappeared..." (2000).

The management of the domain takes into consideration this potential, acknowledges it and seeks for new reference marks. Declaring from the beginning the option for the discovery of the main symbols, on which the culture of a people was edified, we enlarge the perspectives of symbolic communication which tourists expect. This is especially because the symbols considered to be essential for a people frequently have a similar prestige in the culture of other peoples, geographically more close or more remote. Always using the same symbols, people have understood each other better. At the same time, people have spread them on a larger areal, investing them with more significances and thus with prestige within cultural practices. Symbols have such a high prestige that it is not possible to learn about the culture of a people without symbols. Otherwise, in order to understand better what are the best and the most beautiful values of a people, you have to accept the lively experience offered by the symbolic communication.

36.2 Hospitality and Symbols as Cultural Heritage

The field considered here is cognoscible tourism, addressed to active people, those that are eager to learn about new cultural realities, to discover cultural diversity in its most expressive hypostasis. In the Republic of Moldova, a country of villages, the spirit of the traditional culture is still rather strong, because people, especially those from rural localities, but also those living in cities, have a special sensibility towards tradition. This sensibility marks both daily life and the ceremonial, ritual one. However, this traditionalism is neither ostentatious, nor a declarative one. It is experienced naturally, according to behaviour norms prescribed by the community. Traditional norms state that you should offer the foreigner the best, so that he/she would feel like at home.

Hospitality is an essential quality in the Moldovan society. Written records, being in fact opinions of travellers and scholars, witness the practice of hospitality in various forms, during the last three hundred years (Buzilă 2004). People in Moldova have an outstanding artistic spirit that can be noticed in their households (houses), in the objects that decorate the interior, in the art of preparing food and serving meals, in the ways of singing, dancing and in their speech. They are hardworking, endowed with a kind heart, generous and open towards cultural diversity. Their spirit becomes more evident during feasts, when communities assemble to perform their activities.

The calendrical customs, beginning with New Year and ending with Christmas, are based on the stages of the sun and the moon and on the rhythms of the vegetal cycle of nature, which influences the agricultural labour. These customs display, during the year, plenty of occasions to experience feasts together with the entire community. Looking forward for these feasts, families and communities prepare long before, embellish the aspect of households and settlements and undertake considerable expenses in order to prepare special meals. People accept guests and tourists to celebrate together these customs. The interested tourist can see the practice of *cumetrii*, i.e. the customs on childbirth, marriages and funerals.

A feast of special hospitality is the *hram*, i.e. the day of the patron saint of a settlement. In the past, until the 70 years of the twentieth century, it lasted three days, but currently one day. The *hram* is celebrated on the day of the settlement's patron saint. The analysis of the celebrations of *hram* in the region under study proves that these are mostly practised in autumn, less in spring and summer. This temporal choice resulted from the tradition—winter was the season of weddings, offering a good opportunity for hospitality, while in spring and summer people were concerned most of all with fieldwork. In autumn, after they had gathered harvest, people possessed good reserves for celebrating the hram. Because the main activity of villagers is agriculture, the majority of *hram* days are in autumn.

During the *hram*, guests come to the village and villagers invite them to their houses. As a rule, during the first part of the day, different sport competitions and exhibitions take place, while in the second half of the day traditional dances are organized in the centre of the locality, where all the inhabitants and guests participate. Thus, the *hram* day turns into a common feast with food and joy. Nowadays, people prepare for the *hram* day much food so that it would be enough for all the potential guests. In general, the *hram* means the assembly of all the relatives in the same space, under the auspices of the holiness of the feast dedicated to the patron saint who protects the local church.

Hospitality has been and continues to be an outstanding feature of the character of the inhabitants of the Republic of Moldova, becoming a distinct mark of all its inhabitants, due to the social behaviour of Moldovans. During the centuries, Moldovans have been tolerant, generous and hospitable, and continue to be like that, in spite of the historic events that affected their normal course of life. It is the *custom of the land*, i.e. the set of unwritten laws that functioned for centuries before and after the adoption of written law codes, due to the tradition, which imposed hospitality as a social norm. Maybe it was nourished, on one hand, as a remedy or as a capacity to adapt to the constant changes of the cultural alterity and, on the other hand, as a permanent will of strengthening the whole family and the village community. Moldovans have inherited and passed on hospitality not just as a fundamental feature of their group character, but also as an institution of hospitality. It means that hospitality has been and is displayed by all the social layers: from top to bottom. It was imposed and permanently managed by traditional and modern social institutions, functioning on the basis of a very strict complex of syncretic social representations, taken from all the cultural forms. Hospitality comprises several systems of the social domain: morality, ethics, economy, religion, politics, ritual, ceremonies, but also daily life.

In the archaic and the traditional culture, hospitality, as a social phenomenon, is governed by custom and ritual, while in the modern one it is more associated with the field of ceremonies and etiquette. Out of these relationships result the differences between the historical forms of hospitality and the contemporary ones. Although basically this kind of social behaviour has clearly established rules, performers and roles, being respected in various time contexts, the behaviour of the guest also differs from that of the modern guest. The older are the sources concerning the phenomenon of hospitality, the more we discover its code, its symbolic character, bearing numerous significances. On the contrary, nowadays it is simpler, less sacred, more nonconformist and personalized.

Hospitality bears a superior place within the system of values specific for the traditional culture. It designates an indispensable form of human relationship. It may be considered as a proof of the capacity of groups and of their members to be sociable, to accept diversity and the other one's difference in a tolerant way, with respect and generosity, thinking firstly about universal values.

Hospitality may also be understood as a social mechanism directed towards the inner organization of communities, in order to tolerate the differences between your own identity and the alterity of guests, to manage their relationships in the name of the common good. Performing it naturally, i.e. according to the traditions, human communities indirectly strengthen the vitality of their own culture, although they experience a seeming unequal exchange of values.

The model of our hospitality still is a traditional one, with all its defining mechanisms, components and marks. The ritual bread, with all the diversity of forms consecrated through tradition, is present in all customs and traditions. Bread is both an aliment and a symbol, or an objectified symbol with a great capacity of representation. The main characteristic of the ritual bread in Moldova is the intertwining and twisting of two, three and several rolls of dough. After baking, breads become alike sculptures. The specific forms of the ritual bread are baked in order to personify Christmas (also known as Father Christmas), New Year and the Saints. There is a clear link between the significances of these breads and their form, the latter being confined to the sign of the infinite. The fact that the Romanians from other regions of the Romanian cultural area, as well as the Bulgarians, use other forms within the feast of the Saints (Mesnil and Popova 1992) proves that these models of bread have a local character, being confined to a larger context of representations. The most frequent form is the circle and, by general-ization, it is called *colac* (a kind of traditional bread, of circle form). Round, big *colaci* are given to the main performers during all the customs referring to human age: *cumetrii* (baptism feast), weddings, funerals, remembering the dead ones. The cultural practice witnesses over 200 forms of ritual bread, each of them having its form, name and distinct significances within customs. From an iconographic per-spective, these forms of bread make a common system with the folk ornaments (Buzilă 1998).

The Republic of Moldova is one of the 70 countries of the world specialized in the cultivation of wine grapes and in producing wine. Because these are century-old crafts in the Romanian cultural area, they have evidently shaped the traditional civilization and culture. The consumption of wine represents a reference cultural complex. It expresses, by means of rites, customs and ceremonies, deep contents belonging to the folk philosophy and ethics, marked by myths, beliefs and customs. "Wine drinking creates a state of wellbeing, due to its euphoric qualities and it is tranquilising, producing relaxation. It generates pleasant physical impressions, stimulates joy, enriches imagination, mitigates sadness, stimulates communication, eliminates social barriers, creates the sentiment of power, of freedom from obses-sions or depression, influences the moral state of man" (Costea 1995).

Because wine drinking is firstly a social and ritual act, and because of the specific of this drink to produce a state only it can create, it is natural for this action to establish from the very beginning some behaviour norms, some clear attitudes among the participants. These indications are traditionally promoted by means of well wishes. The verbal language is the most explicit and fit for establishing a relationship of communication. The standard of the entire ritual is honouring wine. It concentrates all the moral qualities of the traditional world. To honour wine means more than drinking wine with someone. It means to honour the other person, to welcome and praise that person. The bearers of traditional culture insist on this expression. To honour wine means to have a state of spirit different from the common one. It means to raise above other states of spirit, to be ready for a special communication, required by ritual prescriptions.

The space destined for receiving guests in our tradition is called *casa mare* ("the great house"). It is the largest room in the house, the best fit out, demonstrating by means of its objects the prestige and the age of the family from the community. It is equipped according to the tradition, with different items of furniture, rugs and other emblematic fabrics, inherited or manufactured by that family. These items, made of local raw material, establish the link with nature and have as ornament mainly vegetal motifs. The flowers woven, embroidered or carved on different objects prove the wish of their creators to make the world nicer. We frequently meet on rugs representations of the sun, waters, birds, humans and trees, so that the great house becomes like a small universe. During feasts, people contemplate this universe; they feel at ease in the context of customs, together with their guests.

36.3   The Tree of Life, Ritual Bread and Wine

Having a great capacity of representation, alike some vehicles of time, symbols offer the possibility to travel through time and space, shorten distances, increase the comprehension of the relationships among people, between them and cosmos. Out of several symbols that shape our folk culture, we have chosen three symbols, each of them concentrating rich meanings: The tree of life, ritual bread and wine. Among these three fundamental symbols, there are several similitudes, which tourists gradually discover, playing the role of seekers for spiritual treasures. All of them are symbols of life; this is the reason why they are constantly present in the customs related to human ages (birth, wedding and funeral). All of them link man and nature, because in the folk culture man is perceived as a child of nature. Paradise, as an ideal space, is conceived as a garden with fruit trees, where a river of wine and one of milk flow.

Symbols highlight, through their expressions, essential links between human existence and Mother Nature. They develop the functions analysed by Chevalier and Gheerbrant (1995) and, for this reason, they fit perfectly the options for tourism. Symbols have the function of exploring; they assist the acknowledgement of less known aspects. A ritual bread is the expression of sacred, of folk morality and of the labour of ploughmen.

The function of the symbol, as a substitute, reveals its essence. It always represents something else according to a convention. At first, we discover the symbol as an independent entity and then we perceive it as a messenger, as the substitute of someone else. The tree of life is a universal symbol, bearing several significances. It is known in all cultures, in all civilizations, great and minor, ancient and modern, in all religions. In the Romanian cultural areal, it is known under different names: tree of life, world tree, cosmic tree, world axis. The image of the tree matches these significances through symbolic associations.

These hypostases are illustrated along the touristic route, being centred on the idea of the "tree of life". Its image can be seen in various artistic forms: on rugs, towels, traditional costumes, in architecture, on pottery; it is associated with ritual bread and grapevine. The image of the tree, in a great variety of representations, beginning with the simplest stylized ornamental motifs to the most complex, but also as a ritual object present in the ceremonies related to funerals and to remembering the dead ones, can be discovered and admired in all the locations of the route. Its leitmotif is the same like in folktales: the person in touch with this tree gains eternal youth and life without death. The motif tree of life was attested in Moldova 7000 years ago, and it is widespread in the Romanian traditional culture. It can take the image of the grapevine and bear several significances, starting with sacred ones, cosmogonic and aesthetic. The wine grapes or the wine which joins bread in all the customs has therapeutic and energizing qualities, being perceived as a source of life. Tourists will learn about these traditions by participating in them.

Symbols mediate or intermediate; they have the capacity to support our comprehension across considerable areas and realities. Thus, the cosmic tree comprises and displays the universe through several significant details. The funeral tree from northern Moldova is decorated with several ritual breads, being arranged in a tripartite order, corresponding to the three levels of the world: underground, terrestrial and celestial one. This function of mediating is likewise important; through it, the symbol links phenomena, objects and persons within significant relationships. Thus, the tree branches embroidered on the sleeves of the shirt with *altiță* (an embroidered piece of fabric on the shoulder), in the female costume, create a bridge from the woman wearing this cloth to its alter ego (simulacrum)—the tree. The association between human and tree is frequent in the folk culture. They say that each human has his/her tree. At birth, parents plant a tree, in the name of the baby, and cherish it like a child. During the funerals from Moldova, they prepare the tree of life, in the name of the dead one, and offer it as a gift to a younger person, so that he/she would continue the projects of the one who left for the otherworld. On this tree are hanged all the things necessary for maintaining life: sweets, fruits, ritual breads, cup, clothes and shoes fit for the dead one. When they offer these things, they say: "Take this tree. In this world it belongs to you; in the otherworld it belongs to (they pronounce the name of the dead one)". It is believed that human soul mounts through this tree to the skies. For this reason, they put in it the ladder of the soul, having the form of a bread.

Symbols join known realities and unknown entities, making the latter relevant. The tree of life links worlds. World axis is situated in the centre of the universe, integrating it according to its distinct signs. Wine, alike bread, unites, solidarizes people, making them a part of the community. During weddings, guests are invited to taste the bridegroom's *colac* (traditional bread, of circle form) and the bride's *colac*, in order to be lucky. Several ritual breads accompany the stages of the wedding, gradually mediating the union of the families belonging to the newlyweds, and the creation of a new family. The ritual bread from Moldova is original and imposes itself in the world through the diversity of sculptural and volumetric motifs, taking geometrical, vegetal and zoomorphic forms. During the customs is used a bread of a higher quality than the daily one. The ritual forms of bread are a main symbol in the customs that mark human life and the feasts of the folk calendar. Bread starts to embody the divinity, concentrating all the value vectors of the society.

The consumption of ritual bread is anticipated by the ritual of moulding and baking it with the participation of tourists. Each tourist should know better the taste of the ritual bread and its distinct forms. For this reason, tourists receive everyday a significant bread in the bag and spend the whole day under its sign, discovering pleasant cultural realities. Food communions unite most rapidly people.

The pedagogic function of symbols is the closest to the therapeutic one. Watching, creating, consuming symbols, people feel themselves members of the great communities that bear this heritage, experience it lively and share it generously with guests. This participation makes people simplify their attitudes and get acquainted with the others, gain new experiences and the respect for communities, values and ideals. Symbols are identity marks. We can also experience the joy of other cultural identities, opening new horizons of alterity, accepting the challenges of other identities. Safeguarding the cultural heritage in localities, passing it on to younger generations, takes place by assimilating the symbolic thought, by assuming the cultural marks of the group. The more the marks and the values expressed by them are common for several communities, the more increases the unity of nations.

The touristic route with the generic title *The tree of life* aims the acknowledgement, the preservation and promotion of the values of the cultural heritage of the Republic of Moldova by means of universal symbols, common for several states from the Black Sea region. These symbols are represented through the *tree of life*, the *ritual bread* and *wine* that aim to display the value of important traditions from the local life and culture within an international touristic product, having the impact of stable development of local communities. The new touristic product, supported by modern technological facilities, uses authentic, valuable traditions from Moldova. It offers another form for the development of the cultural heritage and for the touristic development of the localities selected within the project. The route lasts 3 days, when visitors discover diverse aspects of ancestral traditions from the target localities, centred on these symbols.

This heritage route is confined to the communication through symbols and comprises ten different touristic locations: museums, vineyards, a fortress, a monastery, a touristic halt, an archaeological landscape, a rural touristic pension, a cultural centre, a wine collection. In these contexts, the required symbols are essential; they express the creativity as well as the generosity of our people. They will be seen in various hypostases consecrated through tradition, in museums and houses. They will be tasted, drunk and prepared. They will be admired as works of art, but also will be created so that tourists can participate in discovering their significances, alike seekers for treasures. Each of these locations emphasizes either all the three symbols—the tree of life, ritual bread and wine—or one or two of them. But in all the cases, the activities suggest the homage of the natural setting and the triumph of life. Tourists have different possibilities to become "seekers of spiritual treasures" within century-old traditions. By participating in different traditional activities centred on preparing, ritual usage and consumption of the objectified symbols: the tree of life, ritual bread and wine, tourists have the possibility to discover the most interesting cultural manifestations of these universal symbols in various settings where they appeared and are practiced. Like a real seeker for treasures, each tourist will receive a Magic Bag where he/she will gather, along the route, souvenirs–treasures bearing these symbols. First of all, these souvenirs are various ritual breads, wine pots, objects of folk art. The route provides the knowledge of various manifestations of these symbols of life, which address both the artistic imagination of tourists, creating them a pleasant state of spirit, and their gustatory senses, through the ritual bread and wine.

Starting with the visit to the oldest and richest museum of the Republic of Moldova—The National Museum of Ethnography and Natural History—holder of the proofs concerning the local development of the cultural heritage, tourists will be tented to learn about the millennial experiences of life and living of the native inhabitants. Foreign guests will observe them also through active participation in their transmission up to nowadays. Tourists will understand better the meaning of the native soil for the inhabitants of Moldova (from peasant to academic), as well as the perspectives of efficient economic growth of local resources and the amelioration of the level of life of the inhabitants of this zone. The choice of this project, wholly fit to the specific of the work and leisure activities of the inhabitants of Moldova, will draw the attention of local creators and will contribute to the diversification of the touristic product, to the adjustment of the standards of touristic activities to the world ones.

36.4 Conclusions

Being passed on from one generation to another, because they perpetuate visions, practices, experiences and values, symbols can be understood as playing the role of social genes. They appeared from the necessity of people to communicate, at the beginnings of mankind, when people manifested themselves as social beings. Symbols manifest mostly a socializing function, integrating people within communities, helping them build relationships with the others. Tourism supposes a continuous socialization, being facilitated by the use of symbols. The diversity of these symbols offers plenty of ways for mediating socialization. The choice of these three main symbols—the tree of life, ritual bread and wine—as reference points for tourism, is favourable both for the providers of services and for their beneficiaries.

Hospitality is one of the essential values of the Moldovan society and the guarantee for the development of tourism. It takes different aspects in rural communities, as well as among the providers of touristic services in the urban area. This is why the touristic route comprises its numerous manifestations.

The main concern for discovering symbols and their significances pertains to the domain of the feast which involves special human emotions. Feasts enforce sentiments, test the system of values, stimulate communication and human behaviour, solidarize community, assert its social fundaments and prove the prestige of people and values. Tourism is like a feast that lasts as much as tourists, considered to be guests, are hosted. In the scenarios of feasts from the Republic of Moldova are traditionally used several main symbols, bearing rich significances. We considered useful to emphasize some of them in the touristic offer, in order to provide the guests with the key to many other symbols.

The acknowledgement of symbols takes place in the cultural settings of the Republic of Moldova, these being unique due to their natural and anthropic content. The discovery of this symbolic universe takes place also by means of the national cuisine, a varied one, based on local products, verified as a gustative practice for centuries and enriched as a result of living in the neighbourhood of other cultures.

The willingness to learn about interesting places, original cultures, to taste meals and participate in relevant activities maintains tourism on an economic orbit. It helps discover in the cultural heritage generous sources for national and international cooperation.

References

Buzilă, V. (1998). *Pâinea: Aliment şi simbol.* ÎEP Ştiinţa, Chişinău: Experienţa sacrului.

Buzilă, V. (2004). Ospitalitatea românilor—necesitate şi exces. Destin românesc. No. 1–2, pp. 97–116.

Chevalier, J., & Gheerbrant, A. (1995). Dictionnaire des symboles: Mythes, rêves, coutumes, gestes, formes, figures, couleurs, nombres. Edition revue et augmentée. Paris: Robert Laffont/Jupiter.

Costea, V. D. (1995). *"Vinul în existenţa umană"*, in *Discursuri de recepţie.* Bucureşti: Editura Academiei Române.

Cuisenier, J. (1999). Etnologia Europei. Traducere de Marinela Blaj. Iaşi: Institutul European.

Лотман, Ю. (2004). *Семиосфера.* Санкт-Петербург: Искусство СПБ.

Mesnil, M., & Popova, A. (1992). Da gli antenati a i neonati: Il pani della San-Quaranta. In Papa Cr. (a cura di), Antropologia e storia dell'alimentazione. Il pane. Electa Editori Umbri, Perugia.

Stahl, P. H. (2000). Triburi şi sate din sud-estul Europei. Structuri sociale, structuri magice şi religioase. Traducere de Viorica Nicolau, Paideia, Bucureşti.

Printed by Printforce, the Netherlands